BRITISH
CANALS

T0322472

BRITISH CANALS

THE STANDARD HISTORY

JOSEPH BOUGHEY AND CHARLES HADFIELD

The History Press

Cover illustrations from front: A narrow boat on a beautiful, misty morning. (Matthew Troke/Shutterstock.com); Pontcysyllte Aqueduct, which carries the Llangollen Canal 121ft above the River Dee in north-east Wales.

First published 1950 by Phoenix House
This paperback edition published 2022

The History Press
97 St George's Place, Cheltenham,
Gloucestershire, GL50 3QB
www.thehistorypress.co.uk

British Library Cataloguing in Publication Data.
A catalogue record for this book is available from the British Library.

ISBN 978 0 7509 9937 3

Typesetting and origination by The History Press
Printed and bound in Great Britain by TJ Books Limited, Padstow, Cornwall.

MIX
Paper from
responsible sources
FSC FSC® C013056

Trees for LYfe

Contents

List of Maps

Preface to the Paperback Edition

My interest in inland waterways began in the summer of 1963, when my father hired *Kingfisher* from Ernest Thomas at Gailey, in Staffordshire, for a slow fortnight's journey to Ellesmere and back. This journey was repeated in the following summer, towards the end of which my father and I viewed the two lowest locks of the Hatherton branch of the Staffordshire & Worcestershire Canal. Although this had closed in 1955, these were reasonably intact and looked as if they could be used with heroic effort and will. I was curious to know what the canal was like beyond the locks, and from that time, I determined to learn more about the waterways that had so far formed a mere backdrop to a family holiday.

Over the following ten years of family holidays, we explored various less-used and derelict waterways, by boat, and sometimes by road or rail, until I began to explore by road on my own in the mid-1970s. This was driven by my enthusiasms perhaps more than they should, as the youngest family member, although the others took a moderate interest. I encountered a world, much of which, sadly, has long since receded into the past; we saw many vernacular waterside buildings, working narrow boats, and small plywood and fibreglass pleasure boats that no longer exist.

An early encounter was with Charles Hadfield's *British Canals*; I still have a somewhat battered copy of the 1962 edition, which I received on my 10th birthday. This was a good time to begin a lifelong interest in waterways history; David & Charles' *The Canals of the British Isles* regional series, to which *British Canals* formed (and still forms) an introduction, was well under way, with many histories of individual waterways building on their foundations. As I would discover, the "Charles" in David & Charles was Charles Hadfield, leading research and writing in this field, and encouraging publications. He also had a significant role in shaping the progress of history. For instance, he co-founded the Inland Waterways Association (1946), the Railway & Canal Historical Society (1954) and the Inland Shipping Group (1970/1), and was a key member of the first British Waterways Board (1963/6). I would meet Charles in his later years, and would write *Canal Man and More* about his waterways-related work, life and influence. In some ways, we live in a world of waterways that he influenced.

I began as an enthusiast, but later became an academic, carrying out postgraduate research into the built environment until 1984, and as a lecturer between 1989 and 2010. Transport history has a bad name in academic circles, with the term 'anorak' never far away, and I have discovered that many enthusiasts fear that academics look down on their work. In *Canal Man and More*, I presented evidence that this even applied to Charles Hadfield's meticulous work. I later spent several years teaching environmental management, a field in which enthusiasts, professionals and academics often mix with mutual respect, and I hope that transport history will enjoy a similar position one day.

While many assisted me with the 8th and 9th editions, I would detail specific and diverse debts here. My late parents, Joan and Joseph, encouraged me to explore waterways history, although they had many other life interests and could have wished for a very different future for me. My (sadly late) sister Hilarie and surviving sister Christine also provided encouragement in their way. Charles Hadfield placed confidence in me to take over his old book, 'to be completely and radically revised by a fresh mind and a younger head', as he put it. We have now been without him for over 25 years, and I hope that he would be content with a book that is, indeed, so radically revised.

In 1994, I somewhat amusedly described Brenda Heath, my first wife, as bearing 'canal widowhood', little realising the devastation that 'actual widowhood' would bring when she died in 2002. She shared some visits, like that shown in the view of Standedge Tunnel on Page 130, but mostly her love and support helped me to work on writings that could well have awaited a later period, perhaps retirement. A continuing regret is the time spent on writing and a frustrating and unrewarding employment - time that we could have spent together. Finally, my second wife, Sara Richards, has brought new hope and love, but also much practical support, as a stern critic of both Charles' and my words. Our shared interest in historic environments and landscapes, along with the love that has developed despite our major losses, has brought renewed inspiration. I should apologise for such personal comments in a Preface to a book about transport history, in place of the usual British male reticence about feelings but - not on this occasion.

Many people helped both Charles and myself with queries, over the last 75 years. I would commend the assistance and dedication of both reference librarians and (later) archivists, keepers of knowledge whose contribution deserves to be better known. Charles' own interest in waterways had begun nearly hundred years ago, when the family solicitor encouraged him to study documents about his local canal, the Grand Western in Devon. He began *British Canals* with almost no regular public access to archives, yet now there are extensive archives, from digitised newspapers to local record offices, The National Archives, and the Waterways Archive at Ellesmere Port (which now includes many of his own records). Thanks largely to Charles' work in writing and publishing, interest in waterways history now has firm foundations. This does not mean that it is, in any sense, completed. There has been an explosion in sources, online, written and audiovisual, and there is much to be found and further explored, in depth, detail and breadth. At the same time, sources like oral recollections and evidence from engineering and other structures are disappearing, lending urgency to much research. I hope that much more will be written and published, and that this book will provide a useful background.

Introduction to the Paperback Edition

The text from the hardback edition has been left as matters stood in 2008, with minor corrections, but this new edition provides an opportunity to sketch changes over the last 14 years.

The administration of British canals changed markedly in 2012. Ownership of the former British Waterways navigations in England and Wales was formally transferred to a new Waterways Infrastructure Trust, with strategic and everyday management awarded to the new Canal & River Trust. The Trust has moved from an emphasis on powered pleasure boating towards a much broader and general focus on well-being, with a much heavier involvement on the role of volunteers. The Inland Waterways Advisory Council, set up under the Transport Act 1968 to advise government, was abolished in 2011. Relations with government were now very different, while many campaigning groups felt that cooperation rather than confrontation was appropriate.

One intention was for CRT to assume the navigation responsibilities for the Environment Agency waterways, but this failed to take place. The Waterways Trust was absorbed into the Canal & River Trust, including the museums at Stoke Bruerne, Gloucester and Ellesmere Port. British Waterways' Scottish navigations were left with British Waterways, employing a new name of Scottish Canals. The main development was the improvement of the eastern end of the Forth & Clyde, improving access to the Carron and Forth estuary. This new line, which opened in 2015, ran through the Kelpies, two huge horse sculptures.

Effective subsidies continued, with income from government that represented the functions that could not be the subject of charges or other direct payments. For the Canal & River Trust, by the end of 2022, negotiations should determine the renewed level of payments.

From 2010 the separate Trusts for the Lower and Upper Avons, from the Severn at Tewkesbury, to Alveston Weir above Stratford, were amalgamated under a single Avon Navigation Trust, the first unified management since 1717!

Most waterways in Ireland remained devolved to Waterways Ireland. This completed the restoration of the Royal Canal in 2010, and has led the long-term plans to restore the Ulster Canal. The Ulster's first phase of restoration will focus on the section between Lough Erne and Clones; the restoration of an isolated section west of Clones (all within the Republic), costing 12 million euros, was finally announced in 2021.

Restoration completions have been much more limited during this period, in contrast to those completed around the Millennium. Perhaps the most significant completion was that of the Droitwich Canals, in 2011, after which administration was transferred to the Canal & River Trust. The gradual restoration of the Stroudwater Canal and Thames & Severn Canal over the last 50 years accelerated after 2006, using Lottery funding. While British Waterways withdrew promised funding in 2008, support from Stroud District Council secured reopening from Stroud downstream to Ocean, with much progress elsewhere, despite infilling and low road crossings. Further Lottery funding may well see the canal reconnected to the canal network at Saul by 2024.

Some restoration plans were effectively abandoned during this period. This included the Upper Severn and Higher Avon, over which environmental provisions prevailed, as they had on the Yorkshire Derwent, on which there was no progress, with the restored Sutton Lock becoming inoperable in 2015. The Barnsley Dearne & Dove Canals Trust had involved ambitious rebuilding proposals that would have involved extensive new construction. This Trust was wound up in 2020, spurred by the failure of planning protection for the line of the canal within Barnsley, exacerbated by falling membership. Despite greater volunteer involvement in work for the Canal & River Trust, there has been a decline in voluntary organisations. The ageing demographic of key voluntary enthusiasts, and unwillingness to commit to administrative work, provide a partial explanation. This did not just affect canal restoration. The Towpath Action Group also suspended activities in the 2010s, as did the Waterways Craft Guild.

Some smaller-scale restoration works continued, to provide modest extensions to sections of the navigable system. One notable longstanding scheme was the line to Newtown, known as the Montgomery. Progress was gradual and volunteer-led; the line was extended south from Maesbury, reopening to Gronwen. Reconnection to the navigable length at Llanmynech was in sight in 2022, and the final bridge crossing reconstruction under way. South of Llanmynech, much of the section to Arddleen (but not the low A483 crossings at Maerdy and Arddleen, or the Vyrnwy aqueduct) is to be restored under the 2019 UK Government's Community Renewal Fund. In East Yorkshire, while part of the Derwent is now inaccessible, a further navigable two miles was added to the connected Pocklington Canal, upon which full restoration may be achieved in the 2020s.

The restoration of isolated sections in Ireland included the clearance and partial regating of locks on the Newry Canal, in local authority ownership. In the Republic, clearance works on the Boyne, owned by An Taisce, began in 2007. The lowest lock was reopened in 2012, with two more locks completing navigation to Newgrange by 2021, while further works were proceeding on isolated sections upstream.

Schemes of more modest scope have developed outside England. In Scotland, while much of the Monkland Canal has been destroyed, a local Friends group began to clear the towpath and water on a remaining length in 2020. Earlier, the Pontypridd Canal Conservation Group was formed in 2010; this has restored structures on one of the few surviving sections of the Glamorganshire Canal.

The restoration of the Wey & Arun Junction Canal may suggest how future restoration schemes will progress. Most of those schemes that have been completed either did not present major engineering problems, or were able to obtain significant funding around the Millennium, from sources that are much more difficult to access. A campaign for restoration of the Wey & Arun, last used in 1872, had begun just under a hundred years later, with clearance work in the 1970s and 1980s. As much of the line had been sold off and long sections destroyed, works proceeded only when finance and agreements with landowners was obtained. By 2022 a three-mile section north of Drungewick Lock had been made navigable, with reconstructed canal structures and new road crossings, and with short lengths further north navigable by small boats. This may well provide one model for large restoration schemes like the Herefordshire & Gloucestershire, Wilts & Berks, Thames & Severn, Lichfield & Hatherton: gradual environmental improvements, navigation on short but expanding lengths, and perhaps the completion of restoration by the later part of the the present century. Smaller-scale restorations may involve shorter timescales, but this may be disappointingly long-term.

The decline of freight traffics over English waterways continued. For instance, the aggregate traffics between Besthorpe on the Trent to Lafarge at Whitwood, on the Wakefield line of the Aire & Calder, ended in 2013 when Lafarge merged with Tarmac, and closed Whitwood wharf. This left very limited traffic on the CRT Yorkshire waterways - an oil traffic between Goole and Rotherham - as grain and general merchandise had ceased. Plans for a Port Leeds resulted in a new wharf at Knostrop, with a larger scheme in progress, taking renewed aggregate traffic to Leeds, which began in 2019. Elsewhere, traffics remained scattered and minimal, although much potential remains. Among pressure groups, the Inland Waterway Freight Group became dormant in the 2010s, although the Commercial Boat Operators Association, now open to enthusiasts and campaigners as well as operators, has taken up much of its role. Traffic continues to tidal ports, especially in the Thames area; of those East Coast ports listed in the hardback edition, Mistley, Wisbech and Boston are still operational, although Fosdyke Bridge is now a yacht haven. Most of the hoped-for traffic associated with the London Olympics in 2012 did not develop, although this did involve the restoration for leisure use of the Bow Back Rivers.

The Manchester Ship Canal, which had been mooted for closure in 1987, has remained open under Peel Ports, with traffics continuing to Irlam, and grain, cement, and scrap for export, upstream of Barton. It has formed the centre of major proposals by Peel, under the umbrella of Ocean Gateway, which includes a new Port Salford, served by rail. However, the proposed canal to the Trafford Centre did not materialise.

In Scotland, no new traffics have developed on the restored Forth & Clyde Canal (although this had been considered), while Ireland's only inland traffic, in sand mined from Lough Neagh to the Lower Bann, has continued only in the face of major environmental objections that may well lead to its withdrawal.

Local and specialist independent museums, developed strongly from the 1970s, were beginning to decline by the 2020s. For example, the Yorkshire Waterways Museum at Goole, in financial difficulties, closed in 2019. The Canal Museum at Dewsbury and the Canal Exhibition Centre at Llangollen were among smaller attractions that have closed, partly due to changes in the patterns of leisure and tourism and the costs involved. The voluntary organisation that had set up what became the National Waterways Museum, latterly the Waterways Museum Society, was dissolved in 2020. In Ireland, the former Robertstown Canal Hotel remains vacant, although the small museum on the Newry, at Moneypenny's Lock, is still open.

The position with the waterways of the British Isles in 2022 is thus a mixed one. The commercial transport role has become limited, despite the potential for new development, although the latter would require public subsidy. Subsidy is also required to ensure that the majority of waterways that have been retained for leisure boating continue to provide a different form of transport. There are further non-transport purposes, which have developed greatly since the 1960s: to seek the conservation of historic environments, species and habitats, to contribute to landscapes and to informal recreation and amenity. If this is sufficiently recognised and financed, the future of many historic waterways will be secured.

Joseph Boughey
January 2022

Note and Acknowledgements

Some waterways have been through so many changes of ownership and name that it has been difficult to describe them exactly. I have, therefore, tended to retain within the text the contemporary names used at each historical period, while deferring towards more modern names in the illustrations. I have diverged from names recognisable in modern times only in the case of the entirely unhistorical 'Montgomery Canal'.

In the later chapters I have tended towards abbreviations for recurring titles and names: 'BTC' is much more readable than 'Docks and Inland Waterways Board of Management of the British Transport Commission', which was the controlling body for many British waterways between 1953 and 1955!

I have converted pre-1971 British currency to post-1971 equivalents; of course, inflation has removed any real comparability from these. I have resisted the temptation to metricate measurements, since this is largely a work of history; the only exception to this is the reproduction of statistics of tonnages which are now recorded in metric tonnes. In the interests of uniformity, I have used converted statistics which do not treat a multiple chambered lock in Ireland as a single lock; thus the 41 locks on the Grand Canal represent thirty-six sites with changes of level.

For the maps, I would again thank Mr Paul Hodgkinson and Mr Richard Dean. Most of the historical photographs came from four sources: the then Department of the Environment for Northern Ireland (which held the McCutcheon Collection), British Waterways at Gloucester, the then Boat Museum at Ellesmere Port (now the National Waterways Museum) and the Guinness Museum. I would repeat my thanks to various officers who assisted with the supply of these illustrations. For permission to use other illustrations I would like to thank the late L.A. Edwards, Dr Ian Bath, the National Library of Ireland and the Office of Public Works.

Many people have helped with information and comment and I would repeat my thanks for the exceptional assistance of Mrs Ruth Heard, Ireland's principal canal historian, whose help enabled the enlarged coverage of Irish waterways for the eighth edition, which is continued here. For specific assistance with the ninth edition, I must thank Mr Mike Clarke, who always encourages scholarly research, and Mr Ken Fairhurst of the MMBC. As ever, all views expressed in this work, and all errors, are entirely my own.

CHAPTER ONE

Origins

The first edition of this book, which was written largely in 1948, depicted the scene at Boulter's Lock on the Thames, on which boating for pleasure had then been significant for over 60 years. A contrast was then drawn with the river that earlier generations would have experienced, as primarily a means of transport. On artificial canals elsewhere in Britain in 1948, very few pleasure boats could be seen, as what will be termed the Second Canal Age was then only embryonic. On those canals, most boats that could be seen were engaged in carrying the surviving traffics over routes that had been constructed largely during the First Canal Age. To those who now use those routes, for boating, walking, or angling, or who benefit from their less obvious roles in water supply, drainage or nature conservation, their past use for transport may well not be apparent, leaving the reasons for their construction unclear.

This book aims to explain the promotion and construction of canals in the British Isles and their survival into the Second Canal Age. The use of inland waterways for transport long predates the First Canal Age, before which coastal transport and transport by road were supplemented by the extensive use of rivers. Rivers were often used for food, power generation, drainage and water supply and, sometimes, adapted for transport. Then, as now, these purposes could be in conflict, especially under pressure from economic development.

Freshwater fish remain significant in many parts of the world for food as well as for recreational angling, and, before transport developments improved meat distribution, many inland areas relied on freshwater fish for food. In the mediaeval period, fish were often harvested through fish weirs. These comprised dams of wooden stakes with nets, stretched across rivers, to trap migrating fish like eels. Similar examples from the Saxon period have been found in intertidal coastal areas. Weirs were largely created by major landowners, and presented such major barriers to navigation that *Magna Carta* in 1215 provided specifically that: 'All fish-weirs shall be removed from the Thames, the Medway and throughout the whole of England, except on the sea coast.'[1] Most coastal weirs had ceased to be used after the fourteenth century, but many inland ones long continued to impede navigation of rivers. Some still survive, such as those in Durham.

Rivers often provided a major source of hydropower, especially where they were tidal or fast-flowing. Wherever a sufficient fall of water could be exploited, water-wheels could grind corn mills and industrial processes like driving the hammers of ironworks could be powered. Often weirs, mill races and ponds were built to raise river levels and enable a sufficiently large and controllable flow through the wheel. This raising of levels could assist navigation on larger rivers, but both the fall, and the need to maintain levels, provided barriers to navigation. The earliest means in the world by which such barriers were overcome used rough ramps, later known as inclined planes, over which boats were dragged in the dry. Later, opening wooden sections in weirs enabled boats to pass through once levels on either side were equalised. These were known as flash-locks or staunches, early examples being developed on the Thames in the thirteenth century. These had a very limited fall, and provided a 'flash' of water so that a boat could be pulled upstream over a shallow section. At half-locks, or watergates, 'the weir was built of masonry and was equipped with a gate, swinging on rides and equipped with movable paddles, which could be opened against the flow of the river by means of a winch on the bank.'[2]

The larger rivers, like the Thames, featured some such flash-locks until the 1930s, while the last navigable watergate, at Pershore on the Warwickshire Avon, was removed only in 1956. The remains of earlier staunches may still be found on the Little Ouse and Bottisham Lode, in Eastern England.

Few rivers had towing-paths, and it remains unclear which had them, or when the use of animal haulage began. The Warwickshire Avon had no horse path in the 1630s when William Sandys improved it, while the Wey Navigation had paths both for men and horses from 1652. When barges could not rely on sails, they were pulled by gangs of men, known as bow hauliers, who could scramble through obstructions and ford side-streams more easily than could horses or donkeys. Sometimes they would damage property or steal 'Hennes, Geese, Duckes, Piggs, Swannes, Eggs, Woode and all such other Commodytyes'[3] en route. Rivers were rarely dredged or maintained, and barges going upstream would often ground, with the water in each level reach held back to protect the power supplies to each mill. Bargaining with the miller controlling the reach above would be needed in order to release a 'flash' – sufficient water to enable the barge to be floated off. Further bargaining would be required at each weir to allow levels to equalise sufficiently to allow the boat to be pulled through, often with a winch, and sometimes, going downstream, to release enough water for the barge to float over shallow sections. It was reported of the River Lea in 1760 that:

The natural inconveniences of the River [are] made much worse by the practice of those who own the Mills, for tho Flashes from the Mill be in some places necessary, for which the Bargemen pay…for the most part the Millers by deepening and enlarging their bye streams that bring water to the Mill, draw off from the main river very much more than they need, that so they may sell the same water to the bargemen again and help those for money whom they have first themselves disabled. It is certain that some of the Mills do command the streams, that they can lay a whole fleet of Barges on ground upon the adjoining sharps and help them off again upon Composition, and one turnpike there is that lays the whole River dry.[4]

It was written later, that this 'brings on a considerable charge to the Barge-Owner; renders his arrival at any given Place uncertain; and gives the Land Carriage the greatest advantage over that of the River Navigation.'[5]

The records are full of disputes between these interests, over excessive charges, refusals to give a flash, fights and stratagems. The medieval period involved similar efforts to remove fish weirs.

Any economic expansion requires improvements in transport and power, without which progress in agriculture, industry and distribution will be inhibited. Similarly, innovations in transport and power provide opportunities for industry, agriculture and distribution, which may consolidate progress if they are taken, or retard it if they are not. The process known as the Industrial Revolution was characterised in Britain by the mechanization of cotton manufacture, allied to a growing population and colonial surpluses, although the seeds were sown in the sixteenth century. The expansion of industrial production required improved transport and improved means of power generation. The population of England grew from 4 million in 1600 to over 7 million by 1750, and the size of the industrial labour force would almost double between 1780 and 1820. Industry and mining slowly grew in output and variety, as did the range of consumer goods, but before the locomotive railway, their products could only be moved in three ways, by land, sea or inland water.

Land transport has always existed, of course, but, before road engineers emerged in the eighteenth century, roads were often so bad that waggons could not always be used, and much was carried on the backs of horses and mules. For instance, in the early eighteenth century clay coal and flints to the Staffordshire Potteries, and the distribution of finished goods, largely relied on packhorses. The cost of road transport was prohibitively expensive: one horse could draw around 2 tons on a level road but from 50-100 tons on a good larger waterway. Road transport was therefore often limited to short-distance carriage, for instance the transport of coal for a few miles around a colliery, or of goods to and from a river or the sea. It was mainly used over long distances only where perishable or valuable goods were involved, where water transport would damage established interests, or the cost and unreliability of water transit were increased by monopolies or delays. Waggon services in England and Wales eventually grew with the expansion of trade before and during the canal age, with many roads being turnpiked between 1751 and 1772, and further developed to reflect urban and industrial growth, before the railways took much passenger and freight traffic. Some early river navigations were ineffective or expensive; thus various roads in West Yorkshire were turnpiked under Acts of 1741, to bypass the Aire & Calder Navigation that had opened in 1699.

Around the coasts, especially those of England and Wales, ships of the coastal trade moved goods that would be later moved by rail or road. Vessels passed up estuaries to minor inland ports on the smaller rivers of (for instance) East Anglia, or to the larger seaports such as London, Bristol and Kings Lynn. At seaports goods were transhipped to smaller craft – keels, trows or Western barges – in

A somewhat fanciful drawing of a packhorse train. Over the terrain depicted, of course, only horses could be used prior to the development of motorised road transport. This and other drawings from Samuel Smiles's *Lives of the Engineers* tend to overemphasise the advances made by civil engineers in the Industrial Revolution.

which they were transported to smaller ports, such as Bewdley and Bridgnorth, on the Severn.

Other waterways were adapted for navigation merely by the construction of landing-places. In some cases goods carried in larger vessels were unloaded to small boats and then onto the waterside. Estuaries and lakes often presented a barrier that had to be crossed by ferries where there were no bridges or fords. For lakes such as Windermere and Coniston in the Lake District, Llyn Padarn in North Wales, or Lough Corrib in the west of Ireland, the water was used as a means of transport rather than a barrier. Estuarial tidal waterways were often used without recourse to the sea; thus, barges carried lead up the River Dee from Flintshire mines to the leadworks at Chester. In other cases, the river itself was the source of raw materials, such as sand and gravel dredged from its bed, which was then landed nearby.

The River Severn was the main water route to the west side of midland England. Much traffic was carried upstream from the port of Bristol, along with that originating from industries along its length such as the saltworks of Droitwich. Large quantities of coal passed along it from the Shropshire collieries of Broseley, Benthall and Barr. Of around 2–300,000 tons of coal carried on English rivers at the end of the seventeenth century, 100,000 passed along the Severn to Shrewsbury, Bridgnorth, Bewdley, Worcester, Tewkesbury and Gloucester. From Bewdley's warehouses goods

Sand dredged from the estuary of the River Taw at Crow Point being landed on the Yeo at Barnstaple in summer 1993. This was a traffic that had been continuous since at least the sixteenth century, before the canal age. Small creeks like the Yeo (which once served Rawle Gammon & Baker, in the background) carried large quantities of local and seagoing traffic before and during the canal age. This traffic finally ceased in the late 1990s when temporary planning permission expired.

landed from Severn trows were distributed by packhorse and waggon into the countryside of Worcestershire, Staffordshire and Shropshire. A return flow, in goods like Midlands ironware, was sent down river to the seaports and the West Country.

On the other side of England, the Thames was also a distributing and trading river, connecting towns such as Windsor, Reading and Oxford, and forwarding goods from the port of London. Cambridge had long been significant for the distribution of goods by water from Kings Lynn, sending corn and other produce downstream. The nearby Stourbridge fair, which Defoe described in 1724 as the largest in the world, was sustained by water transport, much of it to and from East Coast ports.

The Fens waterways had a special position, as the main highways in parts of Eastern England. They carried goods from overseas and coastal ports up the Great Ouse, Nene, Welland and Witham, sending back countryside produce. They were used to move passengers and goods round their water-dominated district, where roads were few. Stone was brought by water from the Barnack quarries in Northamptonshire to build the Crowland and Ramsey abbeys, and the Lincoln, Ely and Peterborough cathedrals. The fourteenth-century records of Ely show:

...the sacrist and his fellows using the fenland waterways as their normal means of transport; whether it was to synods at Barnwell, or to buy cloth wax, tallow, lead and other necessaries at Lynn and Boston, or merely to conduct their ordinary business at Shippea, Quaveney, Littleport and elsewhere among the fens.[6]

In much of Scotland, Wales and coastal Ireland, rivers tended to be fast-flowing, and not readily adapted for navigation, although in Scotland the deepened Clyde would play its part in the growth of Glasgow, and several tidal rivers around the Welsh coast were navigated upstream.

Before the reign of Elizabeth I most legislation sought to maintain or restore navigation upon naturally navigable rivers, but after her reign there were many more attempts to make new navigable rivers. Beginning with the Lea in 1424, the Thames, Yorkshire Ouse, Kentish Stour and others (but not the Severn) had been put under the care of corporations or other bodies charged with maintaining navigation. Meanwhile Acts authorised the removal of fisheries and other obstructions from the largest rivers, such as the Wye and Medway, the latter without success. Improvement schemes needed bodies which had powers to set aside the rights of private property in the public interest. These were usually corporations in cities like London, Gloucester and York, or Commissioners of Sewers. The latter bodies, set up under a 1531 Act, comprised local landowners with rating powers whose principal concern was land drainage and flood protection rather than navigation.

When rivers were to be made navigable for the first time, the usual practice was to grant letters patent to one or more people who undertook to make the navigation. Thus Thomas Skipwith was empowered in 1634 to make the Soar navigable. In other cases trustees were appointed or powers were given to a company. Those involved were permitted to collect tolls from all who used the improved navigation, and sometimes the exclusive right to carry goods on it. Improvements and operations conferred uneven benefits, and thus attracted variations in support from landowners and merchants.

In the second part of the sixteenth century, the pound-lock, in use since the previous century in Italy, Germany and the Netherlands, was introduced into England. Despite its cost, this invention made it possible to improve river navigation far beyond the level achieved merely by dredging and the removal of obstructions. A Victorian civil engineer described the pound-lock as:

> ... a chamber, placed at the junction of two reaches, in which the water can be raised or lowered so as to be on a level with either the upper or lower reach. The lock-chamber is usually closed by a pair of gates at each end; it is filled by letting in water from the upper pool through sluices in the upper gates or side walls, and emptied by letting it out through similar sluices at the lower end.[7]

If pound-locks were used to pass boats from one level to another, weirs no longer needed a central moveable portion, and could be made continuous. This created such an increased economy in water use that compromises with milling interests became possible. Pound-locks only needed a lockful of water, but a flash given to a barge might have meant lowering the whole stretch of river up to the next weir.

The first known examples of pound-locks in Britain were not on a river but on a short canal. John Trew of Glamorgan, an otherwise unknown engineer, built three on the Exeter Canal between 1564 and 1566. These were very wide basins, with very limited falls; soon replaced, this design does not seem to have been emulated elsewhere. Pound-locks began also to be built on rivers – seemingly one on the Lea and one on the Trent, both in 1576. In the seventeenth century they were constructed on the Thames between Iffley and Abingdon, the Warwickshire Avon, the Wey and elsewhere. Pound-locks were now included in improvement schemes, as with the six 'sluices' built on the pioneering Great Ouse between 1618 and 1625, alongside the older 'staunches' (flash-locks), which continued to be used at lower toll charges.

Opposition to navigation improvements came from many quarters. Those interested in road transport disliked a cheaper competitor. Landowners perceived increased risks of flooding from the raising of water levels for pound-locks, or conversely that improved flood-control would prevent their water-meadows from being flooded. Farmers feared that improved transport would open up wider areas of trade and cause prices to fall, since produce could be obtained from further away. The most sustained opposition to specific schemes came from local authorities in towns that might lose their role as distributing centres for goods. For instance, Nottingham, high up the Trent, bitterly opposed the attempts by Derby citizens to make the Derwent navigable, so that goods would come up the Trent without transshipment at Nottingham. Reading opposed the Kennet Navigation to Newbury, and Liverpool the Mersey & Irwell to Manchester. Parliamentary Bills for navigation improvements thus involved many petitions and compromises with opponents.

When major attempts to drain the Fens were made in the early seventeenth century, towns like Cambridge were concerned that this might damage their navigations. In 1630, an agreement, the Lynn Law, was made with the Duke of Bedford, the chief promoter of the drainage, to preserve the navigation of the 'Ouse, Grant, Nean, Welland amd Glean'[8] and the port of King's Lynn.

While drainage engineers usually sought to keep watercourses as empty as practicable to increase capacity during floods, this often conflicted with regulations to retain a minimum depth for navigation purposes. Despite many disputes, the rights of navigation were preserved in all legislation for the better drainage of the Fens. There were major arguments over Denver Sluice, which was thought to cause the silting up of the channel below it until it collapsed early in the eighteenth century.

Thereafter there were three main periods of activity in the making of river navigations. Before the first, England had about 685 miles of river navigation, including the Thames, Severn, Trent, Yorkshire Ouse and Great Ouse. Several Acts passed between 1662 and 1665, including important provisions to improve the

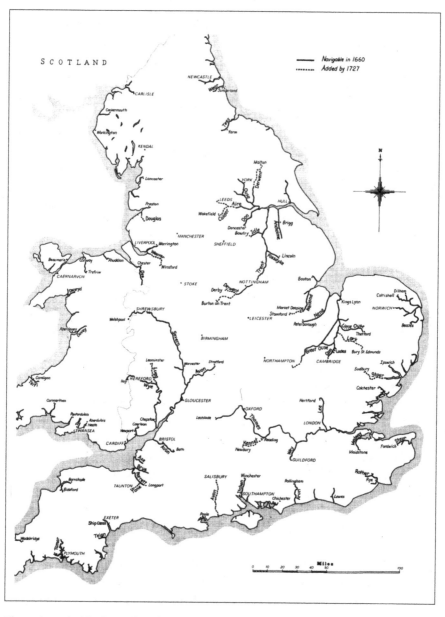

The main navigable rivers of England and Wales, indicating navigation improvements up to 1727. The main coasting ports are also shown. Early editions of *British Canals* reproduced two maps from T.S. Willan's *River Navigation in England*, indicating districts which were more than 15 miles from navigable waterway. This map attempts to replace the earlier maps, indicating a much more modest advance than the Willan maps suggested. Some navigations were short lived (such as the Lugg), while others varied in their condition and usefulness. It is noteworthy that it was the industrial centres in the English Midlands which were not served by water transport.

Worcestershire Stour and Salwarpe, the Wye and Lugg, Medway, Hampshire Avon and Itchen. On 2 March 1665 the Speaker of the House of Commons told the Lords:

> Cosmographers do agree that this Island is incomparably furnished with pleasant rivers, like Veins in the Natural Body…Therefore we have prepared some Bills for making small Rivers navigable; a Thing that in other Countries hath been more experienced, and hath been found very advantageous; it easeth the People of the great Charge of Land Carriages; preserves the Highways, which are daily worn out with Waggons carrying excessive Burdens; it breeds up a Nursery of Waterman, which, upon Occasion, will prove good Seamen; and with much Facility, maintain Intercourse and Communion between Cities and Countries.[9]

Schemes to build canals emerged during the seventeenth century. In 1641, for instance, there was a proposal to make navigable the Wey and Arun rivers, and to join their upper reaches by a canal two miles long, while the Restoration period included unsuccessful Bills to join the Thames to the Severn via the Bristol Avon. These would have used very short artificial canals to join rivers at points where they were extremely narrow and shallow. Andrew Yarranton, a Worcestershire ironmaster and later the author of *England's Improvement by Sea and Land* (1677), advocated the construction of such links in the 1660s, and began work on part of the Severn–Trent route, by canalising part of the Stour.

In the second period of activity, from 1697 to 1700, Acts included the Tone, Aire & Calder, upper Trent, Lark, and Yorkshire Derwent. In the third, between 1719 and 1721, river navigation schemes reflected the boom associated with the South Sea Bubble, including Acts for the Derbyshire Derwent, Douglas, Weaver, Mersey & Irwell, and Bristol Avon. By 1724 there were 1,160 miles of river navigation, although some navigation works were short-lived or ineffective. Most of lowland England then lay within 15 miles of a navigable river, and goods moved more freely, often in new patterns and at lower costs. Before the Aire & Calder was made navigable to Leeds and Wakefield in 1699, wool for manufacturing came from east coast ports or from Lincolnshire or Leicestershire, by road; cloth from Leeds or Wakefield also went by road to the nearest points on navigable rivers, like Selby on the Ouse or Knottingley on the Aire. Most coal to York came, not from the West Riding mines only 20 miles away by road, but from Newcastle, by keel down the Tyne, ship to the Humber, and up the Ouse in lighters – a distance of 200 miles.

Often three or four groups of undertakers would at different times try to make the same river navigable, often defeated by opposition, or by destruction through flooding, as with the Worcestershire Stour to Stourbridge in 1667, and the newly built locks on the Calder & Hebble in 1767 and 1768. Many plans failed because of the lack of engineering knowledge at the time. As will be stressed in Chapter two, it was the building of canals that largely created the profession of civil engineer by producing sufficient demand to foster the development of specialisms, and levels of capital investment that necessitated the reliable and accurate estimating of costs, design, and the supervision of works. However, even after well-known engineers with much practical experience were available, it remained more difficult to make rivers navigable rather than to construct canals, as there were more forces outside the engineers' control. Rivers like the Severn and Trent were not made properly navigable until after the canal age; others, like the Swale, never were.

Poor institutional management and organised opposition sometimes meant that new navigations were less successful. The Kennet, for instance, was to be made navigable to Newbury, but the 1708 Bill was opposed by both the town of Reading, which anticipated the loss of transhipment trade, and by one Finch, a pensioner of the Reading turnpike. Finch presumably feared that the turnpike trust would no longer be able to pay his pension if the navigation was successful. The Act was passed in 1715, making seven partners the proprietors. After a disastrously inexperienced engineer had been dismissed, John Hore was appointed in 1718. He built 21 locks and made 11 miles of artificial cuts to join the 7 miles of river, which, apart from the towpath, was ready in 1723. The navigation had only been completed, however, with many disputes over mills and water left unsettled, deep hostility (sometimes with threats of violence) from parties in Reading, and a severe shortage of money, such that by 1734 the works were in poor order. The original seven partners had soon dwindled to one, and no profit had been made. By 1761 the proprietors asserted that:

> The undertaking has been ruin'd by Idle Servants Extravagant Wages Imbezelments & Loss of materials & by a superfluous & unnecessary number of Hands all of which Evils must be remedy'd by Industry, Frugality great care & application...[10]

Among rivers that had successfully been made navigable were the Mersey and the Irwell. From Liverpool the River Mersey ran past Runcorn and Warrington to Irlam, where the Irwell took up the line to Manchester. By 1697 fish-weirs had been cleared to make the Mersey navigable to Warrington, but in 1721 a company of undertakers was authorised to make the rivers navigable to Manchester, which:

> ... will be very beneficial to Trade, advantageous to the Poor, and convenient for the Carriage of Coals, Cannel, Stone, Timber, and other Goods, Wares and Merchandises, to and from the Towns and Parts adjacent, and will very much tend to the Imploying and Increase of Watermen and Seamen, and be a Means to preserve the Highways.[11]

By 1734 the navigation was open, with eight locks between Warrington and Manchester taking flats, sailed if possible, otherwise towed. However, Manchester needed not only improved trade with Liverpool, but also coal supplies, and in 1737 the company obtained an Act to make the Worsley Brook navigable, to carry coal from mines near Worsley to the Irwell, and so to Manchester. Although this scheme was never carried out, it had significant consequences for the first canal age.

After the invasion in AD 43, the Romans made use of the Fossdyke from the Witham at Lincoln to the Trent at Torksey as a navigation. They may also have used other waterways (the Bycarrsdike and Turnbridgedike) to form a water route towards York. The gradient of surviving remains of the Caerdyke (or Carrdike), running south from Lincoln to the Nene at Peterborough, suggests that its northern part merely served a drainage function and was never fully navigable. However, the section between Peterborough and the Cam at Waterbeach in Cambridgeshire was navigable, and this and the Fossdyke can be said to be the oldest canals in the British Isles. The Fossdyke was partly supplied by tidal water (land and water levels have since greatly changed), but silted up after the Romans left. It was dredged out by 1121, but was unnavigable during most of the thirteenth century. After partial clearance by Bishop Atwater in 1519–21, it declined into decrepitude with only occasional use, until full clearance and a pound-lock at Torksey were provided in 1741.

A new waterway, termed a canal but largely an enlargement of the tidal River Clwyd for three miles under a master *Fossator*, enabled the construction and later supply of Rhuddlan Castle after 1277, as part of works to unify Wales with England. In the twelfth or thirteenth century two short canals were built to carry stone to Rievaulx Abbey in Yorkshire, although, like the Fossdyke, these partly used the former course of a river. Around 1490 Sir Andrew Wood, a retired admiral, appears to have constructed a short private canal at Largo, Fife, for use by his pleasure boat.

The Exeter Canal, effectively bypassing part of the Exe estuary blocked by weirs, was built between 1564 and 1566, at the behest of the local authority in Exeter. Engineered by John Trew, this was a very small canal, 3ft deep, 16ft wide and 1¾ miles long. While Trew had promised to build a canal accessible at all states of the tide, this was not achieved, and the canal was none too successful at first. The canal was rebuilt in 1581, extended downstream by 1677, and then enlarged between 1698 and 1701 to a depth of 10ft and breadth of 50ft, dimensions sufficient for coasting craft and small ships.

The 'Titchfield Canal', built in 1611 in the lower Meon valley in Hampshire, apparently included a sea-lock at its tidal end, but it is unclear whether it was used for navigation. The Wey Navigation of 1651–3 included 12 pound-locks and some 9 miles of cuts in its 15-mile length, including the 'Long Reach' above Weybridge. The navigation began operations amid financial chaos, with unpaid bills and the treasurer heading for the debtors' prison. By 1677 its condition was ruinous, but trade improved after 1680.

The longest improvement to a river line, however, was in rural Lincolnshire. The Stamford Canal extended the navigation of the Welland upstream over 9 miles from Market Deeping to Stamford. After water mills rendered the Welland no longer navigable, an Act to restore the navigation was obtained in 1571 by Stamford Corporation. While no action resulted, it was empowered by a Charter of 1621 to 'make a river or new cut of such breadth and depth as they should see fit for the passage of boats, lighters and other vessels'. This was financed by tolls at each of the 10 canal and 2 river locks, over a 9-mile navigation, the upper section of which comprised 6 miles of canal, with an independent water supply. Construction was delayed by the English Civil War, but was completed by 1673. Using 7-14 ton lighters, the main traffic was seaborne coal, although by 1706 increased taxation had severely reduced it; some traffic lasted until 1863.

However, perhaps the first true artificial canal to be built in the British Isles was in the north of Ireland, to link Lough Neagh and the Tyrone coalfield with the port of Newry.

Ireland's lakes, linked to rivers like the Bann, Erne and Shannon, were used for transport by small boats in the mediaeval period. As early as 1178, navigation along the south end of Lough Corrib was reputedly improved by the construction of Friars Cut by the friars of Claregalway Abbey. This improved access to the port of Galway, and in 1498 a canal was proposed to link the lake westwards through Lough Athalia to the sea.

From the early seventeenth century there were schemes to link the main rivers in Ireland, but it was only after the overthrow of James II in 1688–91 that moves began to promote inland navigations to foster economic development. The Irish Parliament considered several Bills between 1697 and 1700 for river improvements and for a new canal to link Newry and Lough Neagh. None succeeded, but in 1715 an Act was passed to develop the inland counties of Ireland through drainage works and by making 'navigable and communicable passages for vessels of burthen to pass through'.[11] This and later Acts provided for local commissioners who would appoint undertakers to construct works and to levy tolls. Proposals foreshadowed the later Grand Canal from Dublin to the Shannon.

All that resulted was some work on the River Maigue and a disastrous attempt to canalise a fast-flowing part of the Liffey. An Act of 1729 provided for a more centralised control of developments, which led directly to the start of work on the Newry Canal in 1731.

While Dublin was expanding rapidly at that time, it relied on imported coal. Dublin merchants were keen to develop coalfields in east Tyrone, which could be served by way of a coastal route to Dublin, reaching Lough Neagh, through a new canal to Newry. Its form was influenced by Richard Castle (or Cassels), a French Huguenot refugee who had studied waterway engineering in Continental Europe, and arrived in Ireland in 1728. He worked for Edward Lovett Pearce, a Dublin architect responsible for many country houses, who was appointed Surveyor-General in 1730.

Engineered at first by Pearce until his death in 1733, then Castle until his dismissal in 1736, and finally by Thomas Steers of Liverpool, the Newry Canal was opened in March 1742, when it was reported from Dublin that 'the Cope of Loughneaghe, William Semple (commander), came into this harbour laden with coals and being the first vessel that has come through the new canal.'[12]

Lock 11 at Poyntzpass on the Newry Canal in the mid-1960s. While many of the structures on this canal were rebuilt after 1810, this gives an impression of the earliest major canal in the British Isles. (McCutcheon collection)

The Newry Canal was 18 miles long, some 45ft wide and over 5ft deep, with 14 wide locks, with brick chambers, timber floors and sizeable falls of between 12ft and 13½ft. These locks included a staircase pair at the summit at Terryhoogan, and three which made use of ground paddles, which had first been developed in 1561 on the Brussels Canal. Its summit was supplied by a feeder from Lough Shark (now Acton Lake), some 78ft above sea level. Vessels were towed by horses along the Canal itself, but sailed across Lough Neagh and by sea from Newry, although lighterage into seagoing vessels soon replaced the latter stage.

This had critical elements of later canals: locks with solid chambers (some earlier versions, as on the Kennet, had been turf-sided), mitred gates and ground paddles, a towing path for horses, opening bridges in Newry, and a summit reservoir. Castle (Cassels) and Steers may well have been influenced by knowledge of waterways in France. These included the Canal de Briare, opened in 1642 which was the first to cross watersheds, and to have staircase locks, and the Canal du Midi, opened in 1681, which had a summit level, independent water supplies and a short tunnel. By 1750, however, problems with construction and maintenance had limited the Newry Canal's usefulness, and it would be extended downstream of Newry in the 1750s and rebuilt in the early nineteenth century.

Steers had been born around 1672. After a military career in the Low Countries, he became engineer for Liverpool's Old Dock, the first commercial wet dock in Britain, in 1710; from 1717 he was Dockmaster, and Mayor of Liverpool in 1739. He had been approached first to be Newry Canal engineer in 1729, and was later involved in plans for the Douglas Navigation and Mersey & Irwell Navigation.

The first modern canal in England, the Sankey Navigation (later called the St Helens Canal), involved Steers' pupil Henry Berry, who succeeded him as Liverpool dock engineer after Steers died in 1750, and William Taylor. Only the making navigable of the little Sankey Brook from near St Helens to the Mersey

Worsley on the Duke of Bridgewater's Canal, showing entrances to the underground colliery canals, which operated until about 1887. The boats are 'starvationers'. This drawing from Smiles is generally accurate, and the site can be recognised today.

was authorised by the Act of 1755, which, in contrast to most waterway proposals, met with no Parliamentary opposition. Berry had probably decided to build a canal instead of a river navigation, and agreed with the principal shareholder, John Ashton of Liverpool, that 'the work should commence on 5 September 1755, but the project was carefully concealed from the other proprietors, it being apprehended that so novel an undertaking would have met with their opposition'[12]. Most of the canal was opened in 1757, with a further length in 1759. It was 8 miles long with 10 locks, including a staircase pair, using water supplies from the Sankey Brook. The line relied on the use of sailing barges that could transit the Mersey, with opening bridges rather than overbridges.

While Henry Berry and John Ashton should receive their tribute, the credit for beginning the development of the English connected canal system must go to the Duke of Bridgewater and his advisers, John and Thomas Gilbert, and James

The Sankey Navigation Canal between Bradley and Hey Locks, one of the few lengths of the 1757 canal to have survived with anything like its original appearance. This length was in regular use until the sugar traffic ended in 1959 and was closed in 1963. Some clearing works were carried out in the 1970s, but the bridge does not open, and much of the canal above Bradley Lock has been destroyed.

Brindley. The first short length of the Duke's Canal that opened in 1761 demonstrated the engineering practicality of building artificial canals and the economic success that could be generated. Above all, the publicity involved inspired much public support and encouraged investment.

The Duke of Bridgewater had inherited coal mines in Worsley, to which the canalization of the Worsley Brook had been authorised in 1737. Although the number of cotton mills, powered by water, had greatly increased in north west England, domestic coal was not readily available in the growing Manchester area. The sea coal that was available, via the Tyne and the coasts, to towns on the eastern side of England could not reach Manchester, which relied on coal brought expensively from local collieries on horseback or wagons. The Duke had travelled to the Continent on the Grand Tour in 1754 and must have seen the Canal du Midi and other canals there. His land agent, John Gilbert, proposed the line for a canal from the collieries towards Manchester in 1757. The duke agreed, and obtained an Act in 1759 to build two lines to the Mersey & Irwell Navigation. John Gilbert had already been involved in plans to build a canal from the Potteries to the Trent, which had faced financial barriers. The Duke's wealth, which the exploitation of his mines was expected to increase greatly, enabled him to finance the whole undertaking, partly by mortgaging his estates. His political influence and lobbying enabled the Act to pass despite opposition from landowners.

A further Act of 1760 amended the canal's line to one that would cross the Irwell, to join a proposed level line from Manchester to Runcorn. As this presented Gilbert with too much work, he introduced James Brindley to the scheme. Brindley would later be considered to be the most important engineer of the early canals, although he was a millwright by training. He had been born in the High Peak, and practiced as a millwright in Leek. His expertise lay with the use of water, including early experiments with a steam engine, and harnessing water power to drain the Wet Earth colliery near Salford. This had led to his survey of the Potteries-Trent canal in 1758. Brindley surveyed the line to Manchester and gave evidence to Parliament, helping to defeat the Mersey & Irwell opposition, although it was Gilbert who designed the Barton Aqueduct to cross the Mersey & Irwell.

When this canal was being built, in contrast to earlier ones, it attracted great interest. One writer said that 'it will be the most extraordinary thing in the kingdom, if not in Europe. The boats in some places are to go underground, and in another place over a navigable river, without communicating with its waters...'[14] A year later, in 1761, the canal was open to the outskirts of Manchester, and barges were passing over the 200 foot long aqueduct, 38ft above the Irwell. At Worsley a basin was built at the foot of a sandstone cliff, from which tunnels ran into the mine so that coal could be loaded directly into small boats, 'starvationers', possible ancestors of the later narrow boat. Eventually 46 miles of underground canals, on four levels, would be tunnelled, as the Duke's prosperity increased. A further Act, of 1762, much opposed by Cheshire landowners, would extend the line to the Mersey at Runcorn.

The marriage of coal and water transport did not have quite the major advantages that the opening of the canal to Manchester in 1764 suggested – prices at the canal wharves were greatly reduced, but cartage uphill into the city and other destinations greatly added to costs. However, it was the publicity that this scheme inspired, and the demonstration of engineering, albeit elements that had been pioneered elsewhere, that made this scheme formative. The Duke's Canal, the Duke himself, and interests elsewhere, in the Potteries and growing port interests, allied with Brindley's growing reputation, enabled other schemes to proceed against diminished opposition. Chapter four will take up this story.

CHAPTER TWO

Building the Canals

The Duke's Canal fostered the first canal age that ended with the railway mania of the 1840s. When it began the spinning jenny had yet to be invented, and James Watt had not built his first steam engine. When it ended Victoria was queen, the penny post and telegraph were being introduced, and steam power was being applied to industry, ships and the locomotive railway. In those 80 years what was termed the Industrial Revolution took place in Britain.

Before beginning to explore the developments in transport that encouraged major industrial advance, this and Chapter three will provide a composite general portrait of the development of British canals in their prime.

The earliest canals in England and Wales (but not Ireland and Scotland) were essentially local in origin. They were usually projected by manufacturers or mine owners, such as the pottery manufacturers led by Josiah Wedgwood who pushed the Trent & Mersey Canal idea past objectors and pessimists to its successful conclusion, the ironmasters who promoted the Glamorganshire Canal, the Devon copper mine owners behind the Tavistock, and the coalmasters behind the Barnsley and Dearne & Dove Canals. Sometimes leading residents in a town, or manufacturers, who would benefit from coal brought by canal, would promote the canal along with colliery owners; this was the case with the Shrewsbury, Coventry, and Birmingham Canals. The usual arguments put forward for a canal were that it would bring raw materials to factories, carry away products and supply local people with coal more cheaply than by land carriage. Thomas Telford listed the most useful purposes for canals:

> 1st, For conveying the produce of Mines to the Sea-shore. 2d, Conveying Fuel and Raw Materials to some Manufacturing Towns and Districts, and exporting the Manufactured Goods. 3d, Conveying Groceries and Merchant-goods for the Consumption of the District through which the Canal passes. 4th, Conveying Fuel for Domestic Purposes; Manure for the purposes of Agriculture; transporting the produce of the Districts through which the Canal passes, to the different Markets; and promoting Agricultural Purposes in general.[1]

During the canal age many inland counties in the British Isles were almost self-contained. Industries were sited near their raw materials, and sold their finished produce in the surrounding area. Only along the banks of rivers and around the sea coast was it possible to move many products in bulk, although roads were steadily improved during the parallel turnpike era. Local tradespeople and manufacturers would usually support a new canal if it could open up trade to another part of the country, or even to a seaport. The anticipated reduced costs of raw materials and opportunities for the mass production of finished goods suggested prosperity to manufacturers. The prospect of widened markets usually received support from local consumers, as this tended to improve supplies of coal and other commodities. The canal could reduce the dangers of famine and the inconveniences of dearth, whilst almost every account of the opening of a canal refers to reduced coal prices and consequent benefits to the poor.

As most canal projects in Britain were local, much finance was also local. The earlier canals were largely promoted by merchants and landowners, who sought the general economic advancement that a new canal could bring, from which they would benefit indirectly. Later schemes, especially those promoted in the mania period, anticipated that the waterway itself would be profitable. Finance could prove difficult, particularly when money would be tied up in a large static asset like a canal, with no returns for a long time unless interest was paid out of capital raised. Local doggedness completed canals like the Leeds & Liverpool, which took 46 years from start to final completion, while many others took 10 years or more.

Local capital was supplemented by regional funds, as in Wales, where ironmasters, merchants, bankers and landed gentry held shares in a number of companies. When Walter Jeffreys of Brecon died in 1815 he held ten shares in the Aberdare and three in its connection to the Glamorganshire, five in the Swansea, seven in the Brecknock & Abergavenny and shares in the canal-connected Hay and Llanvihangel Tramroads, both of which were connected to a canal. Birmingham and London investors spread their money widely but seldom thickly, and there are occasional oddities of investment such as the group of Leicester people who, during the canal mania, took shares in the Ellesmere Canal and even the Crinan Canal in Scotland.

Not surprisingly, much capital came from colliery and works' owners and merchants, and a great deal from noblemen, landed gentry and the wealthier clergy. Some came from tradesmen and professional people such as doctors and lawyers, while during the canal mania people who were involved in quite small businesses sought rapid wealth through speculation. An example is the four grocers, two coopers, the innholder, mealman, joiner, mercer and perukemaker of Stratford, all of whom subscribed to the Stratford-upon-Avon Canal.

The unreformed municipal corporations played a more limited part in the development of canals than they had in river development. With early canals, councils like Exeter and Stamford took a crucial role. Later, councils often subscribed for shares, as Nottingham, Chester, Carlisle and Swansea did for their local canals, in which case the mayor or another representative would sit on the committee. They sometimes helped to finance surveys, as did Liverpool for the Leeds & Liverpool.

The joint-stock company – one financed by the proceeds of shares sold to the public – goes back to the period before the South Sea Bubble of 1720. It was, however, the frenzy of financial speculation in the Bubble companies of the time that caused Parliament to pass an Act that made it necessary for investors who intended to act as a corporation to be set up by Act of Parliament. The trouble and expense involved in getting a private Act each time that a company was formed meant that few came into existence in order to make rivers navigable.

When canals began to be built, however, their cost was clearly beyond the resources of all but a few wealthy men and partnerships, and thus joint-stock companies were necessary. Compulsory powers to buy land, divert streams, cross highways and so on also required an Act. The number of canal corporations therefore grew rapidly. Early attempts to appoint commissioners to supervise joint-stock companies in the public interest, of which the Trent & Mersey was the best example, were soon defeated.

Many short and private branches were built without an Act, but few bigger waterways were constructed because of the difficulty of acquiring land and securing water supplies without compulsory powers. Longer private canals included the Donnington Wood (Duke of Sutherland's) Canal in Shropshire, the Tennant Canal in Wales and the Torrington Canal in Devon. A notable branch built without an Act was the Hatherton Branch of the Staffordshire & Worcestershire Canal, which opened in 1841.

The formation of a canal company generally followed a similar process, which often began with an advertisement in a local newspaper, like this for the Leeds & Liverpool Canal:

> … whereas such a navigation would be of great utility to trade, especially in time of war, and more particularly to the counties of York and Lancaster, a meeting would be held at the house of Mr John Day, known by the Sign of the Sun in Bradford aforesaid, on Wednesday, the 2nd day of July, 1766, at 10 of the clock in the fore-noon, to consider of the proper ways and means to effect such navigation, at which meeting the nobility, gentry, and clergy of the said several counties, and all others who think it their duty to interest themselves in a matter of so great importance are requested to attend.[2]

Then followed the public meeting (often in the assembly room of an inn), which involved the election of a provisional committee; the subscription for preliminary expenses; the appointment of an engineer to survey and report on a route and give estimates of the costs and probable receipts; the further meeting to receive the report; the resolution to apply to Parliament for an Act; the opening of a subscription book for shares and the payment of deposits; the organization of petitions to Parliament in favour of the project; the despatch by river interests, other canal companies, turnpike trustees, landowners, land carriers and anyone else aggrieved of counter petitions; the expensive battle before the Parliamentary Committees of Lords and Commons, with a full array of counsel and witnesses, including eminent engineers; the various compromises such as clauses to pay compensation tolls, to limit dividends (on the Derby Canal dividends were limited to 8 per cent, after which money had to go to a reserve balance to reduce tolls), guarantees of another company's dividends (as of the Droitwich and Stourbridge canals by the Worcester & Birmingham), or of turnpike trustees against loss, as the Leicester Navigation had to do, and finally the Act, whereupon:

> … on receiving the agreeable news that His Majesty had been at the House of Peers and signed the Bill for making the Navigable Canal from this Town (Birmingham) to Wolverhampton, the Bells were set to ringing, which were continued the whole Day.[3]

All of these promotion expenses were a serious drain on capital.

Opposition to canals came from many sources. Landowners feared that the canal might be carried through their fertile low-lying lands and could drain their water-meadows. They also sought compensation for the inconvenience caused by a canal that might prevent them from enlarging a park, or which divided part of their property from the rest, and brought with it boatmen who did not always respect the game laws.

The local population, while understanding that canals could bring to them cheaply the fuel and goods that they needed, sometimes feared that local produce would be taken away. Cobbett spoke for this kind of opposition when he wrote of the canal at Cricklade:

> … while the poor creatures that raise the wheat and the barley and the cheese and the mutton and the beef are living upon potatoes, an accursed *canal* comes kindly through the parish to convey away the wheat and all the good food to the tax-eaters and their attendants.[4]

Rural millowners feared loss of water from their streams to the canals and were supported by farmers who depended on the mills for the grinding of corn, while owners of industrial mills, driven, for instance, by the Pennine streams, fought bitterly against possible deprivation of their power resources. Road turnpike trustees thought that canals would reduce the tolls on their roads. Road carriers anticipated a loss of livelihood, an argument that they backed up with the accusation that a transport monopoly was being created, and that the reduced demand for horses would lessen the demand for oats and so affect farming. The coasting trade suspected a reduction in the amount of coal and goods carried by sea and the diversion of these goods to the more direct inland navigations. The existing river and canal interests did all they could to make sure that, if they were affected, they did not suffer. On the one hand they demanded compensation payments for loss of tolls, or the erection of physical bars to conserve their water; on the other they insisted on positive inducements, as when the Monmouthshire Canal offered the Brecknock & Abergavenny company £3,000 and ample water if the latter would join its line to the Monmouthshire, rather than build an independent outlet to the River Usk.

All in all there were some bitter arguments before the parliamentary committees. The following is a specimen, from the speech of the counsel for the Thames Commissioners opposing a proposed canal (the Hants & Berks Junction) to join the Kennet & Avon Canal at Newbury to the Basingstoke Canal near Old Basing, so as to avoid the passage of the Thames below Reading:

> Yet even if, which is impossible, water could be procured; and if, which is equally impossible, the repairs [to the Basingstoke Canal] required to an extent little short of beginning *de novo,* could be effected for the sum of ten thousand pounds, instead of ten times ten thousand, where is the money to come from? And what prospect is there of any return for it? Might it just as well be thrown into the sea; and much better thrown *literally* into the Basingstoke Canal, as in all probability there would not be water enough there to cover it? And what guarantee has this Committee that it ever will be forthcoming? The concern has long been bankrupt; its dividends are, as they have always been, naught. There is but one last lingering trader upon it, and he is on the point of flitting, lest his ruin should be consummated. From what quarter can a single ray of hope be expected to break in upon a scene of such utter desolation? This is not a rational project for improving an eligible line of Canal navigation, but is rather like many of those New World schemes, with unpronounceable names, which are so rife these days, distinguished by such a fatuous and headlong rage for speculation that, if any one were to start a Mining Company in Utopia, he could presently dispose of the shares at a profit.[5]

Sometimes the opposition was overwhelmed; sometimes it was persuaded, by conversion of the heart, lining of the pocket or the allotment of shares likely to appreciate quickly in value. For instance, a Bristol newspaper remarks of the opponents of the Kennet & Avon Bill:

> Those who went up to London to petition against it, are returned, and now are most laudably employed in pointing out its beneficial effects, and soliciting the assent of all their late demurring neighbours.[6]

If opposition was overcome and an Act was obtained, a first general assembly of the shareholders was held. At this a committee and officers were appointed: a clerk, often a local solicitor, to do the legal work, write the important letters, and take the minutes; a treasurer, an accountant, probably a banking firm; a principal and a resident engineer; and usually one or two assistants and a clerk of

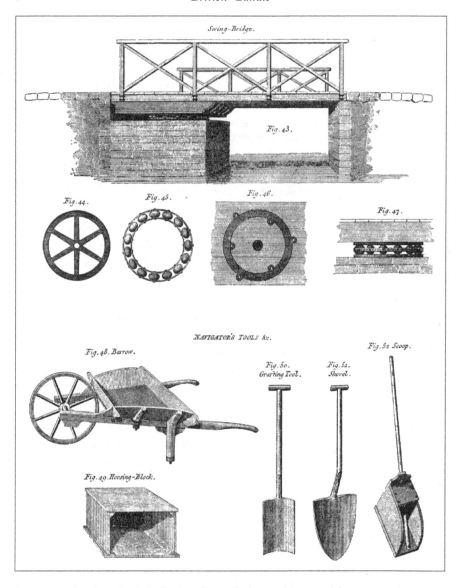

Some examples, from *Rees' Cyclopedia* of 1819, depicting elements of the construction process: designs for a swing bridge, and examples of the simple tools used to build the canals. Horsing-blocks were used to support the planks of barrow runs.

works. Land was bought, contractors and workmen engaged, and then with ceremony the first sod was cut. On 27 July 1766, for instance, the population of the Burslem district celebrated the beginning of work on the Trent & Mersey Canal. After Josiah Wedgwood cut the first sod, Mr Brindley, the engineer of the canal, wheeled it away in a barrow. Then:

... a barrel of old Staffordshire ale was broached on the spot; the healths of Earl Gower, Lord Anson, Lord Gray, the county members, the Committee, and other officers were drunk; and Mr Wedgwood was specially thanked, in the name of the whole assembly, for his indefatigable services in this good cause. Succeeding to this were luncheons and dinners at the Leopard and other inns... A sheep was roasted whole for the benefit of the poorer potters, and at sunset bonfires were lighted in various parts of the town.[7]

Then work began. Local brickworks were set up if suitable clay could be found, stone was brought from the quarries and timber was bought. Gangs of men began to dig with picks, shovels and barrows, occasionally with mechanical help such as that provided by John Carne's cutting machine on canals like the Herefordshire & Gloucestershire. Masons worked on the locks, shafts for the tunnels were sunk to the right depth from the ground above and the tunnels were dug inwards and outwards. This work was often carried out by miners, who set their charges of gunpowder by the light of candles. Water that percolated into the workings was drained off or removed by steam pumps. Ventilation was provided by lighting a fire under a shaft to provide an up draught, which in turn caused a down draught at other shafts.

The skilled workmen who dug the canal navigations – to use the older term – were called cutters or bankers, the unskilled being labourers. The word 'navigator' appeared in the 1770s with two meanings: 'canal boatman' and 'canal cutter'. Both meanings persisted, the first only used occasionally and the second common by the 1790s, though not until 1832, according to *The Shorter Oxford English Dictionary*, was it first shortened to 'navvy'. In England some of these cutters were labourers who had probably left the land because of the enclosure Acts; some were fenmen, used to digging and embanking drains; some were drawn from the vagrants who had been a Poor Law problem since the days of Elizabeth; and many were Scottish or Irish. As the construction gangs moved through the countryside they must have brought consternation to villagers who had not seen such uproar since the days of the English Civil War of the 1640s. They were rough men, and local newspapers and books carry stories of robbery and even murder. The following account records how the navvies working on the improvement of the River Witham under the Act of 1812 were caught up in a dispute with a local baker:

... the riot began on the west side of the river, at a public house with the sign of 'The Plough' – they drove the landlord away from the house, took out his barrels, and drank the beer; having taken his sign down, they also took the baker's basket and bread, and, crossing the river, proceeded up to the village of Bardney... They pelted the baker with his bread, and hung his basket on the top of a tree in the village; they then attacked the 'Bottle and Glass' public house – fetched the barrels of beer out of the house, knocked the ends out and drank the ale; Mr Benson, a person who was then the landlord of the 'Angel' Inn, to prevent them entering his premises, brought or rolled out his barrels of beer himself, and by this means saved himself and his house.

During the time they invested the houses in Bardney, the people were so frightened that they gave them anything they asked for; the navvies went about to the inhabitants of the village demanding money and different articles from them, and proclaiming their own prices for provisions for the future... [8]

The navvies clashed with constables, one of whom died later from his injuries, until the cavalry arrived to read the Riot Act and restore order. The rioters were taken away for trial and imprisonment.

They had some excuse, for some navvies were often not even paid their 2s. (10p) to 3s (15p) a day in cash each week. Those working on the Kennet & Avon Canal in 1797, for instance, were paid in twenty-one day notes, which then had to be cashed at a discount, while in 1804 the tunnellers and cutters working directly for the Grand Junction company at Blisworth were paid monthly. For the Forth & Clyde company, keeping wages to a minimum was a major priority. Truck — the payment in private tokens, often redeemable only by the employers' tommy shops — was not abolished for canal construction workers until 1887, when only the Manchester Ship Canal remained to be built. Pinkertons were among those contractors who paid in truck. Sometimes, as on the Liskeard & Looe Union Canal, a doctor was retained to look after navvies' injuries or illness. More often, workers paid into a fund for sickness payments, as on the Peak Forest, to which the company also subscribed.

More intellectual moments were recorded by the Gloucester & Berkeley Committee in 1794: 'Ordered, That Mr Wheeler pay the workmen who found the Coins £1-1-0 and that he count them over and deliver them to Mr Cheston, who has kindly offered to decypher them, and give his opinion of their value.' [9] Roman and mediaeval remains were uncovered in the digging of the Portsmouth & Arundel Canal, although the navvies' reactions were not recorded.

However, many references by engineers run like the following complaint about contractors in the Sapperton Tunnel: 'Richd Jones ... not in the work at 2 o'clock P.M. nor had been in the work this day. All his men a Drinking except 3 men in the Big Tunnel.' [10]

Now and then a few lines appeared in the local newspaper: 'Early on Saturday morning last, a little beyond Winson Green, in the Birmingham Canal Navigation, the Earth fell suddenly in and killed John Lester, one of the workmen, occasioned, it is thought, by the heavy Rains on Friday evening.' [11]

Just as later most of the railways were built by large contractors like Brassey, so were some of the canals. Beginning in 1768 on the Driffield, the extensive Pinkerton family worked on canals and navigations as widely spread as the Selby, Barnsley, Erewash, Birmingham & Fazeley, Gloucester & Berkeley, Kidwelly & Llanelly and Basingstoke canals. Edward (later Sir Edward) Banks, himself

Token issued by John Pinkerton to the workmen on the Basingstoke Canal. There was a serious shortage of coinage in the 1790s, and contractors had to issue their own. These could be exchanged at a number of public houses, including the George at Odiham.

or through the firm of Joliffe & Banks, built parts of the Leeds & Liverpool, Lancaster, Ulverston, Ashton-under-Lyne and Huddersfield canals, and also the Goole Canal of the Aire & Calder. Hugh McIntosh worked on the Croydon and Grand Western extension, and rebuilt much of the Aire & Calder. Most of the earlier canals, however, were built by local contractors, many of them leading groups of workmen formed for this purpose and often undertaking quite small sections. A few were built by direct labour, or finished by this means after the contractors had withdrawn.

A clerk of works or resident engineer, with his subordinates, was usually in charge of construction, while over him was the principal engineer who had laid out the line and was generally responsible for the work, though he might have been in charge of building half a dozen major canals at the same time. The resident engineer in turn employed overlookers, for, as Robert Whitworth told the Ashby Canal shareholders in 1794, 'neither puddlers or masons ought to be left to themselves, even one Day, in some particular situations'.[12] He also hired checkers to count the men employed by the contractors, in order that 'subsist' money could be advanced by the company to the contractors until the work was periodically measured up and a progress payment made. Cutting went on to the accompaniment of bickering with the contractors over payment on account and accusations of bad work, and also with the men over demands for a rise in pay or the loss of tools. Strikes were not unknown, if short-lived, as with that during the building of the Lune aqueduct on the Lancaster Canal in 1794.

It was during the canal age that the profession of civil engineering came into being. John Smeaton (1724–92), the son of an attorney who began as a maker of scientific instruments, designed the Eddystone Lighthouse and supervised its construction up until 1759, prior to his involvement with waterways. One of the founders of the Society of Civil Engineers in 1771, he was probably the first to adopt what is recognised today as a professional approach to engineering work.

Other great names in engineering came from varied origins and, because of their ability, these people had become expert in the new problems: Brindley learned his trade as a millwright; Rennie was a mechanically minded farmer's son; Telford a working mason; Jessop the son of a foreman shipwright; Outram the son of a 'gentleman'. Others learned from these men. Robert Whitworth senior and Thomas Dadford senior had been Brindley's assistants and in turn fathered engineers, while Hugh Henshall was Brindley's brother-in-law. Jessop had been Smeaton's pupil. Others again, such as Thomas Sheasby, began life as contractors.

It should be stressed that most canals had been surveyed before the first Ordnance Survey map had been issued. The first, for Kent, appeared in 1801, but it was 1844 before the whole of England south of a line from Hull to Preston was mapped; mapping of Ireland was only completed in the 1830s. As there had been no previous detailed survey of England, engineers had to rely on local maps, which may have been inaccurate, and their own special surveys, which were usually later published to encourage prospective investors. The engineers found themselves in greatest difficulty over geology. Not until 1815 was the first detailed geological map of England published. This had been produced by William Smith, who had helped to survey the lines of the Somersetshire Coal Canal in 1793, and was involved in its construction until his dismissal in 1799. Even the most careful survey, including trials of the ground over which the canal was to pass or through which tunnels were to be made, often failed to detect formations that proved difficult to deal with, such as those that caused the abandonment of the first Blisworth Tunnel. Many surveys were sketchy, so that engineers later encountered difficulties that increased construction costs.

Some engineers took on too much. Brindley soon found himself with half a dozen big schemes on his hands at once. He handled them by delegating as much responsibility as possible to his assistants, whom he installed as resident engineers on the Birmingham, Staffordshire & Worcestershire, Coventry and Oxford canals, while he gave most of his own time to the Duke's canal and the Trent & Mersey Canal. This view of his responsibilities did not commend itself to the businessmen of the Birmingham Canal, who observed 'that Mr Brindley hath frequently passed by, and sometimes come into town, without giving them an opportunity of meeting to confer with him upon the progress of the undertaking'. They expressed 'their dissatisfaction at not being able to see him at such times'.[13] A few months later the Coventry proprietors summarily dismissed him. All the same he probably died of overwork, combined with his diabetes and the nephritis he contracted at Ipstones while surveying for the Caldon branch of the Trent & Mersey Canal.

Brindley was primarily involved with narrow-boat canals. Of all those he worked on only the Bridgewater and Droitwich canals took barges, in each case from a neighbouring river. Of his assistants, trained by having responsibility thrust on them, Thomas Dadford senior (and later his sons) and Samuel Simcock of the Oxford and Birmingham canals were also mainly narrow canal builders. A third, Robert Whitworth, did much of his best work on broad canals: the Thames & Severn, Leeds & Liverpool summit, Forth & Clyde and Ashby de la Zouch.

Two other groups were more in the European tradition of bigger waterways. One was headed by John Smeaton, who had travelled abroad before basing himself in Yorkshire. He built much of the Calder & Hebble and the Forth & Clyde canals, and his pupil William Jessop was England's most prolific engineer of broad waterways. These included much of the Aire & Calder; the Barnsley, Rochdale, Trent Navigation, Nottingham, Cromford and Grand Junction canals. Jessop only built one narrow canal, the Ellesmere, and then by accident, for when he was engaged the promoters intended it to be broad. Smeaton's and Jessop's school can justifiably claim John Rennie, builder of two great broad canals, the Lancaster and the Kennet & Avon; the two William Crosleys, first-class working engineers; and later George Leather, who made the Goole Canal and created the modern Aire & Calder. Telford, too, owed much to the Smeaton tradition. His first major canal work was as Jessop's resident engineer for many years on the Ellesmere; his second with Jessop to create, and alone to execute, the great Caledonian; and finally, paralleling in the Midlands what Leather was doing in Yorkshire, to build the new Birmingham main line and the Birmingham & Liverpool Junction Canal.

An Irish group of engineers also drew on experience in continental Europe. English engineers worked in Ireland, notably Steers, Jessop, Rennie and Chapman, and earlier Richard Castle of French, Davis Ducart of Italian and Thomas Omer of Dutch descent. Ireland's own engineers included John Killaly, John Brownrigg and Richard Evans.

The engineering skill and resourcefulness that underlay Britain's canals is striking. No tunnel of any size, other than mining tunnels, had ever been built in Britain before those at Norwood and Harecastle, both over 1½ miles long; even examples in continental Europe were limited. Aqueducts, embankments, cuttings, reservoirs, locks, inclined planes and canal lifts were designed and built as the need arose, albeit sometimes reflecting developments elsewhere in the world. To contemporaries they were a source of wonder. Josiah Wedgwood wrote of the flight of locks on the Bridgewater Canal at Runcorn:

> I was quite astonish'd at the vastness of the plan and the greatness of stile in the execution. The Walls of the Locks are truly admirable, both for strength and beauty of workmanship. The front Lock next the sea (for such it seems when the Tide is in) in particular, whose walls are compos'd of vast stones from 1 to 12 Tons weight, & yet by the excellent machinery made use of, some of which is still left standing, they had as perfect command of these huge masses of Rock as a common bricklayer of the brick in his hands. In short, to behold Ten of these Locks all at a view ... the whole seems to be the work of the Titans, rather than the production of our Pigmy race of beings...[14]

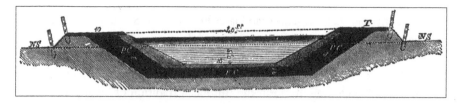

Puddling a canal, from Tomlinson's *Cyclopedia of Useful Arts* of 1866. In porous ground
the bed is given 18in of puddle below, and 3ft at the sides; in retentive soil, puddle is only
needed at each side to prevent lateral leakage, which would weaken the banks.

A more modern canal profile, using metal piling to protect the banks. This length of canal is
part of the Whitchurch Branch of the Shropshire Union Canal, which was filled in during
the early 1950s but re-excavated in 1993 in the first phase of a restoration proposal.

The engineer would ride from one end of the line under construction to the
other, living in inns, working out problems by candlelight, and now and then getting involved in unpleasantness: when the engineer on the Leeds & Liverpool had
to dismiss a contractor, the committee assured him that 'you will be supported in
every proper measure, and that no sinister, envious or ilnatural insinuations will
be listened to.'[15]

   The general meeting of proprietors met once or twice a year to hear reports
on progress, and sometimes to dine at the company's expense. Usually the Act
provided that a certain number of shares had to be present in person or by proxy
if a valid meeting was to be held, and meetings often had to be adjourned for lack

of attendance. Affairs were managed by an executive committee, under which there might be one or two working committees to superintend construction: the Oxford Canal had three such district committees.

On the executive committee the chairman or another prominent member would oversee the engineer and expenditure, and would often negotiate for the acquisition of land, always a difficult process. The land was first valued by valuers employed by the company. If the landowner did not agree with this valuation the chairman or someone from the company tried to reach an agreement. If this failed the dispute was referred to a body of commissioners named in the Act, who were usually all of the landowners of the county over a certain landed income per annum, a quorum of whom had power to judge. Since landowners tended to favour their own kind, the scales were weighted against the canal companies and the obstructive usually got their price. It was therefore often the case that the land for a canal cost more than the estimates allowed for. A further right of appeal, from the commissioners to a jury, was seldom exercised, although in one case on the Leeds & Liverpool in Yorkshire the jury did reduce values put on land by the commissioners.

Most rural land was acquired at around thirty years' purchase, that is, thirty times the annual rent. Special compensation was paid when the canal line cut through land and divided roads and farms. This sum could be increased when a major estate was affected. Thus, the Grand Junction paid £5,000 to Lord Clarendon for the right to pass through Grove Park, plus the price for the land itself. It paid £15,000 to Lord Essex to traverse Cassiobury Park, and thus avoid a planned tunnel. Sometimes accommodation bridges partly compensated for the severance of land, often constructed in ornamental fashion where these cut through landed estates. Sometimes it was cheaper to set out a more circuitous line by agreement, as it was, seemingly, with parts of the Oxford Canal summit at Wormleighton which minimised damage to Lord Spencer's estate. In the case of the Edinburgh & Glasgow Union Canal, a 696 yard tunnel at Falkirk was necessary to avoid the pleasure ground around Callendar House. In some cases, such as parts of the Chester Canal, acquisition was not completed before opening, and rent was due, and paid with difficulty, for unacquired sections near Nantwich.

Canal shares were usually in denominations of £100. A deposit was payable when the shares were first subscribed and then, as the canal was built, calls of so many pounds a share were made on the shareholders until the full amount had been paid. It was not always easy to procure the money for these calls, even if everything was going well, for shareholders often wished to hold on to their capital. Interest was thus usually paid on paid-up calls, although this did increase construction costs; and if paid in bonds, these hampered the company after opening. If the canal's earnings looked much less than anticipated, shareholders were often reluctant to pay calls, preferring to forfeit shares or risk litigation. Canal committees sometimes had to wheedle calls out of shareholders, even to the point of sending their clerk to make a personal visit.

A blank share certificate for the Wey & Arun Junction Canal, authorised in 1815. This illustration was printed from original blocks discovered by Charles Hadfield before the first edition of *British Canals*.

Canal committees often turned for temporary accommodation to their banks, and found, as have many, that bankers took a gloomier view of the future than they did. In 1797 the Kennet & Avon's bankers refused to advance more money against unpaid calls, 'on account of the pressure of the times',[16] but relented after making conditions that slowed down construction expenditure to the pace of the calls made.[16] Calls beyond the nominal amount of each share could be made on the original shares, or fresh shares could be issued, often at a discount.

Alternatively, some sort of preference could be given to those who came to the rescue, in the form of preference shares, bonds, annuities, or promissory notes. Sometimes the tolls of the canal or the waterway itself would be mortgaged. In 1796 the Peak Forest Committee, faced with an overdraft of £4,000, themselves guaranteed £1,000 of this sum and £4,000 more to complete the summit level and the tramroad at Marple that preceded the locks. In 1803 there was the curious case of the Glamorganshire Bank, which made the Swansea Canal a loan on condition of being appointed its treasurers. Finally there was always the danger of bank failure or embarrassment, which was awkward if partners in the bank were also members of the canal committee. For example in 1816 the Shrewsbury Canal switched from a failing Shrewsbury bank to one in Wellington; committee members were involved in both.

The original Act of Parliament always provided for the raising of an additional amount – usually a third as much again – should the original capital prove insufficient to finish the canal. This amount could be found in a number of different ways. On the one hand calls beyond the nominal amount of each share could be made on the original shares, or fresh shares could be issued, the latter perhaps at a discount, or auctioned. On the other hand some form of preference could be given to those who came to the rescue, either by the issue of preference shares or by bonds, convertible or not, annuities, promissory notes or mortgages, either of the tolls of the canal or of the waterway and tolls together. If the canal was later a success the interest payments and later repayments of capital on these prior charges only delayed the dividends on the ordinary shares. In some cases, however, the existence of the prior charges extinguished all hope for the ordinary shareholders, for these canals never succeeded in paying off their debts.

An instance of the removal of prior charges involved the Thames & Severn Canal. By 1808 this concern had accumulated a debt of £193,892, including a principal debt of £117,125 and arrears of interest. Since the company was not earning enough to pay the current interest on the debt, financial reconstruction was essential, and eventually the debt-holders agreed to a scheme by which the old shareholders gained a hope – and later the actuality – of dividends.

Government aid to industry has a long history. In 1784 the Government lent £50,000 to the Forth & Clyde Canal Company and in 1799 it lent £25,000 to the Crinan Canal proprietors out of the repayments. In 1817 the Poor Employment Act set up Exchequer Bill Loan Commissioners with power to lend money to concerns that would employ the poor, especially unskilled labourers, to relieve the unemployment that had followed the end of the Napoleonic Wars. A number of canals were helped in this way. Some, like the Gloucester & Berkeley and the Regent's canals, were successes, and the loans essential to finish the waterway were repaid. Some, like the Portsmouth & Arundel Canal, were not. This company was unable to pay any of the £40,000 loan, but its guarantor, the Earl of Egremont, paid it himself.

In Ireland most inland waterways were financed and constructed with Government support. Even those that were built by private companies, like the Royal Canal, depended on Government loans, and this canal was only completed after the Directors General of Inland Navigation took over in 1813.

Finally, at last the canal would be completed (unless, like the Salisbury & Southampton and the Dorset & Somerset canals, the money that could possibly be raised was not enough to overcome all of the difficulties of finishing the line). Financial troubles would be forgotten, the water would be let in, boats bought, toll and lock-keepers and accounting staff appointed, security bonds arranged and plans made for the opening day.

The opening of a canal was an occasion for considerable celebration. Sometimes verse contributed to the event, as when Elizabeth Davies, who kept a lollipop shop in Wind Street, Neath, wrote a song of nineteen verses, of which two are given below, to commemorate the opening of the Neath & Swansea Junction (usually called the Tennant) Canal:

> O! could I make verses with humour and wit,
> George Tennant, Esquire's great genius to fit;
> From morn until even, I would sit down and tell;
> And sing in the praise of Neath Junction Canal.
>
> I hope when he's dead and laid in his grave,
> His soul will in heaven be eternally saved;
> It will then be recorded for ages to tell,
> Who was the great founder of Neath Junction Canal.[17]

A contemporary newspaper account describes the opening in 1814 of the Thames & Medway Canal. This ill-fated venture was built to connect the Thames at Gravesend with the Medway at Strood opposite Rochester. Its tunnel, 2¼ miles long and the second longest canal tunnel built in Britain, is now used by railway passengers travelling from Strood to Higham:

> There were four barges occupied by the company, and there was a fifth barge, preceding such four barges, occupied with musicians… The most gratifying part of the view, however, was the entrance into the tunnel.
>
> Above the Higham entrance immense crowds of persons were assembled. At the entrance of the Tunnel, the light of Frindsbury Arch at the end could be distinctly seen; and the effect was very curious. The towing-path was thronged with spectators, and the Canal-workers carried lighted torches…
>
> The barges, which occasionally paused in the tunnel, were about forty minutes in passing through it. On passing through Frindsbury outlet, there is a capacious basin, which forms the terminations of this canal. Around this basin there were great crowds

of persons and several of His Majesty's boats, with Officers on board… The Officers greeted the company on their coming out of the tunnel most cordially, giving the signal for huzzas, and the band struck up 'Rule Britannia'. The Officers and others joined the procession on the landing, and proceeded to the Crown Inn, Rochester…

At the Crown Inn a dinner was provided for more than a hundred persons, with entertainment and a series of toasts. Among the latter the chairman:

> … spoke of the magnitude of the work which had been accomplished. There had been united two of the most valuable rivers in the kingdom, and two of the richest rivers of the world, and the importance of the work, he thought, could not well be too highly appreciated. The value of the works they could all understand. If any person's property or comforts had been disturbed, it was the subject of lamentation; and he could state that, if ample remuneration had not already been made, the Company would be happy to make the completest compensation.

Several other toasts followed at this celebration, and 'After the procession the workmen, to the amount of between two and three hundred, had a dinner at the Canal Tavern, &c.'[18]

This composite portrait omits many variations between districts, eras and the ownership and organization of canals. The lines that emerged varied greatly in size, primarily because of the local nature of most projects. In width they can be grouped roughly into ship, broad, narrow and tub-boat canals, although no definite line can be drawn between one class and another.

The early ship canals such as the Caledonian, Gloucester & Berkeley and the Exeter were much smaller than the later Manchester Ship Canal. The largest locks at the time of completion were those of 170ft x 38ft on the Caledonian, in contrast with those of 600ft x 65ft on the Manchester Ship Canal.

The broad canals such as the Kennet & Avon, Leeds & Liverpool, Rochdale, Bridgewater and Forth & Clyde could take craft from 55ft to 80ft long, and between 12 and 21ft wide, carrying about 50-100 tons. Many of them, like the Droitwich, Sir John Ramsden's, Stroudwater, Erewash and the lower Chesterfield Canal formed branches of river navigations and were built broad to take river craft.

Three main routes were built broad: from Forth to Clyde; from Liverpool across the Pennines by the Leeds & Liverpool or the Rochdale to Hull; and from Bristol to London by the Thames & Severn or the Kennet & Avon. Two others failed. In 1793 and 1794 the Grand Junction company sought to build a broad canal from London to Braunston near Rugby, and the Ashby was also built broad. The Grand Junction put pressure on the Oxford, Coventry and Trent & Mersey Canals to widen so that, by building a short link between the Ashby Canal and the Trent & Mersey, a broad line between London, Manchester and Liverpool would result. The Trent & Mersey was opposed, while the others stalled. In 1796 the Ashby and the broad Chester Canal shareholders, helped by dissident Potteries manufacturers, promoted a new broad canal, the Commercial. This was to join the Chester and Ashby canals through Uttoxeter, Hanley and Newcastle, to achieve the same object once the Coventry and Oxford were widened from Braunston to Marston. After this scheme failed, no more attempts were made to provide a national broad route between London and Manchester and Liverpool.

A broad line was also envisaged between Exeter and London, using the Grand Western Canal to Taunton, and then two lines to Bristol and to the Thames & Severn at Cirencester, and on to Oxford. The Oxford Canal would be widened to the junction with the proposed Hampton Gay Canal to London. Later the Kennet & Avon line and a Bristol & Taunton Canal would have provided the line, to enable 50 ton craft to proceed 200 miles from Exeter to London. However, the co-ordination of routes and gauges failed to come about.

Most canals in the English Midlands were built to narrow dimensions, for narrow boats about 70ft x 6'10', carrying 25-30 tons. Brindley and his assistants surveyed many of these canals, and experience in Yorkshire and Lancashire was bypassed when the size of boat was chosen. Although hard evidence is limited, the narrow Worsley mine-boats, or the challenge of barge-sized bores for the long tunnels at Norwood and Harecastle, for which there was no precedent, may have been influential. The critical factors were probably the reduced construction costs and water supply requirements of smaller canals, but without a full appreciation of their limited traffic capacity. In any event, these canals would prove inadequate for the growth in traffics, but sufficient to carry the more limited trade left when railway competition developed.

The tub-boat canals used very small boats carrying about 5 tons and often had inclined planes, by which boats were drawn up and down, instead of locks. There were two groups of these canals, which were suited to hilly country – one in the West Country, the other in Shropshire – and a single canal in Wales, the Kidwelly & Llanelly. Of these, only the Shropshire system was linked to the main Midlands canals, and then only when much of the Shrewsbury Canal was enlarged to narrow boat dimensions.

In South Wales, canals were of varied dimensions, around 60-65ft long and 9ft wide. Those in Scotland varied greatly in dimensions, the Aberdeenshire having locks 9ft wide, but the lockless Glasgow Paisley & Ardrossan taking craft slightly over 7ft in width. No true narrow-boat canals were built in Ireland, although the less successful Ulster canal could only take craft 11ft 6in wide.

These variations in gauge sometimes sufficed to realise the main purpose for which a particular canal was constructed, but they also inhibited the development of a national system of water transport in each country of the British Isles.

CHAPTER THREE

Early Life on the Canals

The opening of a canal often significantly affected the development of the towns which it served. Stourport was indeed created by the trade that followed the opening of the Staffordshire & Worcestershire Canal. The Lancaster Canal's northern end was at Kendal, whose local historian stressed in 1861 that:

> ... the spirit of improvement fully manifested itself in 1818 and 1819. The date of the new town may, we conceive, truly be placed here, at the time of the opening of the Lancaster and Kendal canal. This event gave an impulse to the public spirit of the inhabitants, and formed the commencement of a new era in the history of Kendal... The large warehouses and other buildings at the canal harbour, were all erected at this time; Kent Lane (which before was very steep, and so narrow that two carts could scarcely pass) was thrown open, and the ascent considerably diminished ... in a very short time, the town assumed a new and modern appearance – so very different that any person having been absent a few years, could scarcely have identified it.[1]

Ellesmere Port, and to a lesser extent Goole, were also created by their waterways, much being fostered by the canal company itself. In some places the canal company owned surplus land, and when trade enabled this to be developed, a large income in rents for land and buildings was reaped, as with the Grand Junction's property in Paddington.

Along the lines of the canal and at the basins great changes took place. Factories were built and wharves provided for them, often on side cuts. At the basins warehouses were built, and coal-wharves, sheds, cranes and weigh-houses provided. In Coventry the coal-wharves lay below the boats so that coal could be unloaded directly into carts. Offices were provided for the clerks, often in a specially built eighteenth-century house that still stands, like Beech House at Ellesmere, as a reminder. Along the line of the canal and at basins public houses were now called the Navigation Inn, the Wharf or the Boat and Horses, as those on earlier modes had been called the Pack Horse or the Row Barge. More closely related to a particular canal were the Grand Junction Arms in Praed Street, Paddington; the Calder & Hebble at Salterhebble, near Halifax; and the Grosvenor Basin, which still stood at the side of Victoria Station in 1954.

The administration of a canal was never easy in the days before telephones and telegrams, or even the penny post before 1840. In the canal office, usually located in a main town, were the agent or superintendent; the accountant and chief toll-collector; and the resident clerk, each with their staff, while the engineer often had his own house. Strung out along the line were toll-collectors, who usually had to give security bonds for their honesty; wharfingers; lock-keepers; on the bigger canals assistant engineers in charge of portions of the route; lengthsmen or bank rangers; maintenance craftsmen such as carpenters and masons; and even the mole catcher. When the company did its own carrying, and employed craft and crews, there was also a carrying manager to seek traffic and supervise the boatpeople.

The shareholders would usually meet twice a year to hear a financial statement and declare a dividend which, unlike today, was usually only paid through a bank on application and was therefore advertised in the local press. At one of these two meetings the managing committee was usually elected.

This committee was the real governing body of the canal and met as often as needed – probably monthly on a big canal, three or four times a year on a small one. It had about fifteen members, who were drawn from the more influential shareholders. Occasionally it was constituted regionally, as on the Kennet & Avon Canal, where a number of seats were allotted to each of the three districts into which the canal was divided. The Swansea Canal Committee comprised all shareholders with five or more shares; surprisingly, inefficiency did not result. The quorum for committee meetings was low, as attendances were often poor, although members usually received travel expenses, and sometimes a free meal, 'Beer and a genteel dessert to be included'.[2] Meetings were either at the company's office or a local inn, while many committees had an annual trip to inspect their property, often in a special vessel.

When the canal was a big concern and could afford to pay permanent officials well, business was carried on efficiently. Trouble occurred with concerns too small to pay salaries. Much of the administrative responsibility then fell on the managing committee, which often consisted of country gentlemen and professional men without the time or inclination to undertake the necessary duties. The company's fortunes then depended on the chairman and still more on the clerk. The latter was usually a solicitor from a local and established firm, who might put much more work into the canal company than his salary justified in order to please his clients among the shareholders. If both men were energetic, business went well; if not, it went badly. Energy in chairmen was often helped by their large shareholdings, and often by annual honoraria from the shareholders, or occasional gifts of silver plate. One or two were paid regular salaries, and gave much of their time to the work. For instance the Grand Junction Canal had for many years a paid chairman on its managing committee.

In the bigger concerns the committees faced other difficulties. Their administration was good but their policies, being of such great importance to the economic life of their area, were targets for constant criticism both from inside and outside their number. An example of an inside criticism, which reads with a modern air, comes from the Birmingham Canal in 1769:

That upon examining into the Particulars of a Misunderstanding which happened in the Committee between Messrs. Garbett and Bentley, it appeared, that Mr Garbett did not intend to insinuate Mr Bentley's having wilfully mispent any of the Company's Money, but always thought he did his best; and (taking the whole of Mr Bentley's Conduct into Consideration) that the Public were under Obligations to him. It likewise appeared that Mr Garbett did frequently request for the Poor to be supplied with Coal, in Preference to any Person whatsoever, and that there is no Reason to say, he ever did make a Point for the Brass Work to receive the constant Supply of Three Tons per Day...[2]

The boats used on canals varied widely. On the river navigations sailing boats were the most common: various trows and barges on the Severn, flats on the Mersey and Weaver; keels on the Tyne and in Yorkshire, wherries in Norfolk, lighters in the Fens, Western barges on the Thames and Medway barges on the River Medway. These all differed in size and build, but the following will serve as examples: the trow was nearly flat-bottomed, 16–20ft wide and some 100ft long, carried 40–80 or more tons according to the depth of the river, with a main mast and topmast perhaps 80ft high, sometimes a mizzen mast, and square sails; the barge (sometimes called a frigate) was a good deal smaller and carried 20–40 tons; the Tyne keels were some 42ft long and 19ft broad, while those of Yorkshire were about 54ft long and 14ft broad, and carried upwards of 80 tons. Horse-drawn barges were also used on river navigations. Those of the Kennet were 100ft long and 17ft wide.

On the broad canals horse-drawn barges and river sailing barges were used. On the narrow canals, narrow boats (also known as monkey boats or longboats) were common, each of an appropriate size to fit the locks on the canal where it was used. Those on the valley canals of South Wales were somewhat broader. Most long-distance traffic in the English midlands area bounded by Manchester, Stourport, Nottingham and London was carried in narrow boats, which could be worked singly through narrow locks and in pairs through broad locks. Tub-boat canals had small boats carrying a few tons, often operated in trains. Those on the Bude Canal were fitted with wheels on the bottom so that they could run on the rails of the inclined planes.

Timber, often elm, was the usual building material until iron and steel came later. The first barge made of iron, *The Trial*, was built by John Wilkinson the ironmaster and launched on the River Severn at Coalbrookdale on 9 July 1787. 'It answers all my expectations,' he wrote, and 'it has convinced the unbelievers, who were 999 in a thousand.'[3] Some iron narrow boats were built: Eric Svedenstierna saw several at Wilkinson's Bilston works in 1803.

Experiments were made with steamboats on inland waterways before the end of the eighteenth century. From 1818, however, passenger and goods-carrying steam packets multiplied, especially on the Yorkshire Ouse, Trent, Mersey and

Thames. In 1826 a steam tug began to work regularly through Islington Tunnel on the Regent's Canal, and experimental cargo carriers began to appear on the canals, like the stern paddle-wheeler that arrived at Birmingham from London in 1826 carrying 20 tons. In 1831 the Aire & Calder put a steam paddle tug on their Goole–Leeds run, and thereafter extended steam working rapidly. Tugs followed on other waterways, like the Caledonian and the Norwich & Lowestoft, but not until after the middle of the century were steam canal boats much developed for cargo carrying. The general replacement of horse haulage had to wait until after diesel engines were developed from the 1920s.

The canal company usually provided public wharves in the charge of a wharf-inger. The crane, weighing machine, warehouses and stables were enclosed by a wall and gates. Other warehouses built by the company might be let to permanent tenants – either local traders or one or more carrying concerns like Pickfords – and specialised buildings like salt houses, and warehouses for iron, flour and cheese, were put up when they were needed. Some companies, like the Shropshire Union, also maintained wharves on waterways away from their own, for which goods intended for their line could be collected. Private wharves and warehouses, either on the line of the waterway or on private branches, were built by other users.

Towing on the river navigations was usually carried out by gangs of men, a practice that continued well into the nineteenth century. Thomas Telford, writing about the Severn in 1797, condemned the 'barbarous and expensive custom of performing this slave-like office by men'.[4]

A witness for the Severn Towing Path Bill of 1803 said that about 150 men were employed in this work on the 24 miles from Bewdley to Coalbrookdale. The cost of towing this distance was put at 3s. (15p) per man, each of whom was reckoned to pull 3 tons, while one horse could do the work of six men, at a third less cost. Within the next ten years a horse towing-path was made northwards to Shrewsbury and southwards to Gloucester. On the upper Medway, however, this bow-hauling (said to be so called from the bows of rope attached to the towing line on which the men pulled) continued until about 1838. Sometimes these river towpaths were made by separate towing-path companies, as on the Severn or the Wye, or by a separate public body, as on the Great Ouse from Denver Sluice to King's Lynn, or privately, with access allowed on payment to the landowner, as on the Stour, where haling rents, as they were called, were paid for many years to Abram Constable, the brother of the painter.

In Yorkshire, East Anglia (where many rivers had no towing-paths), on the Medway, the Weaver and the Severn, sailing was commonly employed as an alter-native to towing when it was practicable. The Sankey Navigation was designed for sailing vessels, and had no overbridges until the railway era. Motor barges and tugs are now used on many rivers, often to push other craft.

On canals, also, towing by men was an occasional practice in the early days, for instance on the Trent & Mersey and the Stroudwater. Usually, however, horse towing was used from the beginning. When boats going in opposite directions met, the empty boat dropped its towline under the laden boat or, if both were laden, the outer under the inner. Overtaking of one moving boat by another was usually prohibited by by-laws, with the maximum speed laid down as 2–3mph. A few later and improved canals, such as Telford's reconstruction of part of the Birmingham Canal, had towpaths on both sides.

Horses (or other animals) usually drew a single boat but, when steam and, later, diesel craft were introduced, one boat often towed another. A narrow-boat motor, for instance, towed a butty. In such cases the butty or towed boat had to be worked through a single lock by its crew. Until the 1980s reconstruction push-towed vessels on the Sheffield & South Yorkshire canals were still being bow-hauled through the small locks above Doncaster.

To save construction costs, longer tunnels seldom had a towpath. Boats had to be legged through by boatmen or by special leggers lying on their backs on boards projecting from the boats, and pushing with their feet against the sides or roof. They were recommended to 'strap themselves to a short Cord affix'd to the Boat to prevent their being drown'd'.[5] As a night trip in 1858 through Islington Tunnel by narrow boat recounted:

> A couple of strong thick boards … are hooked on to places formed on each side of the barge, near the head … On these two narrow, insecure platforms, the two venturesome boatmen lie on their backs, holding on by grasping the board underneath, and with their legs, up to the waist, hanging over the water … the operation consists in moving the Stourport through the black tunnel, by a measured side-step against the slimy, glistening walls; the right foot is first planted in a half-slanting direction, and the left foot is constantly brought over with a sweep to take the vacated place, until the right can recover its footing … the four stout legs, and its four heavily hobnailed boots … make a full echoing sound upon the walls like the measured clapping of hands.[6]

On the Grand Junction in 1825 there was a complaint of 'the nuisance arising from the notoriously bad characters of the persons who frequent the neighbourhood of the Tunnels upon the plea of assisting Boats through them'.[7] It seems that later, at Blisworth at any rate, leggers were licensed and carried an identifying armplate. Occasionally boats were poled or shafted through, or a fixed or power-driven endless chain was used. The latter included the steam chain tug on the Islington Tunnel between 1826 and the 1930s.

The earliest tunnel was probably Cookley on the Staffordshire & Worcestershire, or Armitage on the Trent & Mersey (opened out in 1970–1); both short tunnels had towpaths. Longer ones, like Harecastle and Norwood, opened in 1775, had no towpaths. Later, longer tunnels were built with towpaths, such as Berwick on the Shrewsbury Canal, which had a path on wooden bearers over the water, or the second Harecastle. Some tunnels built still later had a path on both sides, like Newbold on the Oxford Canal or Netherton on the Birmingham Canal. Where a tunnel had no path through it, a horse path usually ran over the top. Beside Sapperton Tunnel on the Thames & Severn is *Tunnel House*, a public house where the men in charge of the horses paused while the leggers did their work.

Where bridges had no towpath through their arches the towrope had to be cast off at each bridge and the horse and trailing line taken across the road. On the Stratford-upon-Avon Canal and part of the Staffordshire & Worcestershire Canal some bridges, instead of having towpaths beneath them, had a slot in the centre of the arch to take the towrope. On the Lagan Navigation some bridges had separate arches for the horses.

The most common means of towing was the horse, although donkeys were used in pairs on some canals, and mules were also occasionally employed. A writer about the Birmingham Canal in 1783 shows that the occupant of the towpath did not always enjoy the work:

> The boats … are each drawn by something like the skeleton of a horse, covered with skin: whether he subsists upon the scent of the water, is a doubt; but whether his life is a scene of affliction, is not; for the unfeeling driver has no employment but to whip him from one end of the canal to the other. While the teams practised the turnpike road, the lash was divided among five unfortunate animals, but now the whole wrath of the driver falls upon one.[8]

This was almost 40 years before the first Act of 1822 to prevent cruelty to horses (the first such animal welfare measure in the world), that led to the founding of the Royal Society for the Prevention of Cruelty to Animals in 1824, itself 60 years before the NSPCC.

When a towpath changed sides on a canal a bridge, for this reason called a turnover bridge, was provided to carry the path across, often designed so that the towline did not have to be cast off while the horse changed sides. On rivers, however, there was often nothing so convenient. Horses might be ferried over by a special boat or by the boat they were towing, as on the River Stour in Suffolk, on which short piers were provided for the horse to use to and from the boat carrying it over.

The towing was usually done by the animals belonging to the carrier who owned the boat. Sometimes, however, as on the Tennant Canal and, from 1847, on the Regent's Canal, towing was the responsibility of the canal owners, who provided their own horses and added a charge for the service to the toll. On waterways taking coastal or seagoing craft towing was often carried out by independents – in Yorkshire called horse marines, elsewhere trackers. These waited at places like Goole, Weston Point and Sharpness for incoming craft and then bargained with

An example of a horse which was not ill-treated. The horse was drawing the trip boat *Maria* across the Marple Aqueduct on the Peak Forest Canal, on a somewhat wet day in 1993. This service continued until 2002. Horses are used for pulling pleasure trip boats on a dwindling number of trip operations, but rarely seen elsewhere.

the captains for their services and those of their animals. In the Midlands steering firms existed that would hire boats, horses and men as required.

Stables were provided at wharves by canal companies and carriers, these latter also providing them at their own depots. Canalside pubs, too, had stable accommodation, for boats tended to moor at night where stables could be found. In England animals were never stabled on the boats, as on American canals.

Stoppages or delays caused by floods, ice, repairs or a shortage of water were recurrent hindrances to the passage of boats. The effects could be considerable when canal traffic had to compete with the regularity, even more than the speed, of delivery offered by the railways. Little could be done about floods unless the canal was built above the flood meadows or, on river navigations, special flood-locks or floodgates controlled the water levels inside the lock cuts.

Ice boats, usually short, wide and built of iron, with a high rail down the centre that men could hold, helped to keep traffic moving during frosts, unless the broken ice blocked the locks. When ice formed thickly a team of farm horses was hired to pull such a boat, and men to rock the vessel as it crashed its way forward. In London the ice-cream maker Carlo Gatti, who came to England in 1847, had a contract with the Regent's company to buy their ice. This was stored in several special ice-wells along the line, one of which, used between the late 1850s and at least 1902, was later re-excavated and now forms part of the London Canal Museum. Some of the stored ice came from Norwegian ships, lightered up the Regents Canal.

Stoppages for repairs to lock gates, or the puddling of the bed, always took a week or two each year. If different canals on a through route closed their water-ways at different times, delays to goods could be very serious. Neighbouring groups of canals thus usually arranged stoppages at the same time, often at Bank Holiday periods after these began in the 1870s.

Maintenance consisted mainly of tunnel, lock and bridge repairs, and dredging, the latter laboriously done by manual labour using a spoon dredger or similar device until the power of steam could be harnessed. In 1808 the Grand Junction's engineer, having seen 'a Steam Engine invented by Mr Trevethick on a very simple construction',[9] ordered a 4 hp engine from Bridgnorth, which was to be put on a boat and used to drive a pump. The Stroudwater had a steam dredger in 1815, and by the 1820s they were becoming common.

Water shortages became more and more serious as the traffic carried during the canal age continued to increase, and as the concurrent expansion of large towns caused competition for water supplies. To counteract the effects of leakage, evaporation and the transfer of water from the higher to the lower levels as the locks were worked, a constant accession of supply to the higher levels was needed. This came either from side streams entering the canal or from some big source of supply such as a reservoir, itself fed by streams.

The enabling Acts for canals usually specified the precise streams and other sources from which water could be abstracted. As much industry still depended on water power, mill owners naturally opposed the construction of canals that might reduce their water supplies during droughts. They only gave way if their supplies were protected by the provision of special reservoirs, by compensation, or if the canal company acquired their mills. The supply of the summit or top level was often difficult, especially if a canal crossed a water-shed and sufficient water resources were not available. Reservoirs were built wherever possible, the earliest purpose-built one being that at Pebley to serve the Chesterfield Canal summit. Sometimes the summit level was deepened to provide additional water, as on the Cromford Canal. In other cases water was pumped to the summit level. The Worcester & Birmingham Canal was so strongly opposed by the mill owners that the Bill was twice thrown out, until the company agreed to pump water up 425ft from the Severn. Luckily for the proprietors, however, it proved practicable to build reservoirs at the summit level. The enabling Act for this canal specifically reserved the water from any springs in the bed of the canal and such rainwater as fell on its surface! The Wisbech Canal was entirely dependent for its water on supplies that could enter from the River Nene at spring tides, and it was sometimes hardly navigable just before this water was admitted. Water that needed in any case to be pumped to drain collieries was sometimes an important source of supply, as in the Birmingham area.

Measures were also taken to economise on the use of water at the locks by making boats pass the locks alternately up and down, thus making one lockful do for two boats, by using locks with more than one set of gates or pairs of locks of different sizes, thereby using the minimum of water necessary to pass small craft, or by building side ponds. A side pond was a basin alongside the lock, into which was run not quite half of the water from an emptying lock, instead of into the lower pound of the canal. When the lock had next to be filled the first part of its contents came from the side pond and not from the upper pound. Thus one lockful of water passed two boats. The earliest side ponds appear to have been provided at Berkhamsted on the Grand Junction Canal, most examples being added later, as with those at Atherstone on the Coventry Canal. Most are now disused. A variation on this practice, said to have been first introduced by James Morgan, the engineer of the Regent's Canal, was to build pairs of locks, one for up and one for down traffic, so that as far as possible one could act as a side pond for the other. Another practice was to build stop gates where two canals joined, such as where the Dearne & Dove Canal joined the Barnsley Canal, or even a physical bar, like that at Worcester Bar where the Worcester & Birmingham joined the Birmingham, to prevent loss of water from the better supplied waterway to the other. Lastly, water was sometimes pumped back from a lower to a higher level, as on the Birmingham Canal Navigations, the Tinsley flight of the Sheffield Canal or the Bradford Canal. Backpumping has been incorporated into recent restorations such as that of the Kennet & Avon Canal. Water supplies remain a major problem for several restoration schemes

Some aspects of the design of locks remained unchanged from the earlier days, although on many locks gate paddles were added to supplement ground paddles. Today broader waterways feature power-worked paddles, with some hydraulic gear on narrow locks. There were some early experiments with alternatives to hand-operated paddle gear, such as the compressed-air type that the Peak Forest company seems to have tried. Early locks, however, did not have the usual iron or masonry protection to the sill, nor did boats carry a stem fender, for many by-laws enjoin the boatman to use a piece of timber to prevent the boat striking the sill. Damage to locks was the reason given for prohibiting the double-ended boat, with a detachable rudder hung on projecting eyes at each end, as Brindley had advocated.

Not all early locks had a railed walkway over the gates, or a bridge, to enable the boatman to get quickly from one side to the other. When keel captains asked the Driffield Navigation commissioners to provide a safer passage over the gates, they minuted in 1841 that:

... it was ordered that some little repairs to the tops of the Gates should be made without putting up a Rail which would make the passage over too much of a thoroughfare for persons not concerned on the Navigation, which the Commissioners think they ought not to do.[10]

Many of the most bitter quarrels and lasting enmities between canal companies arose from water questions. The Staffordshire & Worcestershire company was continually preoccupied with efforts to buy cheaply from the Birmingham company the water coming down the Wolverhampton locks, with buying further supplies from the Wyrley & Essington, which was blessed with a superfluity, and with selling dearly what was needed by the Birmingham & Liverpool Junction.

In very hilly country the inclined plane and the canal lift were both used to save water by making the building of locks unnecessary. These followed the somewhat primitive devices in continental Europe. After the Trench plane closed in 1921 there were no boat-carrying inclined planes in Britain, but at one time there were over twenty – many carrying tub boats, as with the Bude, Torrington, Grand Western, Kidwelly & Llanelly, Shrewsbury, Shropshire and Donnington Wood Canals. The first in the British Isles were three in the north of Ireland, designed by Davis Ducart on the Tyrone canal, worked intermittently between 1777 and 1787; these were the only ones in Ireland. England's first was built in 1788 by William Reynolds on the private Ketley Canal in Shropshire. A contemporary description explained how the upper level ended at:

... an abrupt part of the bank, the skirts of which terminated on a level with the iron-works. At the top of this bank he built a small lock, and from the bottom of the lock, and down the face of the bank, he constructed an inclined plane with a double iron railway. He then erected an upright frame of timber, in which, across the lock, was fixed a large wooden barrel; round this barrel a rope was passed, and was fixed to a movable frame; this last frame was formed of a size sufficient to receive a canal boat, and the bottom upon which the boat rested, was preserved in nearly an horizontal position, by having two large wheels before and two small ones behind, varying as much in the diameters as the inclined plane varied from an horizontal plane. This frame was placed in the lock, the loaded boat was also brought from the upper canal into the lock, the lock gates were shut, and on the water being drawn from the lock into a side pond, the boat settled upon the horizontal wooden frame, and as the bottom of the lock was formed with nearly the same declivity as the inclined plane, upon the lower gates being opened, the frame with the boat passed down the iron railway, on the inclined plane, into the lower canal, which had been formed on a level with the Ketley iron-works, being a fall of 73ft... A double railway having been laid upon the inclined plane, the loaded boat in passing down, brought up another boat containing a load nearly equal to one-third part of that which passed down.[11]

This counterbalanced system was only practicable when the predominant traffic carried was downwards. Otherwise a steam engine was used if coal was cheap, and hydraulic power if it was not. Most of the West Country planes had water-wheels fed by a stream, but another and somewhat unreliable hydraulic method was used on the Hobbacott Down plane of the Bude Canal, the biggest of all, with a vertical rise of 225ft. A Victorian civil engineer described the method:

> The barges are drawn up in trains, and are to some extent counterpoised by the descending trains of barges... The water power is supplied ... by two large tubs ascending and descending alternately in two wells, the tub at the top of its well being filled with water, and in its descent drawing the barges up the incline. When the tub full of water reaches the bottom of the well, the water is emptied through a flap-door in the bottom of the tub; and the empty tub in the other well, having been drawn up its well by the descending tub, is at the top ready to be filled with water in its turn.[12]

Later, two larger planes bypassed long flights of locks. That at Blackhill on the Monkland Canal in Scotland, where the locks were also duplicated, worked between 1850 and 1887. The more celebrated example, at Foxton on the Grand Junction from 1900, could carry two narrow boats at a time; lack of traffic and breakdowns meant that it was short-lived, the locks being reinstated in 1910.

The canal lift, or balance lock as it was sometimes called, though invented in Britain, was not successfully used until James Green installed seven of them on the Grand Western Canal's Taunton extension, which opened in 1838. Earlier, in 1796, two inventors, Edward Rowland and Exuperius Pickering, had built

The inclined plane at Ketley, shown on a token.

an experimental lift for use on the Ellesmere Canal. It used the float principle, whereby a caisson holding the boat rode up and down on a float in a well, which could be filled with water or emptied as necessary. It was never used, but the principle is the same as some much later Continental lifts as that as Henrichenburg on the Dortmund-Ems Canal, which operated between 1899 and 1962. Others were later built on the Somersetshire Coal Canal, the unfinished Dorset & Somerset Canal, on the Worcester & Birmingham Canal at Tardebigge and on the Regent's Canal, but none was put to regular use.

A lift usually consisted of a caisson or tank, into which the canal boat was floated, and cables that ran over wheels at the top of the lift, either to counter-balance weights or to another caisson. Chains under each caisson, which coiled or uncoiled as they moved in relation to each other, kept the caissons in balance. In order to raise a boat from one level to another, water was added to the upper caisson, either until the caisson to be lifted began to move upwards, in which case the movement was controlled by a brake, or nearly to that point, the final impetus being given by manual or mechanical power. A lift could have one or two independently operated caissons, or two that balanced each other. The seven lifts on the Grand Western Canal, with rises varying from 12½ft to 42ft, were counter-balanced, one 8 ton boat being raised while another was lowered. These worked successfully for thirty years. Subsequently, in 1875, the Anderton lift connecting the Weaver Navigation with the Trent & Mersey Canal, and capable of lifting two full-sized narrow boats, was completed. Designed by Edwin Clark, this still works, having been restored for leisure use by 2002. Its caissons were counter-balanced, and later independently operated. The Anderton was the prototype for canal lifts later used in lowland Europe, like those at La Louviere in Belgium from 1888, in which Clark was involved, and later ones in Canada.

After all precautions had been taken, however, shortage of water, especially in the summer, was a perennial problem on canals and river navigations. It meant that smaller cargoes were carried than were possible, thereby increasing overhead costs, and that boats ran aground unnecessarily and had to be lightened, to everyone's annoyance and loss. This state of things became increasingly serious. Some industrial canals, especially those around Birmingham, had the advantage that they could draw most of their water from supplies pumped from colliery workings. Others built more and larger reservoirs, or installed machinery to pump upwards from streams or from their own lower levels.

Water was often sold to canalside works, but in the early days of steam engines, when it seems to have been considered that they consumed no water, the following clause was inserted in the Birmingham Canal's Act of 1783:

Whereas such Engines will consume considerable Quantities of Coal, and by the tonnage thereupon promote the Interest of the Navigation, as well as that of the Manufactories of Birmingham, if erected in its Neighbourhood; but as such

Machines can only be erected where cold Water can be obtained to condense the Steam which is necessary to the working of them; and as such Water can be taken from the Navigation without Prejudice thereto, because such Machines, when properly constructed, do not waste or destroy any Water, but may be made to return to the Navigation a Quantity of warm Water equal to the cold Water which they drew from it ... be it therefore enacted... That it may be lawful ... to draw from the said Canal such Quantities of Water as shall be sufficient to supply the said Engines...[13]

Canals continue today to supply water for industrial or agricultural use, much of it being returned for re-use. The transfer of domestic water would be pursued after nationalisation, while the canal water remains available for emergency fire-fighting in some urban areas.

The revenue of canal companies chiefly arose from tolls charged at the rate of so many pence per ton per mile carried, as distinct from the freight charges of the carriers. Milestones were set up along the towpaths so that these point-to-point tolls could be accurately calculated. Charges were lowest for bulk commodities such as coal, culm (slack for lime burning) and limestone, higher for more valuable bulk cargoes such as iron ore, and higher still for finished goods like iron castings, and for groceries and general merchandise. In the case of coal it was the usual practice to allow 21 cwt or more to the ton (a ton is 20 cwt) to cover transfer losses and theft.

The maximum tolls that could be charged on each class of goods were usually laid down in the company Act and could not be increased without further Parliamentary authority. The tendency was, however, in the opposite direction, as increasing trade, together with the competition of road transport, the coasting trade and later railways, worked to reduce tolls. In addition there was always pressure from the industrialists on one canal to get tolls lowered so that they might compete better with factories or mines served by other canals. Small transport concerns, often very dependent on a few businesses for their livelihood, found it difficult to resist such pressures.

Companies were not allowed to discriminate between users by giving special tolls, nor to charge more on one part of the line than another, until the Canal Tolls Act of 1845 gave power to vary tolls. Trade was encouraged by granting long credit: three months was usual, and, with railway competition, it tended to become longer.

Often drawbacks, subsidies in the form of a partial refund of tolls, were paid to those who shipped goods for long distances. They were usually given to encourage the development of markets for coal on other canals than that of the company granting them. The Ashby Canal, for instance, gave a drawback on all Moira, Gresley and Swadlincote coal carried the length of the canal and on to the Coventry Canal. This enabled these collieries, especially Moira, to build up good distant sales, among them to Oxford colleges. Canal companies often competed briskly with one another in this way on the fringes of their territories, sometimes also carrying out raids far into each other's heartlands.

In order to meet opposition to their Acts, canal companies often had to hamper themselves with clauses allowing certain goods to move without payment of tolls. This was detrimental when they came to compete with railways, which were not similarly handicapped. For instance, on the Chesterfield Canal, hay and corn in the straw going to be stacked had to be carried toll-free for five miles, while materials for the repair of parish roads were carried toll-free if no locks were used.

Apart from tolls, some companies reaped a harvest from compensation payments, when a projected canal might cause trade to be diverted from existing navigations. In such cases the opposition of the old proprietors was only withdrawn when the new company had agreed to compensate them for any loss of trade. These payments became a widespread and restrictive network over the waterway system. For example, the Act for the Ashby de la Zouch Canal (1794) provided that the Coventry Canal should collect 5d. (2p) a ton on all goods, with certain exceptions, passing between the Ashby Canal and the Coventry, Oxford or Grand Junction canals, and should have power to place its own toll-houses, stop bars and collectors on the Ashby Canal in order to collect the payments.

The tolls payable were calculated on a written note declaring the type, weight, origin and destination of the cargo, presented by the carrier and endorsed by the toll-collector. Often the latter would suspect the accuracy of the declaration and could make his own check of the tonnage the boat was carrying. This was found out by gauging. When it first came into use on a canal each boat was taken to a dock, where its draught, both empty and when carrying various loads, was found. Figures were then marked on the boat's side in four or six places, being either cut into the wood or cast on a metal plate.

Some canals had weighing machines instead of docks. These substantial structures had a cradle onto which a boat was floated. The water was then let out and the boat weighed empty for record purposes. Once that figure was known it was simple to detect an overweight cargo by sending the boat to be weighed. Indeed, the machine's existence was usually sufficient deterrent. Weighing machines were installed on four waterways, including the Somersetshire Coal, Monmouthshire and Thames & Severn Canals, and in Cardiff on the Glamorganshire. The latter, supplied in 1834, went out of use around 1914, and was later dismantled and re-erected at the Waterways Museum at Stoke Bruerne.

An improved method of gauging was introduced around 1810. Instead of the figures showing different immersion depths for different loads being marked on the boat's side, they were entered in books, which were kept at the toll-houses. The actual depth at which a boat was floating at any given time was found by using a hollow tube, with a rest to fit on the gunwale, which was put into the

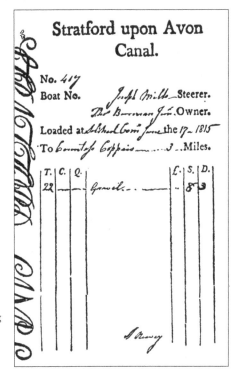

A toll ticket from 1815 for a boat belonging to Thomas Bowman, showing the distance involved, the tonnage of 22 tons of gravel and the toll of 8*s*. 3*d*. (now 41p).

water beside the boat at four or six places. Inside the tube was a rod marked in feet and inches that rose as the tube sank and showed the freeboard in inches. The average of the readings was then compared with the figures in the company's book for the boat concerned, and the tonnage could be read off.

Most waterway concerns insisted that boats coming onto their water from another canal should be gauged by their officers, a rule less onerous in fact than it appeared since most boats worked along well-defined routes. In around 1798, however, eight canal and river companies in the Trent area joined in common gauging arrangements, the printed record books of which now provide researchers with an accurate picture of the boats used at the time in that area.

River and canal companies were rarely empowered to put, or prohibited from putting, boats on their own or neighbouring waterways and carrying goods, so long as there was fair competition with other carriers. Many did carry from the beginning, like the Aire & Calder or the Mersey & Irwell. Others did so intermittently, usually buying barges and running them until independent traders appeared, and then selling them. Yet others organised carrying firms, nominally separate by being run by groups of canal shareholders, as the Trent & Mersey company originally did with its carrying counterpart, Hugh Henshall & Co.

It is probable that, as competition increased after the Napoleonic Wars had ended, canal companies that also ran carrying craft realised that they could, in practice, vary tolls in their own favour by adjusting freight charges, and this could lead to complaints. The Ellesmere & Chester company at that time sought special authority to carry goods, an authority made general in 1845 by the Canal Carriers Act. Many companies, however, remained only toll-takers to the end on waterways that were open to all users. This feature remained until 1987, when the British Waterways Board ceased to be carriers.

Many canal and navigation companies ran businesses in some of the commodities they carried. The Upper Medway Company traded in coal so successfully that it had a virtual monopoly for a century, and it was also involved for a time in timber and iron. The Brecknock & Abergavenny company also traded in coal and thought of acquiring a colliery. Later it transferred its trading interests to the nominally independent Brecon Boat Company. Some companies owned or leased collieries, like the Grand Canal Company, unsuccessfully, for 30 years up to 1830. While many owned limekilns, the Peak Forest company was exceptional. This owned a number of kilns, rented others and also worked large limestone quarries. They used modern ways of encouraging the greater use of limestone: paying part of the cost of new kilns built within a time limit if solely their limestone was used; subsidising publications on the uses of lime; making bulk contracts for sales that included toll, freight and the cost of the stone in one price; and offering loads at special rates to let turnpike trustees experiment with limestone for road building.

Much canal carrying was done by private carrying companies or partnerships. These could be of any size, some running two or three boats, some twenty or more. They paid their workers by the ton carried rather than a weekly wage. Some men worked part-time as boatmen and others full-time, but for different employers. The best-known firm during the canal age was Pickfords, originally road waggon proprietors. The company's activities were widespread in the 1790s: they leased warehouses and wharves, and owned many boats, 'which travel night and day, and arrive in London with as much punctuality from the midland and some of the most distant parts of the kingdom, as the waggons do.'[14] The canals felt the loss severely when, in the 1840s, Pickfords ceased to carry by canal and transferred to the railways.

There were, of course, many other firms, some general carriers and some specializing in fly-boat (express) work. There were, again, trading firms owning their own boats, or hiring them, and carrying their own raw materials or finished products, as on the Swansea Canal, where there were hardly any independent traders. There were firms and individuals that owned boats and equipment and hired these out without any particular interest in canal carrying. Lastly, there were the small men, each owning a boat or two, and plying for hire like a tramp steamer. There were never many of them on the narrow canals, but a few of the 'Number Ones' survived to the 1950s. There were probably more in Yorkshire, where the individually owned keel fitted well into the way that carrying was organised on such navigations as the Don and the Calder & Hebble. Here the

A scene on the Regent's Canal, showing a pair of Pickfords boats passing through City Road Locks, with Islington Tunnel beyond. Note the side paddle, which enabled water from a full lock to be partly transferred to the empty parallel lock.

navigation company accepted goods even though it did not possess its own boats: instead, it contracted carriers, individual owners and partnerships alike, to do the work for them.

Those who work on the waterways today have inherited the remnants of crafts with detailed traditions. It has sometimes been suggested that canal boatpeople had special origins, for instance that they were Romani. It is much more likely that many early boatmen had been small farmers, who had owned horses and carts. Having found good employment carting for local contractors building canals, they would have found their regular road traffic decreasing and moved to the boats. Many boatpeople were recruited in the same ways as other workers were drawn to the new industrial districts of the late eighteenth and early nineteenth centuries. Some doubtless came from river and coastal craft to the canals; many had probably been locally employed navvies, who took to the waterways they had built; others came from canalside towns and villages, places where the building, loading and passing of boats was a familiar sight.

During the canal age boats seem mainly to have been worked by men and boys, the usual bye-laws demanding two men to each boat, or at least a man and a stout boy, the latter to lead the horse. A Stourbridge Canal bye-law of 1789, however, demanded two men and a boy for any boat passing a lock. Males are referred to here literally; women were rarely directly employed, and never in Ireland. Boys were numerous and hard-worked. Wages were relatively good, the profits from carrying were reasonable and many boatmen earned enough money to keep their families in cottages ashore.

A boatwoman carrying a baby and steering a narrow boat, as depicted, perhaps somewhat fancifully, in the tract against family boats, *Rob Rat*, discussed in Chapter Eleven.

Most early boats had no cabins – these began to appear in the 1790s. However, as journeys lengthened, crews often slept ashore in canalside inns or friends' houses, while their horses occupied the inn's stables.

While in the early days boat people were recruited from outside, there soon grew up a largely self-perpetuating boating community, increasingly separated from the populations it served. Then slowly the situation reversed: as carrying declined, younger people left the boats to begin a different life with better prospects.

It is now clear that family narrow boats were quite common by the 1810s. This use of family instead of paid help was the result of several factors: competition between different carriers and different routes; the housing shortage after the Napoleonic Wars; and the increase in length of canal journeys with the system's growth, making it less likely that boatmen would see much of a family ashore. The coming of railways encouraged what was already taking place, until, by the time of George Smith, the canal reformer of the 1870s, the family boat was common on narrow canals, though fly-boats were always worked by men only. Under quite different circumstances many of the sailing keels that traded along the Yorkshire navigations were also family boats, certainly from early in the nineteenth century.

In Scotland, Ireland and in the South Wales valleys the family boat was unknown, although employment on boats was often passed down through generations.

The pressure of time on the boatpeople, toll-keepers and lock-keepers slowly increased through the canal age, as it did with industrial occupations. This was a consequence of the increased development of the transport system that took place especially after the end of the Napoleonic Wars, though symptoms of it had appeared earlier. For instance some fly-boats began running in the 1790s.

The process of increasing hours can be demonstrated on the Staffordshire & Worcestershire Canal, which moved over the years from a near monopoly to a very competitive transport position. Before 1816 the normal hours for boats to pass the locks were 5.00 a.m.–9.00 p.m. on moonlit nights and 6.00 a.m.– 8.00 p.m. otherwise. In that year express or fly-boats were put on, which paid an annual licence fee to be allowed to pass the locks at any time. In 1820 the hours were extended to 4.00 a.m.–10.00 p.m. during the summer, and soon afterwards boats were allowed to pass at any hour if they paid a small extra charge for each trip. Finally from 1830 the locks were open day and night for all boats, the lock-keepers being paid a little extra. For example in February 1832 the man at Stourport lock got 14s. (70p) a week and 4s. (20p) night wages. One sympathises with William Bagnall when the committee minuted in the same year 'That the Bed in the Nighthouse at Heywood be taken away and that our Clerk do warn William Bagnall to be more vigilant in his Duty and not permit any Boat to pass without his knowledge.'[15] Separate day and night men were later employed at the busy points on the canal.

A sign of the increasing pressure of business was the passing in 1840 of the Constables Act, empowering canal and river authorities to appoint their own police, though it does not seem that many companies, bar the Aire & Calder, Sheffield & South Yorkshire, London area waterways and Manchester Ship Canal, did so.

The life of the waterways has always had its hazards. Men, women and children have now and then fallen into a lock, been crushed by a boat or slipped into the canal in the darkness. Boat horses have been drowned or burned in their stables. Of accidents to the boats themselves, two examples follow – one normal enough, the other fortunately exceptional.

The Basingstoke company reported in 1802 that:

… one of the Company's Barges, the *Baxter*, encountered a sudden and violent Storm, about the Nine Elms, as she was going up the Thames, loaded with Grocery and Merchandize, which rendered her totally unmanageable, and she must have sunk in the Middle of the River, but for the assistance of a large Sailing Vessel which kept her floating till she gat near the Shore, when she went to the Bottom and was soon filled with Water… At the same Time another loaded Barge, the Property of a Mr Jones, also going up the River, sunk, after she had been hauled close to the Shore; and Three other Vessels, of different Descriptions, were seen to go down about the same Time…[16]

This accident was not the result of the boatmen's negligence. Neither was the notorious Regent's Park explosion, which was reported in 1874 by the *Illustrated London News*:

> An extraordinary accident, which happened yesterday week at five o'clock in the morning, cost the loss of several lives, much damage to houses and furniture, and a vast alarm to the north-western suburbs of London. This was the blowing up of a barge laden with petroleum and gunpowder for blasting, which was one of a train drawn by a steam-tug along the Regent's Canal... The train of six light barges, of which the first was a steamer, left the wharf in the City-road about three o'clock that morning. Next after the steamer, the *Ready*, was the fly-boat *Jane*, whose steerer or captain was named Boswell. Next to her was the *Dee*, the steerer Edwards; and next came the unfortunate *Tilbury*, whose steerer was Charles Baxton, of Loughborough, in Leicestershire. The *Jane* 'had a little gunpowder on board'. The *Tilbury's* lading is thus described by the official report: 'The cargo consisted chiefly of sugar and other miscellaneous articles, such as nuts, straw-boards, coffee, and some two or three barrels of petroleum, and about five tons of gunpowder.' ... Three or four minutes before five o'clock, this train of barges was passing under the bridge at North Gate, Regent's Park... The *Tilbury* was directly under the bridge when by some means yet unexplained, the powder caught fire and the whole was blown up. The men on board this barge were killed, and the barge was shattered to pieces, while one of the other barges was sunk. A column of thick smoke and a great blaze of fire followed the explosion. The bridge was entirely destroyed; several of the neighbouring houses were half-ruined, their roofs and walls being greatly injured; and in hundreds of other houses, a mile east or west of the place, the windows were broken. [17]

The boatpeople in the past had few friends and many enemies. This perpetually moving population was not welcome to those who lived near waterways, and new canal projects were sometimes opposed for fear of the damage that might be done by them to property or the poaching that might result. The owners of boats also complained of them pilfering, bartering coal from cargoes for food and drink, dumping coal in rivers to lighten barges (and, incidentally, to warm the riverside villagers who dredged it) and spending money in public houses that had been given them to pay tolls. Their good service and hard, laborious work remained unrecorded.

Another hard-working group of people were the lock-keepers and toll-keepers. On the canals lock-keepers were usually given a house as well as their wages, and often a coal allowance (to limit temptation) and perhaps one for candles too. They were sometimes asked to do some gauging and toll-collecting on traffic loading near their locks, inspect tonnage bills, help pass the boats and trim hedges or break ice. They were expected not to leave their posts, unlike Eynon Bowen on the Swansea Canal, who was fined in 1818 because 'A great part of his time is taken up in farming and other concerns'.[18] Some companies, like the Peak Forest, provided 'an upper Waistcoat and a Badge thereupon to distinguish them from other persons...'[19] The toll-keepers had, of course, to be honest in accounting for receipts (they were usually covered by security bonds), for making sure that boats were properly gauged and that their waybills were in order. They also had to refrain from trading with the boatmen or borrowing money from them.

When these men were old they were often given a small pension. In 1823 the Staffordshire & Worcestershire Committee, whose records reveal a long tradition of good works, minuted:

> John Buttery ... being incapable of attending to his Situation owing to Old Age, Ordered that he be replaced, and that an annual pension be allowed him ... and until a Successor be appointed, Ordered that our Clerk write to Crowley and Company requiring them to give notice to their Boatmen not to molest or insult John Buttery in his passing their Boats along the Canal.[20]

Lock-keepers had to be strong characters, for their work was lonely and responsible. Here are two examples of the life they led:

> Tedding^n Lock 28/3/1818
>
> It has been always Customary with me to rise at dawn of day because in general ye Barges move from Richmond then & often do before if the Moon shines till day & this was the Case on ye 20th early. I rose at just past 4 & was Employed in the Office arranging some small matters before ye Craft came when I heard a Man's Voice calling. I open'd one of the Shutters & saw a Man standing about ½ Way between my Window & the lower Gate, and he Pointed with his hand and said here's a Trow coming. I had no doubt in my own mind but that the Trow was very near, & as the Wind blew hard & right into the Pound it was highly necessary the Gates should be opened & ready. I now took my hat & was going out but the Ins^t I open'd the Door a Stout Fellow rushed in & seized me by the throat. While we were struggling in came 2 More & one of them had something in his hand resembling ½ a Sack. I was thrown with Violence over a Chair and we both came rolling to ye Ground & I then felt one of them cover my head & press it so close down that I really began to fear they meant to suffocate me... They then took my Keys from my Coat pocket by rolling me over, and having broke every Lock and Emtied every small Box of Mrs S in the next room they all ran out leaving me locked in & in darkness. By their bad discourse I must (think) them Bargemen of lowest Class. I had about 11 or 12 Single Pound Notes & full six Pounds Silver and ye most part Sm^l Silver & 4 or 5 shillings in Copper. I do indeed much fear that this is only ye beginning, for which ever Lock Receives much value it will be a Temptation to such Villains to make an attempt at ye end of ye Week...
>
> ... Richd Savory.[21]

FELONY

AND

Reward.

WHEREAS on the Night of *Tuesday* the 13th instant, the Hatches of a Boat lying in the Docks at MULLINGAR were forced open, and the TOOLS belonging to four Ship Carpenters taken away; and on the Night of *Wednesday* the 25th instant, Boat No. 49, lying in the Docks upon the BROADSTONE LEVEL, DUBLIN, was attacked by a number of Persons, when they tied the Men belonging thereto, and carried away the TOOLS of six Ship Carpenters that had been working at said Boat. They also made use of expressions threatening destruction to any Carpenter that would work under certain Wages; and that they would destroy the Property of any individual that would not give the prescribed Wages for the Repairs of their Boats. A WRITTEN NOTICE to the foregoing effect was left in the Boat at Mullingar.

NOW the Court of Directors of the New Royal Canal Company, for the purpose of preventing the continuance of such an illegal Combination, do hereby offer

A REWARD OF

Fifty Pounds

for the discovery, and prosecution to conviction, of the Person or Persons who were concerned in the carrying away the said Tools, or in the writing or publishing of the Felonious Threats aforesaid, or

A Reward of Ten Pounds

shall be given to any Person giving private Information, which may lead to the conviction of such Offender, or Offenders, as aforesaid, or of any Person who shall, in consequence of said Notice, conspire to carry into effect the Threats therein contained, or commit any Outrage on the Person or Property of any Trader on the Royal Canal, or any Person in his Employment.

By Order of the Court of Directors,

SAMUEL DRAPER,
Secretary.

ROYAL CANAL HOUSE,
30th July, 1821.

A notice issued by the Royal Canal Company. (Ruth Heard).

On the Regent's Canal in London in 1830 the:

> Eastern division of the Canal, was almost constantly the scene of the most dis-
> graceful Riots. Such were the lawless set that frequented the Canal (to hunt Ducks,
> Swim Dogs, etc.) that a party of the Police were in constant pay, and absolutely
> necessary to protect the Lock-keepers from personal harm; but this did not always
> succeed, for on several occasions, Lock-keepers have been so severely treated, in
> defending the Company's property from damage, that in some cases they were sev-
> eral months in recovering from the Injuries they received.[22]

Quite different hazards to canal workers and boatmen were experienced in
Ireland. The condition of the Irish people in the hard economic environment of
the early nineteenth century affected the working of the Grand and Royal canals.
Both during and after construction, banks were often breached by local people
who hoped to be employed in their repair, while the workers who completed
the western part of the Royal Canal between 1813 and 1817 were attacked by
armed bands. Military protection was needed to prevent the plunder of goods
carried on the Grand Canal, while there was a war between smaller and larger
traders in turf on that canal, which included the burning of boats and threats to
destroy the canal works. In the 1820s and 1830s armed gangs backed the demands
of combinations of horse-drivers on the Royal. Finally, during the Famine of the
1840s, pillaging of boats on both canals led to the re-introduction of convoys of
craft under military protection.

There is evidence of 'collective bargaining by riot' in some instances during
the first canal age, and of the behaviour that a hard life would bring about for
some. Outside reformers would gradually come to take an interest in boatpeople, partly due to the murder of a passenger, Christina Collins, on a Pickford
boat in 1839, and the less-known murder of a boatman, probably by another
boatman, in Manchester in 1840.

There were many variations in conditions between waterways in different
regions, and between different employers. Later chapters will discuss how those
conditions and experiences changed for boatpeople and canal workers.

CHAPTER FOUR

The Arteries of the Revolution

So immediate was the success of the Duke of Bridgewater's canal from Worsley towards Manchester, which had been partly opened in 1761, that he went back to Parliament during the following year for authority to continue to the Mersey near Runcorn, so that his coal might go to Liverpool without using the Mersey & Irwell.

This was a much more ambitious plan. The significance of its promotion by the Duke after his experience with the Worsley canal, and the prominent involvement of James Brindley, was not lost on businessmen, among them Josiah Wedgwood of the Potteries and his partner Thomas Bentley, along with the salt manufacturers of Cheshire dependent upon the River Weaver.

The use of rivers for transport was familiar enough, and it was logical, although startling when it began, that rivers could be joined together so that goods could travel from the sea at either end to any intermediate point, and from any point to either river mouth. Many schemes had been proposed in the past, especially to link the Thames and Severn basins, but now they suddenly seemed practicable. To link the Trent and Mersey would greatly benefit Wedgwood, whose raw material came mostly by sea from Cornwall and Devon to the Mersey, by barge up the Weaver to Winsford Bridge and then by packhorse to the Potteries. It could now be brought from the Mersey to his doorstep, while products could be carried away in either direction as far as Liverpool or Hull.

The upper section of the Trent had already been made navigable to Burton under an Act of 1699, as was later the Weaver to Winsford. These river interests opposed the proposals by Wedgwood and his associates for a canal from the Mersey to Wilden Ferry, on the Trent below Burton. The Burton Navigation pressed for the Grand Trunk (later Trent & Mersey) Canal to end at Burton rather than 14 miles downstream at Wilden Ferry. The Weaver Navigation, which had carried all of the salt and part of the pottery trade, tried to get the western end of the navigation connected to its own river. The promoters were, however, keen to obtain efficient transport by avoiding commitments to join their canal to unimproved waterways or to be charged monopoly rates. The opposition of the rivers was so strong that, at one stage, the Cheshire gentlemen who supported the Weaver surveyed the route for an alternative canal via Stafford to the Trent and fought the Trent & Mersey bill to parliamentary committee stage. The Burton interests continued their opposition until their activity ended in 1805.

To get the Duke's support an agreement was reached by which he would build the Trent to Mersey line between Preston Brook and Runcorn, altering his own line from Manchester to Runcorn to join the new canal. This led to further plans to connect the Trent & Mersey Canal with the River Severn at what is now Stourport, then a hamlet. Both groups of promoters obtained their Acts on the same day, 14 May 1766.

These great projects, the Trent & Mersey, 93¾ miles long and with an authorised capital of £150,000, and the Staffordshire & Worcestershire, 46¼ miles long and with £100,000 of capital, involved major engineering works. The Bridgewater Canal had been built level from Worsley to Manchester and was being continued on the same level to Runcorn, where it would fall to the Mersey via a flight of ten locks. The locks had not yet been built, and the experience of Brindley and Gilbert was limited to the construction of level line, to the embankments and aqueduct at Barton and the mine tunnels at Worsley. Yet 4 aqueducts, 43 locks and 2 short tunnels on the Staffordshire & Worcestershire, and 75 locks, the 2,880yd long Harecastle tunnel and several shorter tunnels on the Trent & Mersey, were planned. In spite of many difficulties the Staffordshire & Worcestershire Canal was completed in 1772 (the year of Brindley's death) and the Trent & Mersey Canal in 1777.

Once the line of the Trent & Mersey had been decided the effort to join it to the Thames began in 1768 with the Act for the Coventry Canal. This Act aimed to supply Coventry with coal from mines along the line, and also to join the Trent & Mersey near Lichfield. Brindley surveyed the line, and was engineer for a time before his dismissal by the Coventry company for inattention. The initial capital of £50,000 only sufficed to complete half of the line, from Coventry to Atherstone, and for ten years the completed portion remained isolated. Meanwhile, in 1769, a canal was authorised between the Thames at Oxford and the Coventry Canal at Longford near Coventry, also to be surveyed and engineered by Brindley. By 1778 the 63¼ miles of canal between Longford and Banbury were open, and it was therefore important to the Oxford Canal proprietors that they should induce the Coventry company to complete its line.

In the same year as the Coventry Act, two tributary canals were authorised. The Droitwich Canal was an artificial tributary, linking Droitwich to the natural river Severn. It was built large, to take river craft, whereas other Midlands canals from this period had all been planned with narrow locks. The Birmingham Canal, which ran from the Staffordshire & Worcestershire Canal at Aldersley, was the first tributary to an artificial canal, and the first of many industrial canals. Completed in 1772, it formed the heart of the early industrial canal network.

The Birmingham Canal not only brought coal to Birmingham from pits along its line, together with goods from the Staffordshire & Worcestershire, and thus from the whole completed canal system, it also carried coal away from the fields around Wednesbury and sent it towards the Severn to compete with that from Shropshire. Before the canal was built it appears that coal brought by land cost 13s (65p) a ton and that it was common to see a train of waggons for miles, with

A romantic picture of Harecastle Tunnel, published in 1785 in John Phillips' *A Treatise on Inland Navigation,* one of the earliest canal books. This says more for the author's enthusiasm than for attention to detail; nothing shown is remotely accurate.

great damage to the road. The canal reduced the price to 7s (35p), while its profits increased the value of its £140 shares to £420 by 1782. This was for a narrow and circuitous line that was later much improved.

In 1776 the process commenced that ended in the Birmingham area's present network of canals. Two new companies obtained Acts on the same day. The Stourbridge Canal joined the Staffs & Worcs Canal at Stourton to Stourbridge, with a line to Black Delph. There it joined the Dudley Canal line to Dudley. These navigations enabled coal from the Dudley area to be carried to the Severn, in competition to that carried via the Birmingham Canal to Autherley.

In 1786 the Dudley Canal proprietors obtained an Act to connect their canal with the Birmingham at Tipton through the proposed Dudley Tunnel. This planned a shorter line from the Birmingham Canal to the Severn, but before the tunnel was completed a further navigation to the Severn was promoted.

To complete this account it is necessary to discuss canals promoted during the canal mania of the 1790s (see Chapter five). These included the Worcester & Birmingham Canal, which provided a direct line from Birmingham to the Severn at Worcester. This line gave the new company a decided advantage over the Staffs & Worcs for Birmingham traffic, including connection to a more easily navigable part of the Severn, and tended to divert Birmingham–Severn trade away from the Birmingham Canal. Both companies strongly opposed the Bill, but this was carried in 1791, albeit with an unusual clause preventing any physical junction between the new canal and the Birmingham Canal. Ostensibly to conserve water, this ruling meant that traffic originating on the Birmingham would have to go by way of Autherley to the Severn, or at least by Tipton, if it was not to be transhipped. This Worcester Bar, as it was called, between the two canals at Birmingham was not pierced until 1815.

The Dudley proprietors took this physical bar as an opportunity to gain traffic from the Birmingham Canal, and thus sought an Act to join their canal to the Worcester & Birmingham at Selly Oak. The Birmingham proprietors realised

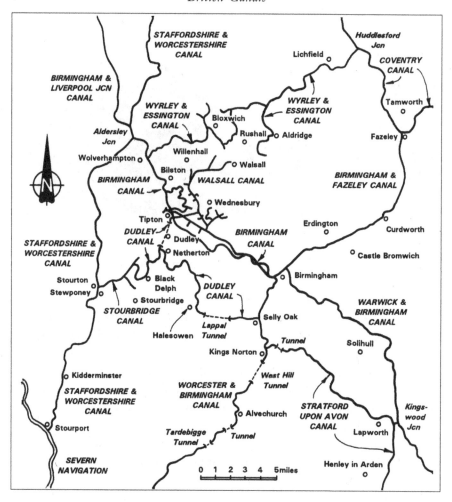

The canals of the Birmingham area as completed by the end of the canal age, before the completion of final links.

that traffic from the south would be able to pass from Tipton down the Dudley to Selly Oak, thus avoiding the Birmingham Canal altogether, while coal from Netherton would cease to pass to their canal through Dudley Tunnel. Their opposition to the Dudley Canal plan was defeated in spite of their cry that:

A parallel Canal, as this [to Selly Oak] certainly is, goes to the almost total Destruction of the Coal Trade on the present Birmingham Canal, and the Coals which ought from their Locality to be brought to the Birmingham Market, may be conveyed into Worcestershire, Gloucestershire, &c. without any equivalent Advantage or Prospect of any of the Inhabitants of Birmingham.[1]

The Dudley extension to Selly Oak through the Lapal Tunnel, at 3,795yd the fourth longest in Britain, was opened in 1798. Later, in 1802, the first part of the Stratford-upon-Avon Canal was opened, from a junction with the Worcester & Birmingham at King's Norton to join the recently built Warwick & Birmingham at Kingswood. This gave water access to London for coal and iron traffic from the Stourbridge, Dudley and Netherton districts, and also from Coalbrookdale on the Severn and from Stourport and other places on the Staffs & Worcs, without using the Birmingham Canal.

Galton Bridge spanning the cutting, 71ft deep, on the improved line of the Birmingham Canal. This was one of the few lengths of canal with double towpaths. The boat appears to be a horse-drawn spoon dredger. By the date of this photograph, the majority of traffic on the Birmingham Canal Navigations was local. (Ware Collection/Boat Museum/The Waterways Trust)

During the rivalry with the Dudley Canal, the Birmingham Canal proprietors increased the capacity of their original line by lowering the old summit level at Smethwick, eliminating three locks at each end, duplicating those that remained at Smethwick, and making a cutting that was 46ft deep at one point. Later, in 1827, the old summit was completely removed by substituting a cutting running up to 71ft deep. By then, there was sufficient trade for all lines, although in time the character of traffic changed as the coal areas around Wednesbury and Bilston became exhausted. The Birmingham canals continued to grow and develop branches, until in 1898 the total length of canals in the area was 159 miles with 216 locks. This network would form the heart of the English midland canal system into the twentieth century.

In 1781 and 1782 the Oxford, Coventry and Trent & Mersey companies supported a project for a canal from the coalmines around Wednesbury to join the Coventry Canal near Fazeley, from where the coal could be taken north or south. The promoters and their supporters met at Coleshill in 1782 and agreed to complete the Oxford Canal from Banbury to Oxford, and the Coventry Canal from Atherstone to Fazeley, while the Trent & Mersey and the Birmingham & Fazeley, as it was called, would each finish half of the Fradley–Fazeley section. The Birmingham company feared losing its monopoly in the coal-carrying trade of the Birmingham area, and its consequent prosperity. It organised a nominally separate company (amalgamated with its parent in 1784) to build from its canal at Farmer's Bridge, Birmingham, to Fazeley, so that Wednesbury coal would not bypass its line. After a major parliamentary battle the Birmingham Canal group won with an Act of 1783. It took over the Coleshill agreement and began construction. In 1790, after some recalcitrance by the rather faint-hearted Coventry Company, the whole Birmingham–Fazeley–Fradley–Coventry–Oxford line was finished. Thus the last link in the interconnection of the four great rivers of Trent, Mersey, Severn and Thames was completed.

That the traffic had only been waiting for the communication is shown by the tolls and weighing charges taken by the Oxford company:

Years	£
1789–90	10,697
1792–3	17,970
1795–6	25,880

Two chains still waited to be thrown across England from river to river: in the north a connection between the Mersey on the west and the Aire & Calder Navigation in Yorkshire that gave access to the Humber; in the south a junction between the Bristol Channel and the Thames by way of the Severn or the Bristol Avon.

The first Act to make navigable the Aire to Leeds, and its tributary, the Calder to Wakefield, had been passed in 1699 as a result of efforts by the mayor and several aldermen of Leeds, and some Wakefield gentlemen. Under this Act, locks were built and a depth of 3½ft was obtained. The northern link between the Aire at Leeds and the Mersey at Liverpool was first planned and in 1766 surveyed by the Yorkshire engineer John Longbothom. This survey was checked by Brindley and his assistant Robert Whitworth, and in 1770 an Act was obtained, the authorised capital being £260,000. The planned line of this Leeds & Liverpool Canal was 108¾ miles long. The Yorkshire side was built as planned, but on the Lancashire side it ran north of the present line by Whalley and the Ribble Valley, then south of Preston and by Leyland to Newburgh and the present line to Liverpool.

The coal of the Wigan neighbourhood had in the past been distributed via the River Douglas, finally made navigable to Tarleton on the Ribble in 1742, from where it was carried by coasting vessels to the Mersey or farther, especially to Ireland. The new Leeds & Liverpool company soon bought a controlling interest in the Douglas Navigation, and later the two concerns were amalgamated.

Before building began there had been controversy between the promoters in Yorkshire, whose interest was in a direct and cheap communication with Liverpool, and those in Lancashire, who wanted a less direct line that would include more Lancashire towns. The Yorkshire promoters, led by the appropriately named John Hustler, carried the day and the Act was obtained for the shorter line.

John Longbothom began construction. By 1774 28 miles on the Lancashire side had been opened from Liverpool to Newburgh, from where there was access to Wigan via the Douglas. Three years later 30 miles on the Yorkshire side had been completed from the Aire & Calder Navigation at Leeds to Gargrave. While the Lancashire part was under construction, however, a group of dissident Lancashire promoters, who had withdrawn from the Leeds & Liverpool company, had promoted a canal from Wigan to Liverpool, stating that the route by the Douglas to Newburgh, and from there by the Leeds & Liverpool, was too roundabout and uncertain. Their Bill was defeated in 1772 and by 1779 an all-canal line had been opened from Wigan to Liverpool. Two years later the Rufford branch from Burscough to the Ribble, to bypass most of the Douglas, was completed.

The Bingley five-rise staircase, opened in 1774, on one of the earliest lengths of the Leeds & Liverpool Canal in Yorkshire. This section featured several staircase locks.

Meanwhile a moment for choosing life or death had come to the Aire & Calder, for in 1772 a newly promoted company, supported unofficially by many

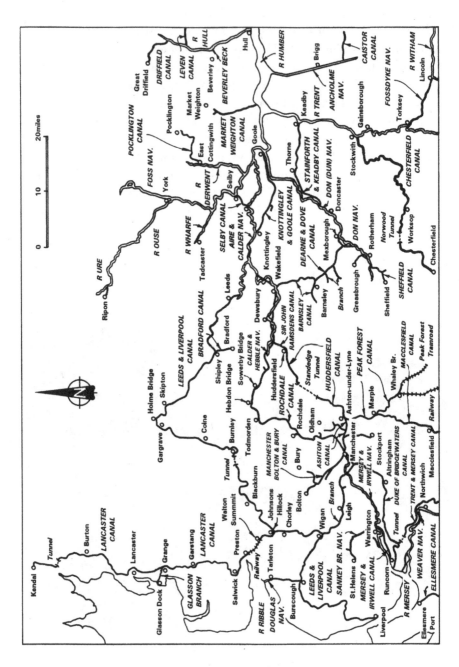

The main inland waterways of Lancashire and Yorkshire, prior to the replacement of much of the Mersey & Irwell Navigation by the Manchester Ship Canal, and the modernization of the line to Sheffield.

concerned with the Leeds & Liverpool Canal, had introduced a Bill to build a canal from Leeds to Selby on the Ouse, thus bypassing the Aire & Calder completely. The latter defeated the Bill and then built a shorter canal from the Aire at Haddlesey to Selby, the present Selby Canal, avoiding the difficult passage of the lower Aire. Other side cuts to improve the river passage were also begun as part of a modernization programme.

Work had stopped, however, on the Leeds & Liverpool as a result of a lack of money, and for 13 years nothing was done. The completed portions were of value, however, for that in Yorkshire joined Bradford (by the Bradford Canal) and Gargrave above Skipton to Leeds and the Aire & Calder Navigation, while that in Lancashire carried rapidly increasing quantities of coal from Wigan. By 1785 nearly 4 per cent was being earned on the capital expended to that date.

In 1790 work began again at the Gargrave end, with Robert Whitworth as engineer, though his estimate of the money needed to finish the canal sufficed for only 14 miles to Barrowford, including Foulridge Tunnel. Meanwhile the growth of new manufacturing districts had made the company decide that a short route between east and west was less important than a route that passed through these areas. The line was therefore altered to run by Burnley, Church and Blackburn to Johnson's Hillock, and work proceeded as the debts of the company grew. The branch canal from Newburgh to Wigan became part of the main line, while the Lancaster Canal, authorised in 1792, was used for 11 miles of the route in Lancashire, from Johnson's Hillock to Wigan top lock. At last, in 1816, 46 years after the canal had been authorised, it was completed by making the last portion below Blackburn. It had cost some £800,000 and had grown in length to 127¼ miles. Though designed for through traffic, its revenue always came primarily from the separate trade of the two ends: from Burnley, Blackburn and the other cotton towns, and from Wigan down to Liverpool, and from the highlands of Yorkshire to Leeds and the Aire & Calder. In 1820 the Leeds & Liverpool Canal was linked by the Leigh branch to the Bridgewater Canal, and so to Manchester. However, although it ran to Liverpool it had no physical connection with the Mersey until 1846. Ironically, although the Leeds & Liverpool was by over twenty years the first trans-Pennine canal to be begun, it was the last of three to be finished: another broad canal, the Rochdale, from the Bridgewater at Manchester to the Calder & Hebble at Sowerby Bridge, was authorised in 1794 and opened in 1804; the narrow Huddersfield Canal, also authorised in 1794, was finished in 1811 through the then 5,456yd long Standedge Tunnel. The Leeds & Liverpool was to outlast the Rochdale and Huddersfield canals as a through route.

The idea of joining the Severn to the Thames is at least as old as the reign of Elizabeth I. The first practical step was taken in 1730 with an Act to make navigable the River Stroudwater from the Severn to the town of Stroud. The owners of the many mills on the river were so strong in opposition, however (they even inserted a clause that no boat was to pass between 14 August and

15 October without their majority consent), that nothing was done. A second
Act, in 1759, is of interest because of the extraordinary scheme that it produced.
To overcome the millowners' objections, it was planned to make the river navigable without locks. Each level was to be divided by a 12ft bank on which a
double crane was fitted. The boats were to contain six to eight boxes of cargo,
each containing one ton of goods, to be lifted from one boat to another by
the crane at each bank, with two jibs to enable the interchange of boxes. John
Kemmett and the other projectors did about half the work (and offered to
make the Calder and upper Don navigable in the same way) and then gave up,
apparently due to a lack of capital.

From 1774 the promoters began to build a canal under the earlier powers, but
were stopped by an injunction. A new Act was obtained in 1776, and the canal, 8
miles long with 12 locks, opened in 1779. It was large enough for Severn trows.

The building of the Stroudwater Canal encouraged action to join the Severn
to the Thames. An Act was passed in 1783, Whitworth was engaged as engineer
with Josiah Clowes under him, and the Thames & Severn Canal opened in 1789.
The main canal was 29 miles long, with 44 locks, and ran from Stroud to the
Thames at Inglesham, above Lechlade. Its length included Sapperton Tunnel, over
two miles long, the third longest canal tunnel in Britain.

The Thames & Severn started life with three handicaps: disordered finance as a
result of loose administration while it was being built; chronic water supply problems worsened by a summit level through the Great Oolite that throughout its
long life lost up to 3 million gallons of water a day in leakage; and the bad state of
the navigation of the upper River Thames. These problems persisted, though the
finances were reorganised. The canal was never more than partly successful and
proved a failure for most of its commercial life.

It was a different story with the second of the three canals built to join the
Bristol Channel to the Thames. The proposal to link the Kennet at Newbury
with the Avon at Bath grew from a 1788 plan to extend the Kennet Navigation
from Newbury by a canal to Hungerford, but got its impetus from the canal
mania of 1792, and was authorised as the Kennet & Avon Canal in 1794.

The project, engineered by John Rennie, was on a grand scale, including a flight of 29 locks at Devizes. The first part of the line, from Newbury to
Hungerford, was opened in 1798 with 'a barge freighted with a wrought Portland
stone staircase, for J. Pearce, esq., of Chilton Lodge, a large quantity of deals, and
nine chaldron of sea coal, in the whole amounting to 40 tons'.[2]

There were many problems and as early as 1800 450 of the 3,500 issued shares
of £120 had been forfeited for non-payment of calls on them, owing to the nervousness of shareholders. The lack of a proper survey before work began caused
much extra expense, and it was not until 1810 that the line was completed, at a
cost of £980,000. Yet the shareholders, already with a controlling interest in the
Avon, went on to buy the Kennet Navigation, followed by plans for expansion

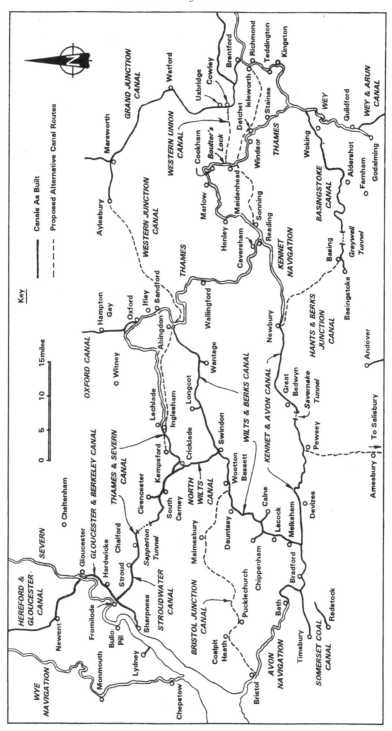

The waterways of southern England, including the Basingstoke Canal, showing a number of proposed connections.

Thames & Severn Canal tokens, showing a Severn trow and the Coates entrance to Sapperton Tunnel.

and through routes. Some Kennet & Avon proprietors took up shares in the Grand Western Canal of Devon, seeing it as part of a through route from Exeter to London.

The Kennet & Avon was a successful canal. Its dividends were small, for the cost of upkeep was high, but in its prime it carried 341,878 tons of goods in a year (1838–9), against 60,894 on the Thames & Severn for the same year. Sold to the Great Western Railway while still a going concern, it survived attempts at closure in 1926 and in the 1950s, and has since been restored for pleasure craft use. Its two competitors remain largely unnavigable.

The Wilts & Berks was a narrow canal, planned not as a through waterway from Bristol to London but as a carrier of coal to the agricultural areas of the Vale of the White Horse. It was built under an Act of 1795 from Semington on the Kennet & Avon to Abingdon on the Thames, by way of Swindon (not then, of course, a large town), and with branches to Calne, Chippenham and Wantage. Its history was that of many agricultural canals, although its high cost of £255,000 was not. It declined after railway competition but had a few years of exciting life.

The Wilts & Berks promoters saw it as a competitor with both the Kennet & Avon and the Thames & Severn, and they made a bid for the through traffic between Bristol, London and the Midlands. The North Wilts Canal was first constructed between Latton and their line at Swindon, effectively bypassing the upper Thames above Abingdon. They then planned a canal to avoid the lower Thames, from Abingdon to the Grand Junction, and one from Wootton Bassett, west of Swindon, to Bristol, to cut out the rest of the Kennet & Avon, and a further canal north from Abingdon to Stratford, for the midlands trade. Given that their main line was narrow and winding, it was wildly ambitious, and the Kennet & Avon proved able to compete for through traffic.

These three canals completed the circuit of Britain, by the Mersey, Trent, Thames, Severn and Mersey again. In time, however, they fall outside the first period of canal building to which the others belong.

Meanwhile two arteries were being built in Ireland to supplement Steers's old Newry Canal, which Thomas Omer, an engineer of Dutch descent, had by 1769 extended via a small ship canal taking craft of 120 tons.

The first, the Lagan Navigation from Belfast to Lough Neagh, was begun by Omer in 1756. While the river section to Lisburn was completed by 1765, there work stopped, partly because of doubts as to whether it was sensible to continue a river navigation so liable to floods as the Lagan. Robert Whitworth then developed alternative approaches to continuing by canal, and a new company took over from the old commissioners. Under the engineer Richard Owen from the Leeds & Liverpool, work resumed in 1782, with the whole line to Lough Neagh opened on the first day of 1794. It was 25¾ miles long with 27 locks, each 62ft by 14ft 6in, very similar in size to the Leeds & Liverpool. Works included the four-arched Spencer's Bridge aqueduct, later demolished, and the Union Locks staircase above Lisburn.

The second artery was the Grand Canal, the line from Dublin to the Shannon, and its major branch to the Barrow. The idea of opening up the centre of Ireland had lain behind the Act of 1715. In 1751 the Corporation for Promoting and Carrying on an Inland Navigation in Ireland was set up by the Irish Parliament to amalgamate the four bodies of provincial commissioners established in 1729. The corporation put impetus behind waterway building but was dissolved in 1787, having spent some £850,000, and separate bodies of commissioners for different waterways were substituted. It had initiated work on the Shannon in 1755, the Grand Canal in 1756 and the Barrow and Boyne in 1759.

The main line of the Grand Canal was to be 79 miles long, reaching the Shannon at Shannon Harbour above Banagher. The chosen line was surveyed by Thomas Omer and work began on a large scale, Omer's first lock being 136ft long and able to take a 175-ton barge. Not long afterwards the city of Dublin decided to draw water supplies for general use from the canal, as would Edinburgh with the Union Canal much later. Canal work proceeded very slowly, however, until, after about 20 miles had been built, it stopped in 1768, with a series of inquiries as to why so much had been spent and so little achieved.

Eventually a company was formed to take over and complete the work on a reduced scale. John Smeaton brought over his pupil William Jessop in 1773. The latter spent some time with John Trail, who had worked mainly as Dublin's water supply engineer, and, supported by Smeaton, recommended that the canal should continue on this smaller scale. This was agreed and construction went on with Trail, William Chapman and other engineers as residents, and Jessop as consultant. The first 12 miles opened to traffic in 1779, and the Bog of Allen was crossed in

The Broadwater on the extension of the Lagan Navigation, on a length of the summit level which opened in 1792. (McCutcheon Collection)

the 1790s. After John Killaly was appointed as engineer in 1798, the whole canal, with its 41 locks of 70ft by 13ft 7 ½ in, was finally finished in 1805, two months after Jessop's Grand Junction Canal in England.

Work on its major offshoot, the Barrow – mainly river navigation, partly canal – had begun under Thomas Omer in 1759, but work went on very slowly until 1790, when a company was formed in 1790. Under this, William Chapman rebuilt some of the old work and created some new, and the navigation was completed with some Government assistance. It was nearly 42 miles between the tideway of the Barrow at St Mullins and the Grand Canal Barrow line at Athy; the latter, 28½ miles long, had opened in 1791.

In 1759 Omer also began work on the lower Boyne from Drogheda to Slane, mostly by building a lateral canal. Though £75,000 had been spent, the section to Slane was seemingly unfinished and semi-derelict when the corporation was abolished in 1787. A new River Boyne Company took over in 1790, and by 1800 it had extended the line to Navan, 19 miles from Drogheda with 20 broad locks.

Back in England, after the Leeds & Liverpool Act of 1770, a short tributary was opened to Bradford in 1774. The Chester Canal, running only to Nantwich, had planned to link Chester with the Trent & Mersey line at Middlewich, but was left incomplete and proved an early commercial failure. This included a five-lock broad staircase at Northgate in Chester, which rivalled the better-known one at Bingley, although it proved short-lived.

The lower reaches of the Chesterfield Canal, that linked that town to the Trent, were built broad, and the upper part narrow. The engineers were Brindley and John Varley. Unusual engineering features included a summit tunnel at Norwood, 2,880 yards long, opened in 1775 just before Brindley's more celebrated one at Harecastle, and numerous staircase locks, those at Norwood totalling twelve in four flights.

Then followed a long period of consolidation, lasting from 1774 to 1788. Capital and labour were being fully employed on the great routes that crossed the British Isles, the War of American Independence was being fought and lost, and investors and Government were watching to see if this new method of transport would be a financial success, so that speculators could take a hand. How successful it was can be seen from the takings on the Duke of Bridgewater's Canal, which in 1791 amounted to £61,143.

The first period of canal development in England saw the authorization of waterways linking the Mersey with the Severn and the Trent, and also with the Aire & Calder, together with some tributaries. Some 16 years elapsed between the Act for the Chester Canal in 1772 and those for the Andover and Cromford canals in 1789 – the harbingers of canal mania. In this period the few canals that were authorised included the Erewash, a tributary of the Trent, a number of small privately owned and privately built navigations from Cornwall to Yorkshire, and the Basingstoke Canal, the first of the agricultural canals.

While the great expansion of canal building was taking place in the growing industrial area around Birmingham, the prosperous landowners of the south had been considering a canal that was not to carry fuel, raw materials or finished goods to or from factories or large towns, but was to open up the countryside and enable the latest agricultural methods to be used on poor land. Suggested as early as 1769, the Basingstoke Canal obtained its Act in 1778, although work did not start until the War of American Independence was over.

This line, 37½ miles long with 29 locks, ran to Basingstoke from the Wey near its mouth at Weybridge. It was partly intended to form a route for goods to pass to and from Salisbury, Bristol and the west by road transport, rather than by the existing route via the Thames and Kennet to Newbury. This hoped for change of through route to the west was, however, not the principal reason for promoting the canal; this was the improvement of agricultural land en route by the carriage of lime and manure.

The canal proved a financial failure, partly due to the requirement to pay interest on capital during construction, and the consequent escalating costs. After it opened in 1794 the estimated revenues were never achieved, and no dividend was ever paid on the original share capital. Despite local benefits, any hopes of it carrying through traffic were dashed by the Kennet & Avon Canal, until railway competition took its toll. Several attempts at revival, some fraudulent, followed.

CHAPTER FIVE

The Canal Mania and the Wars

The earliest period of canal expansion ended in 1778, when the Selby Canal opened, linking the Yorkshire Ouse to the old Aire & Calder line. A year before the Trent & Mersey had opened, while the Bridgewater Canal was finally completed to Runcorn in 1776. However, the effects on the British economy both of existing canals and those under construction, were delayed. At times when results might have been expected, the difficulties during and after the American War did not encourage investment. Gradually trade improved, and even the French Revolution could not disguise the prosperity that resulted from cheaper transport of coal and commodities. The earlier canals had been promoted to improve economic conditions for merchants and industrialists rather than to provide direct returns to canal owning companies. The success of most early canals led owners of capital to see these solely in investment terms, providing a means to tempt less cautious speculation. It was perhaps encouraged by lawyers fostering promotion in order to boost their incomes, and by engineers like John Longbothom, who advertised for:

> The survey of canals by the piece, or examining them by the day. His terms by day are Three Guineas per day, exclusive of expenses. He has men, good surveyors and levellers, very capable of taking the survey of canals, which he charges as common surveyors, and staff-holders, exclusive of expenses.[1]

The boom began in 1790 and was over by 1797. It reached its peak in Britain in late 1792 and early 1793, reflected in legislation of 1793 and 1794. The following table shows its legislative progress:

Year	No. of new canals authorised	Capital authorised (£)
1789	2	131,000
1790	1	90,000
1791	7	743,000
1792	7	1,056,000
1793	20	2,824,700
1794	10	2,037,900
1795	4	395,000
1796	3	585,000
1797	1	18,000

The waterways system of lowland England, as completed in 1789–90, just before the canal mania.

The first cause of the boom was the prosperity of the earlier waterways. It was widely known how profitable, if indebted, was the Duke of Bridgewater's Canal, but the Birmingham Canal paid over 23 per cent for 1789, and others like the Trent & Mersey were very solid concerns. A second cause, perhaps, was the opening of the Thames & Severn Canal in 1789, and the Oxford Canal the next year, both of which completed a national water route between the English Midlands and London and Bristol, together with the completion, in 1790, of a shorter line from Birmingham to London via Fazeley and Oxford. The last cause was, perhaps, the interest taken by industrialists who backed local canal promotions, including the Darbys and Reynolds of Coalbrookdale with the Shropshire Canal, Sir Richard Arkwright and the Cromford Canal, Richard Crawshay of Cyfartha and other ironmasters with the Glamorganshire Canal.

All over Britain the canal mania took hold and raged, so much so that at Leicester and Birmingham special 'Navigation Share Offices' were set up. Because they wanted to keep a good thing to themselves, promoters tended to hold subscription meetings quietly. Thus, whenever a meeting was held, hopeful speculators rushed to the place, seeking to put down deposits on shares that they could immediately sell at a profit, in one case only to find that the supposed canal meeting was really a hunt dinner.

Let us follow the mania in the columns of a single rural newspaper, the *British Chronicle* of Hereford, far from Britain's industrial heart. In 1789 there was to the north of Hereford no canal at all; none of any size in South Wales; none to the west; and in the direction of England nothing nearer than Droitwich. Small barges carrying about 20 tons each brought coal and other goods up the Wye to the city, when there was enough water in the river. There were no locks and no horse towing-path.

In 1790 the Glamorganshire Canal had been authorised, not very far away, and in 1791 two nearer to home, between Hereford and Gloucester with £105,000 of capital, and from Kington and Leominster to Stourport with £190,000, both promoted to bring coal to the towns and villages, and to carry away their goods and produce. These two appeared often in the paper's columns, but soon news from farther away was featured. In May 1791 it was reported that £60,000 had been subscribed in an hour for a canal from Manchester to Rochdale; in June that the Forth & Clyde Canal was open; in September that a meeting had been held at Ellesmere to consider a canal from the Severn to the Dee; in November that the capital of £40,000 for the Grantham Canal had been raised at a single meeting; in December, nearer home, that £51,000 had been subscribed for the Monmouthshire Canal from Newport to Pontypool and Crumlin.

By early 1792 the columns were filling up with canal news; the Gloucester & Berkeley ship canal project was going ahead; so were the Leominster, the Monmouthshire and the Lancaster canals, to the last of which £170,000 had been subscribed at one meeting; and a canal from Birmingham to London was planned. In July, appositely for author and publisher, John Phillips' *General History of Inland Navigation* was published, the first book about British canals as a whole, which must have opened many eyes to the possibilities of water transport. By August an extension of the Monmouthshire Canal was being considered – the Brecknock & Abergavenny – and in September the newspaper

The Herefordshire & Gloucestershire Canal at Monkhide. Although this section of the canal was authorised during the canal mania, it was not completed until 1845, when the canal age was over. The exceptionally skewed bridge carries only a minor road; the earliest canal skew bridge, on the Rochdale Canal, was constructed only fifty years earlier. This section was disused after 1882, but the length into Monkhide, one of the few in water, has been restored, with ambitious plans for the restoration (or rebuilding) of the whole line from the Severn to Hereford.

published a list of canal shares that were standing at a premium. These were headed by the Birmingham Canal, which was open, and projected canals such as the Grand Junction.

On 19 September the paper reported that 'last Saturday's *Gazette* gives notice of applications ... for no fewer than twenty-five navigable Cuts and Canals, many of them of immense extent...' By November and December the paper was full of canal news, which died away before the onset of the wave of merchant and banking bankruptcies of early 1793. For instance, on 13 March 1793 the newspaper recorded that, 'In consequence of the temporary suspension of business of the Monmouthshire bank at Chepstow, the premium on Monmouthshire Canal shares has dropped from near 100 per cent by 25 per cent in the course of last week.' Many who had borrowed to cover their liabilities for shares must have been caught.

Three local canal schemes had been born during the mania and were wound up in 1793. A canal from Brecon to Hay and Whitney quietly died, and one from Abergavenny to Hereford was turned down by a meeting of landowners. (Horse tramroads were built over the general routes of both twenty years later.) A third, from the Leominster Canal to the Montgomeryshire Canal via Ludlow and Bishop's Castle, was seen to be too expensive and was dropped.

So much for Hereford. The following extract from an account of what happened around Bristol helps to bring the canal mania to life:

> The 'canal mania' of 1792, though productive of less important results than the railway mania of 1845, was in many respects a counterpart of that memorable delirium. On the 20th November a meeting to promote the construction of a canal from Bristol to Gloucester was held in the Guildhall, when the scheme was enthusiastically supported by influential persons, and a very large sum was subscribed by those present, who struggled violently with each other in their rush to the subscription book. A few days later, a Somerset paper announced that a meeting would be held at Wells to promote a canal from Bristol to Taunton. The design had been formed in this city [Bristol], but the promoters strove to keep it a secret, and bought up all the newspapers containing the advertisement. The news nevertheless leaked out on the evening before the intended gathering, and a host of speculators set off to secure shares in the undertaking, some arriving only to find that the subscription list was full. The third meeting was at Devizes, on the 12th December. Only one day's notice was given of this movement, which was to promote a canal from Bristol to Southampton and London, but the news rapidly spread, and thousands of intending subscribers rushed to the little town, where the proposed capital was offered several times over. The 'race to Devizes' on the part of Bristolians, who had hired or bought up at absurd prices all the old hacks that could be found, and plunged along the miry roads through a long wintry night, was attended with many comic incidents. A legion of schemes followed, Bristol being the proposed terminus of canals to all parts of the country.[2]

All over Britain waterways had been projected and sufficient money raised to pay an engineer for a survey, however hurried. Many were never embodied in a Bill, and fewer still were authorised by an Act. Those that survived were mostly solid schemes that, though they probably cost much more and took much longer than had been projected, eventually proved successful. These included the Neath and Manchester, Bolton & Bury canals authorised in 1791, the Lancaster, Nottingham, Monmouthshire and Ashton (1792), the Grand Junction, Shrewsbury, Barnsley and Dearne & Dove (1793) and Swansea and Rochdale canals (1794). More of them, while useful, were only moderately profitable: the Worcester & Birmingham (1791), Wyrley & Essington (1792), Stratford, Ellesmere (1793), Peak Forest, Huddersfield and Ashby (1794). Six were failures: the Herefordshire & Gloucestershire took from 1791 to 1845 to reach Hereford from Gloucester; the Grand Western, the Leominster and the Foss never completed their lines; and the Salisbury & Southampton and Dorset & Somerset were abandoned during construction. None of these, except for the Foss, ever paid a dividend during their working lives.

The immediate consequence of the mania was that a great deal of canal building started at the same time, many companies sharing engineers and competing for cutters. In September 1793 Denys Rolle, the Devon landowner and MP, wrote:

> From the Immense Numbers of Canals now coming on and the not only absence of a Multitude of the Labouring Class abroad in the War but the vast suppos'd Diminution that there will arise from the destruction in it, a great scarcity of Hands for the Cultivation will be found at the End...[3]

He proposed that more Irish labourers should be encouraged to come to England. This shortage must have led the Peak Forest Committee to decide in July 1794 to start cutting 'so soon as the Corn Harvest shall be got in'.[4]

The mania fostered a range of useful waterways, significant to the continued industrialization of their areas. The Barnsley and Dearne & Dove provide examples. Promoted as rivals, the Barnsley, a client of the Aire & Calder, and the Dearne & Dove of the Don, met at a junction stoplock outside Barnsley, from where the Barnsley Canal's line extended upwards to the edge of the especially valuable Silkstone coalfield. Their Acts were passed on the same day in 1793 and both opened in 1804. Within fifteen years each was carrying over 100,000 tons of coal, besides stone and timber for building houses and mills, iron and corn. The latter, coming from the fields of Lincolnshire and East Anglia by sea or by the Trent, was carried along the canals in the opposite direction to the coal to feed the Barnsley area and the coalfield.

There was no real canal mania in Ireland, except perhaps with the Royal Canal from Dublin to the upper Shannon, authorised in 1789. Much Irish canal development relied on public funds, with new Directors General of Inland Navigation being appointed just before formal Union in 1800. These had both powers to assist and to take control of any waterways undertakings under local commissioners. Even with a grant the Royal Canal Company became massively indebted and could not complete its line, so the Directors General took over in 1813. They finished the line in 1817 and handed the canal to a New Royal Canal Company, with a greatly written-down capital upon which modest dividends were paid. The Royal Canal had cost over £1.4 million for its 90 mile lines, and in 1836 88,334 tons were carried, with 46,450 passengers in 1837.

One of the less successful canals authorised in the mania produced one of the biggest engineering achievements of the Industrial Revolution. Pontcysyllte Aqueduct, created by William Jessop and Thomas Telford, is 1,007ft long with nineteen arches, and carries the Ellesmere Canal (now known as the Llangollen) 121ft above the River Dee. The piers were built solid for 70ft and then hollow, and over them was laid a cast-iron trough 11ft 10in wide, with a towpath carried over part on iron pillars. Opened in 1805, Pontcysyllte was a monument to canal engineering and to the use of cast iron pioneered at Longdon on the Shrewsbury Canal and The Holmes on the Derby Canal in 1795. It also demonstrates a complete change of mind on the part of a canal company.

The Chester and Ellesmere Canals, later part of the Shropshire Union system, began with the 1772 Act for the Chester Canal. Completed only from Chester to Nantwich, rather than Middlewich, this was the first entirely unsuccessful canal of the early canal age, and much of it became derelict.

In the 1790s two schemes were promoted to link Chester on the Dee with Shrewsbury on the Severn. The chosen line was from Netherpool on the Mersey (now called Ellesmere Port) across the Wirral peninsula to Chester, and then by way of Wrexham, Ellesmere, Frankton and Weston to Shrewsbury on the Severn. Among the proposed branches was one to Llanymynech to join the proposed Montgomeryshire Canal to Welshpool and Newtown. The intention was to serve the North Wales industrial area near Wrexham and distribute its products, and to open up the county by bringing in fuel and manure, as well as commodities carried up the three rivers from farther afield.

Lock 12 at Blanchardstown, on the Royal Canal, the main example of the canal mania in Ireland. This was part of the first length to be completed, in 1796. The photograph was taken on the occasion of the reopening of Lock 12 in 1990; it had been closed since 1961. The section above this lock was the first to be restored, after 1974. (Dr Ian Bath)

A somewhat romanticized view of Pontcysyllte Aqueduct on the Ellesmere (later Llangollen) Canal. The aquaduct was named after the older road bridge in the foreground.

The proprietors started with the broad Wirral line, which opened in 1795, and also began cutting in the middle of their line, from Chirk to Weston, along with the Llanymynech line, while putting in hand the expensive Chirk and Pontcysyllte aqueducts. It was planned that coal from the Ruabon collieries, near Pontcysyllte, would be carried south towards Montgomeryshire.

By 1800 new collieries offered cheaper coal to Chester than the canal could bring. A less expensive route, to link the sections already built or under construction towards Chester, was therefore confirmed. The line went from Frankton east to the Chester Canal at Hurleston near Nantwich, with short branches to Whitchurch, Ellesmere and towards Prees. When this was completed in 1805, it provided a waterway from the Mersey and Dee that was very different from that originally intended.

Though the original main line by way of Wrexham had been abandoned, work continued on the aqueducts at Chirk and Pontcysyllte, although they now lay on a branch. It was thought that coal from the Ruabon collieries made the works worthwhile, and when the great aqueduct was finished a basin and lines of tramroad were built at its far end to handle the coal and other products from Ruabon. The water supply feeder from Llantysilio past Llangollen was also made navigable to provide additional traffic.

The aqueduct was opened with much ceremony, partly re-enacted on its 200th anniversary in 2005. One of its piers still carries the cast-iron plate commemorating the laying of the first stone on 25 July 1795.

By 1805 over £450,000 had been spent and the company had come to the end of its resources. In 1813 an Act was passed to amalgamate the Chester and Ellesmere companies, and in 1826 a new canal, the Birmingham & Liverpool Junction, was authorised to shorten the distance and reduce the lockage between the Mersey and Autherley to 66½ miles and 45 locks instead of 80¾ miles and 75 locks by way of the Trent & Mersey.

A new type of transport now began to serve canals. The financial crisis had dried up available capital, while rising prices caused construction costs to spiral well beyond those estimated. Engineers began to find many proposed branches or extensions unnecessary. Instead, they proposed tramroads.

The use of waggons running on rails dates back to the early seventeenth century in Britain, although these were known in continental Europe, especially in mines. The earliest definitely known were two in East Shropshire carrying coal to the Severn from 1605, the first of many. From the early seventeenth century they were developed to move coal from north-east collieries to staithes on the Tyne. It was an obvious development to use horse tramroads, which had been used as feeders to rivers for over 200 years, as feeders to canals.

Tramroads, which here include all kinds of horse-drawn lines, initially had wooden rails; later the wood was covered with a strip of iron and the waggon wheels were flanged; later still iron edge-rails were used. Then John Curr, followed by Benjamin Outram, introduced the plateway. Instead of rails, this used L-shaped iron plates about 3ft long. The sleeper was a rough cube of granite with a hole in the centre, which was filled with an oak plug, into which a spike to hold the plate was driven. The waggon wheels were flangeless, being held in position by the flanges on the inner sides of the plates. These plateways became very popular and Outram, his assistant and successor John Hodgkinson, and other engineers laid several hundred miles of them. They also converted many of the older railways to plateways between the early 1790s and about 1830, after which these tramroads began to give way to the conventional railway as we know it today, with edge-rails and the flange on the wheel. Some plateways continued in use well into the twentieth century, including that serving the Peak Forest Canal at Whaley Bridge, which only ceased work in 1920.

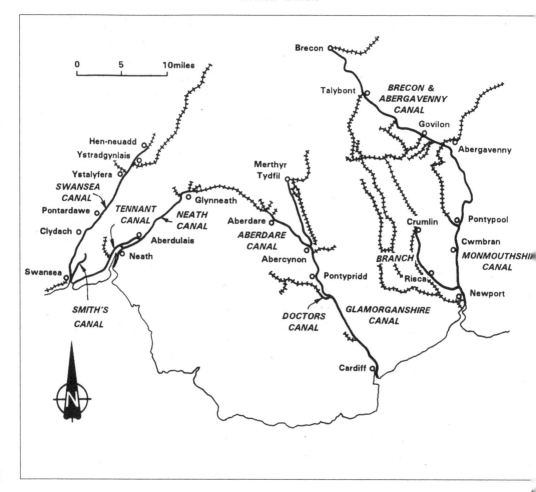

The canals of the South Wales valleys, showing some of their tramroad connections.

These horse tramroads constituted an adjunct to canals, the importance of which is still being established, since they enabled branch lines to be built that would have been uneconomical as canals. For instance in 1794 the Ashby de la Zouch Canal was authorised from a junction with the Coventry Canal to Ashby, with branches to limeworks at Ticknall and Cloudhill, a total of 43 miles with a great deal of lockage. In fact the canal was only cut for 30 lockless miles to Moira, the branches being built by Outram as plateways.

The tramroads extending from the two arms of the Monmouthshire Canal were an outstanding example of such development. In the 1830s a considerable mileage of tramroads ran up the valleys, much of it owned by the canal company. Some of these in turn connected to another tramroad system, depending on the

Brecknock & Abergavenny Canal and extending as far as Hereford. Tramroads
were also developed elsewhere in South Wales, near Coalbrookdale in connection
with the local tub-boat canals, in Derbyshire (notably plateways owned by the
Peak Forest and Derby Canal companies), and in the north, especially near the
Tyne and Wear rivers.

In 1800 Telford advocated the use of iron railways:

> in countries whose surfaces are rugged, or where it is difficult to obtain water for
> lockage, where the weight of the articles of produce is great in comparison with
> their bulk, and when they are mostly to be conveyed from a higher to a lower
> level… Upon the whole, this useful contrivance may be varied so as to suit the
> surface of many different countries, at a comparatively modest expense. It may be
> constructed in a much more expeditious manner than navigable canals; it may be
> introduced into many districts where canals are wholly inapplicable; and in case of
> any change in the working of the mines or manufactures, the rails may be taken up
> and put down again, in a new situation, at a moderate expense.[5]

Tramroads could be double-track or single with passing places. The usual load for
the four-wheeled waggons was 2 tons, a number – called a gang or train – being
pulled by each horse. When the lines could be worked by gravity, as often happened on the Tyne, in Wales or in the Somerset coalfield, a train of half a dozen
or more waggons was run by its own weight to the canalside, a boy applying the
brake and a horse being tied to the last waggon or riding in it to pull back the
empty train.

Outram advocated the use of rafts for the Somersetshire Coal Canal in 1800,
which would take such tramroad waggons without it being necessary to shift
their contents, but the difficulties on the one hand of getting the waggons onto
the rafts, and on the other of navigating the rafts when a wind was blowing,
were too great. Waggon-boats were, however, later used successfully on the Don
Navigation in Yorkshire and on the Forth & Clyde Canal to carry waggons from
the Monkland & Kirkintilloch Railroad.

Tramroads were also used to connect portions of canal. The flight of 16 locks
at Marple on the Peak Forest Canal, and the tunnel at Blisworth on the Grand
Junction Canal, took so long to construct that temporary tramroads were built
to enable through trade to begin. In the case of the Lancaster Canal the difficulties of fulfilling the original intention of carrying the waterway over the Ribble
Estuary were so great that the two parts of the canal were permanently connected
by a tramroad.

Sometimes these tramroads were built and owned by canal companies: the
Brecknock & Abergavenny, remarkable for having completed and worked a tram-
road before having cut a yard of canal, the Monmouthshire, Peak Forest, Trent &
Mersey and others were important tramroad owners. Sometimes they were built

by independent companies, such as the Surrey Iron Railway or the Oystermouth, or by companies having many common shareholders with a neighbouring canal, such as the Hay Railway. Often these were privately owned by the proprietors of the collieries or works they served; thus the Hills of Blaenavon or Crawshay Bailey of Nantyglo owned lines from their works to the canals.

In Ireland the only significant tramroad to be constructed served one canal, the Coalisland, and superseded another, the Ducarts Canal. John Smeaton had suggested that the latter should be replaced by a tramroad, and one was built between the Drumglass Colliery and the basin at Coalisland in about 1790. It was still operating in around 1830.

Many canal Acts gave companies the power to make tramroad branches, usually to a distance of 4–8 miles from the canal. If the owner of a mine or works within the specified distance applied and the canal company refused to build a tramroad, the powers of construction were transferred to the applicant. Some canal companies, like the Swansea, steadfastly refused to make tramroads and left them to the businessmen; others like the Monmouthshire built many. These powers were included to avoid the system of wayleaves in force on the Tyne and Wear, where railway owners had to make a payment to the landowner for everything that passed over his land. In the Chesterfield Canal Act, instead of tramroads, power was given to make toll-free roads up to a mile long, and in other Acts the power to make 'stone-roads' was an alternative to that for making tramroads. Many roads were general purpose feeders to canals throughout the country, and canal companies spent much time complaining to the town and country local authorities that such feeder roads were inadequate or badly maintained.

When the canals were built, the takings of turnpike trustees of the roads that ran parallel with canals fell sharply. For example those of the Loughborough to Leicester road fell from £1,800 in 1792 to £1,162 in 1802, after the Leicester Navigation had opened in 1794. Not until 1830 did the takings again equal the earlier figure, and then only because of the increase of passenger traffic. On the other hand, roads whose location made them natural feeders to canals gained in revenue. Thus the tolls of the Hinckley road in Leicestershire rose from £602 in 1792 to £888 in 1802. Roads that suffered from canal competition had two consolations: the removal of heavy traffic reduced upkeep costs, which were greatly affected by the type of traffic and vehicles; and the waterway was useful for carrying roadstone, usually toll-free unless water was short. In some cases, such as the impecunious Chester Canal, the parallel road competed successfully and contributed to the canal's failure.

The outbreak of the French Revolution in 1793, and the accompanying financial crisis and inflation, put a brake on developments at a time when industrial and transport expansion was taking place. A number of canals begun during the mania soon found themselves with lines uncompleted and capital exhausted owing to rising prices, at a time when money was difficult to borrow.

In 1797 the Kennet & Avon Company said 'the distress of the times during the last year ... has increased the pressure on your committee for money to carry on the work', and in 1798 'not only the rise of labour and the increased price of almost every article employed on the Works, have occasioned a considerable excess beyond the original estimate',[6] while in 1800 450 of the company's shares were forfeited because the owners either would not or could not pay further calls on them. In the north the Huddersfield Canal's shareholders were being told that, 'from the bankruptcy of several of the proprietors of shares ... the deaths of other proprietors insolvent, and ... several of the proprietors having left the kingdom, it is become impossible to procure payment of the whole of the money subscribed'.[7]

Five problems raised by the war especially affected the canals. French privateers lay in wait around the coasts, reducing the reliability of the coasting trade. The diversion of coasting trade to inland navigations was investigated in 1800 by a House of Commons Committee, which considered whether enough coal could be brought to London by inland waterway or road, should the Tyne colliers be unable to make the sea passage. There was support for schemes to provide alternative routes to those by sea, such as plans for a canal from London to Portsmouth, and for a connection between the Basingstoke, now acting as a carrier of Portsmouth and Southampton trade, and the River Itchen to Southampton. Schemes for a canal across Somerset and Devon were pursued to enable traffic to get to the south coast from Wales without having to pass around Land's End, thereby risking the privateers who waited there and along the south coast. Projects between the Tyne and Solway Firth to move troops more quickly should the French attack Ireland or the east coast were also considered. The great state enterprise of the Caledonian Canal was commenced partly to enable warships to cross quickly from one side of Scotland to the other.

The second problem was that of possible invasion. The Government built the Royal Military Canal from Shorncliffe to Winchelsea along the south-east coast. It was designed originally both as a barrier to an invading army and to move troops and stores quickly along the stretch of coast most threatened by the enemy.

Some canal companies and their employees, felt they might be affected. In July 1797 the Grand Junction Committee received a joint letter from:

> ... the Engineer, Inspectors, Foremen, Hagmasters, and Workingmen, employed on the banks of the Grand Junction Canal ... think ourselves called upon, as Englishmen, to stand forth in support of our Laws and Property, and that of our Honourable Employers ... with our firmest assurances that we will spill the last drop of our blood, in the cause of old England, against all Foreign and Domestic Enemies.[8]

Later, in 1803, the Basingstoke Committee recorded that:

> Several of the London Proprietors having called upon the Committee, recommend-
> ing, that after the Example of other corporate Bodies, the Company should offer
> such Assistance, as they may be able to give to Government, towards transporting
> Baggage, or Stores up or down the Canal, and the consent of Mr George Smith and
> the Rest of the Bargemasters, having been obtained, a Letter was written … to Lord
> Hobart, offering Ten of the Basingstoke Canal Barges, in Case of Invasion, or the
> Appearance of the Enemy on the Coast, to transport Stores, free of Expence, from
> London to any Part of the Canal.[9]

In 1803 Pickfords, at that time both canal and road carriers, also offered the
Government the use of 400 horses, 50 waggons and 28 boats.

The third problem was that of obtaining quicker transport around the country
for troops and stores, and for the first time the usefulness of canals to speed up
movement became clear to the authorities. On 18 June 1798 the Grand Junction
Company issued a notice to its men that a considerable body of troops was to
embark at Blisworth for Liverpool, and that the locks and canal were to be kept
clear for the urgent movement of fifteen boats on each of two days. Another example, from *The Times* of 19 December 1806, announces that the first troop division

> for Liverpool, and thence by transports for Dublin, will leave Paddington to-day,
> and will be followed by others to-morrow and Sunday. By this mode of conveyance
> the men will be only seven days in reaching Liverpool, and with comparatively little
> fatigue, as it would take them above fourteen days to march that distance. Relays of
> fresh horses for the canal boats have been ordered to be in readiness at all the stages.

Indeed, when invasion threatened, a central fortified citadel was built at Weedon,
to which king and cabinet could be moved, served by a short branch from the
Grand Junction Canal, with portcullises against water penetration of the defences.
It was completed in 1816, the year after the war ended.

The fourth problem was inflation, especially of food prices. While this led in time
to a rise in wages, the time-lag caused distress. For instance, on 1 September 1800
the town clerk of Nottingham drafted a letter to the home secretary, in which he
said 'riot has been occasioned by the Difficulty of obtaining Flour & the Price at
which the small Quantity that could be procured was obtained… They seemed
Disposed to plunder the Warehouses & some Boats laden with Corn'.[10]

Nervousness of what the working class might do, if it ceased to 'stand forth in support of our Laws and Property, and that of our Honourable Employers', also showed
itself. The Grand Junction employees' loyal sentiments of 1797 did not extend to the
men working on the Wolverton Embankment in 1801, who faced the engineer with
a strike for higher wages. The Grand Junction Committee told him

An early illustration of the Grand Junction Canal at Paddington Basin. On this occasion, a passenger packet boat is leaving; a more familiar sight than the carriage of troops.

to discharge at all risque these offenders, and to use his utmost endeavours to bring them to Justice, and to call on the Magistracy and Yeomanry of this County to repress and punish all acts of Outrage and Violence and an illegal conspiracy or combination for increase of wages.[11]

The fifth problem was that of increasing output from the homeland. This was achieved under the inducement that rising prices gave to producers and led to many kinds of new enterprises. The story of the Tavistock Canal is one such enterprise.

During the early nineteenth century 25 per cent of the world's copper supply was mined in Cornwall and Devon. Prices of ore rose steeply in wartime, but the output from Wheal Crowndale near Tavistock in Devon was limited due to the difficulty of getting the copper to the River Tamar, from where it could be taken to coasting ships at Devonport. In 1803, therefore, a meeting was held to consider connecting Tavistock to the navigable Tamar at Morwellham Quay by:

... a CANAL to be taken up from the River Tavy, near the Abbey Bridge, in Tavistock, and carried from thence to Lumburn Valley, from thence by an Embankment across that Valley, and a TUNNEL through MORWELL-DOWN, and a BRANCH or SIDE-CUT to the Slate-Quarries, at MILL HILL.[12]

The proprietors produced an unusual canal. Though only 4 miles long, 1½ miles lay through a tunnel. At the far end of this tunnel was a drop of 237ft to the level of the Tamar, and:

> … after duly weighing the merits of various plans … the Committee … adopted that of an inclined Plane, furnished with iron railways, on which carriages fitted to transport boxes which may contain ores, coals, lime, etc., are made to ascend and descend by the application of a machine driven by water supplied from the canal.[13]

The water in the canal was deliberately given a current flowing downwards to the plane from the intake on the River Tavy at Tavistock. On its way it drove the mining machinery, carried the boats filled with ore down through the tunnel and finally worked the wheel of the inclined plane.

The canal company obtained from the Duke of Bedford, owner of the surrounding land, the right to mine any copper or other mineral found in the course of making the canal, and copper was indeed struck soon after the tunnel was begun. This lode became Wheal Crebor, and until 1828 the mine was managed in conjunction with the canal.

It took 13 years to cut the tunnel. One may indeed agree with the report of the canal committee for 1816, which says:

> The Tavistock Tunnel will be a lasting monument of the patience of those who executed and of the spirit and enterprise of the Proprietors who supported the work and who have so steadily pursued their object through the disheartening circumstances which have of late attended all mining pursuits.[14]

The canal was opened on 24 June 1817, but the boom in copper caused by the war had given way to a depressed state of trade that never fully passed away, and which led in the third quarter of the century to the disappearance of the Devonshire copper industry. The canal had cost some £62,000, but it seldom returned to its owners more than £600 a year in net profit. Yet for forty years it carried about 17,000 tons of goods a year in its 8 ton boats: merchandise for the town of Tavistock up against the stream, and copper ore, limestone, slate and granite downwards to the Tamar.

Eventually railway competition and the decline of mining led to the canal's disuse, and it was sold to the Duke of Bedford for £3,200. It remains in use today, however, in that the water supply drives a hydroelectric plant alongside Morwellham Quay. The tunnel, still in use, is close to the Morwellham Quay open-air museum.

Except for the great Caledonian Canal, nearly all of the new waterways authorised between 1800 and the end of the war in 1815 were near London, or were

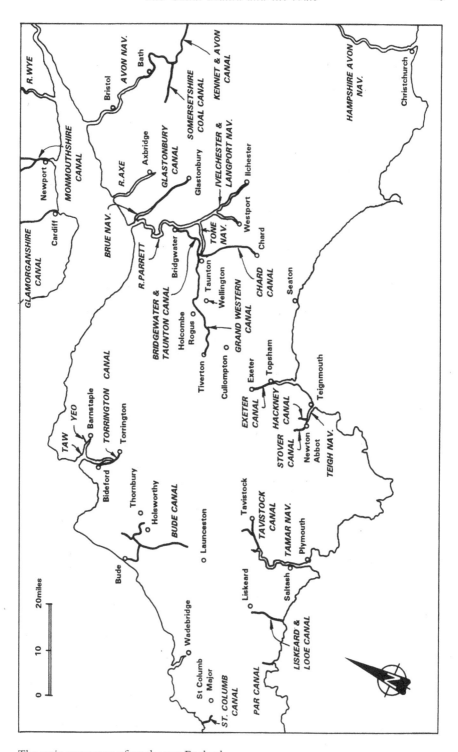

The main waterways of south-west England.

connected to the Grand Junction line, which joined the Midlands to London by a more direct route – from Braunston on the Oxford Canal – than the older one by way of Oxford and the Thames.

The Grand Junction Canal had been authorised in 1793 with a capital of £600,000. The Duke of Grafton, the Earl of Clarendon, the Earl of Essex and Earl Spencer were on its board, with the Marquis of Buckingham a strong supporter. Later, when the Commons became more important in relation to private Bills, there were fewer peers and more members of parliament on its managing committee. This political influence, supported as it was by the considerable connections the committee members had with shareholders in other canal companies, was a grievance to those who got in the way of the Grand Junction company.

The chairman was William Praed, who, after having been a partner in the Cornish Bank at Truro, had in 1803 started Praed & Co. in London. William Jessop was chief and James Barnes resident engineer. The canal, 93½ miles long with 101 locks, ran from the Oxford Canal at Braunston through Braunston and Blisworth Tunnels to the Thames at Brentford. It was completed in 1800 bar the 1¾-mile-long Blisworth Tunnel. After the first boring for this tunnel failed, Outram linked the ends temporarily by a double-track tramroad, after which the second tunnel was completed in March 1805. By then there were branches to Old Stratford and Buckingham, Wendover, the military depot at Weedon, and one built by an independent company to Newport Pagnell. Later, branches were made to Aylesbury and to the Nene at Northampton, the latter, in 1815, replacing a plateway from 1805.

The opening of the Grand Junction gave the Birmingham–London route its final form. The line completed via the Thames & Severn Canal, a roundabout route of 270 miles, was soon superseded by a more direct route of 227 miles via Fazeley and Oxford in 1790. The completion of the Grand Junction and the Warwick & Napton and Warwick & Birmingham Canals reduced this mileage to 138 miles. The Oxford Canal, now reduced to a 5-mile link in this new through line, was compensated for the lost tonnage, but the Coventry did lose some of its trade. By 1825, however, these losses had been more than recouped by its rapidly growing coal trade, and its share price, which had declined from £400 to £350, rose to £1,230 in 1825. Finally, in 1801, a branch from Bull's Bridge on the main Grand Junction line was opened to Paddington Basin, and the last river section in what was then an all-canal route into London disappeared. In turn this branch was in 1820 connected by the Regent's Canal, authorised in 1812, to the Thames at Limehouse.

Other developments were taking place around the upper end of the Grand Junction. During the time of the mania the Leicestershire & Northamptonshire Union Canal had been projected to link Leicester, itself connected to the Trent through the Loughborough and Leicester navigations, with the Nene at Northampton. Building began from the Leicester end, and in 1797 was completed to Debdale Wharf, 17 out of the proposed 44 miles. There the project rested for a time, apart from the building of a branch to Market Harborough in 1809. The construction of the Grand Junction Canal re-animated the project, and eventually it was decided to join the uncompleted Leicestershire & Northamptonshire to the Grand Junction at Buckby Wharf (Norton Junction) by means of a new company's line. Known as the Grand Union (not to be confused with the later amalgamation of the same name), this was authorised in 1810, promoted partly by Leicester interests and partly by the Grand Junction. The canal opened in 1814, completing the route between London and the Trent, but its two flights of narrow locks at Foxton and Watford prevented the development of through services by wide boats.

Around London several canals were authorised: the Grand Surrey (1801), was planned to run from the Thames at Rotherhithe to Mitcham, but got no farther than Camberwell; the Croydon, from Rotherhithe to Croydon; the Thames & Medway, from Gravesend to Frindsbury opposite Rochester; the Isle of Dogs Canal, built by the City of London and designed to shorten the passage around the Isle of Dogs from Limehouse to Blackwall; and the Wey & Arun Junction, to create a through communication from the Thames to the south coast at Littlehampton. In addition to these canals the Surrey Iron Railway from Wandsworth to Croydon and its extension, the Croydon, Merstham & Godstone, which was only partly built, were parts of the same development of communications around the rapidly growing city of London.

A final project is within the scope of this chapter. Although the main rivers of England had by now been joined, only in 1815 was the narrow Northampton Branch opened to link the Fenland waterways that served the dual purposes of drainage and navigation. One suggestion for a link was the Stamford Junction Canal to link the Nene and Witham to the old Stamford Canal, and the Welland to the Oakham Canal. This agricultural canal had opened in 1802, an extension of the Melton Mowbray Navigation, that linked to the Leicester Navigation. A further suggestion was a link from Stamford to Market Harborough.

It was another scheme that got as far as an Act. As early as Whitworth, acting for the Common Council of the City of London, surveyed a line to join the Cam near Cambridge to the Stort, and thus via the Lea and Thames to London. The plan was revived in wartime and in 1812 the London & Cambridge Junction Canal was authorised, to run for 28 miles from the Stort to the Cam near Clayhithe Sluice. The authorised capital was £870,000, but the Act provided that £425,500 must be raised before work began. This failed to materialise, but in 1814 permission was granted to build only part of the line, from the Cam to Saffron Walden. This was not built, and the last of the great river connections, between the Thames and Great Ouse by way of the Cam, was never made.

CHAPTER SIX

Canals, Seas and Ports

Sea transport continued to be important during the canal age, both in supplying the ports that provided traffic, often transhipped between ships and canal craft, and in the promotion of canals to link the seas.

Two notable areas in Britain where canals to link the seas were proposed were Scotland and the Somerset and Devon area. In the first area canals were built; in the second no plan succeeded.

One consequence of the '45 rebellion in Scotland was that the British Government sought to break up a clan system that had supported rebellion, and also to create a network of good roads through the Highlands to make them less inaccessible. Landowners were replacing cattle farms with large sheep farms, leaving no place for the old peasant economy. At the same time the building of the new roads gave Highlanders news of easier lives to be led to the south or over the seas in America, as well as the means to get there.

Many were dismayed by this trend and sought to develop the Highlands to relieve the distress and slow emigration. Among them was John Knox, a Scotsman who had made his money in England and who, when retired, used it to further the prosperity of the north. He saw that the promotion of fisheries and manufacturing, which he and others had suggested, depended on improved transport. Writing in 1784 about the proposed establishment of Highland fisheries, he advocated the construction of three new lines of canal – from Fort William to Inverness, from Loch Fyne to the Atlantic and from the Forth to the Clyde – which would 'open up a circumnavigation within the heart of the kingdom to the unspeakable benefit of commerce and the fisheries'.[1]

All three canals had been suggested, and in fact surveyed, before he wrote. One, the Forth & Clyde, had been partly built. However, he had much influence on events, which in time provided all three of the sea-to-sea canals he advocated. They are now called the Caledonian, the Crinan and the Forth & Clyde canals.

A glance at the map of the Highlands shows the Great Glen, that astonishing rift across Scotland from Loch Linnhe north-east to Inverness. With a sea loch at either end and with four lochs in its length, the Great Glen seemed made for a canal that would save ships from the great dangers of passing round the north of Scotland. The natural delays and difficulties of a passage in the days of sail from one side of Great Britain to the other, both for merchant ships and fishing vessels, provided a good argument for a canal, as did the Napoleonic Wars, which drove ships everywhere to keep close to the land. Yet the high cost and uncertain returns involved in the project did not make it commercially attractive. For these reasons, and also because the Government saw the providing of public works as a means of preventing wholesale emigration from the Highlands, Telford was sent by the Treasury to report on the cost and practicability of such a canal, along with other works such as roads and bridges.

Telford's 1802 report in favour of a ship canal led to the appointment of commissioners. Jessop was called in, and the two engineers re-surveyed the line, Jessop alone signing the final estimate. Soon afterward the proposed dimensions were enlarged and, using Jessop's working drawings, cutting began. The canal was planned to be 20ft deep with 23 locks, to run from sea to sea through the Great Glen, connecting lochs Lochy, Oich, Ness and Dochfour, at a cost estimated at over £500,000. Jessop worked as senior engineer until 1812, shortly before his death.

An excitable contemporary chronicler of canals, writing in 1803 and recalling what water transport had done for Wales, asserted that:

> Undoubtedly in digging this canal veins of minerals will be found that will incite artists and manufacturers to flock to a place where land can be had at a cheap rate, and will induce the land owners to give pecuniary assistance where wanted to forward undertakings, by which the riches of the bowels of the mountains may produce ten or twenty-fold returns, eight or ten times a year. The mountains in Wales continued unexplored, barren, and useless for ages, but are now found to contain lead, iron, copper, coals, marble, &c. &c. in the greatest plenty, and some hundreds of people are employed, and whole villages built to accommodate them on a spot which a very few years ago was an uninhabited waste.[2]

The Caledonian Canal never met these kind of hopes. In 1804, work began inwards from the sea locks. Given the problems posed by size, terrain and climate, progress was bound to be slow. Whilst estimating had been good, war had caused major increases in the costs of labour and supplies. There were also construction troubles, the worst in the middle district – Fort Augustus to Loch Lochy – the last to be built. By the time work seriously started there in 1817, John Simpson, who had been in charge in construction, had died, as would Matthew Davidson, another engineer in 1818. Deprived of these two experienced men from Pontcysyllte days, and with heavy pressure from above, work went on too fast: there were slips in the Laggan cutting and the side wall of the bottom lock at Fort Augustus fell in.

The canal had cost over £900,000 when, two years after Telford had ceased to be engineer, it opened on 24 October 1822, unfinished, at the insistence of a Government annoyed by continuing expense and public criticism. The canal had only 12ft depth in the cuts and 15ft at the locks – enough only for fishing boats and small ships. However, this did not mar the opening ceremony, with the first vessels passing through. The *Inverness Courier* reported that:

The termination of the voyage was marked by a grand salute from the Fort, whilst the inhabitants of Fort William demonstrated their joy by kindling a large bonfire. A plentiful supply of whisky, given by the gentlemen of Fort William, did not in the least tend to damp the ardour of the populace.[3]

The canal proved for Telford a comparative failure; for the State a perpetual drain of money, and for the inhabitants of the Highlands something of a white elephant. It would not take the larger ships from which Telford had expected much of the canal's trade, while the working of sailing ships through the lochs proved difficult. There was no towing-path along their sides, and the Great Glen acted as a wind funnel that, when adverse, could hold ships up for weeks, thus preventing the hoped-for savings of time over the route through the Pentland Firth. On the canal sections alone there was a horse towage service.

After almost twenty years of inefficient operation the commissioners asked James Walker to report, and in 1839 he pointed out that the traffic was only about 2½ per cent of that rounding the north of Scotland. He recommended that the canal should be completed, deepened to 17ft and provided with steam tugs to assist sailing ships. After three years of reports and select committees, the Government finally decided it was better to complete than abandon the canal. Work on deepening and reconstruction began in 1843, and the canal reopened in 1847 for craft of up to 500 tons, at an additional cost of £228,000. However, the age of steam removed the best argument for the development of the canal, and in later years toll receipts rarely covered maintenance costs.

During 1918 wartime traffic proved to be considerable, and those who foresaw its value in war were justified. Mines and sinkers were brought from America to Corpach at the western end of the canal, transhipped into 100 ton lighters and passed through the canal to Muirtown basin near Inverness. Here, at US Naval Base 18, they were assembled before being taken out into the North Sea to form part of the Northern Barrage, the minefield planned to stretch from the Orkneys to the coast of Norway and to cut off German submarines from the Atlantic.

In 1920 the management of the canal passed to the Ministry of Transport. There were discussions over a much larger replacement canal with a lower summit level which would avoid most of the lockage on the old canal, including the eight locks at Banavie known as Neptune's Staircase, which acted as a bottleneck to traffic. During a time of economy, however, such a proposal had no chance of success. During the Second World War the canal again experienced increased activity. After nationalization it passed to the British Waterways Board, which considered closure, as revenues did not even cover maintenance costs, but it nevertheless remained open, taking small ships, fishing vessels and pleasure craft.

The second of John Knox's proposals was for a canal from Loch Fyne to the Atlantic. The Crinan Canal was to cut through the great peninsula of Kintyre,

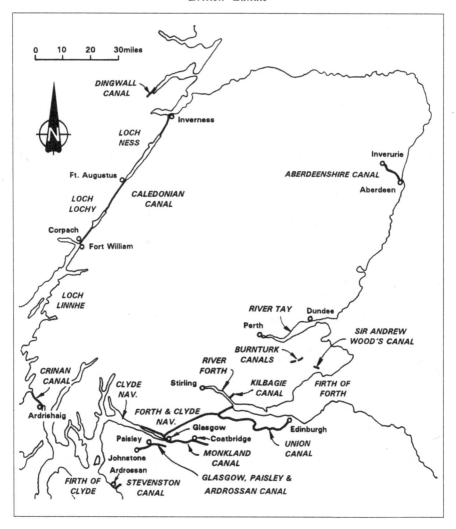

The main waterways of Scotland. The Glasgow, Paisley & Ardrossan Canal was only completed to Johnstone. There were some smaller waterways elsewhere in Scotland.

which blocks off the direct route to the north, thus shortening voyages by 85 miles and avoiding the passage of the Mull of Kintyre. It was considered partly as a continuation of the Forth & Clyde Canal, so that vessels proceeding from the west coast of Scotland to the east coast, or vice versa, could use both navigations, but also partly to help the prosperity of the western coasts and isles by making them more accessible to the Glasgow market.

The Crinan projectors put out their prospectus ten years before the state had agreed to build the Caledonian Canal. Their scheme was much smaller – the estimate was £63,628 – and it is clear that the promoters had philanthropic rather than commercial motives in mind:

While the extensive prospects of the present existing trade of the kingdom, passing through the Crinan canal, and the natural increase which may be expected from a greater facility of communication, hold out a probable return for the money to be expended in making and maintaining it, the inestimable benefit which must arise therefrom to the inhabitants of the Western Coasts and Islands of Scotland, are extremely interesting to a benevolent mind, and may alone be an inducement to many to subscribe without an anxious regard to future profit.[4]

Rennie, the engineer, revised the estimate to £107,512 for a canal now to be 15ft and not 12ft deep. An Act was obtained in 1793 and a capital of £150,000 was authorised. Philanthropy in fact raised £98,000, and to complete the canal the proprietors had to borrow £25,000 from the Treasury, to whom the canal was mortgaged. It opened in 1801, but owing to a shortage of money it remained unfinished at the western end, where a shallow and awkward channel remained to damage and discourage ships. Because the canal was built as economically as possible it also had inadequate depth (10ft) and a very short summit level (1,114yd), approached by four locks on one side and five on the other. The expense of cutting through this short summit would have simplified the navigation of the canal.

The Crinan was always in financial difficulties. Money was lent by the Treasury on several occasions to pay for repairs and in 1817 the management was vested in the commissioners of the Caledonian Canal. In 1848 it was formally transferred into state ownership. The commissioners retained control until superseded by the Ministry of Transport in 1920, and later by the British Waterways Board. Yachts, motor cruisers and fishing boats are now the principal users.

The third of the sea-to-sea canals of Scotland, and the most successful in its time, was the Forth & Clyde Canal. To join the seas with a waterway across the narrow isthmus between the two firths was so obvious a proposal that it had many times been made, for instance by Defoe in his *Tour* (1724–6), when he wrote:

… it would take up a Volume by itself, to lay down the several advantages to the Trade of Scotland, that would immediately occur by such a Navigation, and then to give a true Survey of the Ground, the Easiness of its being perform'd, and the probable Charge of it, all which might be done. But it is too much to undertake here, it must lye till Posterity, by the rising Greatness of their Commerce, shall not only feel the Want of it, but find themselves able for the Performance.[5]

Some forty years later, the need for the canal had arrived. Posterity, however, divided itself into two groups. Some, including interests in Edinburgh, were concerned to enhance the general prosperity of Scotland, and sought a sea-to sea canal to link the trade of the western and eastern coasts which could take coasting vessels. Against this, Glasgow merchants did not want trade to pass through their city, but to be centred in it. They therefore supported a barge canal from the east coast to Glasgow.

In 1764, John Smeaton reported on two routes, the first roughly as the canal was later to be built, the second by way of Loch Lomond. The first, 5ft deep, he estimated at £74,000. Glasgow interests then got Robert Mackell and James Watt (of steam kettle fame) to bring Smeaton's line nearer Glasgow and, with depth reduced to 4ft, the plan reached Parliament in 1767. Meanwhile the supporters of a 'great canal' had been holding meetings as far away as Perth and Aberdeen, and succeeded in obtaining subscriptions of over £100,000. The original Bill was withdrawn, whereupon the disgusted Watt wrote to his wife: 'I think I shall not long to have anything to do with the House of Commons again – I never saw so many wrong-headed people on all sides gathered together.'[6]

Smeaton reported on a canal 7ft deep and costing £147,337. Some supporters wanted a depth of 10ft so as to take sloops, but the 7ft proposal went through in 1768, the Act authorizing £200,000 of capital. Smeaton, with Mackell as resident engineer, began work that year, and by 1775 the canal, built

The *Anzac* unloading barrels on the Glasgow Branch of the Forth & Clyde Canal towards the end of its working life, in the 1950s. This illustrates the small seagoing craft able to pass through this canal, necessitating opening bridges throughout. (British Waterways/The Waterways Trust)

from the Forth end, had reached Stockingfield, 3 miles from Glasgow. Two years later most of the Glasgow branch was opened. Glasgow had got what its merchants wanted – a canal to the eastern coast – but the through sea-to-sea communication was still lacking. In 1784, however, £50,000 was advanced to the company by the Government and work resumed, this time with Robert Whitworth as engineer. At last, in July 1790, the canal was fully opened. It was 35 miles long with 39 locks and Whitworth's four-arched Kelvin aqueduct. Thenceforward the company became increasingly prosperous. Receipts rose from some £8,000 a year to £50,000. The construction of the Monkland and later the Edinburgh & Glasgow Union Canal to join it brought additional traffic, and it flourished until the opening of the Newcastle & Carlisle Railway, and later the Edinburgh & Glasgow, reduced its receipts. The Forth & Clyde Canal was finally bought by the Caledonian Railway in 1867, largely to acquire its harbour at Grangemouth, and continued to decline in usefulness: the tonnage carried fell from 3,022,583 tons in 1868 through 817,836 tons in 1908 and 27,751 tons in 1942, to 14,839 tons in 1953. The canal was closed in 1963, but was restored for pleasure use by 2002.

The Forth & Clyde Canal is memorable partly because, on its waters in 1789, Symington tried out the second of his steam paddle-boats, and, as he records, 'in presence of hundreds of spectators, who lined the banks of the canal, the boat glided along, propelled at the rate of five miles an hour'.

This experiment interested Lord Dundas, the governor of the canal company, and he later employed Symington to prepare a new engine to be fitted to a hull specially built as a tug, the *Charlotte Dundas*, and to drive a stern paddle-wheel. In trials in March 1803 the boat pulled two laden barges from Lock 20 to Glasgow in 9¼ hours. Though the trials had been successful, the proprietors decided not to use the vessel owing to the damage that the wash might cause to the banks. So the *Charlotte Dundas* was beached in a creek off the canal, till the hull was broken up by the weather and souvenir hunters. It was not until 1856 that the first steam craft was introduced on the canal.

The possibility of a mid-Scotland ship canal was promoted by a special association after the 1914–18 war. In both 1930 and 1946 Government committees reported adversely on the project. In 1946 a 32ft deep sea-level canal was estimated at at least £109 million, and it was doubtful that revenue would even cover maintenance costs, while its strategic importance would be small.

The Humber-Mersey route involved three trans-Pennine canals, and in the twentieth century there were schemes to link the Manchester Ship Canal and Aire & Calder. A line between the Tyne to the Solway Firth and Maryport was proposed for over forty years after the canal mania, but only the Carlisle Canal portion was built. A sea-level canal was proposed even at the end of the twentieth century. Rather than examine these in detail, a less well-known sea-to-sea scheme will be considered.

Of all the capes in England, the crews of small coasting sailing ships, before the days of steam, feared Land's End the most, both for its rocks and for its contrary winds. So from early in the canal age plans were made to cut a waterway across Somerset, Devon or Cornwall to avoid the dangers and shorten the voyages. The coal exporters and merchants of South Wales wanted to sell more goods along the south coast of England and in London, while the landowners and merchants of south-west England stood to gain from cheap goods brought by waterway to their harbours and countryside.

Two ways of sending goods across the south-west peninsula were suggested: by barge canal, with transhipment into ships at each end of the canal, and by ship canal.

There were many plans for a barge canal, from 1769 when Whitworth, under Brindley's supervision, first surveyed two routes. This included one from the River Exe to Taunton, from where barges would use the Tone Navigation to Bridgwater, where they would enter another canal to pass via Glastonbury and Axbridge to Uphill near Bristol. Two of the many that were planned were partially built. Both were products of the canal mania.

The Grand Western Canal was intended to run from Topsham to Taunton in Somerset, from where traffic could work to Bridgwater by way of the navigable rivers Tone and Parrett. This was to be 46 miles long, including branches to Cullompton and Tiverton, and its total cost was estimated at £166,724. After the Act of 1796, the projectors viewed it as too risky due to wartime inflation, and the project was laid aside until 1809, when it was revived. An allowance of 50 per cent for increased costs was made to reflect increased prices, and a start was made upon the original plan for a barge canal.

Two disastrous mistakes were made at the outset. To capture the trade in stone – overestimated at £10,000 a year from the Burlescombe quarries to Taunton – work began in the middle, on the Tiverton branch and part of the main line, a total of 11 miles. If construction had begun at either the Taunton or Topsham ends, a trade in coal would soon have developed over the first few miles of canal, while construction materials could have been carried easily and cheaply.

The second mistake was made by Rennie, who had been appointed as engineer after several others had reported. He decided to improve on the original plan by lowering the summit level at Holcombe Rogus by 16ft to save lockage on the main line and the Tiverton branch, and also to save the cost of a reservoir by using the Lowdwells springs. He did save these costs, but only at the expense of much heavy and difficult cutting and embanking. The next three years were spent in happy optimism by the local committee, which represented the shareholders, and in a struggle against physical obstacles by the engineer. In 1812, the short section was open to traffic. Without a lock it had cost £244,505 for 11 miles – more than the 1793 estimate for the whole 46 miles of the canal with its branches. Coal had to be brought by road from Taunton to the end of the canal at Holcombe Rogus, and from there to Tiverton by water, while the stone traffic for which the section had first been constructed never yielded £1,000 in any one year.

The proprietors of this self-contained section of a sea-to-sea canal, that they could not afford to finish, resisted the blandishments of engineers who wanted to complete the canal at trifling cost. Eventually James Green, an Exeter engineer who had done competent work on the Exeter, Bude and Torrington canals, and had even been called over to Wales to advise on the Kidwelly & Llanelly Canal, made a proposal that sounded workable. He suggested that the canal should be completed to Taunton on a smaller scale, so as to obtain the benefits of connection with the newly built Bridgwater & Taunton Canal, and thus with a seaport. He estimated the cost at £61,324, a figure just within the remaining resources of the committee.

On the Bude Canal inclined planes had been successfully used instead of locks. Green therefore convinced the committee that the new section should have no locks, but instead an inclined plane at Wellisford and seven vertical lifts. Unfortunately for his reputation, Green not only failed to make the inclined plane work using the hydraulic power for which it was designed, resulting in the installation of a steam engine, but he was so confident of the design of his lifts that he went ahead with construction before he had made the necessary practical experiments. Too late he found difficulty in equalizing the levels of water in the two pounds of the canal and the two caissons, so that the stop gates could be raised and the boats pass easily in and out of the lifts. He eventually cured the trouble, and at his own expense, but the delay in opening the canal cost the proprietors their last capital. To get traffic started the committee was forced not only to raise an additional subscription among themselves, but also to borrow from their own superintendent.

The extension opened in 1838, and a modest prosperity set in for the Grand Western Canal, until the railway came a few years later. However, nothing more was heard of extending it to Topsham to join the English and Bristol channels.

The second project begun but not completed was the Dorset & Somerset. This 49 mile long canal was planned from beside the Dorset Stour to join the Kennet & Avon Canal near Bath, from where traffic could work down the Avon to Bristol. Like the Grand Western, the Dorset & Somerset obtained its Act in 1796 and, similarly, chose to begin work on a 9 mile long branch in the middle of the line in order to carry coal to Frome from the collieries at Nettlebridge. A lift was built near Mells and others were begun, but by 1803 the working capital was exhausted and 1¾ miles of the branch still remained to be cut. Shareholders, fearful of rising costs, failed to pay further calls on the shares, no one would take up promissory notes and so work stopped, never to start again. Today, only limited traces remain of this canal that probably never carried traffic.

The principal ship canal project was surveyed by Thomas Telford and James Green along the same general line as many previous proposals. The canal was planned to carry ships of 200 tons along a line 44½ miles in length from Stolford near Bridgwater to Beer near Seaton. There were to be 60 locks, and harbours at each end of the line. It was estimated that 1,095,527 tons of goods would pass through the canal each year and that receipts, including harbour dues, would be £210,847 from the through traffic alone. Of the proposed capital of £1,750,000, the sum of £1,518,000 was actually promised, and an Act for the English & Bristol Channels Ship Canal was passed in 1825. Soon after, however, a slump set in, and in 1828 the committee reported sadly:

> The severe shock … which was given to public confidence shortly after the passing of the Act, and the consequent aversion to almost every speculative activity, have not failed to affect the Ship Canal, so as to render it highly improbable that so large a capital as £1,750,000 will now be raised for the accomplishment of this object.[7]

The idea of cutting a waterway through the peninsula continued to attract enthusiasts into the twentieth century. One of the most charmingly optimistic was Mr Hern of Cardiff. In 1922 he suggested a canal for 15,000 ton ships, costing £37 million. He contended that:

> … a source of considerable profit to the canal whichever route it follows, will be the pleasure traffic which will pass through beautiful country having near its banks many places of historic and other interest, providing for tourists a pleasant and useful journey, appealing more to many people than trains and motor chars-a-banc or even motor cars, to places of rest and beauty in South Devon, such as Torquay, Teignmouth, etc., and to the delightful neighbourhood of Bournemouth, Southampton, and the Isle of Wight.[8]

In reality the project of a ship canal became unviable once steam replaced wind as a motive power. Whereas sailing ships could spend days or even weeks waiting for the wind to take them around Cape Wrath or Land's End, and often came to grief from the tides of the Pentland Firth or the rocks of Scilly, steam power made such voyages both regular and safe. The saving of time and insurance premiums was therefore not enough to make it worthwhile for shipowners to pay the dues of the Caledonian Canal or the proposed English & Bristol Channels Ship Canal. For that reason the first lost money and the second was never built.

Apart from the sea-to-sea canals, we can envisage the waterway system of Britain as a network of canals and rivers joining together the principal towns, and linking sources of raw materials with industrial areas. Some of the traffic was purely internal, originating at one point and being carried to another; much, however, had either arrived at a port via a coasting or foreign-trading vessel, or was destined for shipment from a port. This trade passed to and from the ports at the edges of the network, where the navigable waterways ended and tidal water began. Many of these ports, like Bristol on the Avon or London on the Thames, had been distribution centres where goods were transhipped either into river barges or road waggons, before the advent of the canals. The arrival of artificial waterways merely increased their commercial importance. Other ports, like Goole on the Aire & Calder and Ellesmere Port on the Shropshire Union, were creations of the canal age. While ports in Ireland played a somewhat different role, trade serving Belfast, Newry and Dublin was enhanced by the development of waterways upstream.

Some rivers, like the Severn, had always been difficult navigations in their tidal stretches. Some – the Thames, the Tyne, the Tees and the Wear – were quite suitable for small craft but had to be dredged and possibly embanked in places to take the larger ships that were coming into use, especially after the introduction of steamships. Others, especially in the fenlands, silted up so much that extensive training works had to be carried out, as on the Great Ouse to King's Lynn, or an artificial cut provided in place of an unusable river channel, as on the Nene below Wisbech. Training works aimed to narrow and straighten a river channel to increase the speed of the current and thus its scouring effect on the river bed. In one case, Bristol, William Jessop cut a new channel for the Avon river, the old one being cut off by locks and turned into a floating harbour. In other cases nothing was done, and the small ports that once flourished, like Hedon on the Humber, became no longer accessible. It sometimes proved impossible to preserve or improve the navigation of a river channel. Therefore, to prevent trade deserting a port on that river, a canal, such as the Exeter Canal, was cut from the sea to the town to take the place of the river navigation. Now and then a town near the sea, but without a harbour, decided to turn itself into a port by building a canal to salt water, like the Ulverston Canal.

The Exeter and the Gloucester & Berkeley Canals are similar in that both ports suffered from a difficult river navigation; they differ in that the Exeter led only to the city, while the Gloucester & Berkeley made Gloucester not only a port of import for the country around it, but also a place of transhipment into river barges and canal boats, which then went up the Severn into the Midland inland waterway system, or by way of the Stroudwater and Thames & Severn Canals towards Oxford or the Vale of White Horse.

The early history of the Exeter Canal was outlined in Chapter One. After it became clear that the port of Exeter would not become, like Gloucester later, the focal point of canals running throughout the south-west, the corporation decided that its canal must be improved, both in the interests of the city itself and to attract capital to canals that might be connected with it.

James Green was called in, and between 1820 and 1827 he completely reconstructed the canal, making it 15ft deep and carrying the entrance 2 miles farther down the estuary to Turf, where 12ft of water was available at all tides. The canal could take vessels of 400 tons, but by now Exeter's most important business, the export of woollen goods, had ceased. However, the corporation supported an early railway Act of 1832 for a line from the canal basin at Exeter to Crediton, and,

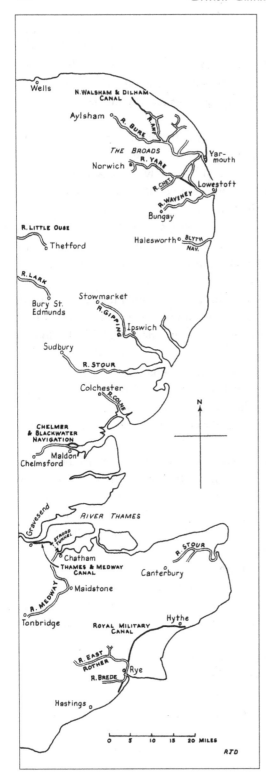

The waterways of Kent and East
Anglia did not form a connected
system and, apart from the Royal
Military Canal in the south, were
mostly river navigations which relied
on ports and seaborne traffic.

when action failed, agreed with the Bristol & Exeter Railway that its line should come to the basin.

Then two great changes took place. The corporation changed its mind about the terminus of the railway, which in fact ended at Red Cow (St David's), and it was not until 1867 that the basin had railway communication via a branch line near St Thomas's. The coming of steamships made the canal's dimensions inadequate. Competition from railways, instead of the cooperation that might have been possible, and the falling-off of traffic caused the tolls received to fall below the interest charges on the money that had been borrowed to reconstruct the canal. The creditors then took over the canal, and its ownership did not revert to the city until 1883. The canal failed to make Exeter an important port, and its final traffic ended in the 1990s. Until 1996 the terminal basin was used to display part of the Exeter Maritime Museum collection.

A ship canal from Berkeley Pill on the Severn to Gloucester was planned in order that shipping bound for Gloucester could avoid the difficult and dangerous passage of the river between those points, and that the transhipment of goods from ships to barges, or vice versa, could take place in the basin at Gloucester, into which craft could pass from the river by means of a lock. The Act for this canal was passed in 1793. Two years later John Phillips wrote in his *History of Inland Navigation*:

> This undertaking for its magnitude and accommodations, deserves to be considered
> as of the first importance; its magnitude is intended for the passage of vessels of
> more than three hundred tons burthen; and its accommodations to commerce, by
> uniting the city of Gloucester, by an easy and certain water carriage with the port of

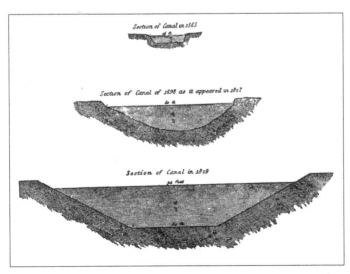

Successive cross-sections of the Exeter Canal, showing how it was enlarged in 1701 and 1827 from its original dimensions. Very little remains today of the original canal engineered by John Trew.

Bristol, and from thence with all the world, may justly be deemed an object of great magnitude to trade. The whole of this scheme evinces an extent of idea, known only in a free country; and an ardour of enterprise, which none but an industrious and commercial people could endure...[9]

When he wrote that last sentence John Phillips spoke more truthfully than he knew. The ardour of enterprise of the proprietors of the Gloucester & Berkeley Canal carried them to success through great difficulties. It was 34 years after they obtained their Act that the canal was opened, and, because they had needed to borrow heavily from the Government and to mortgage their property in return, it was 78 years before the descendants of those who first subscribed for shares were in full control of their property.

Much in this canal's construction reflects the histories of many other canals built during the canal mania, although this was the biggest built at the time. The minute books record the letter from Boulton & Watt saying that they could not have immediate delivery of a steam engine for pumping water out of the channel during cutting because of the great demand for steam engines; the agreement with the Herefordshire & Gloucestershire not to attract each other's workmen; the insistence by landowners on written authority for all surveyors coming on to their lands, and on compensation for all damage; and trouble with workmen, engineers, estimates, surveys and contractors.

Relations with the workmen started off well, the committee recording:

It being understood, that it is customary, at the commencement of every Canal, to allow some liquor to the Workmen, and Mr Edson having reported that the number of Workmen now employed are fifty –
Ordered, That he do give one shilling, to each of those men...[10]

Trouble with engineers was chronic until just before the canal was opened, when the family of Clegram moved in, the father as engineer and the son as clerk, and they remained until, in 1885, the son, now the engineer, retired and took a seat on the board. The usual practice was followed of appointing a 'Chief and Principal Engineer', in this case Robert Mylne and a resident engineer. During the mania the few canal engineers who had reputations took on far more work than they could carefully deal with. Mylne was not, in fact, one of them, but rather, as engineer of London's New River Company, an expert on water provision and supply, as well as being an excellent architect. He was, however, as busy as the others, and thus seldom visited the site unless a crisis occurred, depending on the reports of the resident engineer as a basis for advice. Often committees found it hard to engage competent resident engineers, given the number of schemes under way, but with an incompetent resident the damage was often done before the chief engineer was aware of it.

The first resident engineer on the Gloucester & Berkeley was Dennis Edson, who lasted only nine months before he was dismissed. He had been dismissed twenty years earlier from the Chester Canal, and he was to suffer the same fate at the Grand Surrey seven years later. Already the committee were in difficulties as a result, for they took on the 26-year-old James Dadford, who at any rate came from a competent engineering family, and wrote anxiously to Mylne:

> … and they are so very anxious to have doubts removed, that much embarrass them, and as they conceive very much affect their future operations, that they cannot be satisfied, but by your personal attendance, which they trust you will not defer longer than next week.[11]

Eventually the company's affairs reached such a state that a proprietor complained that he thought that Mylne was to oversee everything, the resident engineer merely carrying out instructions, instead of which:

> … but a small quantity of his personal attendance has been necessarily occupied by the Works, and since our engagement with Mr Dadford, scarcely any… As for the Idea which in the Days of our ignorance was broached, with some success, that an Engineer may render us sufficient services, by thinking and contriving for us, while sitting at his ease in London: I will not suppose any member of the Committee is now amused by it.[12]

Mylne came down to face the committee and agreed in future to accept payment by the day.

From this it may be understood that the company was in trouble. The original plan had been for a canal 17¾ miles long, 70ft broad at top (or water level) and 18ft deep, estimated by Mylne to cost £121,330, to cover which the Act authorised £140,000 and a further £60,000, if necessary. Work began in 1794 at the Gloucester end in excavating the dock and cutting down towards Berkeley. By 1799 available cash had run out and the canal had only been cut to Hardwicke, about 5¼ miles from Gloucester. Confidence had almost gone, and the efforts that the committee made to interest shareholders in putting up further money were in vain, either for a narrow canal to continue to the junction with the Stroudwater Canal, which would open trade through the Thames & Severn, or to change the final junction with the Severn from Berkeley Pill to Hock Crib, which was nearer but less convenient. The shareholders, like those of so many other canals of the mania who had been caught by the effects of the war and the results of inefficiency and over-optimism, refused to budge, and the partly finished canal lay useless. Dadford was given notice: there was nothing for him to do.

The committee spent the next 20 years alternating bursts of enthusiasm with long spells of inactivity, trying to decide where to end the canal (they finally chose Sharpness Point, rather than Berkeley Pill or Hock Crib) and to raise the necessary money, at one time even by a lottery scheme that was turned down personally by William Pitt.

Government assistance, through the Exchequer Bill Loan Commissioners, eventually enabled work to resume. Telford pronounced the canal a good risk, and work began with a loan of part of the estimated costs.

So work began again. There were problems with John Upton, who had been clerk but became engineer in 1815, and his replacement John Woodhouse, both dismissed for financial irregularities. Further trouble with contractors included the bankruptcy of one, while in 1820 only the junction to the Stroudwater Canal was complete and much of the works remained incomplete. The Commissioners threatened to take over the canal as mortgagees, unless money was raised to pay interest and repayments of capital. Meanwhile all work had stopped.

A frantic search for money ended in the raising of capital in preference shares and further loans from the commissioners, who now administered the funds of the company jointly with the committee. Civil Service control in this case led to a great increase in efficiency. A new contractor was appointed, warehouses were built and the canal was finally completed.

In 1827 the canal opened in a flurry of settling debts to contractors, arranging for market passenger boats, dealing with the now numerous applications from traders to erect warehouses or wharves, looking for more water supplies and making terms with the organization of trackers, the men who hauled the sailing ships along the waterway until a regular service of tugs was introduced in about 1862. It was the greatest canal in Britain: at a depth of 18ft, deeper than the Caledonian at that time, and taking ships carrying 600 tons of cargo. Trade increased – 2,360 vessels used the port in 1827, rising to 7,981 in 1830, but then the commissioners threatened to take steps to dispose of the property to recover the public debt, unless the company could arrange its early liquidation.

Indeed, it was nearly 20 years later before the company was free from periodical threats to sell up, as a result of raising the money to repay the commissioners through the creation of first preference shares and by borrowing from an insurance company. The mortgage to the insurance company was not finally repaid until 1871, when the committee's report triumphantly read: 'this Company became free from the restrictions of the mortgages originally imposed by the Government, and received the whole of their title deeds into their own possession.'[13]

Thenceforward the policy of the company was made up of three strands, which met in the 1870s. The first was cooperation with railways.

It is so natural to think of railways as competitors of canals – as, indeed, they proved – that it is not at once realised that canals like the Gloucester & Berkeley, which were primarily ports, had much more to gain from good

The docks at Gloucester, with Gloucester Lock, leading to the Severn in the distance. 'S.N.D. No. 4', on the dredger, signifies the Sharpness New Docks company. This is moored outside the National Waterways Museum, where it forms an exhibit.

railway connections to their docks than might be lost from rail competition along their route. This applied especially to ports having a foreign trade, for the general result of the coming of railways was to increase foreign and decrease coastal trade. As far back as 1806, three years before the Gloucester & Cheltenham Tramroad received its Act, the Gloucester & Berkeley agreed to have rails laid to its basin at Gloucester (where they remained until 1862). In 1843 it gave permission to the Birmingham & Gloucester Railway to lay its rails to the docks, and by 1862 the railway connections to the Gloucester basins were complete.

The company was also anxious to build up a coal export trade, at first from Gloucester and later from Sharpness Docks. Thus it gave every encouragement to a company formed to build a Severn railway bridge near Sharpness, and so to bring Welsh and Forest of Dean coal. When the bridge company got into difficulties the Gloucester & Berkeley subscribed a considerable amount to its capital. The bridge was opened in 1879.

The second strand of policy was the promotion of inland waterways. It must be remembered that Gloucester was a terminal port with respect to the country around it. It was also a place of transhipment of cargoes from seagoing craft to river lighters going up the Severn to Worcester, to barges working through the Thames & Severn Canal to the Thames, and to narrow boats bound for the Wilts

& Berks, by way of the Thames & Severn, for the Staffs & Worcs (from Stourport) and for the Worcester & Birmingham (from Worcester).

The Gloucester & Berkeley company opposed the improvement of the Severn by various proposed private navigation companies, nominally in the cause of a free river, but in fact because it feared that the improvement of the navigation would cost more in tolls to craft on the river than the added facilities were worth, thus discouraging traffic. When the Severn Commissioners were set up as a public body, however, the canal company supported them financially.

Its interest extended beyond the Severn. The Staffs & Worcs Canal was a prosperous concern that maintained its independence of railways without difficulty. The Worcester & Birmingham, however, was not, since it both had an expensive line to keep up and suffered severely from railway competition. As early as 1858 a proposal to lease this canal to the Oxford, Worcester & Wolverhampton Railway was opposed and defeated, and after this there were bids for control by both railway and waterway interests. The Worcester & Birmingham passed into the hands of a receiver in 1868, but in 1874 the latter finally won when the Gloucester & Berkeley leased it, together with the Droitwich canals, both of these having formerly been leased to the Worcester & Birmingham. The canal company now possessed two separated waterways, one a ship canal and one a partly narrow, partly broad, canal, connected by the Severn in which they were financially interested, and which provided a through water route to Birmingham.

The Gloucester & Berkeley company started well by giving its new acquisitions a thorough overhaul and dredging. On the Droitwich 73,000 tons of mud were removed, according to the engineer 'the accumulation, I should think, of the last half century'. Nevertheless the new purchase never earned enough for its parent to cover the mortgage debt that had been taken over and in payments to shareholders guaranteed under the terms of the lease. By the end of the century the tolls received were hardly balancing the maintenance costs. Traffic had left both Droitwich lines by the late 1920s and both closed in 1939.

The company also did its best to keep open the canals towards the Thames, successfully opposing in 1897 the abandonment of the Wilts & Berks by its owners. It became a stockholder in the Thames & Severn Canal Trust, which took over the waterway from the Great Western Railway, and ran it until funds gave out and it was passed to the Gloucestershire County Council.

The two threads of cooperation with the railways and encouragement of waterways were intertwined with a third, the improvement of the port at Gloucester and the harbour at Sharpness. New basins were built at the former, and many developments took place as warehouses and wharves were constructed. Sharpness, a port built for sailing ships, which could not take the bigger steamers, had been suffering heavy competition from the newer steamer docks in the

The docks at Sharpness, looking south. Only occasional shipping passes through the swing-bridge in the foreground, while the original terminal is used by pleasure craft alone.

Bristol Channel ports: a larger harbour and entrance lock were opened in 1874, and steamers carrying over 1,000 tons of cargo navigated the canal. A rate-cutting war with Avonmouth to attract the Bristol Channel trade was ended by agreement in 1882. After that the canal continued to serve Gloucester, although port traffics there finally ended in the 1990s.

The estuary of the Leven had receded from Ulverston, in North Lancashire, so in 1793 an Act was obtained to build a small ship canal from the town of about 1¼ miles length. The first sod was cut on 23 August and the canal opened in 1796.

The Ulverston Canal was a substantial affair, 15ft deep and 66ft wide at water level, and provided with two large basins. It was used largely for the export of iron and copper ores and slate, and the import of coal, timber and the merchandise needed in the town and its district. At first, trade was small, with 94 vessels entering in 1798, totalling 4,704 tons. By 1821 this rose to 259 vessels and 13,960 tons, and then between 1829 and 1834 an average of 531 vessels and 35,009 tons. Then came two years of great activity as ships entered with materials for the building of the Furness Railway. When that line was opened in 1846 trade at once fell away: 388 ships and 25,220 tons in 1849. Thenceforward it declined, until in 1862 the Furness Railway Company bought it. Since the authorised capital was £7,000, to which must be added the cost of subsequent works such as the pier and a weir, and the railway paid £22,005 for it, the proprietors were probably not out of pocket. The last ship entered the canal in 1916, after which it was used for some yacht storage and water supply. After a very early campaign to revive navigation for trade, in 1938, the canal was abandoned in 1945.

This account of a short canal illustrates the local economic importance even of such a minor work as the Ulverston Canal. Later in the nineteenth century a plan for a greater inland port was put forward and successfully carried out by a larger town than Ulverston. The story of the Manchester Ship Canal is told later.

Finally, one freak deserves a mention: the Grand Surrey Canal, which began as a canal and became an extended dock. The canal grew out of various proposals, among others one for a waterway from Deptford to Kingston, with branches to Epsom and Croydon. In 1801 a canal from the River Thames at Rotherhithe, through Peckham, Camberwell and Kennington to Mitcham, was authorised. The engineer, Ralph Dodd, got to work at once, and cutting began on the Rotherhithe section. In April 1802 Dodd was dismissed, and thereafter the company became less and less interested in extending the canal, which was slowly cut past the junction at New Cross with the Croydon Canal (opened in 1809) to Camberwell, together with a later branch to Peckham, while the entrance lock into the Thames opened in 1807. At Camberwell and Peckham the canal remained, while the company developed as a dock concern, though for a long time not a prosperous one, mainly owing to the competition of other docks.

The use of the Grand Surrey as an inland waterway really ended in 1836, when the through traffic from the Croydon Canal ceased. The Croydon was sold to a railway company, the earliest example of the use of a canal line to construct a railway. Thereafter the wharves that had sprung up along the Grand Surrey must be thought of as extensions to its docks. In 1855 the company became the Grand Surrey Docks & Canal Company and was authorised to build the Albion Dock. In 1864 it amalgamated with the Commercial Docks Company, which had bought the old Greenland and other docks, and the combined company became the owner of the Surrey Commercial docks system. Soon afterwards the canal was connected to the Greenland dock. In 1908 the canal, together with the docks, was transferred to the newly formed Port of London Authority, and in January 1971 the whole canal closed, a minor casualty in the ending of the long service to London of the whole Surrey Commercial docks system.

CHAPTER SEVEN

The Golden Years

The slump that followed the Napoleonic Wars affected all waterways, but especially those that had gained abnormal traffic during the war as a result of the danger from privateers that had faced the coastal trade. The Basingstoke Committee welcomed the return of peace with the remark 'That from the facilities afforded in peace to the conveyance of goods by sea, some considerable injury must be sustained by the Canal...'[1]

The general system in the British Isles was now evolving into a settled form. The evolution of some groups, such as the arterial canals connecting the estuaries and the network around Birmingham, have been considered. Other groups will now be examined to complete a reasonable picture of the waterway system as a whole.

Firstly, two in Lancashire and Yorkshire had grown up largely during the war, and were almost complete by its end. On the Lancashire side the great Leeds & Liverpool, not yet finished, curved through Blackburn, Burnley and Colne on its way to Yorkshire. Part of its route lay over the Lancaster. This broad canal route began at Wigan and ran north through Preston and Lancaster, then over Rennie's great Lune aqueduct and through Hincaster Tunnel to Kendal in Westmorland. Completed in 1819, the Lancaster was an oddity because it was broken in the middle by a 5-mile-long tramroad that crossed the valley of the Ribble just south of Preston. This tramroad, which necessitated the double transhipment of goods, formed an obstacle to through traffic greater than its value. It was last used throughout in January 1862, after which the canal was divided into two separate sections, the southern part leased to the Leeds & Liverpool.

From Manchester there ran out a spray of canals, climbing into the valleys where factories were still driven by water power. Even in 1831, possibly half of the cotton mills in Britain were on the banks of the Goyt or the Etherow. The earliest trans-Pennine route to open throughout was the Rochdale Canal, in 1804. This left the Bridgewater Canal in Manchester and crossed from Lancashire to Yorkshire without a summit tunnel. At Sowerby Bridge it joined the Calder & Hebble, which itself linked to the Aire & Calder system at Wakefield. The Ashton also left Manchester and met the Huddersfield Canal at Ashton. This narrow route then climbed the Pennines through the Standedge Tunnel, the longest (5,456yd, now 5,698yd) in Britain, and one of the world's five longest. Its construction delayed the canal's full opening until 1811. This reached the highest point (637ft) of any canal in the British Isles. The canal ended at Huddersfield, linked to the Calder & Hebble by the short private Sir John Ramsden's Canal.

The southern portal of Standedge Tunnel, which was extended to this point when the adjacent railway was enlarged in 1892–3. At 648ft above sea level, this was the highest summit level in the British Isles.

The Ashton also joined the Peak Forest Canal, which crossed the Marple Aqueduct to reach Whaley Bridge, where it joined the Cromford & High Peak Railway. This railway, with many inclined planes, was envisaged as part of a through canal-rail line from London via Leicester and the Cromford Canal (which it joined near its terminus at High Peak), but it never did so. It did threaten competition that kept down rates lower on the Trent to Manchester route via the Macclesfield Canal.

Although the Leeds & Liverpool was the first of the three Pennine routes begun, it was the last completed, in 1816. The Rochdale proved the largest carrier of trans-Pennine traffic, while the Leeds & Liverpool flourished more on highly-developed local traffics, and the Huddersfield's traffic was far less than either.

North out of Manchester ran the Manchester, Bolton & Bury, to the west the Bridgewater Canal to Runcorn for Liverpool, to the north-west the Worsley branch, connected to the Leeds & Liverpool by the Leigh branch of that canal, while to Liverpool there was also available the old but efficient river route of the Mersey & Irwell Navigation. The Rochdale was connected to the Bridgewater Canal, but not to the Mersey & Irwell Navigation until, towards the end of the canal age, the Manchester & Salford Junction was built to join the two. From

In contrast to the Standedge Tunnel (opposite), the summit level of the Rochdale Canal reached 600ft without any need for a tunnel, although the parallel railway line used a tunnel. Although this canal was closed in 1952, the lock in the far distance was restored in 1980, and the canal to the north was fully restored by 1996. This length had been polluted with toxic silt from a chemical works, one of the canal's last customers.

Marple on the Peak Forest was to run the Macclesfield Canal, not yet built, to join the Trent & Mersey to the west of Harecastle Tunnel, and thus shorten the distance between points on that canal and Manchester at the cost of additional lockage.

Though rivers played a small part in the waterway system of Lancashire, in Yorkshire they were the basis of the network, canals or river cuts being used to improve the river navigations. The base line lay from west to east. The branches of the Aire & Calder from Leeds and Wakefield joined at Castleford, whence the line used the Aire and the Selby Canal. The older navigation had yet to be improved and extended to the Ouse via the Ferrybridge and Goole Canal. At Selby it joined the Yorkshire Ouse, giving access to Hull and the Humber, and York and the Ure to Ripon. North of the Humber estuary the navigable River Hull led to Beverley, Leven and Driffield, all on branch canals.

To the south the Stainforth & Keadby Canal ran from the Trent at Keadby into the busy River Don, passing by Doncaster and Rotherham to Tinsley, from where a canal climbing to Sheffield was opened in 1819. The older route for Don traffic by the Dutch River to Goole and the Ouse was little used afterwards, most vessels going instead via Keadby. From Swinton on the Don the Dearne & Dove Canal ran past branches to Elsecar and Worsbrough (for iron and coal) to a junction with the Barnsley Canal, coming down from the Silkstone coalfield on its way to the Calder at Wakefield. The Trent provided access to the Chesterfield Canal at Stockwith, and at Torksey to the Fossdyke, and through the Witham Navigation to the Wash at Boston.

Several canals were specially cut to carry coal or iron to the nearest artery or to the sea. These waterways usually had no town at their inland end but instead terminated at an ironworks or a colliery. Their construction contributed to the output of the two raw materials on which industrial development relied more and more heavily into the nineteenth century. There were isolated examples, such as the Monkland near Glasgow and the Somersetshire Coal Canal, which connected with the Kennet & Avon not far from Bath, but there were also three notable groups: the Welsh canals, the Derbyshire group and the Shropshire group.

Small private canals existed in South Wales before 1790, including a number of very short-lived waterways around Llanelli, which lasted only until their sole industrial traffic disappeared. The table below details the canals built from the 1790s onwards, to carry coal, limestone, copper ore and other industrial raw materials up and down the valleys, and to carry iron and industrial products to the ports. It also shows how heavily locked the earlier canals were:

Canal	Opened	Miles	Locks
Swansea	1798	16	36
Neath	1795	13	19
Glamorganshire	1794	25	50
Monmouthshire	1799	9 (main line)	31
Brecknock & Abergavenny	1812	33	6
Aberdare	1812	7	2
Tennant	1824	5	2

Among these, the Tennant enterprise grew remarkably. It began in 1790 with a small private canal from a colliery at Glan-y-wern to the River Neath at Red Jacket. This was leased in 1818 to George Tennant, who extended part to the Tawe at Swansea. It aimed to supply coal from the Neath Canal with a better shipping place at the Tawe than at Giant's Grave. This proved unsuccessful, so Tennant extended it upstream to join the Neath Canal at Aberdulais, and built new wharves at Port Tennant, at the Swansea end. The opening of this canal in 1824 was that eloquently commemorated by Elizabeth Davies in her verses.

A further canal intended importance but did not achieve it. This was the Kidwelly & Llanelly, which had lines to Pembrey New Harbour and Burry Port, and another to Cwmmawr up the Gwendraeth Valley. The latter had three inclined planes engineered by James Green, although one was never used.

The South Wales valley canals, served by an extensive network of horse tram-roads, proved profitable and of great industrial value, helping to found their respective ports. Before they were built the products of the iron industry had been carried on horseback or muleback over the mountain and into waggons to be taken to ports. The table below demonstrates how two of the canals made possible the growth of the industry. It also shows the influence of coal carrying by the Glamorganshire on the growth of Cardiff, whose population increased tenfold between 1798 and 1841 with the growth of coal exports:

Year	Glamorganshire		Monmouthshire	
Tons	Iron	Coal	Iron	Coal
1807	–		23,019	
1817	39,497		43,407	
1819		34,606		–
1827	84,946		91,618	
1829		83,729		471,675
1837	124,810		144,277	
1839		211,214		484,993

A second group of canals ran north of the Trent near Nottingham into the Erewash valley. These comprised the Erewash Canal and its continuation the Cromford, with the Nutbrook as a tributary of the Erewash. From this central line, offshoots led on the one side to Nottingham (the Nottingham Canal) and on the other to Derby (the Derby Canal), so that the coal, iron, limestone, paving-stones and other goods coming down the main line could be diverted to either of these towns or to places beyond them on other connecting navigations. Alternatively they could pass into the Trent to go down river as far as Gainsborough (for shipping by sea) and Torksey (for Lincoln), or across it into the Loughborough Navigation and so to Leicester and the south. In 1808 269,456 tons of coal were carried on the Cromford, Erewash and Nottingham canals and this figure grew steadily until railway times.

The third group comprised the Shropshire tub-boat canals. The Shropshire coalfield was one of the earliest to use river transport and tramroads. Iron had been smelted in the district with charcoal since at least the first half of the seventeenth century, but, when Abraham Darby first learned to smelt iron with coke at Coalbrookdale, he laid the foundation of a tight little industrial pocket of collieries and ironworks. The country was so hilly, however, that to build ordinary canals was out of the question. William Reynolds of Ketley, one of the works in the Coalbrookdale group, provided the answer when he introduced the inclined plane at Ketley.

The earliest canal in the area, the Donnington Wood (or Duke of Sutherland's Tub-boat) Canal, had been built by 1767. It ran from collieries at Donnington

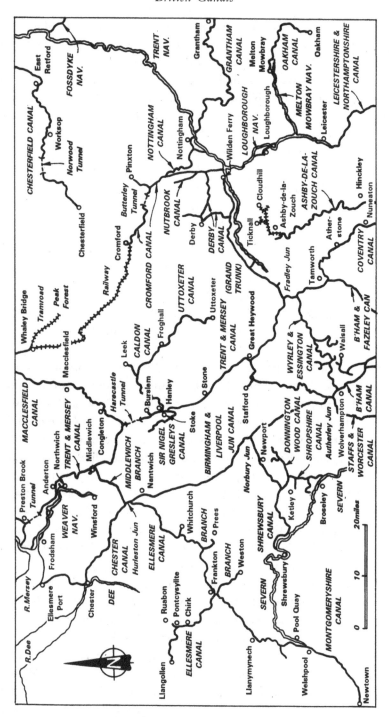

The waterways of the West and East Midlands of England, with their connections into Wales and the North West. These include the Shropshire group and those around the Erewash valley.

Wood to Pave Lane near Newport, and was promoted by Earl Gower, the Duke of Bridgewater's brother-in-law, and the two Gilberts, Thomas and John. William Reynolds's little Ketley Canal led to the formation of the Shropshire Canal Company, which built 8 miles of canal from the Donnington Wood Canal past the Ketley Canal to the Severn at Coalport, with a branch to Coalbrookdale, and three inclined planes. This canal carried the industrial output of the area to the river, where it was transferred to river craft. Later the Shrewsbury Canal was built to carry coal more easily from Donnington to Shrewsbury. It also had an inclined plane, at Trench, which was to work until 1921 and was the last to operate in Britain. Lastly, a plane was built on a branch of the Donnington Wood Canal, which had previously had a vertical lift for the cargo, though not for the boats.

These canals were small in size and cheap to construct. Their small tub-boats holding 5–8 tons each were navigated in trains between the planes, and the cost of operation was low. Not until 1835 was this self-contained tub-boat system connected to the main canal network by means of the Newport branch of the Birmingham & Liverpool Junction. The Shrewsbury Canal was then partly converted for narrow boat use. Cargoes from the rest of the system had to be tran-shipped to special 'Trench' narrow boats at Trench wharf below the plane there.

It would be possible to trace in detail the new patterns of trade encouraged by this wide and interlacing system, and even to assess what developments might have emerged had this system not been fostered. However, this would be to stray too far into economic history. Some consideration of the coal trade in England and Wales may give some idea of what happened to every raw material and fin-ished commodity, and of the repercussions on manufacturers, their employees and the towns where work was carried out.

Before the canals, coal went by sea from the north-east coast to those towns accessible to small coasting vessels. This sea coal came up the Thames to London and up the many rivers of the east coast into the heart of East Anglia, Lincolnshire and Yorkshire. Land coal was usually supplied by road transport only in the neigh-bourhood of the collieries, for the cost of carriage rose steeply as the distance increased, whether in waggons or on horseback. Where there was a river to help the distribution, as with the Severn in Shropshire, land coal could usually be transported far afield. There were therefore parts of Britain that found it difficult to get coal at all, except at a prohibitive price.

The motive of cheap coal was important in the history of canal development and, after the waterways were built, land or sea coal was transported by water everywhere south of Lancashire or Yorkshire, except to parts of North Wales. Yorkshire coal went east via the Aire & Calder or the Don, until it met the sea coal in from the Humber, although Yorkshire coal also went south along the coast; Wigan coal also crossed the Pennines, as well as going south to Liverpool and west on its old route down the Douglas Navigation on its way to Ireland; Welsh coal came down the valleys by canal and was then shipped to Bristol and

Coal being carried on the Bridgewater Canal over the Barton Swing Aqueduct, which crosses the Manchester Ship Canal. This unique structure replaced the earliest major aqueduct. This view was taken in the late 1940s, showing both wide and narrow boats. Coal provided one of the last major traffics on the smaller canals. Over this section, coal was moved to power stations from the Wigan and Leigh areas as late as 1973. (De Mare Collection/Boat Museum/The Waterways Trust)

the south-west; Forest of Dean coal went to Gloucester and Cheltenham, and through the Thames & Severn as far east as Oxford; Somerset coal, through the Kennet & Avon and the Wilts & Berks, also moved east, until at Reading it met the sea coal coming up the Thames, or at Abingdon or Oxford met Leicestershire or Warwickshire coal from the Oxford Canal. Coal within the Midlands competed freely – Leicestershire mainly against Derbyshire, Staffordshire against Warwickshire – and pressed down the Grand Junction towards London. Via main canals or their branches, such country places as Buckingham, Newport Pagnell, Oakham and Ledbury found themselves supplied with fuel for domestic and industrial use, while the growing manufacturing towns had a constant supply, not dependent on the output of a single colliery and at a cheaper price, which naturally drew coal-using industries to the canal side.

In Scotland coal from the Monkland or the Forth & Clyde went by boat to Glasgow and then by ship from Bowling or Grangemouth up and down the coast: before long it would go by canal to Edinburgh too.

The coal trade played a much smaller part in Ireland, where turf (peat) was, and remains, a more significant indigenous fuel. Coal imported through Dublin did, however, traverse the Grand and Royal canals. The first had opened to the Shannon in 1805, and the Barrow Navigation to St Mullins 15 years before. The Grand Canal Company leased a colliery near Athy and carried coal to Dublin for a time after 1805.

To the north, imported coal from Newry and Belfast was carried up the Newry Canal and the Lagan, the latter being completed to Lough Neagh in 1794. Coal from the Tyrone collieries was carried down the 4⅔ mile long Coalisland Canal, although by 1787, when it had opened, the earlier Ducart's tub-boat canal, with its three primitive inclines, had closed.

The end of the Napoleonic Wars brought a slump and inhibited canal development. Men and horses that had been used in the wars returned and competed with the navigations by taking traffics onto the improving roads. From that time road transport presented serious competition for the trade in merchandise and groceries, which, while small in volume compared with that in raw materials, earned high tolls and was the support of the fly-boats. Prices fell as unemployment rose. The years from the peace of Waterloo, in 1815, to 1822, when the coming boom made investors willing to venture capital, were a time when little was done to expand the canal system and competition for the existing business was keen. In 1822 the Basingstoke Committee stated:

> that one hundred weight of goods is conveyed from London to Farnham by land, for one shilling and sixpence, which by the Canal, the same quantity must cost one shilling and threepence, and where the difference is so slight, it may be readily imagined the land carriage will be preferred, for its rapidity.
>
> In ordinary times, the expense of conveyance on land was about three times as much as by water...[2]

Of the biggest projects of this period, the Aire & Calder's Ferrybridge and Goole Canal is described in Chapter Eight. The Edinburgh & Glasgow Union was authorised in 1817, with a capital of £290,000 to connect Edinburgh with the Forth & Clyde Canal near Falkirk by a line 30 miles long, all on one level bar the flight of locks that descended 110ft to the Forth & Clyde. This project had first been mooted in 1793, and since then, pamphlets advocating various proposed routes had poured out.

Another project, the Portsmouth & Arundel, proved unlucky. In 1813 the Wey & Arun Junction had been authorised, to bring goods from the Thames and Wey, over the canal to the Arun and then to Arundel and Littlehampton. This probably spurred the promotion of the Portsmouth & Arundel to provide a direct water route to London. A canal was to link Ford, on the Arun, to Chichester Harbour. Then a tidal channel was to be dredged past Thorney and Hayling islands to a short canal across Portsea Island into Portsmouth.

Before completion an agreement for through tolls on the waterways to the Wey was made, and the Wey & Arun Junction altered its works to allow the same barges to make the whole passage. The whole canal opened throughout in May 1823, with some through traffic. However, in December 1824 an indignant meeting in Portsmouth protested that the saltwater in the Portsea Canal was leaching into wells that provided drinking water. Three weeks later, the proprietors stated that, while some compensation had been paid, the company 'were not to be dictated to by any set of individuals, however respectable'.

The company survived but, despite efforts to build up the through trade, this languished and died, and the Portsmouth & Arundel Canal with it. The Portsea portion had hardly been used, and around 1855 the rest of the canal was disused, except for the short branch from Chichester to Chichester Harbour, which had been built on a larger scale. The company was finally wound up under an order of 1888.

The third of the new projects was the Bude Canal. Authorised in 1819, this was planned to run from Bude on the north coast of Cornwall to Thornbury, with branches to Launceston, and elsewhere, with a total length of almost 46 miles. The promoters envisaged a tub-boat canal to carry sea-sand, to be used as fertiliser, into the interior. It was therefore planned on the model of the Shropshire Canal, without locks, except on the entrance section, and with six inclined planes, the biggest of which, at Hobbacott Down, was 225ft high and 907ft long. The boats, to carry some 4 tons each, had wheels permanently fixed beneath them so that they could run directly on to the rails of the inclined planes. Because coal was expensive in Cornwall the planes were worked hydraulically, five by waterwheel and that at Hobbacott Down by the bucket-in-the-well system, supplemented by a steam engine on the numerous occasions when one of the bucket-chains broke.

By 1826, 35 miles of the canal had been built at a cost of about £118,000. For many years this carried some 50,000 tons of sea-sand anually, but only much later was any dividend paid. In 1891, the whole canal, bar a wide length at Bude, was closed. The reservoir and part of the line were used for public water supplies for many years.

During the prosperity of 1824 three ship canal projects emerged. The English & Bristol Channels Ship Canal did obtain an Act, but that from the Dee estuary to Manchester, a forerunner of the Manchester Ship Canal, was not well supported. The most ambitious scheme, a ship canal from London to Portsmouth, failed to attract support.

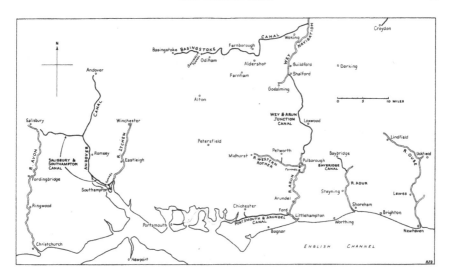

This map shows the line from London completed by the Portsmouth & Arundel Canal, and the system centred on Southampton. Of these waterways, only the Wey has remained continuously navigable, although most of the Basingstoke to Greywell has been restored, along with short lengths of the London–Portsmouth line.

In 1825 the first public railway to be successfully operated by locomotive engines was opened between Stockton and Darlington. Originally a canal had been projected, but the proposal had then been changed to a railway. As we have seen, horse railways and tramroads were not a new idea in Britain. Starting as coal lines to feed the Tyne and the Severn, they had been extensively constructed to serve canals. Later, more ambitious lines were planned and built, notably the 33-mile-long Cromford & High Peak Railway, which was authorised in 1825 (after the Stockton & Darlington had opened) as a horse-operated line and opened in 1831, and the Stratford & Moreton, completed in 1826 as a branch of the Stratford-upon-Avon Canal. Extensive mineral lines such as the Sirhowy had existed for many years in the Welsh coal and iron districts.

In all some two dozen railways had been authorised by special Act of Parliament before 1824, along with many lines sanctioned by canal Acts or built privately. In the years 1824 and 1825, however, there was a tremendous outburst of speculative activity in railways, usually for locomotive routes. In those years most of the great lines of the next decade, such as the Great Western and the London & Birmingham, were first projected. In total, proposals for some sixty railways in the British Isles were put forward, and a number were authorised by Act of Parliament. A second outburst followed in 1830.

The use of locomotives on the Stockton & Darlington marks the virtual beginning of railway history. To contemporaries, however, this was an interesting

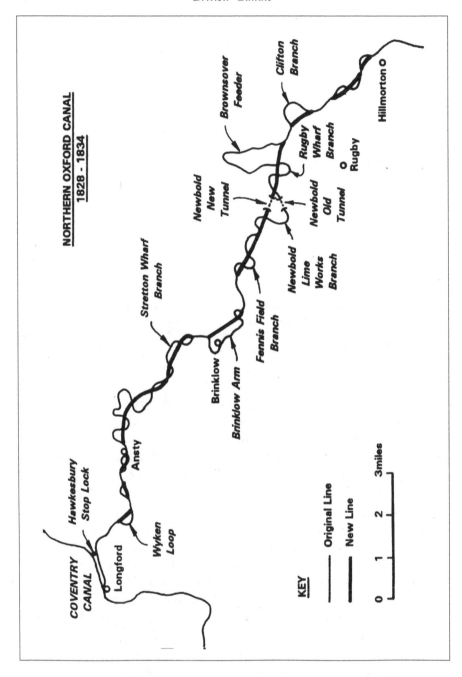

The shortening of part of the Oxford Canal. (Lengths further south, including a long loop near Braunston on the Grand Junction Canal, were also bypassed.) Some sections were retained as branches off the main line; only the Stretton Wharf Branch is now in regular use, as moorings.

development that increased the utility of railways but did not alter the general view: that railways were essentially feeders to waterways, useful in hilly country where the making of canals was impossibly expensive or over country where the expected traffic was light. Later informed opinion was to swing to the other extreme: that waterways had no longer any part to play in the future of transport. This situation justified the legendary assertion of the old Duke of Bridgewater, that canals would last his time 'but I see mischief in those damned tramroads'.

The extension of the railway idea, and the faster operation of railways that followed the introduction of locomotives, was one cause of an increase in the efficiency and enterprise of the waterways.

One response was an effort at improvement. For instance the Harecastle Tunnel on the Trent & Mersey Canal was doubled in 1827. The first tunnel – 12ft high and 9¼ft wide – had taken nine years, whereas the new tunnel – 16ft high and 14ft wide – took only three years to build, so greatly had engineering technique improved in the meantime. In other cases the distance between two points was reduced in order to save time and wages, since competition was becoming even more fierce than that between water and road transport. Some early canals had adopted the principle of following as far as possible the contour of the ground, and had sacrificed shortness

The two tunnels at Harecastle, the older one, in which Brindley was involved, on the right. The drawing somewhat overemphasizes the more modern appearance of the second tunnel. The Brindley Tunnel was used until the First World War; the bore has now subsided to minimal headroom.

to ease and cheapness of construction and water conservation owing to the absence of locks. Later ones such as the Birmingham & Liverpool Junction were made as straight as possible, even at the expense of considerable cutting and embanking to maintain the level. The northern Oxford Canal provided an extreme example of the straightening of a rural contour canal. Between 1829 and 1834 it was shortened from 91 to 77½ miles, with many short lengths left as branches.

The Birmingham & Liverpool Junction (now the Shropshire Union main line) was a 'modern' narrow canal. Authorised in 1826, opened in 1835 and engineered by Telford and Cubitt, it was intended both to shorten the distance between Birmingham and Ellesmere Port on the Mersey, and to provide a waterway less obstructed by tunnels and locks. It proved expensive to build, for it completely deserted the contours and drove across country from the end of the old Chester Canal at Nantwich on embankments and through cuttings to a junction with the Staffs & Worcs at Autherley. After using ½ mile of that canal, boats from Ellesmere Port passed into the the Birmingham Canal. Much of this system had itself been reconstructed by Telford, with further improvements to follow in the 1850s.

Efforts were then made to extend this new model right through to London by building a canal from a point on the Stratford-upon-Avon accessible from Birmingham to Highgate with a minimum of lockage. But by 1835, when the Birmingham & Liverpool Junction opened and the extension was being advocated, it was no longer possible to raise capital to build new canals: investment was going into new railways. Even the more modest Central Union proposal, to improve the London–Birmingham route by a cut from the Worcester & Birmingham to the Warwick & Birmingham, and another from the Warwick & Birmingham Canal to the Coventry, was not seriously supported, though it would have reduced the number of locks between Birmingham and Braunston from 54 to 17 by avoiding the heavy lockage down to and up from the Avon valley at Warwick.

In Ireland, too, a great through canal line was projected to link Belfast and Newry with the Shannon. As these cities were already connected to Lough Neagh, the new line required a canal from the Blackwater River west of the lough to the River Finn, which led to upper Lough Erne. Another line would link Lough Erne to the Shannon at Leitrim, above Carrick-on-Shannon.

In 1825 the Ulster Canal Company was empowered to build the first of these links, from the Blackwater to the Finn. Much of the money was found not by shareholders but by the Exchequer Bill Loan Commissioners, whose engineer, Telford, worked with John Killaly on construction. Between them they made the serious mistake of building the locks to take craft of the same length as those on the Newry or the Lagan canals but 3ft narrower – 11ft 6in against 14ft 6in, so that it could only be used by specially built craft. Finished in 1841 at a cost of £231,000, over half of it public money, and being 45¾ miles long with 26 locks, the Ulster was hardly being used twenty years later.

Meanwhile the second link in the through route, the Ballinamore & Ballyconnell Canal from upper Lough Erne to the Shannon, stimulated by the completion of the Ulster but with the additional aim of improving drainage, was begun in 1846. This time with 16 locks taking craft 82ft by 16ft 6in, the new canal was built by the Board of Works and opened in 1858, the navigation works having cost some £229,000. Traffic was negligible, but nevertheless the board closed the Ulster, which they now owned, in 1865 and spent £22,000 on improving it, though without widening the locks. The Ulster was re-opened in 1873, by which time the Ballinamore & Ballyconnell was, in turn, almost impassable. The through line was therefore never achieved in practice. Even if it had been it is improbable that much traffic would have appeared on such an unlikely route.

There had also been a change in Irish waterway organization. The Directors General of Inland Navigation, who on the whole had done well, were replaced in 1831 by a new Board of Public Works to oversee all Government works. In 1839, however, the Shannon was given its own commissioners, but in 1852 the navigation reverted to the Board.

Back in England just before the railway age, the running of fly-boats became important, although some had run since the earlier days of canals. These express boats ran to a timetable using relays of horses and double crews, carrying merchandise and parcels, setting down and picking up at wharves along the line with priority over all other traffic and permission to work all through the night. They were usually light boats, carrying less cargo than their slower brethren. Excerpts from the rules adopted by the Kennet & Avon Canal in 1840 for the operation of fly-boats show the conditions under which they worked and the surprisingly good service they gave:

> The following Resolutions relative to the passage of Fly Boats from Bath to Reading and vice versa are recommended for adoption:
>
> 1st. That Boats not exceeding 15 Tons Tonnage will be allowed to trade on the Canal between Reading and Bath.
>
> 4th. In case there shall be more than 15 Tons in one Boat, the same shall be liable to all the Charges and penalties imposed by the Company for false entries.
>
> 5th. In consideration of and to participate in the above terms, the parties must engage to start one Boat at least every day from Bath and from Reading whether having a complete Cargo or not, to deliver goods from Bristol to London and Vice Versa in 36 hours [36 hours from Bath to Reading], unavoidable stoppages excepted, the Boats to have every facility granted for their passage.[3]

At the same time experiments were tried with fly-boats to carry loaded carts and loaded tramroad waggons, put on the Forth & Clyde Canal in order to save transhipment costs.

During this period passenger-carrying on canals reached its peak. The full extent of passenger-carrying remains relatively unknown, but modern trip and hotel boats did have their antecedents. This had been a common practice even on the old river navigations. For instance the River Wey Act of 1651 laid down a maximum fare for passengers from Guildford to London. Soon after canals were first built passengers were carried on them, and this business grew until, during the 1820s and 1830s, it became very large on certain waterways. In 1773 Josiah Wedgwood wrote:

> From Warrington to Manchester the Duke has set up two passage boats, one carries passengers at a shilling each. The other is divided into three rooms, & the rates are 2/6 p head for the best room, 10*d*., and 12*d*., and it is the pleasantest and cheapest mode of travelling...[4]

While a year later the Leeds & Liverpool Canal Company enacted:

> That every person passing in any boat between Wigan and Liverpool, or any other part of the line, shall pay for every two miles or under, one half-penny; each passenger to be allowed fourteen pounds weight of luggage; and in case any boatman shall neglect to give a just account of the number of passengers he shall at any time carry on his boat, with the distance each passenger shall have passed, he shall forfeit the sum of ten shillings.[5]

In lowland Scotland, passenger-carrying reached a high degree of efficiency. On the Forth & Clyde itself, and later on the Edinburgh & Glasgow Union, regular services were provided by both the company's own boats and by others, although in England the usual practice was to allow private carriers to operate passenger services, the canal company merely taking tolls. The Forth & Clyde introduced two track boats, carrying both freight and passengers, in 1786, and these grew to carry about 5,000 passengers annually. In 1809 the company introduced a daily service for passengers only. Each boat had cabin and steerage accommodation, the cabin being provided with newspapers, books and games, with meals and drinks obtainable on board. These boats did the 25 miles between Glasgow and Lock 16 (Falkirk) in 5½ hours, later reduced to 3 hours. They were pulled by two horses, the second ridden, which were changed every 2 miles at the stables, many of which are still to be seen alongside the canal, now converted into houses.

Passengers found the boats cleaner and more comfortable than the stage-coaches, and the numbers carried on the Forth & Clyde Canal rose from 44,000 in 1812 to nearly 200,000 in 1836. In 1831 sleepers were put on between Glasgow and Edinburgh, which made the journey of 56 miles in under 11 hours, and a handbill of 1841 shows that four passenger boats a day were then leaving Glasgow,

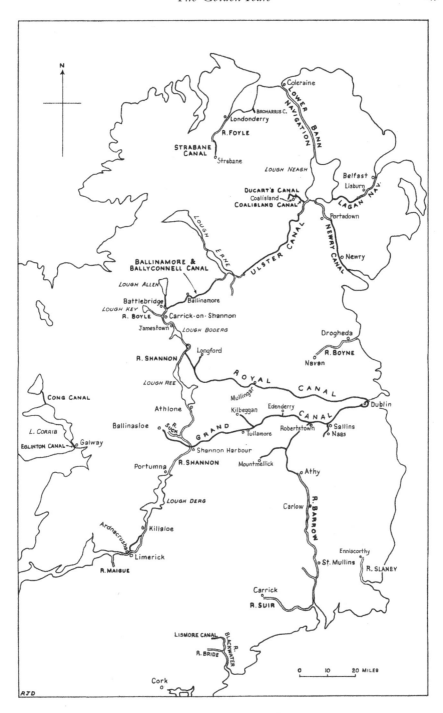

This map shows the waterway system in Ireland, as finally completed by the Ballinamore & Ballyconnell Canal. (Since restoration, this has been known as the Shannon–Erne waterway.) One waterway which is not shown is the short Tralee Ship Canal, in the extreme south-west of the island.

with through bookings by canal or canal and coach together to Edinburgh, Stirling, Alloa, Falkirk, Perth and Kirkcaldy.

Even the mainly industrial Monkland Canal featured passenger boats, although here there were separate services to Port Dundas and Sheepford from Blackhill Locks, with through passengers having to walk down the busy lock flight in between. The Lancaster Canal and Runcorn Locks would feature a similar arrangement.

The achievement of the Glasgow, Paisley & Ardrossan Canal is even more striking. This narrow waterway had originally been planned to run from Glasgow through Paisley to the sea at Ardrossan, and it obtained its Act in 1806. Funds ran out when it had reached Johnstone beyond Paisley in 1811, and eventually it was completed by a railway.

Before 1830 the passengers carried on it between Paisley and Glasgow, a distance of 8 miles, did not exceed 30,000 a year. William Houston, who had money in the company, determined to build up the traffic through the use of fast, light boats of special design carrying between eighty and ninety passengers, and by charging about 3s 4d. (17p) a mile. The boats were built of thin iron sheets, with a fabric cabin covering supports. They were some 70ft long, 6ft wide, weighed only 33 cwt and drew 19¼ in when fully loaded. Houston achieved the following results:

Year ending 30th September	Passengers carried	No. of boats each day each way
1831	79,455	4
1832	148,516	7
1833	240,062	9
1834	307,275	12
1835	373,290	12

In this last year Houston cut the fares for the 8 miles from 9d. (4p) to 6d. (3p) cabin and from 6d. (3p) to 4d. (2p) steerage, and still further increased his trade, until his long white boats and scarlet-jacketed postillions became well known. Other canal companies heard of William Houston's boats and ordered similar ones, or bought them second-hand: we find them on the Don, Lancaster, Carlisle and Bridgewater canals, the Grand Canal of Ireland and even the Kennet & Avon.

A writer of 1835 says of these Scottish canals:

If any one had stated five years ago, that by improvements, in the build of Canal Passage Boats, a speed of ten miles per hour would be regularly maintained on Canal routes; and that the charges to passengers, carried at this speed, would be the same as at the previous slow speed, of four or five miles per hour; that in one small district of Scotland alone, distances amounting in all to nine hundred miles each

Various forms of carrying craft on the Forth & Clyde Canal, taken from a prospectus for the proposed Stirling Canal; these drawings indicated uses to which the proposed canal could be put. From top to bottom, these illustrate a boat to carry loaded carts; a boat to carry loaded tramroad waggons; and a swift passenger boat. The growth of railway transport halted the development of these imaginative uses of water transport.

day ... should be performed by these improved light Boats at the above speed ... the assertion would have been received with unlimited ridicule. Yet such is now the case.[6]

When railway competition came prices were cut, until both canal and railway were carrying passengers from Paisley to Glasgow for 2*d*. (1p). Then, in 1843, the canal company gave up passenger and parcel carrying in return for an annual payment, and its horses and boats were sold.

In England passenger carrying is recorded on many canals such as the Lancaster:

… for safety, economy and comfort no other mode of conveyance could be so eligible; for there the timid might be at ease and the most delicate mind without fear.[7]

A daily service between Kendal and Preston was operated from 1820 with boats that covered the 57 miles in 14 hours. In 1833 an express boat was introduced to compete with the stagecoaches, which cut the time from Kendal to Preston to 7¼ hours. In the first six months 14,000 passengers were carried. Passenger boats did not finally leave the canal until 1846.

Regular services were operated on such waterways as the Bridgewater, Mersey & Irwell, Leeds & Liverpool, Aire & Calder and Yorkshire Ouse; for shorter periods on the Birmingham, Chester, Ellesmere and Grand Junction; while on others market boats were run, as on the Gloucester & Berkeley and the Derby Canal, on which 'a market-boat, decked over, with seats, and a fire-place, for the accommodation of passengers, starts from Swarkestone every Friday morning, to carry market-people to Derby, at 6d. each; which again leaves Derby at 4 o'clock for Swarkestone.'[8]

The oddest collection of passengers was perhaps that reported in the Derby Mercury of 19 April 1826:

> On Saturday last arrived in this town by canal, a fine Lama, a Kangaroo, a Ram with four horns, and a female Goat with two young kids, remarkably handsome animals, as a present from Lord Byron to a Gentleman whose residence is in this neighbourhood, all of which had been picked up in the course of the voyage of the Blonde to the Sandwich islands in the autumn of 1824.

In South Wales, passenger-carrying seems to have been confined to the Tennant Canal, with a packet boat operating between 1827 and at least 1850.

In Ireland the Grand Canal Company maintained long-lived passenger services between Dublin and the Shannon, later Ballinasloe, and to the Barrow, and also built fine hotels, though these proved less successful than the boats. First put on in 1780 between Dublin and Sallins, packet-boat services were extended and then curtailed, until they ended in 1852. The importance given to packet-boats is shown in the following rule for lock-keepers made by the Royal Canal Company in 1813:

> If a Lock-Keeper has not his Upper-Chamber full, and his Gates open to receive the Packet-Boat the moment she arrives on her Passage to Dublin, he shall be liable to a Fine of Two Shillings & Six Pence.

Excursion travelling by canal was also quite common. As early as 1776 the Chester Canal company was running special boats from Beeston to Chester Races. A handbill of the Edinburgh & Glasgow Union in 1834 offers 10 miles

The Grand Canal at Shannon Harbour, with the ruins of the company hotel on the left. This hotel was built in 1806, shortly after the main line was completed in 1804. Not a great success, it seems to have been used as a hotel only until 1847, has been vacant since 1925, and is now a roofless shell. Shannon Harbour was a new settlement built to service passenger and transshipment traffic between the Canal and the Shannon. (Ruth Heard)

for 6*d.* (3p) amid most pleasant scenery and over highly interesting aqueducts, at one of which fruits, confectioneries and a variety of refreshments could be had.

The prospectus for the Stirling Canal in 1835 suggests that the superiority of railways for passenger-carrying was not yet fully appreciated:

> In regard to the comparative amenity of the two modes of travelling, the noiseless smoothness of the Canal boats is unequalled. Nor must it be forgotten, that while a very large portion of the Liverpool Railway passengers are conveyed in uncovered waggons, exposed to wind and weather, all the Canal passengers have the privilege of well-lighted, comfortable, and elegant cabins.[9]

Since the canal was never built, presumably the investing public thought better of the railway.

Although a boat drawn by horses on a canal may not seem a dangerous mode of travelling, accidents did occur. The following newspaper account in 1810 tells of one incident:

> Paisley. Nov. 11. Yesterday about half-past 12 the boat which tracks on the Ardrossan Canal, was about to set off for Johnstone: it was one of the days of our quarterly fair, and a great many boys and girls being off work – were attracted by its novelty (being

the fifth day it had sailed); some had not got out from Johnstone, while others were crowding on board to go there; the boat was lying at the quay in the basin; the water about six feet deep, some were below, but most part on the top of the cabins or the deck. The boat was raised pretty high out of the water, and the weight getting too great above, she suddenly swayed on one side, and all on deck fell over. Some were able to leap upon the quay on the first motion: but upwards of 100 persons, men, women, boys and girls, and even children were precipitated into the basin. A few swam out, and others were got out before they sunk: but the greater number sunk to the bottom. Drags were got, and before one o'clock about 50 were got out. Every aid was given by the surgeons and inhabitants, and on Saturday night 18 or so were recovered. The dragging continued all the afternoon. About 90 have been dragged out in all; but owing to the great number of families the sufferers belong to, it is not accurately known how many are dead… Those in the cabin of the vessel were safe, the boat uprighting as soon as the crowd fell off.[10]

A Bury historian related another incident on the Manchester, Bolton & Bury Canal in June 1818 when 6 people died:

The catastrophe … was caused by the insensate folly of a party of passengers, drunken men, numbering near twenty, who overawed the quieter portion on board, and persisted, for amusement and to frighten the women, in swaying the boat, heavily laden and overcrowded, from side to side, until the window-sills of the cabin, below the deck, were almost on a level with the water of the canal. The brutal wretches, maddened with drunkenness and riot, paid no heed whatever to the remonstrances of the captain, the shrieks and piteous entreaties of the women, or the tears and cries of children who were on board; for the journey was a favourite Sunday trip, many families going that day to visit friends or relatives in Bolton. Opposition led only to more strenuous efforts, and they were blind to danger; and at length the dreaded apprehension was changed to reality. The heavily laden boat, urged by powerful impetus, gave one fatal dip below the water-line, turned upon its side, with its living freight, a hopeless multitude, and rose no more…[11]

Such events were, fortunately, rare, but there were accidents to the passenger boats on the Royal Canal in Ireland. In 1845, 6 people died when a boat full of emigrants at Longford harbour keeled over and capsized; while 16 perished when a packet-boat, in the hands of an inexperienced steerer, struck a rock in Clonsilla cutting and sank.

The carrying of passengers and the working of fly-boats were affected by experiments in 1832 and 1833 on the Forth & Clyde, Oxford and Grand Junction canals to increase the speed of boats. It was found with specially built light boats that if speed was increased beyond the normal 3–4mph a wave was built up in front of the boat, but that a further increase in speed enabled the boat to pass the

GRAND CANAL.

Cheap Travelling,

Between DUBLIN and ATHLONE, by TULLAMORE,

Commencing on Friday, the 15th day of November, 1811.

FARE.

Boat, between Dublin and Tullamore, 45 Miles.			Coach, between Tullamore and Athlone, 19 Miles.			Total.	
	s.	*d.*		*s.*	*d.*	*s.*	*d.*
First Cabin,	13	0	Inside,	5	0	18	0
Second Cabin,	8	8	Outside,	3	4	12	0

Coach Fare, from Tullamore to Clara, Inside, - 1s. 8d.—Outside, 1s. 8d.
Ditto, - - - to Moate, - - 3s. 4d.— - 2s. 1d.

LUGGAGE allowed in Coach——Inside, 40lb.—Outside, 20lb.

Extra Luggage to be paid for, at the rate of one penny per lb.

A Passage-Boat departs from Dublin, every morning, at seven o'clock; and arrives in Tullamore, at ten minutes after eight o'clock, in the evening;—and another Boat departs from Dublin, every afternoon, at two o'clock, and arrives in Tullamore, at half after three o'clock, next morning. – And a COACH, capable of conveying six inside and ten outside Passengers, departs from the Company's Hotel at Tullamore, every morning, at five o'clock; and, passing through the towns of Clara and Moate, arrives at half after nine o'clock, at Mr. JOHN GARTY's Hotel, in *Athlone.*

NOTE.—Under this arrangement, a passenger, leaving Dublin in the Boat, at two o'clock in the evening, will arrive in Athlone, about nine o'clock next morning.

The Coach departs, from Athlone, every afternoon, at half after two o'clock, and, passing through Moate and Clara, arrives at seven o'clock, in the evening, at Tullamore Hotel; whence a Boat proceeds, at half after nine o'clock, for Dublin; where it arrives at twenty minutes after eleven o'clock, next morning:— and, another Boat proceeds from Tullamore, every morning, at seven o'clock, and arrives in Dublin at ten minutes after eight o'clock in the evening.

N. B. No charge made in the Boat for any child, under the age of one year; and only half price charged for the passage and ordinary of any child between that age and seven years.

Breakfast, Dinner, and Supper, provided in the Boats, as usual.

Small parcels carried in the Boat and Coach, between Dublin and Athlone, at moderate rates.

Seats for the Coach, from Tullamore to Athlone, may be engaged from the Boat-Masters on the Passage; and Seats from Athlone to Tullamore to be engaged at Mr. JOHN GARTY's Hotel, in *Athlone.*

By Order,

15th November, 1811. DANIEL BAGOT, *Sec.*

DUBLIN: PRINTED BY WILLIAM PORTER, GRAFTON-STREET,
Printer and Stationer to the Grand Canal Company.

A notice for a combined boat/coach service run by the Grand Canal Company between Dublin and Athlone. This had to compete with direct coach services, but some combined services lasted until they were overcome by railway competition.

wave, rise in the water and to travel at a speed of 11–12mph. Frequent changes of horses were, of course, necessary. As a result of these experiments, fast passenger services were operated successfully on the Glasgow Paisley & Ardrossan and other canals.

In 1839 the Forth & Clyde Canal experimented with locomotive haulage from the bank, but concluded that it would prove too expensive. Half a century later more trials were held, this time on railway initiative, when Francis W. Webb, the mechanical engineer of the London & North Western Railway, initiated trials on the Middlewich branch of the railway-controlled Shropshire Union. These showed that loaded boats could be towed at 8mph. Mechanical towage from the towpath using tractors was used on British Transport Commission waterways in the 1950s, but on the Continent both locomotive and tractor towage had a long life until self-propelled craft made them unnecessary.

Just as it is difficult now to realise the canal activity of those times, when much of the heavy goods, some of the lighter merchandise and many passengers were all moved by water transport, so it is not easy to generalise about the prosperity of the canals without complete figures for every company. A few concerns, which were extremely prosperous, are often quoted as examples of the high profits made by navigation companies in the days before their monopoly was threatened. In 1833, for instance, the figures for seven of the leading companies were as follows:

Name	Nominal value of shares (£)	Dividend paid (per cent)	Market value of shares (£)
Loughborough Nav	142	108	1,240
Erewash	100	47	705
Mersey & Irwell	50	40	750
Trent & Mersey	100	75	640
Oxford	100	32	595
Coventry	100	32	600
Forth & Clyde	100	25	545

A number of other companies provided very satisfactory investments, such as the Staffordshire & Worcestershire, Cromford, Shropshire, Shrewsbury, Swansea and Grand Junction. Others were paying only small dividends, but would have had good prospects had railways not intruded. These included the Brecknock & Abergavenny, Peak Forest, Macclesfield, Ashby de la Zouch, Kennet & Avon, Rochdale, Stratford-upon-Avon and the Regent's, none of which paid as much as 5 per cent in 1833.

Much had, however, been spent on canals that were financially unsuccessful, and which never paid a dividend in their working existence, such as the Grand Western, Salisbury & Southampton and Leominster. Canals in Ireland and high-

Two of the *Queens*, passenger excursion vessels on the Forth & Clyde Canal. (British Waterways)

land Scotland had, of course, not been built in the main by investing companies. The following details of the dividends paid by three important companies are fairly representative. The Oxford was built before the wartime rise in prices, and its high dividends reflect its low construction cost of about £300,000. The Grand Junction and the Kennet & Avon were both built during the war, and each cost around £1 million. One was financially very successful, the other less so. Nevertheless all three were of great commercial value:

Year	Oxford (opened 1790) Dividend on £100 shares (per cent)	Grand Junction (opened 1805) Dividend on £100 shares (per cent)	Kennet & Avon (opened 1810) Dividend on £40 shares (per cent)
1809	25	5	–
1819	32	9	$2^{1}/_{4}$
1829	32	13	$3^{1}/_{8}$
1839	30	10	$3^{3}/_{8}$
1849	20	5	$^{15}/_{16}$

The dividend figures should be compared with those of toll receipts. These are roughly, but not exactly, comparable with each other:

Year	Oxford (£)	Grand Junction (£)	Kennet & Avon (£)
1809	78,848	127,404	4,472 (not yet opened)
1819	78,876	157,633	35,595
1829	89,992	181,144	43,818
1839	85,570	138,263	44,328

(The Kennet & Avon figures include tonnage receipts from the Kennet Navigation from 1814.)

It is odd that waterway interests met the threat of railways bravely and progressively up to a point, and then resigned themselves to passive defence of their positions or to active efforts to get themselves bought out at favourable prices. The force of private enterprise in railways overcame that of the waterways, and the latter succumbed. In France, Germany and lowland Europe, on the other hand, State or local authority intervention early in the struggle led to partial nationalization, the coordination of water and rail transport, and the modernization and standardization of the waterways.

Here and there a canal company believed in itself, for a time at least. In 1841 the Birmingham Canal company wrote:

> The circumstance ... of the Birmingham Canal being kept in a navigable state during the winter, whilst the neighbouring Canals were closed, affords strong proof of what can be done by energy and determination, and is well calculated to add to the impression, now rapidly gaining ground, that the low price of Canal stock and diversion of Traffic, is less to be ascribed to opposing railways, than to the inactivity, want of foresight, and absurd jealousies of the Canal Companies themselves.[12]

A striking example of inactivity was the Staffs & Worcs company, a neighbour of the Birmingham. This was a very prosperous concern in a key position, run by a small group of apparently able proprietors. Yet throughout its long career from its opening in 1772 it spent nothing substantial to improve its winding narrow line and single locks, except to build reservoirs and rebuild the Bratch Locks. It watched the Worcester & Birmingham take part of its Birmingham–Severn trade, and the Birmingham & Liverpool Junction take most of the Liverpool trade, with no action more effective than petitions against the Bills and in the second case, provision for heavy compensation payments.

A few concerns stood up, fought and succeeded. It never seems to have occurred to the Aire & Calder proprietors that they might be defeated, although even they were willing to sell to a railway group at one time. They were broad-based, prosperous and well-managed, and they showed what could be done. Had other companies been more like them, much could have been saved. Across the Pennines, the Weaver's reactions were much the same. This navigation was publicly owned, by Cheshire County Council, and provides the main British example of what often happened in continental Europe. The Weaver trustees were indeed so formidable that railway companies treated them with respect. Significantly, both navigations, many times modernised, were later among British Waterways' most important waterways.

The problem was that on the whole each waterway lived for itself. Very few working agreements were made to pass traffic, and those that were often broke down. There were few canal amalgamations in pre-railway or early railway times. Only the Ellesmere with the Chester, and later with others to form the Shropshire Union, the Mersey & Irwell with the Bridgewater, the Birmingham with the Wyrley & Essington and the Dudley, and the North Wilts with the Wilts & Berks spring to mind, though sometimes canal ownerships were interlocked by shareholders prominent in the affairs of more than one company. Even during the railway period amalgamations were few.

So ended the first canal age, which had made the already navigable rivers a basis for an inland waterway system of some 4,000 miles in all, serving nearly all of the important towns and industrial areas as well as many country districts. In the eighty years to 1840 the system had provided an important means of transporting goods in bulk and had helped to foster the process known as the Industrial Revolution. Britain and Ireland now stood on the threshold of a new era – the Victorian or railway age.

CHAPTER EIGHT

The Rivers during the Canal Age

As was outlined in Chapter one, over a thousand miles of river had been made navigable before the Sankey Navigation and Bridgewater Canals were promoted. This mileage was enlarged during the first canal age by work under Acts for small rivers, and by improvements to drainage, which also provided better navigation facilities.

River navigations were built in a variety of ways. In some very early cases individuals were appointed to do the work, while later some river Acts named commissioners, local people with property near the river, who in turn appointed undertakers, sometimes called trustees, to do the actual work. Money was then borrowed, usually at a fixed rate of interest. The Weaver to Winsford was made navigable in this way. In other cases commissioners themselves undertook the work, as on the River Ure, Calder & Hebble and, indeed, the Thames. Where drainage was involved, trustees were sometimes given local rating powers, as under the River Axe Act of 1802 and the Adur in 1807.

Joint stock companies were also formed, as for building the Aire & Calder, the Don and the Mersey & Irwell. During and after the second half of the eighteenth century, the joint stock type of company organization became more usual, the Calder & Hebble and later the Ure changing to this type.

The development of canals greatly changed patterns of inland water transport, usually to the benefit of river navigations, for they became the trunks from which the canals branched. Some promoted linking canals, as the Aire & Calder did with the Barnsley, and the Don with other links. Others found their interests so closely linked with canals that they amalgamated, as the Kennet and Bristol Avon did with the Kennet & Avon Canal – or the river was let to the canal, as was the Upper (Warwickshire) Avon to the Stratford-upon-Avon Canal.

Some, however, found themselves in bitter competition with a canal – like the Tone with the Bridgwater & Taunton Canal, and the Upper Trent Navigation with the Trent & Mersey Canal – and a battle took place that often ended with the new canal buying the old river, as later in other circumstances new railways bought old canals. Finally there were the great rivers of the Thames, Severn and Shannon, throughout the first canal age always to some degree navigable, yet never fully so until after that era was over.

In 1778 the opening of the Aire & Calder company's new Selby Canal provided an artificial bypass to the difficult natural navigation of the lower Aire. Almost fifty years later the Selby Canal was itself bypassed when the company opened a new large-scale canal from Ferrybridge on the Aire to Goole on the Ouse, engineered by George Leather junior. Immediately afterwards the Aire & Calder's routes upwards from Ferrybridge to Castleford, and then to Leeds and Wakefield, were rebuilt to the same standard, to a depth of 7ft and with locks 18ft wide. This rebuilding included the tied-arch aqueduct at Stanley Ferry (completed in 1839, and itself bypassed in 1981).

The port of Goole was the creation of the Aire & Calder. Starting in 1826 it grew throughout the nineteenth century and into the twentieth, new lock entrances being added as traffic – by canal and later by rail – increased. This company demonstrated how a river company that was connected to canals, and that used the science of canal building to shorten and make easier its own line, could attain and maintain prosperity. As we shall see, the Aire & Calder remained a leading waterways concern upon nationalisation and parts of its routes are still active.

To the south the Don Company, controlling the river from Tinsley near Sheffield to the Dutch River, was nearly as energetic. Authorised in 1726 and 1727, the line to Tinsley was finished in 1751, with 17 locks and a number of cuts bypassing river sections. During the canal mania the company took the lead in getting the Dearne & Dove and Stainforth & Keadby Canals built: the first connected the Don to the coalfields north of Barnsley, the second provided an outlet to the Trent more efficient than the Dutch River passage to the Ouse. Later, in 1819, the Sheffield Canal was opened to the Don at Tinsley, and from 1821 onwards the Don company rebuilt much of the line so that, when the railway age began, they were well placed to meet it.

The Kennet, whose early history was outlined in Chapter One, provides an example of a river closely connected with a canal, into which it was later incorporated. It had been developed under an Act of 1708, but was not successful until after 1767, when Francis Page purchased the shares from the commissioners whose disagreements had prevented viability. He, and later his sons, did their own carrying. By 1798 traffic was 20,000 tons a year and tolls (apart from freight) up to £2,140 a year. The building of the Kennet & Avon Canal greatly increased the Pages' profits, and by 1802, although the canal was incomplete, tolls had risen to £3,150. Traffics then included malt, flour and timber to London, coal, and Baltic and West Indian goods, from London to Bath, Bristol and Salisbury, by land carriage from Newbury.

In 1809, when the Kennet & Avon became interested in a link from Newbury to Old Basing on the Basingstoke, which would have by-passed the Kennet, Frederick Page opposed this proposal on behalf of the Thames Navigation and himself. This opposition, probably combined with some pressure behind the scenes, caused the canal company to buy him out for £100,000 in 1812. In 1798 his interests had been valued at less than £28,000, so he drove a hard bargain, although the increased prosperity brought by the canal had increased the Kennet's value.

Frodsham Bridge on the Weaver, on a formerly tidal length which was bypassed by the construction of the Weston Canal which extended the Weaver Navigation to Weston Point. The boat was the *Panary*, used to carry grain from Seaforth for forwarding by road to a mill in Stockport.

Amusingly, in 1824 Page opposed a new Basingstoke link against his former ally, the Thames Navigation, and he became chairman of the canal company shortly before his death in 1834.

A number of rivers were physically independent of the main waterway systems of Britain and Ireland. Some were great rivers, like the Tay, Tyne and Tees; others were small affairs, like the Adur, Eastern Rother, Boyne and Slaney. All to their capacities performed a useful service in opening up inland areas to trade. Of these, a prosperous example was the Weaver. This Cheshire river was first made navigable in 1732 under an Act of 1721; a further Act of 1760 placed it under the control of a body of county trustees, which continued to be responsible for the waterway until the Transport Act of 1947.

The first locks were made of wood, taking boats of about 40 tons, while the river itself could only be entered from the Mersey estuary at highwater ordinary spring tides. From 1760 onwards, however, the locks were rebuilt and the navigation improved, with a new lock built at Frodsham, close to the confluence of the river and the Mersey, so that it was accessible at most states of the tide. At this time the trustees made great efforts to connect their river to the proposed east–west canal that later became the Trent & Mersey. Failure, however, hardly affected the salt trade, which was the staple of the Weaver, and in 1810 the trustees opened an improvement, the Weston Canal. This avoided the difficult navigation of the lower Weaver by linking it to a new basin at Weston Point (the ancestor of the later docks), where craft could wait for the tide, with a river lock.

By 1830 the waterway was receiving some £30,000 a year from its trade and was handing considerable sums to the county authorities in relief of rates. Traffic was mainly in salt (432,000 tons) and coal (124,000 tons). From 1832 onwards the trustees carried out major improvements by increasing the depth from 6ft (itself an increase on the original 4ft 6in) to 7ft 6in and enlarging the locks to 88ft by 18ft, so that vessels carrying 100 tons or more of cargo could pass. Oddly, not until well into the railway age was this well-managed river connected to the canal system. From 1859 the short Runcorn & Weston Canal linked it to the Bridgewater docks at Runcorn, and, from 1875, the Anderton Lift connected it to the Trent & Mersey Canal, enabling narrow boats to pass up and down the river to Weston Point.

The most interesting of the failures among river navigations was the Norwich & Lowestoft. The ancient communication of Norwich with the sea had been by way of Yarmouth, but this line of waterway grew so shallow as to be of little use. In order to make Norwich once more a port, therefore, a plan was put forward for a ship canal to Lowestoft. After great opposition from Yarmouth this was authorised in 1827. The River Yare was deepened from Norwich to Reedham, from where a cut of 2½ miles was made to the River Waveney, taking the line to Oulton Dyke, which was enlarged to Oulton Broad. A short cut took the line into Lake Lothing, which was made into a tidal harbour by cutting through the bank separating it from the sea. The ship canal, which cost £150,000 to build, was opened in 1833 and proved a financial failure, the expenses of maintaining the channel exceeding the revenue. Money borrowed from the Exchequer Loan Commissioners could not be repaid and the canal was sold by the commissioners to a new company, which soon afterwards resold to a group of railway promoters. The older route to Norwich continued to be used and in 1908 there was a further proposal for a major ship canal to Norwich.

The rivers that were either independent of the canal system or fitted well into it were a large group. Some, however, found themselves directly in competition with canals. In Chapter nine we will see what effect the competition of railways had on waterways, with the price-cutting and acquisition of waterways by railways that resulted from the impact of a more efficient means of transport over an older, less efficient, one. During the canal age, a similar development involved the impact of newer canals on old river navigations. This impact was very local and often occurred when a canal was projected at the very end of the first canal age.

Where the pattern of river and canal development was quite different, as in Ireland and Scotland, there are no examples of such competition, unless the progressive improvement of the tidal Clyde Navigation, that removed some Forth & Clyde Canal traffic from the Clyde into Glasgow, is cited.

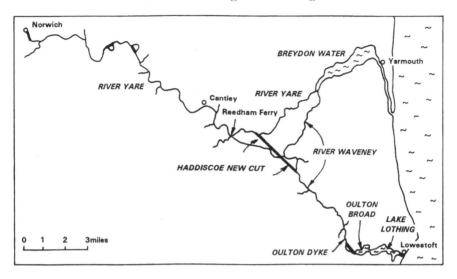

Map of the Norwich & Lowestoft Navigation, the thick lines showing the new cuts created to improve the navigation.

The case of the River Tone illustrates the course of canal competition in England. This small river, linking to the tidal Parrett near Bridgwater, had been made navigable up to Taunton under an Act of 1699, which set up conservators to keep the navigation open. Their General Proposals of 1697–8 provided that after a set rate of profit of 7 per cent, the remainder 'shall be to the said Company and every one of them, their Heirs and Assigns for ever, in Trust for the use of the Poor of Taunton and Taunton St. James'.[1]

The navigation to Taunton, completed in 1717, with one lock and at least two half-locks, had been a small affair but had slowly increased in prosperity through the eighteenth century, and more rapidly in the nineteenth, toll receipts increasing from £388 in 1728 to £668 in 1789 and £2,369 in 1821.

When the Bridgwater & Taunton Canal Bill was put forward the conservators bitterly but unsuccessfully opposed it. The canal was opened in 1827 and price cutting followed. The tolls became absurdly low and the canal company felt the strain to such an extent that, in spite of strong opposition from the conservators, they sought to acquire the Tone and thus control its trade. During Parliamentary proceedings the parties agreed that the canal company should discharge the charitable trust for the poor. The conservators' sole remaining powers, to ensure that navigation from Bridgewater to Taunton was maintained, were used up to nationalization.

In some cases the river navigation succumbed to the competition and ceased to be used. The River Salwarpe gave way to the Droitwich Canal, as did the River Idle from Bawtry to the Trent when faced with the Chesterfield Canal. In other cases amalgamation took place. For instance in 1783 the Leeds & Liverpool

Canal bought the Douglas Navigation. When it was authorised in 1795, the Derby Canal bought the Derwent Navigation and closed it.

The purchase by the Bridgewater of the Mersey & Irwell ended longstanding competition. The navigation company had unsuccessfully opposed the building of the Duke of Bridgewater's Canal from Manchester to Runcorn, and since then the companies had competed for Manchester traffics. During this time the river company shortened its line by artificial cuts and overcame shortages of water. During the last years of its life it took such a progressive line that it proved worthwhile for the Bridgewater trustees to acquire it. The river company started a plan to deepen the rivers to allow vessels of 300 tons to reach Victoria Bridge, Manchester, and successfully promoted the Manchester & Salford Junction Canal (buying it in 1840), which joined their navigation to the Rochdale, already linked to the Bridgewater.

Another type of river navigation usually had a more fortunate history: that which formed an integral part of a through line of canal. The Kennet & Avon proprietors, for instance, found that, if traffic was to be efficiently handled, they needed to own the two rivers connected by their canal. As we have seen, they bought the Kennet Navigation at a high price, and at the Bath end they acquired a majority of Avon shares.

The outstanding example of a river that prospered from the connection it made with canals was the Soar, usually known as the Loughborough Navigation. Originally built during canal times as an inexpensive project to make navigable the River Soar from the Trent to the town of Loughborough, this company, with an authorised capital of only £10,000, had the good fortune to find itself connected in 1794 with Leicester, and then in 1814 with the Grand Junction Canal by means of the Leicestershire & Northamptonshire Union and (old) Grand Union canals. As a result its earning capacity was greatly increased, the average dividend rising from an average of 1½ per cent in 1782–94 through 40 per cent in 1797–9, 108 per cent in 1812–14 to 154 per cent in 1827–9, before falling to 107 per cent in 1839–41.

During the canal age works to improve drainage in parts of lowland England also provided better navigation facilities, as with the Ancholme, Witham, Nene and Great Ouse. One unusual scheme, which featured conflict between navigation and flood protection, was the improvement of the Lower Bann, very much at the end of the first canal age.

Several rivers drain into Lough Neagh, the largest inland lake in the British Isles, but its shallow nature resulted in flooding when its only outlet through the Lower Bann could not discharge all flood waters. In 1822 it was proposed to remove the locks on either side of the Newry Canal summit in order to allow floodwater to drain through the Upper Bann and down to Newry, with navigation retained. No work resulted, but instead the Lower Bann was made navigable, under a scheme that included lowering the level of the Lough, works on the Upper Bann and Blackwater (themselves linking to the North's canals) and a new 32-mile-long navigation with 6 locks.

The lowest lock on the Lower Bann Navigation, at The Cutts, near Coleraine. The railway bridge above the lock was completed in 1860, only two years after the navigation opened. (McCutcheon Collection)

Work proceeded slowly between 1847 and completion in 1858, with over £144,000 spent on drainage works and £101,000 on navigation. Control of the Lower Bann passed to a trust whose deficits were made up by two local councils. Railway competition soon reduced annual receipts to £70, and navigation inhibited effective drainage, while £10,000 could have been saved had the navigation been abandoned. Despite this, it was kept open in case significant traffics might develop, until 1929, when the Trust was abolished and continuing losses were met by the Stormont Government. Later, control would pass to the Rivers Agency and then to Waterways Ireland in 2000.

Three great rivers, the Shannon, Thames and Severn, need to be dealt with. The latter two were vital to the English canal network, yet neither was improved to a good navigation standard until after the first canal age was past. This failure not only prevented parts of the canal system from functioning as efficiently as they might, but also contributed to their inability to compete with the railways.

The Shannon had much more attention paid to it before 1842, albeit with limited results, and will be dealt with first. The longest river in the British Isles, this includes canal sections and also lakes or loughs, some of considerable size. The upper navigation begins at Lough Allen, with a section to Battlebridge and then via Carrick-on-Shannon to Jamestown. Four loughs, including Lough Ree, 18 miles long, take the navigation to Athlone, whence it passes Shannon Harbour and Lough Derg, (24 miles long) to the end of the middle section at Killaloe. The final section runs to Limerick, below which the estuary begins.

This great river has several natural tributaries, including the Boyle, joining above Carrick-on-Shannon, itself made navigable into and just beyond Lough Key. Eventually three canals were to join it. The Ballinamore & Ballyconnell Canal, an ambitious attempt to connect with Belfast and Newry, opened in 1842, proved a disastrous commercial failure. The Royal Canal from Dublin, completed in 1817, joined 7 miles above Lough Ree. At Shannon Harbour, the Grand Canal from Dublin was opened in 1805, continued from 1828 across the river to Ballinasloe.

Athlone Lock on the Shannon about 1910, part of the improvement works carried out in the 1840s. By this time, traffic above Athlone was minimal. (National Library of Ireland)

Early proposals to make the Shannon navigable preceded even the general Act of 1715. However, work only began in 1755 when Thomas Omer began work on both the Limerick-Killaloe and Upper Shannon sections. The first was an example of opportunistic estimates, insufficient technical supervision and thus highly intermittent progress. It was transferred to the Limerick Navigation Company in 1767, but did not open until 1799, and even then only for small boats. The Directors General of Inland Navigation took over this section in 1803, completed it with three bypass canals, and returned it to the company in 1829. It had cost £96,000 and took craft 74ft by 14ft, but was still imperfect.

Higher up, work on the length from Battlebridge to Lough Allen was not completed until 1822. Between Roosky and Killaloe the river was reputedly navigable in 1769, with locks and half-locks (the latter seemingly the only ones in Ireland). After the remaining by-pass, the Jamestown Canal, was navigable, the whole Jamestown-Killaloe section had been canalised, although the top and important lower sections had to wait until the 1820s to be perfected.

In the 1790s the directors of the Grand Canal considered taking over and improving the middle section from Portumna to Athlone, on the basis of grant assistance. William Jessop reported on the river up to Lough Allen, and the company sought a Government grant of £130,000; a modified scheme received a grant of £54,634 in 1806, just after the Grand Canal opened, and was complete by 1810. However, even after the whole river was open, tonnage was negligible: under 9,000 tons north of Athlone and under 20,000 on the middle Shannon in 1835, with 36,000 tons on the Killaloe-Limerick section in 1836.

Concerns for public works to relieve unemployment, combined with pressure from passenger steamboat interests, produced reports that led to the appointment of Shannon Commissioners under an Act of 1845. They took charge of the whole river, but focused on the middle section, from Killaloe northwards to Battlebridge. They rebuilt this to take steamers of 102ft by 30ft, but left the rest of the river with smaller below dimensions. Traffic improved, so that in 1845, when 16,113 passengers and 105,084 tons were conveyed, 31,537 tons were interchanged with the canals, mostly the Grand. To gain this increase, nearly £600,000 had been spent.

The Severn, but not the Thames, was a free navigation at the beginning of the canal age. Before 1730 the City of London had general responsibility for the Thames, but only strictly exercised this below Staines. The only other authority was the Oxford-Burcot Commission set up in 1624 to improve the navigation between Oxford and Abingdon by building three pound-locks. In 1695, a commission was set up for the river, but only in 1771 did this gain powers to borrow and to regulate charges. Three years later the river downwards from Staines was formally transferred to the City of London. The commissioners were now able to build pound-locks and make towpaths, to buy the old flash-locks and to arrange for regular flashes, on the part above Staines. However, it was provided in the Act that the same tolls as before had to be paid to the owners of the old flash-locks, even though barges passed through new pound-locks on which tolls were also payable. A result of improvement was therefore to turn some old lock owners from mill owners into landowners or publicans, with a second and substantial source of income. Only very slowly over the following decades were the flash-lock owners bought out.

The navigation of the Thames at that time entirely used flash-locks, except for the three pound-locks built in the previous century by the Oxford-Burcot Commission (absorbed by the Thames Commission in 1790). So bad was it in the light of the improved waterway standards set by canals that, in 1770, Brindley proposed a London Canal to avoid a long stretch of the river from Monkey Island below Maidenhead to Isleworth. This project, and another for a Reading-

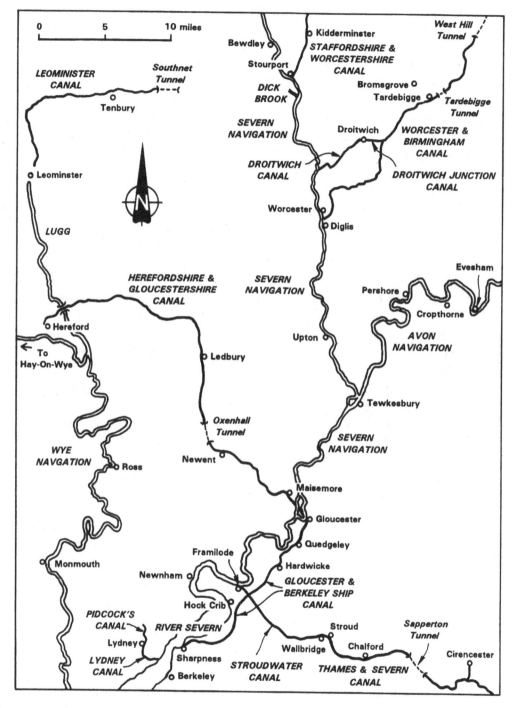

The waterways associated with the Severn, along with those of border England.

Monkey Island canal, gave place to the Act of 1771 to improve the navigation of the river itself. Under this, 8 timber pound-locks were built between Reading and Maidenhead, and then between 1777 and 1795 a new series from above Reading to Oxford. The river between Oxford and Maidenhead, was then in fair condition, but much dredging and the replacement of the old weirs was still needed. This had not prevented the building of the Grand Junction from London to the Oxford Canal at Braunston, providing a broad route that diverted much traffic from the older route via the narrow Oxford and the Thames. Jessop surveyed the upper river, which at that time had no pound-locks, and four bridges with small navigation arches. Osney lock was then built and Radcot bridge enlarged. Five more locks followed, by which time the Thames Commissioners reckoned they had done well by the new and unproven canal. However, they called in the elderly, rather cantankerous but expert Robert Mylne to make a survey. On behalf of the commissioners he wrote: 'I consider the Navigation, across the Island, from the Severn to the Thames, is totally barred and locked up; unless, it is opened by the means herein recommended.'[2]

This question was taken before a Commons committee in 1793, which concluded that the commissioners had both neglected the upper river and opposed canal improvements. One witness, a Thames & Severn shareholder, had complained about the condition of the Thames:

> … that if the Thames was put into as perfect a State as possible he thinks he should receive a fair Dividend for his Money, but now receives none; that the Canal was made in full Confidence that the Commissioners of the Thames Navigation would complete their Navigation by the Time it was opened, but the Proprietors have been disappointed.[3]

Despite this, in 1811 the commissioners stated unrepentantly that the only improvement above Oxford that they favoured was the provision of towing paths, as:

> … the favourable expectations formerly entertained, of the accession of trade, to be expected from the Thames and Severn Canal, have not yet been realised. Of the four canals, namely, the Kington and Leominster, Hereford and Gloucester, Berkeley, and Worcester and Birmingham, which were stated by Mr Josiah Clowes, in his evidence in 1791 [sic], before the House of Commons, as then forming; and all the goods from which were expected to pass down the Thames and Severn Canal, not ONE has yet been finished.[4]

This tactless expression of home truths was too much for the Thames & Severn company, which in 1813 joined with the Wilts & Berks to promote the North Wilts Canal to join them together and so allow narrow boats to avoid the upper

Thames altogether. Much trade then left the Thames, but it is doubtful that it lost much profit. It was not until the 1890s, in the last active days of the Thames & Severn Canal, that a number of new locks were built to bring the upper river to the standard of the lower, or until the twentieth century that the last flash-lock disappeared from it.

By the time that the Thames Conservancy was set up (in 1857 for the part below Staines, until then controlled by the City of London, and in 1866 for the whole river) and modern administration established, the Thames & Severn, Wilts & Berks, Basingstoke and Wey & Arun tributary canals were moribund. The Kennet & Avon had passed into railway ownership and the Londonwards traffic brought from the Midlands by the Oxford Canal had long ago been diverted to the Grand Junction. So low had the commissioners fallen through railway competition that, in their last year of existence, the £100 stock units were valued at 2s. (10p) and the annual income from tolls, which had once been £13,000, was only £3,000. From that time the development of pleasure boating became the main priority.

The story of the Severn shows even less movement still. Throughout the canal age the river had no controlling authority at all, for the Severn Commission was not set up until 1842, and then only for the portion between Stourport and Gloucester. Before the canals the river had been a great artery of trade in spite of its imperfections, and such it remained. For instance in 1797 seventeen trows went weekly between Bristol and Bewdley, and twenty-eight between Bristol and Stourport. Although for the rather abnormal year of 1796 Telford claimed that barges could only be navigated for two months with a paying load, only two serious efforts were made to do something about the river's condition, by the Staffs & Worcs and Gloucester & Berkeley companies.

The Staffs & Worcs Canal entered the river at Stourport, and, when another canal from Birmingham to the Severn, the Worcester & Birmingham, was projected to join the river lower down, the former company obtained an Act in 1790 to deepen the river channel between Stourport and Worcester. This it achieved not by using locks, but by building projecting jetties to increase the speed of the current and thus its scouring effect on the river bottom. However, the boatmen found these obstacles to navigation and they were removed. Lower down, the Gloucester & Berkeley Canal (see Chapter Six) was promoted in 1793 to bypass the worst stretch of the river, where shifting shoals and strong tides made navigation difficult.

One other improvement was carried out under various Acts between 1772 and 1811 to incorporate companies to build horse towing-paths from Shrewsbury to Gloucester. On the Severn, as well as on the Thames and many smaller rivers, the towpath was an addition of the canal era. Before the building of the Gloucester & Berkeley Canal, which was opened in 1827, the trows went up to Gloucester under sail and with the tide, and from there to Worcester and Stourport, partly under sail on the tide and partly by bow-hauling, using gangs of men who could get past the obstructions of the river bank better than horses before the towpath was built. The heavy river barges needed gangs of men just as later they needed teams of horses – as many as twelve horses on one barge was usual on the Thames when working upwards. Before the opening of the Gloucester & Berkeley Canal goods going downstream were normally transhipped to trows at Worcester or Stourport, though a few narrow boats that worked from Stourport or Worcester to Maisemore for the Herefordshire & Gloucestershire Canal, or to Framilode for the Stroudwater and the Thames & Severn canals, were given sails or bow-hauled. Later, bow-hauling died out, and many narrow boats worked down from Stourport or Worcester to Gloucester without transhipping their cargoes.

The only effort at this time to deal with the river channel was by the Severn Navigation Company, formed at Worcester in 1835. Its proposal, for a series of locks and weirs to give 12ft of water to Worcester and 6ft from there to Stourport, affected a number of interests. In favour were the merchants of Worcester, who would have found themselves at the head of a ship canal made up of the Gloucester & Berkeley and the newly deepened Severn from Gloucester to Worcester, and also the Staffordshire & Worcestershire Canal, which was always in trouble because of the lack of water below Stourport to carry its Midlands' goods down to Worcester. Opposition came from the Gloucester & Berkeley Canal and the merchants of Gloucester, who foresaw that the transhipment trade of Gloucester would be transferred to Worcester, and feared that the imposition of charges on the river would in any case injure traffic by waterway. This was also feared by the Worcester & Birmingham proprietors, who sought to divert Midlands traffic from the Staffs & Worcs. After the Bill was thrown out, the Navigation Company proposed a smaller scheme, which was also defeated. The Worcester & Birmingham promoted a Severn Improvement Company to get a depth of 4ft to Worcester only, using two movable weirs.

A compromise was agreed, that the Gloucester & Berkeley would support a Bill for the improvement of the river by public commissioners. The Navigation Company dissolved itself, and a Bill was introduced in 1841, but by then all but the Staffs & Worcs had withdrawn support, fearing damage to the river. Only when it was agreed to put no lock lower than Diglis was the Bill passed in 1842. A commission was then set up, representing the towns and navigation interests, and at last the Severn had a controlling authority. This was to build locks up to Stourport, but the length above, over which it had no authority, steadily lost traffics up to the 1890s. The cause of this decline, railway competition, will be examined in the next chapter.

CHAPTER NINE

War with the Railways

Even before the development of steam locomotion, railways and canals had sometimes competed. Many early railways had been built as feeders to canals, and the early locomotives had been used on such lines – Trevithick's on a canal feeder in South Wales, Stephenson's on a coal line to the Tyne. However, the Surrey Iron Railway had struggled to compete with the Croydon Canal for traffics from the Thames to Croydon. Although a canal had first been proposed, no existing navigation interest was affected by the Stockton & Darlington Railway. During 1824–5 while this was built, a number of railways Bills were promoted, some successful, which foreboded the coming struggle.

For example, in 1824 a meeting in Gloucestershire promoted a railway, for which locomotives were recommended, from Framilode or Frampton by the Severn to Stroud, to be called the Stroud & Severn Rail Road.

It is not quite clear whether the promoters seriously intended to proceed with a railway, for they authorised their committee to begin negotiations with the Stroudwater Navigation for a reduction in rates of tonnage. When the canal company refused to do so, the railway committee decided to go ahead with the promotion of a Bill. This attitude of the railway promoters seriously alarmed the canal company, which stressed that for over forty years their average profit had been less than 6 per cent. However, they agreed to reduce their tonnage rates over the whole length of their navigation from 3s. 6d. (18p) to 2s. 9d. (14p) per ton, and to reduce it by 6d. (3p) if the railway project were abandoned. The railway promoters nevertheless insisted on presenting their Bill in the 1825 Session, saying that:

> … they did not consider the suggested reduction of Tonnage to be a sufficient inducement to them to enter into any negociation [sic] for the abandoning the Railway.[1]

The Bill was opposed by landowners, the Stroudwater and the Thames & Severn Canal companies, and was defeated.

The lesson, for traders, was that only competition could reduce canal tolls, if companies did not exceed those laid down by their Acts. The very high profits of many canal companies, and the refusal of reductions when railway competition threatened – for not all companies were as accommodating as the Stroudwater – led to railways being regarded by the trading public as their saviours from a canal monopoly. The story of the Erewash valley coal trade, told at the Canal Conference of 1888, illustrates the point. While in the 1790s there had been an abortive attempt to link the Leicestershire collieries to Leicester by means of tramroads and a canal through Charnwood Forest, Leicester had only been supplied by the Derbyshire and Nottingham collieries. Then:

> ... the opening of the Swannington line, in 1832, placed the trade in the hands of the West Leicestershire colliery people. A reduction of 3s. 6d. per ton on coal delivered at Leicester, from the Erewash valley, was needed to enable the Derbyshire and Nottinghamshire proprietors to retain the trade. As this traffic amounted to 160,000 tons a year, it was a great question ... whether coal-owners or canal proprietors should make the sacrifice. The Erewash Canal received, for toll and wharfage, 2s. per ton for 12 miles; Loughborough, 3s. per ton for 8 miles; Leicester, 1s. 8d. for 14 miles – total, 6s. 8d. per ton (exclusive of boating and haulage charges) for 34 miles, or 2¼d. per ton per mile. Conferences were held with the canal committees, who decided each to allow a drawback of 6d. per ton 'on such coal only as shall be delivered at Leicester at 10s. per ton'. The coal-owners, who held that the canals should allow 1s., 'promptly rejected' these proposals, and the meeting broke up, with the colliery proprietors determined to free themselves from the monopoly of these canals by making a railway... The result was, the railway secured the traffic to the detriment of the canals, who are now, in 1888, glad to pass coal at 2d. per ton each, or 6d. per ton for the whole 34 miles.[2]

Some felt that the development of railways would overcome the disadvantages of canal transport and foster further industrial growth. As a prize-winning essay at the Ystalyfera Eisteddfod of 1860 asserted about the Swansea Canal:

> It is very often the case for managers of collieries, iron and tin-works, etc., to fail to produce the articles demanded by the order at the specified time for shipment in consequence of the slowness and difficulty of conveyance by canal; and the result is that they have to defray the expenses of the vessel as long as it is detained, and sometimes to make up losses. Now, by railway, these things could be brought from the works to the vessel in less than an hour's notice and this expense prevented. Also, conveyance by rail is safer than by canal. Most merchandise brought and taken along the Canal is liable to be damaged, either by water bursting into the boat, which is seldom devoid of that element, or from exposure to the weather... The Railway, also, is vastly superior to the Canal from its being open for traffic in all kinds of weather. But extremes of heat or cold prevent all communication by canal, the warm weather from scarcity of water, and the cold by reason of the water being frozen up. At such periods traffic is not only checked but the Ystalyfera Forge and Tinworks are stopped from want of coal, which can be obtained no nearer than Pontardawe, it being carbon; and the blast furnaces cannot remain for long without it in the shape of coke. It greatly hinders every work in the Valley; and if these stoppages continue long, they occasion the most pitiful misery by making many a pantry empty.[3]

The lower section of the Swansea Canal, some sixty years after it was acquired by the Great Western Railway, whose line was built so close here as to overshadow the canal. This length was closed and drained after 1928, while the middle portion remained in use by trading craft until 1931. (Boat Museum/The Waterways Trust)

The Swansea Vale Railway was completed up the valley shortly afterwards, and in 1872 the Great Western Railway Company acquired the Swansea Canal, which nevertheless retained much traffic into the twentieth century.

The use of locomotives on a railway that competed directly with navigations began in 1830 when the Liverpool & Manchester Railway was opened. With it a new situation was created, for steam traction brought to the railways two advantages: speed and the ability to haul heavy loads. The waterways bitterly opposed the early railway Acts and made it expensive for the railway shareholders to obtain them. Indeed, inducements had to be offered to them to persuade them to withdraw their opposition.

A curious situation then developed. Early railways were thought of much as if they were land canals: proprietors said they only wished to be toll-takers; and Parliament in some cases empowered any interested carrier to run trains, landowners to make branch lines to connect with the railways, and lords of the manor to use free of charge those parts of the lines that passed through their property. In 1845 the Upper Medway Navigation indeed bought its own locomotive to haul coal trains on the South Eastern Railway, but quickly found that parliamentary powers were little use against the railway's determination not to allow their locomotive to run. On the London & Birmingham all carrying was done by private carrier for a time, the company only providing waggons and engines, while on the Great Western and the Grand Junction Railways carriers competed with the railway company.

Nowadays trade is usually considered in national or international terms, so it is difficult to realise that both early canals and early railways began as essentially local affairs. While many canals had joined up with each other and national systems grew, they continued to be owned by small, independent and jealous units, often competing with one another as well as with rival methods of transport such as roads, coastal shipping and horse tramroads. They were constructed of all sizes and shapes, and traffic passed between them with difficulty.

The railways began in a similar way, as local affairs. The Stockton & Darlington, Liverpool & Manchester and the Canterbury & Whitstable were built to improve communication between two towns, or along a single route. Even the bigger projects, such as the London & Birmingham, were still local in the sense that they were not thought for practical purposes to be part of a national scheme.

Competition therefore began between local waterways and railways for the same passenger and goods traffic between two points, as happened between Manchester and Liverpool. In the 1830s the annual reports of almost every canal company indicated that a railway in competition with that undertaking was projected. An extraordinary general meeting of the Basingstoke proprietors, for example, was called for 22 September 1831: 'to adopt such measures as may be necessary for the Interests of this Company, in regard to the proposed Railway, from London to Southampton.'[4]

Just as the river navigations had bitterly opposed the development of canals, so now canals opposed railway Bills in a way which, until the railway mania of 1845–7, followed a similar pattern. First, pamphleteering, meetings and a little misrepresentation; then petitions and the organizing of parliamentary opposition; then, if the canal was important enough, compensation or possibly purchase. In 1835 the Kennet & Avon Committee reported that

> The necessity of watching and opposing the Great Western Railway Bill, during the last two years, has materially added to the law expenses of the company; but the committee beg to inform the proprietors, that such arrangements have been made as rendered unnecessary a continuance of opposition to the Bill, and as cannot, in the opinion of the committee, fail (if the bill should pass) to be satisfactory to the proprietors.[5]

These arrangements consisted of a payment of £10,000 by the railway company, less the value of lands transferred to the railway. Since the gross annual receipts of the canal company for the previous five years had averaged £45,213, the compensation payment was not large and reflected the bad bargaining position of the canal.

The railway Bills having been obtained, the canal companies then gained a few years of extra prosperity by carrying the materials to build their rivals' lines. One bizarre instance of new traffic was the carriage of a railway engine, in sections, along the Newry Canal to the Great Northern Railway at Portadown, just before the parallel railway line was completed in 1852. Competition affected passenger-carrying and fly-boat services first.

The receipts of the Kennet & Avon grew to a peak of £48,269 in 1840. Then the railway opened, and takings dropped in three years to £32,045, caused not by a loss of tonnage but by the drastic cut in tolls necessary to keep the traffic.

Price cutting was the most common competitive weapon, and it was sometimes taken to the point where a weak canal company charged no toll at all, only freight charges being taken by the carriers. At the same time steps were taken to improve the service, as when in 1844 the Gloucester & Berkeley Company agreed to a proposal from Pickfords, the carriers, that trows should be permitted to move at all hours of the night to expedite carriage and so enable water carriers to compete more successfully with the railways.

This lengthening of permitted hours for lock and tunnel working, sometimes to the extent of 24 hour working, combined with the religious revival and moral reform movements of the 1830s, brought pressures on canal companies against Sunday canal work. In 1839, for instance, 140 boatmen at Shardlow petitioned the Trent & Mersey Company to close the canal on Sunday, and in the next year the company in turn petitioned Parliament 'for the general prevention of Traffic on all Canals and Railways on Sundays'.[6] The Lancaster and Worcester & Birmingham companies took the same view. Protests against Sunday working also came in from canalside towns, such as Stourport in 1839. Companies varied in their attitudes: on the Manchester to Wakefield line the Calder & Hebble closed its line on Sundays from 1836, but the Rochdale did not agree and, in one instance, defended a boatman accused by the Calder & Hebble of contravening their by-law.

Most of the revenue of the early railways was made from passenger carrying – rather against the railway companies' expectations – the heavier goods remaining for the time being on the canals, though at a lower rate of toll. In 1843 the railways received £3,110,257 from the carriage of passengers and £1,424,932 from goods. In 1848 the receipts from passengers had risen to £5,720,382 and those from goods had reached £4,213,169. Canal dividends had by then suffered little from the railway competition that so far existed: the Oxford paid 25 per cent in 1846, compared to 32 per cent in 1833; the Trent & Mersey 30 per cent compared to 37½ per cent.

There are close parallels between the development of canals and early railways. The building of isolated lines demonstrated the success of the new form of transport, followed by an investment mania. Between 1830, when the first really successful locomotive railway opened, and 1844, was a time of construction of

BRECON AND ABERGAVENNY
CANAL NAVIGATION.

REDUCTION
of
TONNAGES.

From and after the First day of February, 1863, the Rates, Tolls, & Tonnages, payable to the Company, in respect of their Canal and Railways, will be as follow:

Coal & Coke ....heretofore 2d. per Ton per Mile, will be ¾d. per Ton per Mile.					
Lime & Limestone	»	1d. »	»	»	¾d. » »
Pitwood, Cordwood, & Sleepers	»	1½d. »	»	»	1d. » »
Round Timber, Deals, Pine, Lath, Helves, &c.	»	1½d. »	»	»	1¼d. » »
Iron, Iron Mine, Iron Ore, Cinders, Slates, } Stone, Clay, & Bricks.................... }	»	1d. »	»	»	¾d. » »
Hay, Straw, & Compost.	»	1d. »	»	»	1d. » »
Goods and other Merchandise not above described.	»	2¼d. »	»	»	1½d. » »

Canal Office,
Llanelly, Nr. Abergavenny,
January, 29th, 1863.

By Order,

GEORGE L. HILEY,
Clerk to the Company of Proprietors

PRINTED BY J. HILEY MORGAN, HIGH STREET, ABERGAVENNY.

An example of heavy price-cutting, in the face of railway competition which was affecting traffics on the Brecon & Abergavenny. Two years later this amalgamated with the connecting Monmouthshire Canal, which was in turn acquired by the Great Western Railway in 1880. There was very little traffic on either canal after that.

varied lines. Towards the end of this period the importance of through routes and the need to capture spheres of influence were seized on by such enterprising railway directors as George Hudson, and so the railway mania began. This involved a mad scramble to promote companies and to acquire competitors. 23 railway Acts were passed in 1843, 48 in 1844 and 108 in 1845. Competitors were either other railways or canals. Railway directors saw little difference between either type of competitors, both of which threatened the aspirations created by the dividends of the Stockton & Darlington or the Liverpool & Manchester.

The Government at first doubted the wisdom of allowing an unrestricted amalgamation policy, whether of railways with railways, or of railways with canals, and it was laid down that the Board of Trade must examine all amalgamation Bills to determine whether they were in the public interest. The tide was, however, coming in too strongly, and the decision was soon reversed, with no further attempt to control the leasing or sale of one line of transport by another until the railway mania was over. The policy of control had, however, reversed the leasing in 1843 of the Calder & Hebble to the Manchester & Leeds Railway, following protests by the Aire & Calder.

In 1846 a Commons committee recommended precautions to be taken before railway and canal amalgamations were allowed, such as the provision in authorizing Acts to ensure low maximum canal tolls, and to ensure that railway-owned canals were kept in repair and supplied with water. Although an Act then set up a policing Railway Commission, laissez-faire ideas led to the transfer of its duties to the Board of Trade in 1851.

Parliament then sought that railways and waterways should compete on an equal footing. Canal companies' Acts had bound them to charge the same tolls for each mile of the line, and not to discriminate between customers. This rigidity was somewhat lessened by drawbacks on tolls for cargoes carried a minimum distance, and discounts for those passing a minimum annual tonnage over the canal. However, when a railway Bill of 1844 sought powers to vary tolls, representatives of canal companies, led by the Aire & Calder, met in London, calling themselves the United Body of Canal Proprietors.

Canal companies' Acts, unlike those for railways, neither specifically authorised nor forbade them from operating carrying craft. Some companies had carried extensively, others occasionally, while companies like the Trent & Mersey had operated through nominally independent firms, like Hugh Henshall & Co. In their carrying role they could quote ad hoc rates, which they could not do as toll-takers. This anomaly must have worried the United Body, which drafted two Bills. What became the Canal Tolls Act of 1845 allowed canal companies to charge different rates per ton-mile on different parts of their line, though these varied rates had to apply equally to all. The Canal Carriers' (or Clauses) Act enabled companies to carry and provide towage services on their own or other waterways, though not to discriminate between customers in doing so. This second Act also empowered companies to make traffic agreements with railway or other canal companies and to lease themselves to any other canal or navigation company. The implications of this were not then seen. In 1847 a third Act enabled companies to borrow money to set up carrying departments.

Very few companies seem to have perceived any general waterway interest opposed to a general railway interest, or any war between both kinds of transport. An exception was the Staffs & Worcs, which in 1845 drafted this circular letter (probably never sent) to other companies:

An experience of seventy years has established the utility and importance of Inland Water Communication. It has become intimately interwoven with the great manufacturing, trading, and agricultural industry of this country, and has been mainly instrumental to the development of its resources and the growth of its power and importance. But although your Committee are quite ready to admit the advantage and necessity of Railways as a great step in advance of the old modes of conveyance for passengers and many articles of commerce, they conceive that a stoppage of any part of the great chain of inland water communication, would cripple the whole system and produce irremediable mischief to the interests of the Canals and Navigable Rivers and to those of the Community at large … they afford to the public the only salutary check to and control over those charges and regulations which the Railway Companies may at pleasure impose if left uncontrolled by such check.[7]

A month later, however, when it seemed likely that the Regent's, Warwick & Birmingham and Warwick & Napton canals would all be bought for conversion to railways, such a powerful company as the Grand Junction could write mildly to the Board of Trade saying that:

> … altho' this Committee is not aware that any reasonable objection can be urged to the whole, or even the greater portion, of any thorofare line of Canals being converted into Railways, it is to be hoped that with a view to protect the inland navigation of the Country Her Majesty's Government will be disposed to oppose in Parliament, the principle of partial conversion.[8]

The first incident of the war with the railways was a case of desertion to the enemy, for in 1831 the Manchester, Bolton & Bury Canal proprietors obtained an Act authorizing them to make a railway at or near the line of the canal, and altering their name to the Company of Proprietors of the Manchester, Bolton & Bury Canal Navigation & Railway. Following a successful takeover bid by a group of railway promoters, it was decided not to turn the canal into a railway, as intended, but to build a railway, opened in 1838, alongside the waterway routes. The com-

The Royal Canal at Pike Bridge, near Maynooth, in 1965 (shortly after closure). The second bridge carries the parallel railway, demonstrating how closely it followed the canal. After closure this would prevent the blocking of the canal by the removal of road bridges, since any new road crossings between Dublin and Mullingar had to clear the railway line, and culverting, which affected several crossings in County Longford, did not take place. (Ruth Heard)

pany amalgamated in 1846 with the Manchester & Leeds Railway, which soon changed its name to the Lancashire & Yorkshire.

Other canal companies later followed this example and turned themselves into railways, among them the Ellesmere & Chester, Liskeard & Looe Union, Thames & Medway, Monmouthshire, and the Carlisle. The important Don company followed its own path in order to dominate south Yorkshire traffic, on the one hand absorbing three other waterways – the Stainforth & Keadby, Dearne & Dove and Sheffield canals – while on the other encouraging the formation of what became the South Yorkshire, Doncaster & Goole Railway. In 1850 the Don Company amalgamated with this line to form the South Yorkshire Railway & River Don Company, which operated as a combined rail-waterway transport concern until it was leased in 1864 by the Manchester, Sheffield & Lincolnshire Railway, after which the waterway side of the business became much less important.

Before the mania, only two more waterways had been sold or leased to a railway company. The Croydon was bought in 1836 by the London & Croydon Railway for conversion, and the Kensington was vested in the West London in 1839 and partly converted. By 1845, two factors were at work, the first being the railways that wished to eliminate a competitor, and used their shareholders' money to this end. The second were canal proprietors who had seen the early warning of what railway competition implied, and who were often anxious to sell out before profits declined. In 1845 five navigations, beginning with the Norwich & Lowestoft, with a total length of 78 miles, came under railway control; in 1846 seventeen totalling 774 miles, and in 1847 six totalling 96 miles. These figures include the canals that turned themselves into railways. In these three years about four-fifths of the mileage of all railway-controlled canals was acquired, amounting to one-fifth of all the navigable waterways in Great Britain. These included the 160 miles of the Birmingham Canal Navigations and the 204 miles of the Shropshire Union system, on which railway control did not become effective for some time.

There was one curious case of the reverse process – of a canal company that leased a railway. Carrying on the Lancaster Canal had risen from 459,000 tons in 1825 to 617,000 tons in 1840, when it was seriously affected by the opening of the Lancaster & Preston Railway. In 1842 the canal company therefore acquired a 21-year lease of the Lancaster & Preston, for an annual rent of £13,300. From 1846 the Lancaster & Carlisle Railway threatened trade, so in 1848 the Lancaster & Preston agreed to sell itself to the Lancaster & Carlisle, paying the canal proprietors £4,875 annually for the surrender of their lease. In 1859 the lines were leased (and later sold) to the London & North Western Railway, and in 1864 the northern part of the canal too was leased to the LNWR and sold outright in 1885. The separate southern part from Walton Summit to Wigan, which was used by the Leeds & Liverpool Canal route, was leased to that company.

Whereas railway competition greatly affected Irish waterways, most of which were economically less secure than those in Britain, only one waterway was bought by a railway, and another leased for a time. The Royal Canal, less prosperous than the Grand Canal, accepted an offer to purchase from the Midland Great Western, at some £300,000, 40 per cent of its written-down capital and over one-fifth of original cost. The railway needed canalside land to build their line for over 50 miles between Dublin and Mullingar. The purchase was authorised in 1845, and the Royal stayed open, but in decline.

The same railway then tried to acquire the Grand Canal. The Grand had been working a haphazardly observed rates agreement with the rival Great Southern & Western since 1847. In 1850 the GS&WR ended the agreement, and offered to buy the canal in 1852, but the Grand accepted a higher offer from the Midland Great Western. The Bill to authorise this purchase was defeated by GS&WR opposition, and the MGW then leased the Grand Canal for 7 years from 1853. While the lease was in force, the two railways agreed to buy the canal jointly, but the MGW had been losing money on it. Thus, when in 1860 the proposed canal rates seemed too low, the acquisition Bill was dropped and the Grand Canal Company took over again, negotiating rates agreements with both railways.

Railways bought canals for three reasons: because they could not get their Bills without coming to an arrangement with their principal opponents; because they were actual or potential competitors; and because they wanted to use the line of the canal for a railway.

The purchase of some canals was authorised as part of the Bill giving powers to a railway company to construct its line. These included the Stratford-upon-Avon, the Stourbridge Extension, the Ashby de la Zouch and the Cromford, which were in a strong bargaining position and also able to ensure that the railway acquisition did the least possible harm to other waterway interests. For instance in the Act for the sale of the Ashby Canal, in 1846, it was laid down that the maximum tolls charged should not exceed the railway charges, and that:

> … if, owing to railway competition, coal from the Moira collieries is diverted from the Oxford Canal (which is a continuation of the Coventry Canal, and is in communication of course with the Ashby Canal), and in order to meet such diversion the Oxford Canal lower their tolls for this traffic, then the Midland Railway must lower the tolls on the Ashby Canal proportionately, provided that the tolls shall not be reduced below ¼d. per ton per mile… There is a further clause to this effect, that if any one or more of the canals forming the route to London, combine to reduce their rates, the Midland Company are bound to reduce the tolls on the Ashby Canal correspondingly.[9]

The situation envisaged in this Act later came about.

Many canal companies, when opposition to railway Bills had not brought an acceptable offer, or which were at first prepared to 'ride the whirlwind', later doubted their ability to compete and tried to move the railway companies to make a proposal. One way of doing this was to promote a Bill for a rival railway. Thus, in 1845, the Kennet & Avon considered converting their canal to a railway. It was with crocodile tears the following year that:

> The Committee regret to report the loss of the Bill which was applied for in the present Session of Parliament ... for making the London, Newbury and Bath Direct Railway, in conjunction with the Kennet and Avon Canal, but they trust that as a General Meeting will be shortly held, the explanations which will there be given, of the arrangement come to with the Great Western Railway Company and the Wilts, Somerset and Weymouth Railway Company, will be satisfactory.[10]

In 1852 the Great Western Railway finally agreed to take over the canal for a payment capitalised at £210,415. The capital cost of the waterway had been just over £1 million, but the highest dividend paid had been 3¾ per cent, and since the railway had been opened the usual distribution had been under 1 per cent.

Railways were sometimes forced to acquire canals after competition developed, and caused railway losses. The completion of the Bristol & Exeter through Taunton in 1844, and especially its Tiverton branch in 1848, brought direct competition with the Grand Western Canal from Taunton to Tiverton.

After 1845 the Grand Western was unable to pay its mortgage interest and had to maintain itself with further loans. It became a matter of life or death to defeat the railway, but a forlorn hope. The canal proceeded to cut rates against the railway, the Grand Western cutting tolls on coal from Taunton to Tiverton around 1851 to enable the canal traders to sell coal at Tiverton at the same price as the railway delivered. Later the traders were able to carry coal free of any toll. The railway lost money, but was able to recoup losses elsewhere. Only the Tiverton coal consumers benefited.

The extent of the price cutting can be seen by comparing the figures for tolls and tonnage in the years 1849 and 1853. In each year the canal carried 37,000 tons, but while it received £2,351 in tolls in 1849, this had fallen to £734 in 1853. The canal company had, however, succeeded in raising the tonnage carried on the through haul from Taunton to Tiverton from 1,961 in 1850 to 4,373 in 1852.

It was estimated that the railway was losing £6,000 a year as a result of the competition, so both parties were anxious to come to terms, and did so after the railway had opened negotiations with the Bridgwater & Taunton Canal, so threatening the source of the Grand Western's coal supplies.

The railway refused to buy the canal but agreed to lease it for £2,000 a year, and in 1853 the tolls on it and on the Bridgwater & Taunton were raised to the full parliamentary levels, while the railway charges rose also. Traffic then left the canal almost entirely, and ten years later, when it was clear that the canal company was unable to revive its business, the railway made an offer for its purchase of £30,000, which was accepted. The Taunton to Holcombe Rogus portion was

HEREFORDSHIRE AND GLOUCESTERSHIRE CANAL.

In the Matter of The Newent Railway Act, 1873, and

In the Matter of The Ross and Ledbury Railway Act, 1873.

TAKE NOTICE, that in pursuance of the powers in that behalf contained in the Newent Railway Act, 1873, and the Ross and Ledbury Railway Act, 1873, it is intended on and after the 30th day of June, 1881,

TO STOP UP AND CLOSE

so much and such part of the CANAL known as the Herefordshire and Gloucestershire Canal as is situate BETWEEN the Worcester and Hereford Railway at LEDBURY in the County of Hereford and the River Severn in the City of GLOUCESTER, and that all rights of way or navigation and other rights and privileges if any along, upon, or over such part of the said Canal with the Banks and Towing Path will as from the said 30th day of June cease and determine accordingly.

AND FURTHER TAKE NOTICE, that all persons who will be affected by the closing of the said portion of the Canal are required, on or before the said 30th day of June, to remove their Barges, Boats, and other Craft accordingly.

Dated this 2nd day of June, 1881.

BY ORDER,

Waterlow and Sons Limited, Printers, London Wall, London.

One of the later closures of a canal to allow a railway to be built along its site. It was rumoured that the section from Ledbury to Hereford, which opened in 1845, was constructed so that its line could be converted to a railway. However, it was the older section which was converted to a railway. The isolated section north of Ledbury remained in use until 1882.

dismantled, but the part that carried the stone traffic from Holcombe Rogus was preserved. This isolated local traffic continued until 1924.

Lastly, in a few cases canals were bought or leased in order that they could be converted into railways, the rails being laid along their banks, such as the Croydon, Aberdeenshire, Glastonbury, Oakham, Andover and part of the Leominster. Others were proposed for this purpose, like the Shropshire Union.

Financially the waterways that sold out made no bad bargain for their shareholders, who fared far better than did most of those who remained owners of independent canals. For instance the Stratford-upon-Avon, owing to construction costs far above the estimate, had never been a great success. Authorised in 1793, it was not completed until 1816 and paid no dividend until 1824, after which this rose to a maximum for seven years. The Oxford, Worcester & Wolverhampton Railway paid the owners of bonds and shares £160,434 for their interests, when the canal had cost £300,000. However, it acquired the small Stourbridge Extension Canal for more than its stated capital value. The proprietors of the Cromford Canal, which had cost about £79,000 to build before the wartime rise of prices had become severe, judiciously agreed during the railway mania to sell to the Manchester, Buxton, Matlock & Midlands Junction Railway before the most seriously competitive line, the Erewash Valley Railway, was opened in 1847. Since by 1850 the canal tolls had fallen from £14,198 in 1840 to £7,588, although the traffic had only fallen from 346,208 tons to 284,889 tons, the Cromford Canal Company was perhaps lucky to get £103,500 for the property.

The Fossdyke and Witham Navigations were both leased to the Great Northern Railway, for 999 years at £10,545 per annum, and interest on mortgages in the latter case. These rents were calculated on the basis of the previous three years profits, plus 5 per cent. These payments continued after nationalization, the right to receive the Fossdyke rent, of a 894 years' unexpired lease at £9,570 per annum, being auctioned in 2004.

The canals that the railways acquired while they were consolidating their position became, in most cases, an embarrassment to them. The companies were bound to maintain them in good order by statute, and therefore many waterways were fortunately kept in more or less navigable condition up to the time of nationalization; they would have decayed if they had remained in private hands.

Railway companies naturally wished to carry traffic by rail and not by water, since otherwise they would have been maintaining a competition with themselves. Partly by intention and partly by neglect, the general effect of high tolls, a lack of dredging, closures for leisurely repairs, failure to provide ice-breaking, and a general failure to modernise and develop, decaying warehouses and wharves, failure to provide or maintain cranes and no effort to obtain business served to divert trade from the water to the land.

There were exceptions, either because the canals were indispensable for certain purposes or because they served an area or attracted traffic not otherwise available to the railway company. The two most important were the Birmingham Canal Navigations and the Shropshire Union system.

The Birmingham Canal Navigations came under railway control by deferred action. The canal company was a powerful one with a near monopoly position in the Birmingham area. This had been strengthened by its amalgamation in 1840 with the Wyrley & Essington, followed by two new links between the Walsall and Wednesbury lines of each. Yet the beginnings of railway competition caused strain, and when the London & Birmingham Railway Company proposed a joint venture for a railway taking in Birmingham, Wolverhampton and Dudley, the canal company agreed. Because the Dudley Canal Company would obviously be affected, an amalgamation was arranged in 1846 between the two waterway concerns, a second railway, the Shrewsbury & Birmingham, being taken into the partnership. In 1846 the canal company subscribed to the new railway, the Birmingham, Wolverhampton & Stour Valley, and at the same time came to an arrangement with the London and Birmingham Railway, by which the latter would guarantee the dividends of the canal company at 4 per cent. If the canal company earnings were sufficient to not require this guarantee, the canal directors had the casting vote; if not, the railway directors would have the casting vote.

The railway/canal interchange basin at Hockley, off the Soho Branch of the Birmingham Canal, opened at the same time as the adjacent railway. Cargoes were exchanged here with the Great Western Railway; railway-owned craft were used until 1954. (Boat Museum)

After 1874 the canal income never reached a sum enough to pay 4 per cent, and the company came under continuous railway control. However, in the original agreement a clause provided that the canal company should not vary its tolls without the consent of the railway, which thus gained much immediate advantage in the competition for business.

In 1878 the then chairman asserted that:

> The company would concur in thinking that the directors had done wisely in placing themselves under the tutelage of the L.& N.W.R. instead of leaving themselves to contend against the continually increasing encroachments of the railways, which were now more than ever going on in the district. They might rest under the shadow of the £4 per share which the L.& N.W.R. Company guaranteed to them.[11]

The Birmingham Canal case illustrates that any united waterway interest was hard to sustain, given the different problems faced by each self-interested company. In December 1844 the Staffs & Worcs, one of the few canals that maintained an anti-railway policy throughout the mania year of 1845, proposed a meeting with the Birmingham 'to confer on the propriety of arranging a Coalition of the Canals in this District, in opposition to the projected Lines of Railway'.[12] The meeting took place, a joint fund was set up and agreement reached to oppose railway Bills at

Chirk Aqueduct on the Shropshire Union Canal, with Chirk Tunnel in the distance. The parallel railway viaduct, opened in 1848, was constructed by the Shrewsbury & Chester Railway, which rapidly became a rival to the London & North Western Railway Company which owned the Shropshire Union. Traffic, including regular flyboats to Llangollen, was organized in Shropshire Union craft until 1921.

any rate up to second reading. Sadly, only a fortnight later the Birmingham had had second thoughts, in the light of the moves by the London & Birmingham Railway, and wrote to say that 'under all the Circumstances ... [it is] no longer expedient to carry on any united opposition to the various projected Railways'.[13]

The BCN remained busy after railway control began and into the later twentieth century. To access the growing Cannock coalfield, the important Cannock Extension and Wyrley Bank branches were built from the 1850s, as was the Netherton Tunnel with a double towpath, that opened in 1858. However, the large tonnages carried on these canals mask a major change in the nature of traffic. Birmingham and the Black Country area were intersected by this elaborate network of 160 miles of canal, with over 500 private basins, and hundreds of works located on their banks. These depended on the waterway for their coal and raw material supplies, and in many cases for the removal of their finished products. It would have been impossible to divert all of this traffic from canal to rail without causing intense dislocation, since in many cases the construction of rail sidings was impossible in such a crowded area. Instead the railway policy was to use the canal like the road – for a collection and delivery service. Instead of goods being sent from the canalside works for long hauls by waterway to London, Hull or Liverpool, they were sent by water to a railway basin, where they were transferred to rail for the remainder of their voyage. In 1905 it was suggested that between 53 and 63 per cent of goods transhipped could not have completed their journey by waterway. Taken in reverse, the figures show what a large tonnage could in fact have remained on the water for long hauls.

The earliest BCN railway basin opened in 1845, but their provision accelerated from 1855, with the last significant one built in 1908. Goods only remained on water for short distances in the BCN area. In 1905, 7,546,453 tons were conveyed on the BCN, but 1,108,127 tons involved railway basins, and only 1,376,165 tons moved outside the system. Three major railway companies, the Midland, Great Western and London & North Western, built basins.

Within these limits the Birmingham Canal Navigations were well maintained and improved. The widening and deepening of channels, widening under bridges, installation of new pumping machinery and extensive walling of banks were all carried out under railway control. This showed a gross profit on canal working as well as an indirect gain to the railway system. Thus, in 1905 gross receipts were £190,873 and the working expenses £99,207, but the balance was enough to pay the guaranteed 4 per cent dividend to the shareholders and £39,861 was paid to the canal company by the railway company.

Railway interchange basins were also developed on other waterways outside the West Midlands, such as the Ashton Canal and canals in London.

The Shropshire Union system, which afterwards controlled over 200 miles of waterway, was authorised in 1846 to include the Ellesmere & Chester (already united with the Birmingham & Liverpool Junction), Shrewsbury and the two parts of the Montgomeryshire Canal. The object of the company, in which two railways were given powers to hold stock, was to convert part of the canal line to railway and to build certain new lines of railway. One of these lines, from Wellington to Stafford, was in fact built. Then in 1847 the whole system was leased to the London & North Western Railway, and later part of the Shropshire Canal was added. Since this system covered an area not fully served by the railway owner it was encouraged to receive trade. Later, when the Manchester Ship Canal was built, Ellesmere Port, which had been the outlet on the Mersey for the canal system, now became a port on the ship canal. This fact was important enough to persuade the railway to operate the canal as fully as possible, as supplementary to their own system, and to avoid a loss on the heavy maintenance cost of the waterways. The railway company spent over £250,000 on new quays, warehouses and a barge dock at Ellesmere Port, and themselves became carriers on the canal. In 1905 469,950 tons were carried, having increased from 371,978 tons in 1898. After deducting the cost of maintenance and the carrying business the company was still making a trading profit of £6,765, but without any contribution towards interest on capital.

When the railway mania ended in 1847 the greater part of those canals that were destined to pass into railway ownership had already done so. Only fifteen more, with a mileage of 300 miles, were subsequently transferred, though others came

DERWENT NAVICATION.

NOTICE IS HEREBY GIVEN,

That it is intended to commence some Repairs and Alterations at **Stamford-Bridge Lock** on the River Derwent, on *Monday the 16th of July instant;* On and after which day no Vessels can pass the said Lock to and from Malton until further Notice.

The stoppage is expected not to exceed a Month.

MALTON, 2nd July, 1849.

C. SMITHSON, PRINTER, YORKERSGATE, MALTON.

A stoppage notice for the rural Derwent Navigation, some five years before its owner, Earl Fitzmilliam, sold out to railway interests. When the threat of railway competition first became evident, the earl had improved the river by dredging; but by 1849, despite reductions in tolls, traffic was so light that a lengthy stoppage would not prove a major inconvenience.

under railway direction for a time. Of three taken over by the end of the nineteenth century, the lines of the Glasgow, Paisley & Ardrossan, Forth & Cart, and Somersetshire Coal canals were all extensively used to construct new railways. On the former, the Blackhall Aqueduct, completed in 1811 and now a viaduct, is the oldest such structure still in use on a functioning railway.

On the rest of the canal network, which continued an independent existence in competition with railways, long hauls fell away, and those canals which had many factories and other customers on their banks tended to survive. Often most earnings came from only small parts of the line, in urban and industrial areas. These benefited from the long period before users changed to better forms of transport. In cities such as Manchester, Birmingham and London, factories had lined canals for up to 80 years, and it was often impossible to build sidings. As was written in 1836 about Manchester:

Railroads have one disadvantage in the carriage of coal for manufactories, which appears likely to give the canals a permanent superiority over them in this branch of traffic. The banks of the latter being generally studded with manufactories (to which such a supply of water as canals afford is indisputable); coals conveyed in boats is lodged without any second expense, at their very doors. The railroads are otherwise circumstanced. The coal is necessarily deposited regularly at the 'stations', whence it must be carted to its destination...[14]

The advantage sometimes lay with the canal, though usually only if it reduced both freights and tolls. It was clear to most manufacturers, however, that the railways were more efficient and offered a wider distribution system. Therefore new factories tended to be situated alongside the rails rather than the waterway, and branches were built where a change in the type of transport used was practicable. Indeed, it was often the case with an industrial canal that it was not the original line of competing railway that did the serious damage to traffic, it was the subsequent building of branches and sidings into successive works which had formerly sent their goods by canal.

While the industrial canals kept their tonnage at the expense of their receipts, the independent waterways that ran through agricultural districts and had few works on their banks (like the Wilts & Berks), or the heavily locked long-haul canals such as those over the Pennines (like the Rochdale), mostly succumbed sooner or later to the competition of the railway. During the railway mania, and afterwards, the railway companies had brought under their control over one fifth of the navigable waterways of Britain. In the century between the mania and nationalization another quarter was driven out of active existence by the competition of newer forms of transport: first railways, then motor lorries. It was the relentlessness of this pressure, quite as much as the actual purchase of waterways by railways, that broke up the waterway system and forced it back to the regional and local trade from which it had sprung. The expansion of trade would leave the waterways with a significant but declining share of specialised traffics.

CHAPTER TEN

The Years of Decline

The completion of the Birmingham & Liverpool Junction Canal in 1835 marked the end of major developments in the first canal age. This canal represented Telford's attempt to show that an improved form of canal, straight and comparatively level, even if narrow, could compete with a railway. However, it cost so much more than the estimate and involved embankment problems that it became doubtful that it would open.

Some waterways were built later, including the Tame Valley and Netherton Tunnel lines of the BCN; the Chard Canal from the Bridgwater & Taunton Canal to Chard; the final section of the Herefordshire & Gloucestershire Canal to Hereford; the Droitwich Junction to join the Worcester & Birmingham and older Droitwich Canals; the Ballinamore & Ballyconnell Canal in Ireland; and later, the unfinished Romford Canal, and the New Junction Canal (see Chapter Eleven) in Yorkshire. In addition, some branches were built to existing lines, notably the Bentley, Rushall and Cannock Extension Canals on the BCN system, and the Slough Branch of the Grand Junction.

The previous chapter dealt with those canals which were acquired or defeated by railways. Some independent waterways continued to compete, through choice or because no railway company was rich enough to buy them out.

The Oxford Canal had been built before the Napoleonic Wars inflated construction costs, and had been prosperous as soon as it was completed in 1790. It also benefited when the opening of the Grand Junction made part of its line a link in the through route from London to Birmingham, because of the substantial compensation payment to which it became entitled. If by 1870 the affairs of the waterways had attained some sort of stability with the railways, it is clear that the Oxford had in fact lost no traffic. The 450,000 tons carried in 1828 increased to 520,000 in 1838, partly due to the carriage of railway construction materials. Then the railway drove down traffic for twenty years, after which improvements in trade and to the waterway itself brought a revival to 482,000 tons in 1868.

However, the Oxford's financial position deteriorated, as its tonnages were maintained at the expense of a steady decrease in tolls and compensation receipts, and thus in dividends. It had been in a good position at the beginning of this period, shown by toll receipts of £92,962 and a dividend of 32 per cent in 1830. Receipts halved by 1850, with the dividend reduced to 20 per cent. Although traffic increased, by 1870 tolls amounted only to £23,632 and a dividend of 8 per cent. No exact comparisons can be made, however, because of variations in tolls on the kind of goods carried and in the length of hauls, but trade changed and traffics became more local.

The three great interchange points of Hawkesbury (to the Coventry Canal), Braunston (to the Grand Junction Canal) and Napton Junction (for Birmingham) had accounted in 1830 for 67 per cent of the total receipts. By 1869 the long hauls had fallen away so far that the proportion of total receipts taken at these three points had dropped to 47 per cent, Hawkesbury having suffered least and Napton Junction most. Oxford had little interchange traffic with the Thames within the period of comparison and must be counted as a local centre. Trade to Oxford, Enslow, Aynho, Cropredy and Hillmorton (for Rugby) had fallen away heavily owing to railway competition, but where that competition was less, takings could be maintained, as at Banbury, or indeed increased, as at Stretton.

The Oxford was a major canal that formed part of important through lines of waterway. The Stour was a minor river not joined to any other navigation. Yet this small concern, through whose minute and account books run the names of Gainsboroughs and Constables, met the railway threat, made the most of a good competitive position and survived into the twentieth century.

The Stour Navigation from Manningtree to Sudbury had been authorised by an Act of 1705 and by 1835 was paying a dividend of 14 per cent on its nominal capital of £4,800. On 10 February of that year the minute book recorded the appointment of a surveyor to investigate and report on the state of the river, and stated:

> That it be a particular instruction to the surveyor that his attention be drawn to the possibility of there being shortly established two lines of Rail Roads through Colchester and Bury Saint Edmunds to Yarmouth and Norwich, and how they are likely to affect the interests of all parties concerned.

The proprietors at once got back the lease of the tolls from a lessee who had held them for many years, and proceeded to manage the river themselves. They decided to abolish all staunches, build a number of new locks, dredge and clean the river, improve the towing-paths, cut tolls and revise schedules of rates. The improvements were paid for partly by issuing new shares and partly by taking considerable amounts from revenue during two and a half years when no dividends were paid. The result of these measures of reconstruction was to increase the rate of dividend on the larger capital to 20 per cent in 1840 and 30 per cent in 1846.

In 1845 a railway company offered to buy the shares, and the proprietors with spirit offered them at £1,000 each, the market price having reached £850. They seem to have been sure that the railway would accept the offer, but it was refused, and the proprietors began a long and losing battle. They had the advantage of connection with the sea, and thus could handle seaborne imports, mainly of foreign corn for the mills along the river, and coal for Sudbury and other towns. Exports, chiefly flour, and also bricks from Sudbury for the building of the suburbs of south London, also went by sea for many years. They reduced tolls when they had to, attained every possible competitive advantage from quoting special rates, kept the river in good repair and even experimented with a steam barge. Though the gross income from tolls, which had reached £3,415 in 1847, was less than £2,000 in 1849, it did not actually fall below £1,000 until 1869. A dividend of 15 per cent was still being paid in 1863, and of 6 per cent in 1871. The last, of 1½ per cent, was declared for 1890.

Renewed interest in waterways in 1888 brought a moment of hope, when a vague proposal was made to join the Stour with the Ouse and the Cam. Thereafter mills began to close, the new county councils set up in 1888 began to insist on more expensive standards of maintenance for bridges, and money to keep the navigation alive and in repair was only found from sales of land and property. At last, in 1913, the shareholders resolved to wind up the company. It was revived, unsuccessfully, as a public trust in 1918, and again collapsed in 1935. While a campaign for revival began in 1947, only limited restoration has resulted.

Other concerns, which at the onset of railway competition lacked the small capital burdens and high earning power of waterways such as the Oxford and the Stour, found that, by being forced to cut their tolls, their receipts gradually became less than their maintenance costs. Such costs became a significant factor as they rose through the century and often accompanied falling revenue per ton carried. The Basingstoke company, for example, had estimated in 1787 that 30,700 tons were carried for £7,783 receipts, or 5.07s per ton carried. In 1801–2 actual tonnage was 18,737 and tolls 4.08s. In the boom year of 1825–6, tons carried were only 15,258 and 4.06s, but by 1838–9 tonnages had risen to 33,717 as railway building materials were carried, but at tolls of 3.2s. By 1865–6 tons had fallen to 20,598, and tolls at 1.03s, and the company finally went into liquidation, although it would later be revived under various names.

All canals suffered from this tendency. For instance the revenue of the very prosperous Somersetshire Coal Canal fell from 2.61s. per ton carried in 1828 (113,442 tons and £14,809) to 0.84s. per ton in 1868 (140,112 tons and £6,120); and that of the Leeds & Liverpool from 1.59s. per ton in 1828 (1,436,160 tons and £114,518) to 1.13s. per ton in 1868 (1,884,140 tons and £94,207). Notably, the tonnage carried increased in both these cases, as it did in many others.

Some smaller concerns went into voluntary liquidation, retiring early from a contest in which they had no prospects. Thus the Wey & Arun Junction Canal paid a dividend in all but three years between 1830 and 1865, but went into liquidation in 1864 while there were still assets to divide. Many followed, especially in the 1870s, such as the Coombe Hill, Ivel, Melton Mowbray and Sleaford Navigations. A few, like the Ballinamore & Ballyconnell Canal, or the Wilts &

Berks, just faded away. Receipts became less and less, until meetings ceased to be held and offices were closed with no means to pay wages. The long pounds and locks became steadily unnavigable and proved a nuisance. Then some public authority, like Swindon Corporation in the Wilts & Berks case, would take steps to stop the inconvenience and close the canal.

In the Fens, where the waterways had been built or enlarged primarily for drainage reasons, a great waterborne trade had grown up before and during the canal age. The coming of the railways saw this traffic up and down the rivers and drains of the fenlands slowly die away, except here and there where the railways did not quite serve local purposes. In these cases, however, the waterways themselves continued to be maintained for their primary purpose of drainage.

By the early 1850s a considerable mileage of canals was railway-controlled. The Railway & Canal Traffic Act of 1854 specified that these railway canals should provide 'reasonable facilities' for traffic and should not hinder through freights to or from independent waterways. Complaints were to go to the courts. The Act was well-intentioned but had no teeth, and not until the appointment of commissioners under the Regulation of Railways Act of 1873 did policing become effective, or the quotation of through rates compulsory.

Some canals were bought by railways long after the railway mania. This was not unlawful, given parliamentary approval, but during the 1850s Parliament became much less inclined to see canal companies absorbed. Railways therefore sought expedients whereby they could control canals without having to go before Parliament. One way was to use the leasing clause of the 1845 Canal Carriers' Act in an unintended way. If a railway already owned a canal company, that company could legally lease others. Thus a consortium of three canal owning railways in 1850 jointly leased the Leeds & Liverpool Canal for 21 years, and in 1855 another consortium of four companies leased the Rochdale Canal for 36 years, thus killing the trans-Pennine canal trade in finished textiles. As the Huddersfield was already owned by the London & North Western Railway, all three Pennine canals were for a time railway-controlled.

The Aire & Calder took the Rochdale case to the Board of Trade, and the Gloucester & Berkeley similarly took the Worcester & Birmingham Canal case. In the latter case the Oxford, Worcester & Wolverhampton Railway tried to use the Canal Carriers Act to lease the canal. This led Parliament to change the law to prevent this except by a special Act.

Another approach was never prevented. In 1855 three officials of the North Eastern Railway bought, in their own names, the Yorkshire Derwent Navigation from Earl Fitzwilliam, then leased it to their own company. The same technique was used in 1859 when the Upper Avon was sold to an individual who resold it to the Oxford, Worcester & Wolverhampton Railway. More importantly, but with a different approach, the Bridgewater trustees sold their waterways to the chairmen of the Midland and the Manchester

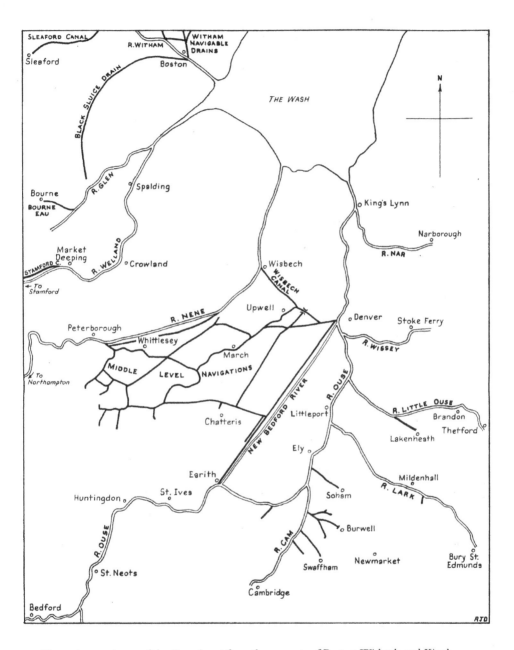

The main waterways of the Fens. Apart from the seaports of Boston, Wisbech and King's Lynn, navigation was generally an incidental adjunct to drainage by the end of the nineteenth century.

Sheffield & Lincolnshire railways in 1871.These then formed the Bridgewater Navigation Co.

Between the 1840s and the 1870s waterways seem to have been seen as increasingly outdated and unable to cope with the changing world of trade, industry and commerce.The independent canals had been created as local lines of communication and so they largely remained.There was little evidence of any pressure to amalgamate and form national routes, in contrast to the development of railways. Occasionally, however, the larger companies met to try to evolve common policies.Thus in May 1841 all the companies on the routes from London to Manchester and Liverpool met to complain about the excessive tolls demanded by the Oxford company, and the Oxford's acute competition.The lines from the Regents through the Coventry to the Ashton Canals were represented, but not the Oxford.The meeting discussed the following figures of the companies' share of the through toll from Manchester via Preston Brook, Fradley and Braunston to Paddington:

Canal	Miles	Toll		
		s	d	
Bridgewater	25	1	0	(5p)
Trent & Mersey	67	2	9½	(14p)
Coventry (Fradley section)	5½	0	2¼	(1p)
Birmingham (Fazeley section)	5½	0	5½	(2p)
Coventry	21¼	0	11	(5p)
Oxford	23¾	2	11	(15p)
Grand Junction	101	4	2½	(21p)
Total	248¾	12	6¼	(63p)

These figures are for tolls only.At the time the freight charge for the distance made by the carriers was £2 2s 5¼d. (£2.12), making £2 15s (£2.75) in all, which was a quite inadequate differential in favour of the canals compared with the railway charge of £2 17s 6d. (£2.87) for the same distance, which had recently been reduced from £3 5s (£3.25).

The meeting resolved that 'the course which the Oxford canal is pursuing is destructive of the thoroughfare trade'.[1] The Oxford did nothing, and the situation deteriorated. In July 1845 there was another meeting, this time with the Oxford present.The Oxford took the offensive, complaining that the Grand Junction was giving preference for coal traffic to the Leicestershire line over its own.The Grand Junction cited differences in tolls, such as the Oxford Canal's tolls on coal for London at 1¾d. (0.7p) per ton, against the Grand Junction's at ¼d. (0.1p), 'by which exactions the Oxford Canal Company had been and were still enabled to Share a Dividend of 30 per cent, while the Grand Junction Canal Company were sharing one of only seven per Cent'.[2]

The Oxford still refused to lower its tolls or go to arbitration, until the Grand Junction approached the Warwick canals and others 'for a general amalgamation of their common interests'.[3] This threat to isolate the Oxford worked, and it agreed to arbitration and a lowering of tolls. Nothing more was heard of amalgamation for many years.

This shows the difficulties faced by a number of long-established and independent companies in competing against railways. For a time tonnages carried were unaffected, but price cutting caused major falls in revenue. Amalgamation into larger units, or at least a common policy, might have counteracted the fall in revenue and overcome the conservatism of management and engineering policy.

There was one water line where such a policy was pursued with a good deal of success: that from Birmingham or Liverpool by way of the Staffs & Worcs Canal to the Severn and the Gloucester & Berkeley. The initiative came from the Staffs & Worcs, the energetic management of which combined much foresight in respect of other waterways with a reluctance to improve its own canal. From the beginning in about 1835 of serious proposals to improve the navigation of the Severn, the Staffs & Worcs had supported them with money and parliamentary influence. When the Severn Commission was at last set up in 1842 the canal company agreed to guarantee the commission's bonds up to £180,000, which enabled locks to be built between Stourport and Diglis, and the river to be dredged lower down.

When the railway mania began, two or three railway companies interested themselves in the Severn, offering to guarantee its revenue in exchange for a clear run with their Bills. Of these the offer of the Oxford, Worcester & Wolverhampton Railway was accepted, so that the Severn bond-holders were doubly protected: the railway company guaranteed the revenue of the waterway, and the Staffs & Worcs the capital and interest of the bonds.

Through many years and manoeuvres the Staffs and Worcs, which had meanwhile guaranteed additional capital for improvements to the Severn, aimed to remove the railway influences over the Severn. It took the canal company until 1890, and at heavy cost, to secure an independent waterway route to Gloucester. Ironically, most of the feeder waterways to this route, including the Trent & Mersey and BCN, were railway-controlled, while the Staffs & Worcs main water rival for the Birmingham–Gloucester trade, the Worcester & Birmingham, was not, and had preference due to its ownership by the Gloucester & Berkeley. Only the small and extraordinarily supine Stourbridge Canal was independent, though its feeder, the Stourbridge Extension, was not.

Again, a waterway company could stay in business if it could encourage traffic originating on its line to remain, was largely self-contained, well managed and had reasonable access to funds. This was the case with the Aire & Calder. The company was well-placed to meet competition for, between 1820 and 1826, it had built the broad and deep Ferrybridge & Goole Canal as a more modern alternative to its older line to the Yorkshire Ouse via the Selby Canal, and had then developed Goole as a port. It had also enlarged and straightened its main lines from Castleford to Leeds and Wakefield between 1828 and 1839, so that it entered the railway age with a recently modernised waterway.

The navigation's basic traffic was coal, much of it from collieries beside its own waterway, with East Anglian corn as back carriage upwards. To enlarge the area from which coal could be drawn the company leased the largely coal-carrying Barnsley Canal in 1854 (purchased in 1871 and its locks enlarged) and the Calder & Hebble for 21 years in 1865. To keep traffic on the water it followed a vigorous carrying policy. Steam tugs had been used since 1831, and by 1855 the company was steam-hauling two thirds of its own carrying mileage, after which it put on public tugs to haul bye-traders' craft. Its self-sufficiency, however, was essential, since railway company discouragement, and differences in gauge and haulage reduced trade with the Rochdale and Huddersfield routes.

It is difficult to say that railway ownership of or influence over important canals prevented a movement to bring the waterways closer together, because there were so few signs of such a movement even along routes that remained independent, but it was undoubtedly one of the factors working against an energetic canal policy. The difficulty in getting a quotation for a through toll from a railway-controlled canal such as the Trent & Mersey, for instance, was a discouragement in itself. By the time the law compelled railways to quote through tolls, under the Railway & Canal Traffic Act of 1888, the possibilities of keeping long-haul traffic on the canals had largely gone.

Canal traffic was partly inhibited by variations in gauge, while rural canals lost much trade when large mills relocated near ports after the repeal of the Corn Laws. Changing industrial processes also ended traffics, such as the development of a few large steelworks served by railways and ports, in place of many small ironworks served by canals.

Many canals fell behind because of the failure of investment, and the difficulty of obtaining capital when investors no longer believed in inland water transport. Railways were seen as more efficient, faster, and more flexible. They were also more densely and widely spread in Britain than in other countries in which the state took a greater hand. Many canal proprietors and officials lost heart.

Throughout the period the canals that were successful in retaining their trade did so by keeping the short hauls, which remained because old-established industry was located on the canal banks. The long-distance trade decreased a good deal, not only because of the difficulty of passing goods from one company to another with different tolls and classifications, different lock sizes and depth of waterway, but also because portions of many through routes were in railway hands.

This tendency towards the short haul can also be seen on the system of a single waterway. In 1905, on the 145 miles of the Leeds & Liverpool, for instance, the average haul for a ton of goods was 19.6 miles; on the 189 miles of the extended Grand Junction it was 23.2 miles; and on the 144 miles of the Thames Navigation it was 16.7 miles.

Canal companies were hampered by several factors in any effort they made to extend their hauls. The first was the old distinction between toll-taking and carrying.

A number of navigation and canal concerns had always had their own carrying fleets, like the Aire & Calder, the Mersey & Irwell and the Bridgewater. Others had organised the business of carrying by accepting goods freight-paid, and then themselves employing independent craft to carry them, like the Don or the Calder & Hebble. Others again had agreed with carriers that they would run regular services – the so-called contract vessels of, for instance, the Rochdale Canal. However, the majority of companies had only intermittently or never been concerned with carrying, and had confined themselves to taking tolls from independent carriers. This system was abandoned in the early days of railways, but its continuance on many canals kept traders from the benefits of the necessary business organization of offices, regular services, warehouses, cranes and so on.

The carrier might have been the owner of a single boat, a manufacturer, or a carrying company such as Fellows, Morton & Clayton, which carried goods over many canals. As the canal, unlike the railway, did not usually do its own carrying it did not have the same vital interest in the state of its line. Thus, if a carrier's boat went aground the company did not feel the same urgent sense that a railway company did when a train was derailed. Again, manufacturers who wanted goods moved by water had to go to more trouble: they had to find carriers and then entrust them with the necessary money to pay tolls and charges. Sometimes the money was otherwise spent, especially by small carriers, or there was pilfering from the cargo, compensation for which was difficult to recover.

A number of companies continued to carry; others adopted the powers of the Canal Carriers' Act; while others made no attempt to go beyond their toll-taking functions. One well-managed concern, set up by the Grand Junction company, is however worthy of examination.

Before 1848, when it set up a carrying business, the Grand Junction's interest in rate cutting against the railways derived only from pressure from independent traders for toll reductions. As early as 1851 it agreed with the London & North Western Railway that neither would cut rates against the other. The Grand Junction thus pegged its own freight charges, but found that it was unable to control those of the independent carriers. Once it informed the railway of this, the LNWR began to cut its rates, and canal tolls and rates had to be cut. In October 1857, at a meeting of canal companies and carriers, the GJ chairman reported that the managers of the LNWR and GWR had complained that 'they could not retain their fair proportion of the heavy Trade in consequence of the Carriers on the Canal being enabled to carry at such low rates.'[4]

The meeting must have decided not to fight further, for in December a rates agreement was concluded with both railways that gave small fixed differentials to the canal carriers, which the Grand Junction accepted for itself and undertook to enforce on the independents. This was perhaps made easier by some rises in rates on both railway and canal as a result of the agreement. Over this tendency the (old) Grand Union company warned that 'any decided combination between the Railways and Canals may materially affect the interest of the Canals with the Board of Trade',[5] refusing to join the understanding on tolls that the Grand Junction, in the light of its agreement with the railways, had now reached with the Oxford and other canals.

Price cutting by the independent carriers caused further trouble, however, and for a moment the company thought of following the example of the Bridgewater trustees, controlling the Duke of Bridgewater's Canal. Faced with the same difficulty, they had converted the independent carriers on their canal into their agents, to whom certain working expenses and a commission were paid in exchange for agreements to charge uniform rates.

After 1857, all seems to have gone well, until the Regents Park explosion of 1874 (see Chapter three), which, although on the Regents Canal, involved Grand Junction craft. The damage brought 632 claims totaling £74,418, and the final costs proved so great that the Grand Junction closed its carrying business in 1876.

Not until the 1880s were serious efforts made to negotiate through tolls, even on lengths of waterway that were not interrupted by railway ownership. At no time did the canal companies set up an equivalent to the Railway Clearing House for the settlement among themselves of mutual debts (although this had saved railway companies and railway users immense time and trouble), though they were expressly authorised to do so by the Railway & Canal Traffic Act of 1888. There was not even an association to promote the interests of the waterways during the critical early period of their history. In the canal age there had from time to time been ad hoc meetings, or groups of meetings, between representatives of canal companies, such as the group of proprietors of inland navigations who called a meeting in 1797 to protest against a proposed tax on goods carried by canal.

Common action had to wait until 1844 and the United Body whose pressure helped further the Canal Tolls and Canal Carriers Acts of 1845. This continued in loose form to watch Bills and consider the future of canals. In 1855 it became the Canal Association, with an Aire & Calder Navigation chairman and secretary. This lasted until nationalization. There was no journal devoted to canal affairs until the short-lived *Canal Journal* of the 1890s, though several periodicals covered railway interests.

Meanwhile a steady deterioration of the condition of many canals took place. As receipts fell, maintenance was cut in order that dividends might still be paid. Money for capital expenditure was hard to find in the face of dropping revenues with which to pay interest on borrowings. Canals began to look less prosperous,

Boating for pleasure on the tidal Arun in 1867, from J.B. Dashwood's account of his voyage in *Caprice*. The journey was not without difficulties, given the decaying condition of the Wey & Arun Junction Canal, and the problems involved in persuading the horse to negotiate the gates across the towing-path on the Arun.

and this did not attract new customers. Mud accumulated, boats could not carry full loads, delays increased and even long-standing customers began to look for alternative transport.

The decline of many canals was accompanied by the arrival of tourists, who often arrive when the ordinary is becoming exceptional. Earlier, there were occasional references to short pleasure trips on canals, such as the 'Barge with a party of Ladies and Gentlemen'[6] for whom tolls on the Swansea Canal were remitted in 1809. There may have been much local use for day trips, although no special pleasure craft, except for the directors' boats that started to appear. The Reverend John Skinner, rector of Camerton in Somerset, described a trip in 1823 on the Somersetshire Coal Canal:

Having engaged one of the coal barges, I had it fitted up for the ladies with an awning and matting against the sides, and tables and chairs from the public-house, in which we proceeded to Combe Hay...As the day was delightful, the whole party very much enjoyed the excursion.[7]

Loading sugar beet at Ludham Bridge on the Ant, some 7 miles south of its junction with the North Walsham canal. The tractor indicates that this dates from as late as 1959, but otherwise the vessel is similar to those operating in the late nineteenth century. This photograph was taken in October, towards the end of the pleasure boating season; the traffic was itself seasonal and loading rarely took place in summer. (L.A. Edwards)

Much longer trips had generally to wait until the 1860s, but in 1821 a lengthy voyage in the *Joseph* was taken by Josiah Baxendale, a surgeon whose son was a director of Pickfords'. They travelled 434 miles in 16 days, usually sleeping ashore. Beginning in Manchester, they travelled via Fradley, Wolverhampton, Worcester, Braunston, Coventry and back to Manchester. Diversions included nights spent in inns and visits to various 'gentlemen's seats'. Two extracts may provide some of the flavour, the first through the Ogley Locks:

… we left the Trent & Mersey Canal [sic] and entered the Wyrley and Essington Canal on which there appears to be little or no trade. The number of locks on this canal are immense, I believe not less than thirty, a considerable number of them are on Cark Heath [sic], one of the most dreary places I ever passed over. We arrived at Wolverhampton early in the evening, and slept at the Swan, a moderately good inn.

We left Wolverhampton, a most uninteresting and dirty town about 11 o'clock a.m. and passed thro' a dreary and unpleasant country filled for many miles round with Iron furnaces…The trade and number of boats on the Birmingham Canal are beyond any thing I could have imagined. We met and passed upwards of four hundred boats full or empty on our sail from Wolverhampton to the locks at Birmingham.

By contrast, later on:

We passed thro' a beautiful country and stopped at the bridge at Leamington... and took a survey of that pretty place...The sail from Leamington to Warwick is delightful as independent of the beauty of the country, you have continually a view of the Castle of Warwick and the grand steeple of the Church, and the view is constantly varying as you sail nearly round that town.[8]

Journeys for holiday purposes only seem only to have started in the 1860s. In 1867 a party led by J.B. Dashwood, rowed and pulled *Caprice* through the Wey & Arun Junction Canal and to the sea at Littlehampton just before that canal closed; they had intended to follow the Portsmouth & Arundel Canal, but learnt en route that it had been drained. Dashwood's account, *The Thames to the Solent by Canal and Sea*, was published in 1868. The following year *The Waterway to London* described a canoe trip by three young men from Manchester to London via the Mersey, Shropshire Union, Severn, Thames & Severn Canals, and the Thames. One feature was the limited use they made of canals, using the Shropshire Union only from Ellesmere Port to Perry Aqueduct, whence they followed that river to the upper Severn; a friendly boatman put their canoe on board for much of the canal journey. Both authors write as if they were pioneers in this kind of amusement. This may have been so, given the ability of the railways to move passengers over long distances in England by the 1860s.

The railways also encouraged day pleasure trips by visitors, such as those to the Wye at Tintern (recorded in use in Wordsworth's day, in 1798) and the Dee above Chester, whose use expanded after the 1860s. Some of this made use of smaller boats. After 1866 the new Thames Conservancy soon concerned itself with pleasure users, the Thames Preservation Act of 1885 aiming at 'the preservation of the River above Teddington Lock for purposes of public recreation, and for regulating the pleasure traffic therein'. From the 1880s regular services of steamers ran up to Oxford, mainly for pleasure rather than travel purposes, while boat rollers for small craft began to be provided at the new locks built by the Conservancy.

The Thames, with its many locks, some still only half-locks, tended to attract pleasure boaters who could develop a familiarity with the navigation, whether by small craft or steamboats. The first developments towards the modern hire industry began on the Norfolk and Suffolk Broads, where trading wherries were being hired out from the 1860s. Visitors were attracted in large numbers from the 1880s, and in 1888 Press Brothers of North Walsham advertised five trading wherries for hire. Unusually, these millers also owned the North Walsham Canal, which they had acquired in 1866; when they sold their interests in 1907 there remained some income from pleasure tolls. This hiring operation was still in being in 1899, when four craft were in use; even pianos could be hired. Purpose-built Broads craft were first advertised in that year, although special cruising boats had been built at Wroxham since 1880.

All of these hired craft were sailing vessels, and hire charges usually included a skipper and a steward who would act as cook. The crew was essential on larger trading craft, but optional on smaller craft, which were sometimes rowed. The general lack of locks made hiring more feasible. Visitors sometimes found it difficult to organise bookings at a distance, and one recalled of the 1900s that 'the novice might....find on his arrival that he had booked a boat which had halyards and sheets in a deplorable condition, several important items of gear missing, and a 6ft tiller occupying the whole of the cockpit.'[9] One solution was the development of booking agencies, which could ensure minimum standards. The year after his Broads holiday in 1906 with members of a Dulwich tennis club, Harry Blake set up a booking agency, whose catalogue listed 43 sailing yachts from over a dozen boatyards in 1908.

Interest in canal journeys was more limited and more occasional, with numerous Sunday School trips over short lengths. The advent of bank holidays from 1872 encouraged day trips, and one destination, Llangollen, was visited by boats on bank holidays from the 1870s. A long-standing service of horse-drawn day boats began there in 1884 with *Maid of Llangollen*. Trips ran to Berwyn and Chirk, the latter crossing the Pontcysyllte Aqueduct. The growth of leisure on canals was to reflect the development of railways, which both brought visitors on excursions and inhibited traffic growth so that the amenities of lightly-trafficked sections could be enjoyed.

CHAPTER ELEVEN

Time of Hope

Until the 1870s the development of the railway system was so extensive and so apparently beneficial that many thought the waterways obsolete and overlooked the dangers of railway monopoly. A letter written at the time of the Canal Conference of 1888 asserted that: 'Sixteen years ago anyone advocating water transport was promptly accused of galvanising a corpse...'[1] In Britain, a change of heart was brought about by a number of factors all operating over the same period.

The dangers of a railway monopoly in Britain began to be perceived when foreign manufactured goods began to compete in the British market with those made at home, for the first time since the industrial revolution. Free trade made this possible, and the reduction of transport costs began to be critical. In continental Europe, where state influence was greater, railway and (especially) waterway transport was much cheaper than that in Britain. It was alleged that railway rates on imported goods were less than those on home manufactures, so that manufacturing was relocating from inland locations to ones closer to ports to avoid the high railway rates. Some suggested that railways were raising new capital to carry unprofitably heavy traffic, some of which could better go by water.

The 1873 Regulation of Railways Act attempted to control railway influence over canals. It set up a Railway Commission to which disputes were to be referred, which was seen as the guardian of the public interest, and aimed to ensure that through rates were fair. Railway and canal companies were forced to quote and publish through tolls and rates, and railways would only be allowed to acquire any controlling interest in a canal if the Commission agreed. Those railways that already owned canals had always to maintain them 'at all times kept open and navigable for the use of all persons desirous to use and navigate the same without any unnecessary hindrance, interruption or delay.'

Between the 1870s and the 1900s arguments raged between two groups of interests. Supporters of waterways transport argued that it could play an important part, but only if existing companies were amalgamated, probably with the help of the central or local Government, followed by modernization. This would ensure a uniform gauge on the major through waterway routes, an enlarged sectional area to increase speed, the substitution of lifts for flights of locks, the protection of canal banks by walling and the use of steam haulage. On the other side railway supporters pointed out that the canal network was not nearly as comprehensive as that of the railways, that storage in railway waggons was an essential convenience to coal and other merchants, that speed of conveyance was becoming increasingly important as traders held smaller stocks and traded on less capital, and that the enormous expenditure involved in any major reorganization of the waterways system would be out of all proportion to the possible benefits.

By the 1880s, interest in revival had been spurred by railway controversies and journals like *Engineering* and *The Engineer*, which featured major waterways developments outside the British Isles. In 1888 the Royal Society of Arts held a major conference on the subject, involving leading waterways engineers and managers. It was revealed that private enterprise was unlikely to raise the necessary capital and that, in any case, a strong hand was needed to make sure that railway influence was still not exercised over waterways. Several speakers supported nationalization, or the formation of public trusts under local authorities. Nationalization had not then acquired its later political contentiousness and proposals for state acquisition were judged on their merits in furthering transport improvements. As one speaker put it: 'The traditional independence of Englishmen is opposed to Government interference, and yet the descendants of Englishmen in Canada and the United States are now enjoying the benefits of artificial waterways provided by their Governments.'[2]

The conference endorsed the use of state acquisition and amendments to the Railway & Canal Traffic Act to empower local authorities to form public trusts to take over and develop canals. Controversies continued, but with little state action until a Royal Commission was appointed in 1906 to study the whole matter.

The revival of interest from the 1870s led to several lines of development. These included proposals for ship canals and enlargements, influenced by the progress of the Manchester Ship Canal scheme. The Worcester & Birmingham purchase of 1874, and the negotiations by the Staffs & Worcs over the Severn by 1890, both removed railway influence, and showed that waterways concerns could protect and develop waterways.

In Ireland, in contrast to the British mainland, the railways took a large share of a much slower growth in trade, and there was a continuing conflict between the interests of navigation and drainage. The Monck Royal Commission of 1880, which considered the very unsatisfactory north–south route between Limerick and Belfast or Newry by way of the Shannon, Ballinamore & Ballyconnell and Ulster Canals, tended to favour navigation. Later commissions felt that navigation, drainage and other water interests should be the responsibility of a single Government department. Subsequent commissions – the Allport of 1887 on Irish Public Works and that of 1905 on Arterial Drainage – thought navigation, drainage and other water interests should be the responsibility of a single Government department.

The Manchester Ship Canal provided a major improvement over the existing barge routes from the Mersey to Manchester. The early Mersey & Irwell Navigation, whose line it largely subsumed, had not been prosperous even before the opening of the Duke's Runcorn extension in 1776. In 1779 it had sold out to a new group, which improved the navigation, including the Runcorn and Latchford Canal to bypass part of the Mersey. The company was also a carrier, and thus built up its fleet and began a passenger service.

The Liverpool & Manchester Railway had opened in 1830. Its promotion was prompted partly by the inability of the two waterways, despite improvements, to carry the increasing traffics brought by growing trade. The promoters also envisaged rich pickings from a new line. However, the railway company, as would others, found that its main source of revenue lay in passengers rather than the anticipated freight. Ten years after the Liverpool & Manchester opened it was still only carrying a third of the total goods traffic available.

As early as 1824 a small ship canal was proposed, to carry 400 ton vessels to Manchester – not from the Mersey but from the Dee, by a 45 mile long route. Parliament rejected this scheme, which would have been strongly opposed by port interests in Liverpool, in 1825, but Manchester remained interested in a ship canal. Into the late Victorian period there was increasing criticism, both of the exactions of the Liverpool port authorities and of the growing railway transport monopoly between Liverpool and Manchester. This was exacerbated from 1872, when the new railway-dominated Bridgewater Navigation Company bought the canal, carrying interests and waterway property of the Bridgewater Trustees for £1.15 million.

The movement towards a ship canal began in 1876 when George Hicks, an insurance agent, began a process of letter-writing to the *Manchester Guardian*, pressing for improvements to the Mersey & Irwell line. Initial proposals were both dashed and fostered by the trading slump of 1881. Some political support for the scheme resulted, but, contrary to accounts like that of Bosdin Leech, it was not supported by the largest manufacturers and merchants and political interests in the Manchester area. After Hicks met Daniel Adamson, a successful businessman and engineer, a detailed mass campaign of meetings and pamphleteering began in 1882. Much support came from Liberals and their trade union allies, who felt that this could represent a new kind of popular capitalism. However, two successive Bills were thrown out, amid opposition from railway companies, the Bridgewater Navigation Company and Liverpool interests.

Parliamentary assent was finally granted in 1885, after alterations to placate Liverpool interests. The route was altered so that it would no longer pass down the Mersey estuary, which the Liverpool interests felt would damage its navigation further down, but would leave the river at Eastham and run alongside it. The cost of works was estimated at £6.3 million, added to which was the cost of acquisition of the Bridgewater Navigation Company for £1.71 million, nearly £600,000 more than the railway interests had paid for the company some years before.

The Act provided that £5 million in shares, along with the BNCo. price, must be raised by 6 August 1887. Only £750,000 was raised, and a further Act was required to allow the payment of interest on capital. Even so, a further share issue failed, mainly because investors were unimpressed by the soundness of the estimates or of the Board of Directors. A consultative committee on the Ship Canal scheme found the estimates satisfactory and the project commercially sound. It suggested the strengthening of the Board, and Adamson resigned in favour of Lord Egerton, a kinsman of the Duke of Bridgewater.

A rush to raise the money began, with meetings all over the Midlands. Before 6 August 1887 two-thirds of the authorised share capital had been raised. An agreement was signed with T.A. Walker, the contractor for the Severn Tunnel, and on 11 November 1887 the first sod was cut by Lord Egerton on the site of Eastham Lock.

Within a year 11,000 men were at work and cutting was on schedule. Then Walker died, and there followed arguments between the company and his executors, and natural disasters in the form of floods, that delayed work and increased costs. At the end of 1890 the company had to take the work into its own hands, but at a time when bad weather caused further difficulties, and when costs of labour and materials had risen above those estimated.

It soon became clear that the company had insufficient capital to finish the canal, and Manchester Corporation, aware of the consequences of non-completion, promoted a Bill allowing it to lend the company £3 million in debentures, and to have five directors on the board. Its influence led to a tightening of the canal administration but, while work progressed, by 1892 yet more money was needed, and Manchester offered a further £2 million, which was accepted in debentures. It was agreed, in an arrangement that would last until 1988, that Manchester Corporation should appoint a majority of the directors until half the total of £5 million was repaid.

Among the last works to be completed was the Barton Swing Aqueduct, a unique structure that carried the Bridgewater Canal over the Ship Canal. At the same time Brindley/Gilbert's old aqueduct, that had inspired so much interest 130 years before, was demolished. Most of the Mersey & Irwell Navigation works outside Warrington also disappeared to accommodate the canal line.

On 1 January 1894 the Canal was opened by a procession of boats headed by the *Norseman* carrying the directors, followed by a trail of merchant ships, 71 of which entered the docks. The formal opening was on 21 May. The total cost was £14.35 million, compared with the estimated cost of £8.4 million. In consequence, it would be many years before the Ordinary shareholders saw a dividend.

The new Canal had 179 acres of water space in its docks at Manchester and Salford alone, and over 5 miles of quays. The largest entrance lock to the canal was 600ft by 80ft, the upper locks being 600ft by 65ft.

The Canal's early years were filled with difficulties, and for the first year or so it was thought possible that it might have to close. Problems included a lack of

The Irlam Locks, looking west, as pictured in the *Illustrated London News* on 30 December 1893, just before formal opening. The railway bridge was one of the five bridges built on the elevated deviation lines. The Ship Canal Railway passed through the arches on the right (now occupied by a main road); it is not yet shown on this drawing. The Partington Coaling Basin lay shortly beyond the railway bridge.

cooperation from the railways, which caused the slow handling of goods. The practice of shipping companies' conferences bound shippers by means of rebates to use certain channels, that proved difficult to change.

Its fortunes slowly changed. Cheaper imports attracted import trade to Manchester, and the total tonnages handled rose between 1896 and 1898 from 1,826,237 tons to 2,595,585. The indirect benefit in lowered freight rates to Manchester was great, both on canal-borne and railway goods, since the railways had lowered Liverpool–Manchester rates when the Canal opened. This and the direct benefits from the Canal improved Manchester's prosperity.

Early developments included its close association with Trafford Park Estates in 1896, which was developed to serve new industry likely to use the canal, and in 1898, with Christopher Furness of the shipping line, the formation of Manchester Liners, which aimed to increase the carrying of Canadian produce to industrial England, and which soon added services to the United States.

This was followed by the provision of facilities especially for the import trade, mainly in timber, grain, cotton, oil, cattle and, later, woodpulp. Since outside interests were reluctant to provide the necessary warehouses for raw cotton, grain elevators, cattle lairages, cold stores and oil tanks, the MSCCo. had to act, directly or indirectly, to provide them. Manchester was to remain a largely importing port;

The largest entrance lock at Eastham, looking out onto the tidal Mersey. The approach channel also serves the Queen Elizabeth Dock, which is part of the Port of Manchester but not part of the Manchester Ship Canal..

imports as a proportion of total traffic were 60 per cent in 1900, and would rise to 70 per cent in 1920 and 71½ per cent in 1950. Manchester never succeeded in gaining a dominant share in raw cotton imports despite many battles with Liverpool. Exports were mainly coal, salt, manufactured goods and machinery, the mechanised Partington Coaling Basin of 1894 being the forerunner of a continuous development of mechanised handling of varied cargoes.

The later history of the Manchester Ship Canal will be outlined in subsequent chapters. Its influence on proposals for improved navigation elsewhere was almost as great as that of the Canal on the prosperity of Manchester.

Plans for a ship canal from the sea to Birmingham arose from complaints about high railway rates from Birmingham during the trade depression of 1885. On 5 April 1887 Birmingham Town Council passed the resolution:

> That this Council deems it to be of the utmost importance to the trade and commerce of Birmingham and the surrounding district that improved canal communications should be opened up, which should connect this great centre of industry with the sea...

In 1888 its Committee reported that while the Severn was the greatest source for Birmingham's imports, its exports went to Liverpool and London, and it was these lines that needed most attention. One suggestion was the Birmingham & Liverpool Ship Canal project. This would be 64 miles long from the Weaver at Winsford through the Potteries to Stafford, Wolverhampton and Birmingham.

The Birmingham committee recommended that new public trusts should rebuild the main lines of canal – to the Trent, Thames, Mersey and Severn. These would be of a uniform depth of 8–10ft, to take steamers of 600 tons, with lifts to replace locks wherever possible. The cost of acquiring and converting these links was put at £8–12 million each. While similar proposals would arise from the Royal Commission of 1906–10, little was done. The North Staffordshire Railway did obtain an Act in 1891 to enlarge the Trent & Mersey to Stoke-on-Trent, but only enlarged the canal between Anderton Lift and Middlewich to barge standard. Further schemes for ship or barge canals would emerge in the 1920s and 1940s.

One perceived means of limiting the railway monopoly was to develop waterways, and release them from railway control. The 1883 Select Committee, the last in a series to make this recommendation, also recommended that the Irish canals should be taken over by public trusts or local authorities. Legislation up to 1888 provided some protections and powers for canal companies and traders on railway-owned canals, but little action resulted.

An instance of the ineffectual nature of protective legislation was Butterley Tunnel on the Cromford Canal, owned by the Midland Railway. This was badly affected by mining subsidence and was closed between 1889 and 1893, when £8,000 was spent on it. When H.R. De Salis went through in 1897, he found it very low and in a bad condition 'unsurpassed by any other I have ever seen'. The canal below the tunnel, which connected with the collieries and the Erewash, was also 'in a very bad condition'[3], affecting traffics to Nottingham via the Nottingham Canal, itself also railway-owned and in poor condition. In July 1900 worse subsidence closed the tunnel completely, and it was not reopened.

An appeal could have been made to the Board of Trade to compel the Midland to reinstate the tunnel, but, even the hard-headed Grand Junction admitted that 'there would be a very great deal of risk for one independent canal to endeavour to compel a railway company or to make it navigable.'[4] Others concurred, and a Board of Trade Inquiry of 1907 determined that the tunnel should remain closed.

Apart from the acquisition of the Worcester & Birmingham canals, two important canal amalgamations took place. In 1894 the Grand Junction Canal Company, one of the most powerful, bought the old Grand Union and Leicestershire & Northamptonshire Union Canals. These acquisitions were followed by an agreement on through tolls with the Leicester, Loughborough and Erewash companies, under which the Grand Junction offered a guarantee of tolls. The agreement sought to obtain the coal trade of the Erewash valley, but this was partly frustrated by the bad condition of the Cromford and the abandonment of most of the privately owned Nutbrook, and partly by competition with other coalfields in the Grand Junction market. As a result, the Grand Junction had to pay out on its guarantees of receipts, relinquish its options to purchase and drop its 1895 proposals to amalgamate with the Warwick Canals on the Birmingham route.

In Yorkshire, local interests sought to remove the navigation linking Sheffield to the Aire & Calder from railway control. The River Don Company had encouraged the building of the Stainforth & Keadby and Dearne & Dove Canals, and had later absorbed them along with the Sheffield Canal. Amalgamations with railway interests had brought the navigation into the hands of the Manchester, Sheffield & Lincolnshire Railway (later the Great Central) in 1864, which then built a line from Mexborough past Rotherham to Sheffield. This used part of the navigation's Rotherham Cut, which was replaced by a more circuitous route via two new cuts and a section of the old river, which opened in 1868.

In 1888, as a result of strong local initiative, a new company, the Sheffield & South Yorkshire Navigation, was formed to purchase the former navigation from the railway, and to modernise and enlarge the main line. Agreement was finally reached in 1894 on a price of £1.14 million, payable as £600,000 in cash and the balance in ordinary shares, to be held by the railway until bought from them at par by the Sheffield & South Yorkshire Navigation. However, investors' enthusiasm for waterways had diminished since 1888, and the company could not raise the capital to acquire all of the shares. The railway therefore retained a very strong influence on the company; in turn this inhibited the Aire & Calder from offering possible financial support for the Sheffield & South Yorkshire.

The Aire & Calder was the most successful of the independent concerns. Its prosperity largely depended on traffic generated on its own system, that to and from the Barnsley, Calder & Hebble and Leeds & Liverpool adding palatable icing to an already satisfactory cake. It had been fortunate in being managed from the late 1770s onwards by an energetic board and served by highly competent officials and engineers, who had overseen the founding of the port of Goole and the rebuilding of the lines to Leeds and Wakefield.

Steam tugging had been introduced in 1831. By the 1850s most of the company's own craft were steam-hauled. The resultant barge trains suggested much longer and wider locks. The first of these, Pollington – 206ft long and partially widened to 22ft – opened in 1860, followed by all others to Castleford by 1867, and throughout the navigation by 1873. Meanwhile, in 1862, the company's engineer, William H. Bartholomew, obtained the board's approval for the experimental construction of his newly patented invention of compartment boats. These, later called 'pans' or 'Tom Puddings', were rectangular iron boats that could be built up into trains. Each was then fitted with spring-loaded buffers and a protruding vertical iron bar, in front of which fitted a corresponding slot at the back of the boat ahead. By putting a steam tug at the back, running cables through fairleads on each boat to a false bow at the head of the train and working the cables by windlasses it was possible to bend the train to pass round curves in the waterway. At Goole these coal-carrying compartment boats were then separated, raised in a hydraulic hoist and tipped into ships' holds.

Over the years Bartholomew modified his invention: he dropped push-towing from behind, together with his elaborate steering system, in favour of a tug in front pulling a long train of boats that adjusted themselves to curves. The boats' design was also simplified. The system was a tremendous success. By 1897 0.5 million tons a year were being carried in four hundred boats, and 1.5 million tons in 1913 in some thousand pans, which operated, of course, alongside conventional barges and steam tugs. From the 1880s onwards locks began to be further enlarged, and in 1896 the company began to build the New Junction Canal, 5¼ miles long with one lock, to join the Sheffield & South Yorkshire to the Aire & Calder, mainly to introduce to the Don line compartment boat trains working to the Goole hoists. Finally from 1884 onwards the company took control of the River Ouse from Goole downwards to its junction with the Trent at Trent Falls, and enlarged it so that bigger ships could reach Goole, where the port facilities had been greatly enlarged and extended in the previous half century.

The effect on revenue of operating a large modern waterway with big barges or long barge trains, compared with narrow-boat canals, whether highly industrialised and short-haul like the BCN, or long-haul on a good sized waterway like the Grand Junction, can be seen from the following figures of revenue earned and tonnage carried in 1905:

Company	Tonnage	Revenue
Birmingham	7,546,453	£190,873
Grand Junction	1,794,233	£101,926
Aire & Calder	2,810,988	£317,468

In the last thirty years of the century, therefore, there were prosperous concerns such as the Aire & Calder and the Weaver, viable but less secure companies like the Grand Junction, and one or two efficient railway-owned canals like the Trent & Mersey and the Shropshire Union main line. However, there were also many canals in difficulties. Some became entangled in railway companies; others just died. Perhaps the story of the later years of the Thames & Severn will epitomise the first process, and that of its neighbour, the Wilts & Berks, the second.

As early as 1836 the Thames & Severn had sought to turn itself into a railway, when the broad gauge Cheltenham & Great Western Union Railway was promoted to run from Swindon along a route that paralleled the canal between Cirencester and Stroud. The ready-made line and existing tunnel led the canal company not only to oppose the railway Bill but to promote its own. It also supported a rival scheme for a standard gauge line between Tring, Oxford, Burford and Cheltenham, as this would not affect canal traffic. However, the latter two

Bills were lost, and the Swindon scheme was authorised, and completed in 1845, by which time it was owned by the Great Western.

This seriously affected the canal's revenues, and by the early 1860s the canal company was in difficulties, with the last dividend paid in 1864. As several railway schemes were in prospect, it sought to incorporate the canal line in a new railway that would use Sapperton Tunnel and the line to South Cerney. The canal between Stroud and Brimscombe would have been retained, with water piped from Thames Head. This provision, diverting Thames water to the Severn valley, was one factor in the failure of the Bill.

Richard Potter, a director of the Great Western Railway Company, resigned as chairman in 1865. Between 1876 and 1882, he bought shares in the Thames & Severn until he had a controlling interest. He and the company then promoted a railway from Stroud to near Cirencester, which would have benefited from the traffic in Welsh coal that had developed since the Severn Bridge opened in 1879.

This scheme would have meant the closure of the whole canal. Spurred by part of the Gloucester & Berkeley Canal board, several navigations approached the Board of Trade and opposed the Bill, which failed when Potter was unable to persuade the navigations that the Thames & Severn could never compete with the railway. The Great Western, keen to prevent any rival railway scheme, sought to ensure that the Thames & Severn remained a canal by buying control from Potter at a comfortable profit to him. Shares were acquired through nominees to avoid contravening the 1873 Regulation of Railways Act.

The railway had not bought the canal to work it but to make sure that it was not converted into a rival railway, and would instead remain a canal until it could safely be abandoned. The associated navigations had been discussing rather vague proposals for leasing the canal and now offered to do so for 21 years, but the railway asked a prohibitive price and instead allowed the canal to deteriorate. On local initiative a Board of Trade inspection took place in 1886, recommending the canal's transfer to owners more committed to keeping the canal in good repair, for 'the harmonious working and development of the Canal system … cannot be effectually carried out if this duty is neglected and the interests of the public will suffer so long as it is neglected'.[5]

Nothing happened until 1893, when a memorial was presented to local MPs, signed by 152 traders, boat owners and others. The GWR soon countered with notice to close 26 miles of the canal, leaving only 4 miles open. Thereupon the local authorities approached the Board of Trade, reiterating the willingness of the associated navigations to take over the canal. In 1895 a Trust for the canal was set up by an Act, which empowered the associated navigations and local authorities to take over the canal, with powers to raise finance to repair it. The latter proved insufficient to restore the canal, and during the five years before 1900, when Gloucestershire County Council took it over, it was only open throughout for three months.

The main hindrance was the chronic leakage on the summit level, so the council spent some £20,000 in completely clearing out and repuddling about 2¼ miles. The waterway re-opened in 1904, but traffic never recovered, and it was closed in 1927, except for 6¼ miles between Stroud and Chalford, which were transferred to the management of the Stroudwater company and finally closed in 1933.

The Wilts & Berks had remained an independent canal. Until the Great Western came along the Vale of White Horse, it brought in coal and took away produce from the area between its junctions at Semington and Abingdon. The coming of the railway ruined the concern, which struggled on until 1876, when the annual tolls had fallen from some £15,000 to £1,158. After the Great Western decided not to acquire the canal, the original company sold out at a major loss to a new group. This new company leased the waterway in 1882 for 21 years to a group of Bristol merchants, who thought that they might make the canal profitable. After 6 years, having lost £16,000, they paid £1,000 to surrender their lease. The previous company then worked the canal until 1891. Tolls then brought in only £671, but a new company was formed, which spent about £7,000 on dredging and other improvements, and put on a fleet of twelve fly-boats, which ran regularly to Bristol.

Once again no money could be made from the canal, and in 1897 the company applied for a warrant of abandonment. Neighbouring waterways and landowners (who needed the water for their farms) opposed the closure, which broke down on a legal point. The company survived but traffic did not, and it ceased entirely by 1906. Swindon Corporation found their local canal such a nuisance that they applied for, and obtained in 1914, an Act for closure, taking over Coate Water, the canal reservoir, for local purposes. Shortly after, road bridges in Swindon were removed, parts there were filled in and the line was sold to local landowners.

It is very noticeable during this period that the best progress was made by the river navigations, though more could have been done had the non-tidal portion of each river been under the control of a single authority. Some rivers, like the Severn, for a long time had no authorities, while others had several: in the case of the Witham, at one time seventeen. Increases in capacity could be obtained more easily and at less cost on rivers, even if partly canalised, than on pure canals. However, the smaller river navigations still suffered from the old trouble of the rights of millers to draw off or withhold water and to charge tolls, but nevertheless the improvement of large rivers was general. The Severn and the Weaver will serve as examples.

The Severn Commission, representing interested local authorities and neighbouring navigations, was set up in 1842 to improve the waterway from Gloucester to Stourport, the rest of the river being left without a controlling authority. Its work was, however, hampered by the existence of two factions, one representing the interests of Gloucester and the other those of Worcester. The former wanted no other improvement than dredging to be carried out below Worcester, in order to keep tolls low; the latter, supported by the Staffs & Worcs Company, wanted locks to be built in order to increase traffic above Worcester, both on the river and on the canals. Work proceeded under the enabling Act, the bonds of the commission up to £180,000 having been guaranteed by the canal company. Four locks were built between Diglis (near Worcester) and Stourport, while below Diglis the river was dredged to a depth of 6ft, thereby meeting Gloucester's wish that the channel should not be obstructed. It was found impossible to maintain the dredged depth and, after much opposition, a proposal for a lock and weir at Tewkesbury was sanctioned, and completed in 1858.

In 1864, the Severn Commission's engineer, Leader Williams, advocated major improvements to bring a foreign as well as a coasting trade to Worcester. Gloucester interests withdrew their opposition and supported a plan to obtain a depth of 6ft to Worcester through new locks at Gloucester. Clegram, the Gloucester & Berkeley engineer, pointed out that the shallow depth inhibited the use of steam tugs, necessitated the lightening of vessels at Gloucester, and reduced the ability of the river to compete with the railways for traffics above Gloucester.

The waterway interests had seen where the danger lay. When in 1868 the commission announced its intention to apply for an Act, the Gloucester & Berkeley agreed to guarantee £750 a year to the commission, and the Staffs & Worcs helped also. The Act provided for complete canalization through the construction of two locks and weirs at Gloucester.

When the Oxford, Worcester and Wolverhampton Railway obtained its Act in 1845 for a railway that largely paralleled the river and the Staffs & Worcs Canal from Worcester to Wolverhampton, the Severn Commission represented that £180,000 had been spent on the river and that the estimated annual yield from tolls was £14,000. The railway therefore undertook to make up the tolls to this amount should they fall short of it. However, further bond guarantees for improvements to the river with the encouragement of the Staffs & Worcs put the railway guarantee into abeyance. It was renewed in 1868 by an agreement between the Staffs & Worcs and the Great Western Railway, which had absorbed the Oxford Worcester & Wolverhampton Railway, and was, as we have seen, eventually commuted in 1890 for cash payments and mortgage cancellations totalling £129,000, much of which was used to repay part of the debt owed by the commission to the Staffs & Worcs Company.

In 1888 the river had a minimum depth of 6ft, with 9ft in most parts. Tugs towing ten or twelve boats navigated it and in that year carried 323,000 tons. While in 1890 further improvements were made to the river, including the enlargement of the lock at Gloucester, which connected the river to the ship canal basin, and the condition of the navigation remained adequate, the tonnage carried declined to 120,000 tons in 1927, in spite of great efforts by the Severn Commission and the Severn & Canal Carrying Company to obtain traffic.

The Anderton Lift, photographed from the Weaver below. This was still in regular use when this photograph was taken; the lift continued in commercial use until 1968. The Visitor Centre is now sited on land to the right of this photograph. (British Waterways)

The River Weaver depended for its traffic on an export trade in salt and an import trade in coal, raw materials and china clay, much transhipped at Anderton for the Potteries. From the late 1840s to the 1870s the eleven locks were reduced to nine. Most were also doubled, new 100ft by 22ft by 10ft locks being built alongside the old 88ft by 18ft by 7ft 6in ones. An additional dock and Mersey entrance lock were also built at Weston Point, and opened in 1856. The result was to increase both tonnage and revenue by 50 per cent between the 1840s and the 1870s.

Then Edward Leader Williams jnr, son of Leader Williams of the Severn Commission, was appointed engineer. Further dock extensions began, a steam tugging service for Weaver traffic was inaugurated on the Mersey, and the Anderton vertical boat lift opened in 1875, thus providing a direct connection between the docks, the Weaver and the Trent & Mersey Canal to the Potteries. This structure, the prototype of many lifts on the Continent, raised boats 50ft 4in, each caisson being 75ft by 15ft 6in by 5ft, and able to take two narrow boats or one barge. In 1903 electricity replaced steam power at the lift, and in 1908, when the hydraulic rams and cylinders were worn out, the lift was provided with a new framework that enabled each caisson to be separately worked using counterbalance weights.

In the early 1870s, following recommendations Leader Williams had made in 1865, the Weaver trustees began to build new locks of 220ft by 42ft 6in by 15ft, able to take craft carrying 1,000 tons and, except for the Manchester Ship Canal, the biggest inland waterway locks so far built in Britain. Four of these were constructed in parallel with the larger of the earlier pairs, to replace all existing locks down to the old entrance at Frodsham, and the new one at Sutton, where a new duplicate lock was also built. The gates of these new locks were power-operated by two Pelton wheels to each gate. The programme was completed by 1885, the year a further dock was opened at Weston Point. By the 1880s the income of the Weaver Navigation had reached £60,000 a year, and £10,000 or more was being handed over to the relief of the Cheshire rates by the 105 trustees. The principal traffic was salt, carriage of which had grown from 14,524 tons in 1732 to 1,250,543 tons in 1880–1, when another 500,000 tons were being sent by rail. Thereafter the salt traffic tended to move to pipeline and rail. Coal carrying fell also, but thanks to modernization these losses were replaced by a rapid growth of traffic for the chemical works that had been built near the Weaver from the 1870s.

The last half of the century saw a number of major engineering projects on waterways. In 1850 the Blackhill incline had been completed on the Monkland Canal, supplementing the duplicate lock flights. This drew empty barges uphill, while loaded boats continued to use the locks. It was steam powered, rising 96ft, with twin caissons carrying barges longitudinally down its 1 in 10 slope. It ceased working around 1887, however, as coal traffics had greatly reduced. Foxton inclined plane, on the amalgamated Grand Junction's Leicester line, aimed to replace the ten Foxton Locks permanently. It too was steam-powered, and rose 75ft, each caisson taking two narrow boats sideways down its slope. This opened in 1900, but the anticipated increase in trade failed to materialise, so the incline was largely abandoned in 1910 and the locks reopened.

Some waterways themselves were also improved. For instance the Bridgewater Canal was walled and a depth of 7ft obtained on the towing side, many road bridges were rebuilt to give greater canal width, and additional water supplies were found. Traffic was by then normally worked by a tug towing four boats with a total cargo of 200–240 tons. A more modest but valuable improvement was the opening out of the two lengths of the Fenny Compton Tunnel, totalling 778yd, on the Oxford Canal in 1868 and 1870, and their replacement by a cutting – the longest such tunnel to be opened out.

Though steam-driven craft had been used experimentally on canals from early days, and soon came into use as tugs in tunnels and on the bigger waterways, they did not seriously threaten horse-drawn boats on the narrow canals until about the 1870s. These 'steamers' were similar in design to diesel-engined craft, with an engine room separate from the living accommodation and an overhanging counter to protect the propellor. The earlier craft were adapted from horse-drawn boats by adding a separate counter. Later they were specially built.

A contemporary drawing of the Foxton Inclined Plane.

Coke-fired boilers were designed to take up the least space: they were 6ft long by 4ft in diameter, and worked at a pressure of 140 lb to the square inch. The boats had tall brass funnels, hinged so that they could be lowered under bridges if necessary, and a brass steam whistle. The engines usually had one high-pressure and one low-pressure cylinder in tandem vertically, operating on a single crank, and were fitted with Stephenson link motion for reversing.

Two main disadvantages of 'steamers' compared with semi-diesel-engined craft were the greater space needed for the engine, boiler and coke supplies, and the heavy crew. There were usually two men on the 'steamer' and two on the butty, or, if the boats were working 'fly' round the clock, four on the steamer and three on the butty, of whom three were off duty at any one time. The whole crew was employed by the captain. Later a family sometimes took over the butty, but not the steamer.

In about 1910 the biggest canal carriers, Fellows, Morton & Clayton, began to fit single-cylinder two-stroke semi-diesel units to their boats, and other carriers followed. The last 'steamer' was to leave the Grand Junction in 1932, but on the northern canals occasional steam-driven craft, usually maintenance boats, lasted much longer. From the early 1930s two-cylinder four-cycle diesels began to be fitted, which did not need the pre-heating of the older type.

One great operational reform in the late Victorian period was the reclassification of the freights carried on waterways and the fixing of new tolls for each waterway. An inquiry on rates resulted in the Railway & Canal Traffic Act of 1888, which laid down that each waterway company had to submit a revised classification of traffic and schedule of rates to the new Railway and Canal Commission,

which succeeded the Railway Commission set up by the 1873 Act. Much work
was done by the commission, and in 1894 a series of Acts gave the new classifications and charges (generally lower than before) the force of law. This Act was
damaging to some of the smaller canals, and to the Leeds & Liverpool, since it
reduced their already small revenue, collected perhaps from a single article over
which they had a local monopoly.

One feature of waterways was the lack of any information infrastructure, so
that potential traders might know what routes were available and under what
conditions. This was partly rectified by Henry Rodolph de Salis, a director of
the carriers Fellows Morton & Clayton, who sought greater efficiency. In 1887
he began an examination of the waterway system of England and Wales. Over
11 years, he travelled 14,340 miles (much of this in repeated journeys along and
around the Thames) in three private boats, each named *Dragonfly*, with shorter
journeys by narrow boat. His survey was published in 1904 as *Bradshaw's Canals
and Navigable Rivers of England and Wales*, a handbook to inform commercial users
about the possibilities of water transport. The third and last edition would appear
in 1928, not long before his death.

About those who worked on canals during, and after, the long time of decline,
much went sadly unrecorded, and some impressions must suffice here.

The canal boat people – men, women and children who lived on the boats
– brought up children, aged, died and were ignored by legislators, reformers,
and clerks of canal companies alike. Because they moved about they did not fall
within the jurisdiction of any local authority; they were not covered by the developing factory legislation, or protected by Acts prohibiting the employment of
young children, or Sunday work. In any event, many waterways workers were not
employed directly, but by very small firms or partnerships that were hard to regulate. No Engels investigated them as he studied the condition of the Manchester
working class in 1844; no Charles Kingsley took canal boatpeople for his theme.

Now and then an early glimpse of their life appears: of the part played by canals
in spreading cholera, as at Braunston in 1835, 'it appearing that the disease first
attacked a woman who had been employed in washing the bedding of a boatman
who had died of it' ;[6] of poachers, as when a Cromford Canal by-law prohibited
any boat from stopping at night in Crich Chase, or any wood or coppice; of
drunken boatmen, when the lock-keepers on the Staffs & Worcs were told to
report them to the committee; of sober boatmen on the same canal, at a temperance meeting at Penkridge in 1891, when some took the pledge.

One effect of railway competition was the ending of much fly-boat carrying
and a renewed focus upon the carrying of goods of low value. During the 1850s
and 1860s the numbers of boatpeople declined, especially among younger boatpeople, who sought opportunities elsewhere. Although the former assumption
that falling incomes led more women and children to join family boats in Britain
(but not Ireland) is now in doubt, slow boats tended to feature families more,

THE PADDINGTON

CANAL BOATMAN'S

Magazine.

No. 1.]   APRIL, 1829.   [Vol. 1.

INTRODUCTORY ADDRESS.

In commencing a new Periodical, it is usual to state the necessity that exists for such a work, and also the end likely to be promoted by such a publication.

The necessity of the work is simply this: There is no publication, at present, for the specific purpose of placing before the Christian public an account of the means employed to promote Christianity among those useful labouring men, who are employed on the Canal and on the various Wharfs at the Paddington Basin. Nor is there any publication which records the proceedings of that Society, whose members are so interested in the welfare of this class of men;—and those friends who have contributed to its support, know not whether the efforts used are successful or not. To supply this information, and to establish a publi-

The churches were interested in canal people from before the Victorian era. This is the title page of a church-backed magazine, which ran until December 1832.

and thus family boats became more common on the narrow canals of lowland England. There is evidence that carriers and owners encouraged the family boat in order to reproduce workforces that would otherwise prove costly to recruit and train, and by the end of the nineteenth century there was an established way of life among boatpeople on narrow boats, set apart from other workers of the time. Their experience of this world is difficult to discern, and it was often described by outsiders, hostile in tone like the Birmingham newspaper of 1875 that depicted:

> … the grimiest of low-ceilinged taproom, a truly savage and barbaric 'tap' wherein is dispensed the thinnest and flattest beer I have ever yet come across…Greasy wooden 'settles' and battered wooden tables furnish the apartment, and there come the 'jolly bargemen' to make merry. The walls have two distinct and clearly defined rows of black lines, indicating the presence of greasy backs and heads…[7]

This distaste at squalid living conditions would apply to many pubs in Victorian cities, and the concern for moral welfare when lives seemed to be dominated by alcohol was shared for many 'on the land'. There were pubs in rural areas that depended mainly upon the trade of boatpeople, as were some small shops. The availability of credit for regular customers may have been a significant factor.

The existence of a people with a separate life, and the lack of influence upon them of organised religion or (later) formal education, led some to take an interest in changing their conditions. As evangelicalism grew, from the 1820s onwards various religious bodies attempted to address the perceived welfare and spiritual needs of this population. These organisations were aware that few boatpeople would attend churches, and so set up chapels and mission rooms, sometimes floating. The earliest boatman's chapels seem to be those which opened in 1827. One was near City Road Basin on the Regents Canal, and the other at Paddington on the Grand Junction. Both catered for others in the district as well as boatpeople, and included Sunday schools in which boatchildren could be taught to read. Other chapels soon followed at Leicester and various locations in Yorkshire. These were strongly influenced by, and often overlapped with, missions to seamen. Much of their early history is obscure, but they were mostly inter-denominational, and attempted to address the welfare of boatpeople as well as to convert them to Christian beliefs and secure temperance and improved morals.

Canal owners' views of religious involvement varied, and much depended on whether they were also carriers. Some, like the Shropshire Union company and the Bridgewater Trustees, were concerned for their employees' moral (and perhaps physical) welfare, and assisted in the setting up and support of bethels and mission rooms at a number of locations.

Much publicity resulted from George Smith ('of Coalville'), a Nonconformist who took a well-publicised interest in boat people. After he secured an Act of 1872 to regulate the work of children in brickyards, he lost a well-paid job as manager of a large brickyard in Coalville, and was boycotted by employers for the rest of his life.

In 1873 he turned his attention to the plight of boatpeople, especially children. He confirmed and propagated a general image in two influential books, *Our Canal Population* (1875) and *Canal Adventures by Moonlight* (1881). These painted a lurid portrait of a population that was largely illiterate and irreligious, with widespread drunkenness, immorality and overcrowding, and with children worked hard for seven days a week. Later research has pinpointed many inaccuracies in Smith's books, notably their over-estimates of the numbers who lived on board (100,000, he insisted, against census evidence of about 30,000 at most) in the 1870s, but they did spur legislation. While public health legislation of 1848 and 1875 had provided for the inspection and minimum standards of housing, this did not apply to canal boats until the Canal Boats Act of 1877. Under this, a system of registration and certification limited the numbers of adults and children who could live aboard. While this system provided later researchers with invaluable data for boat genealogy, it had little impact. It was permissive only, and rarely enforced, and failed to achieve Smith's goal to prevent any children from living on boats.

Smith's continued campaigning, helped by another Nonconformist, the Reverend Guy Mark Pearse, influenced a further Canal Boats Act of 1884. This provided for the central supervision of local authorities, which were instructed to ensure that children attended school, a requirement that dated only from 1870.

A somewhat fanciful portrait of an oppressed canal child, from the tract *Rob Rat*; note the bearded sailor ogre-figure on the boat!

This view, showing the work of the London City Mission at Brentford early in the twentieth century, indicates conditions much more clearly. The children do not look impressed. (K.C. Ward/Boat Museum/The Waterways Trust)

This did much to improve conditions on boats and to reduce overcrowding, although school attendance continued to be limited. One effect of the Act was to reduce the number of women and children living on board, although reductions in many traffics and length of hauls had reduced the demand for their labour in any event. Smith next focused his attention, unsuccessfully, on Romani people, until his death in 1895.

Smith's campaigns publicised the poverty and unwelcome behaviour of some boatpeople, unintentionally enlarging existing prejudices and creating new ones. One beneficiary was the revival of religious involvement. Much of this was promoted by the Seamen & Boatmen's Friend Society, founded in 1846 but renamed in 1851, and the London City Mission, founded in 1835. The latter was concerned with the poor in general but appointed a canal missionary in 1878. Neither body favoured the banning of children on boats, but they did seek to improve their moral position. The LCM succeeded in starting a school for boatchildren at Brentford in 1896, with a new purpose-built building from 1904. Some canal companies, like the Leeds & Liverpool, gave support to missions, whilst from the 1870s the Shropshire Union company provided craft, sites or buildings on its own canal and encouraged activity elsewhere. It seems that these were generally more effective in providing rudimentary social services in health and education, albeit patchily, than in religious conversion or the securing of social control.

The advance of unions in some industrial occupations, and on the railways, was not reflected in the growth of union activity among boatpeople or canal company employees. However, in the last two decades of the nineteenth century there were at least twelve strikes among boatpeople. One factor that contributed to relative industrial peace was the tied nature of accommodation, on boats or on the bank, where the loss of employment would also lead to the loss of a home. Another was the paternalism of some small employers, who had been boatmen themselves, and conversely, the oppressive threats by others, such as those around the Humber waterways who sought to circumvent the effects of the Canal Boats Acts by deducting the cost of improvements from the boatpeople's earnings. However, a company like the Shropshire Union, while not recognising unions, did negotiate rates informally with its employees in the fluxingstone trade in the 1890s, as it was fearful that higher negotiated rates elsewhere would tempt away more employees and lead to labour shortages.

Long hours certainly persisted, as this example from the Glamorganshire Canal indicates. After 1887 the Glamorganshire Canal Company began carrying in its own right, although only for a decade to Aberdare and Merthyr Tydfil until subsidence closed these sections. Bill Gomer, a boatman in the 1890s, described this:

James Street Harbour on the Grand Canal, around 1949, with a Grand Canal Company boat loaded with barrels of Guinness porter. There appear to be four boatmen on board; a very long and hard voyage lay ahead for them. The last barge, bound with Guinness for Limerick, left here on 27 May 1960. The harbour has now been filled in. (Guinness Museum)

The Cardiff-Pontypridd boatmen got a monthly wage from the company for making their three trips a week whatever traffic had to go. On the up-along work we did not get the monthly wage, because the Aberdare and Merthyr runs were too long a distance. The company paid us 1s 8d a ton for boating goods to Aberdare or Merthyr. They would pay you a bonus. Suppose I left West Wharf in Cardiff at 5 pm. They could pay me a bonus of 2s 6d if I could get the boat to Merthyr by 7 o'clock tomorrow night. It was not all easy going and there were places on the Merthyr side where it was hard to make the boat swim but when you got to Aberfan the water was so deep that you could drive on the gallop![8]

For those who decided not to work for carriers, but to become owner-boatmen, the position was also mixed. The 1895 diary of Harry King, then a 'number one', on the Grand Junction, shows long periods totalling 31 days inactive through frost, but surviving with 'docking money' intact, travelling empty (and unremunerated) for 37 days, finding cargoes and backloads wherever possible. Later he returned to 'company boating'.

The position in relation to other occupations is unclear; mortality statistics from 1897 suggested that the death rate from accidents was almost four times the average, and twice that of other transport workers, whereas that from suicide was half the national mean.

While the waterways themselves would require modernization in the twentieth century, so would the conditions of those who worked on them. The next century would bring only limited progress on both track and craft modernization and working conditions, and would see waterways involved with new purposes as well as quite different kinds of people.

CHAPTER TWELVE
Towards Nationalization

The construction and completion of the Manchester Ship Canal increased public interest in waterways, while a greater knowledge of the achievements of overseas waterways was provided by such books as J. S. Jeans' *Waterways and Water Transport in Different Countries* (1890), and the second edition of L.F. Vernon-Harcourt's engineering work, *Rivers and Canals* (1896). The development of waterways was seen as one means of reducing railway rates, especially on those serving ports, and on the raw materials on which British industry increasingly relied. From 1900 the Association of British Chambers of Commerce pressed the Government to appoint a Royal Commission, and submitted a series of Waterways Bills, the preamble to that of 1906 conveying their general object:

> To constitute a strong Central Canals Board for the purpose of obtaining provisional orders authorising the board to take over, improve and manage, in the first instance, certain canals which form a chain of navigation between the principal ports of England .[1]

The report of the Royal Commission of 1906, presented in 12 volumes in 1911, provided a comprehensive study of the waterways system of the British Isles, along with studies of the waterways of continental Europe. The latter tried to balance the undoubted progress there, much of it under state ownership of infrastructure, against the very different commercial, economic and topographical conditions in the British Isles. They summed up the position as follows:

> On a few waterways or sections of waterways, favoured by special conditions, combined in two or three cases with enterprising management, traffic has been maintained and even increased. On other waterways it has declined, on some it has virtually disappeared. Everywhere the proportion of long-distance traffic to local traffic by water has become small. Considered as a whole, the waterways have had no share in the enormous increase in internal transport business which has taken place between the middle of the nineteenth century and the present time. Their position, so far as regards their total traffic, has been at best one of a stationary character, since the development of steam traction on railroads and on the sea, while the whole transport business of the country, including that taken by railways and that taken by coasting vessels, has multiplied itself several times over.[2]

It recommended the widening and deepening of the trunk waterway routes of lowland England, connecting the Thames, Severn, Humber and Mersey to a centre in Birmingham. After this was completed, one of the trans-Pennine routes could be enlarged. The widening of the Birmingham area canals was considered impossible, and these were seen as a collecting ground for the enlarged waterways.

Enlargement would have involved complete reconstruction to handle much greater traffics and larger barges. For instance, consulting engineers for the route from Birmingham to Sharpness suggested that 7 inclines and 6 locks should replace 62 existing locks. These reconstructions were expected to result in large savings in time and thus labour costs.

It was clear that, if the waterways were developed on the lines recommended, certain users would achieve major savings in transport costs. For instance, the cost of carrying coal from Leicestershire to London would reduce from 6s. 8d. (33p) to 3s 10d. per ton.

The cost of improving 534 miles of main waterways and some improvement to 514 miles of connecting waterways was estimated then at £17.5 million (*cf.* £15 million for the Manchester Ship Canal to 1894), excluding the costs of acquisition, and new terminals, wharfage and warehouses. The expected return on the investment suggested that revenues on the waterways involved would have to double.

The Commission was clear that 'private enterprise cannot be expected to take the improvement of canals in hand, because, as things stand now, there is no prospect of adequate remuneration, except perhaps in a very few cases.'[3] The nationalization of trunk waterways and their branches in England and Wales, adding to the two existing state-owned canals, the Caledonian and the Crinan, was recommended. This would be under a Waterways Board, which would not have powers to act as a carrier, like many waterways authorities in continental Europe.

The Commission was deeply criticised in two books by Edwin Pratt, who was employed by the Railway Companies Association to present, *inter alia*, the case against its work. In *Canals and Traders* (1910), he virtually accused the Liberal Party of attempting to nationalise all transport; by investing in new canals, the value of railways, and hence the costs of their acquisition, would fall. This might have been the effect, if not the intention, while the idea of a state-owned waterways system competing with a privately-owned railway system contrasted with the practice in parts of continental Europe, where both railways and waterways were state-owned or state-assisted, and the transport system was planned as a whole.

In the event the attention of the Liberal Government was diverted away from the problems of transport towards the problems posed by Irish home rule and the long struggle with the House of Lords, up to the outbreak of the First World War. The Waterways Association was formed in 1912 to press for waterways improvement under state ownership, but despite support from many Midlands local authorities and MPs, this made little progress.

The Commission's report was less radical in regard to Ireland. Noting the drainage problems on the Shannon and Lough Neagh, it recommended State control of both drainage and navigation by a single water authority. It considered proposals to enlarge the line between Limerick and Belfast, but only approved the enlargement of the Shannon locks between Limerick and Killaloe, and a replacement for the Newry Ship Canal. The new Irish Free State appointed a Canals and Waterways Commission in 1922 which also recommended public ownership and the same Shannon enlargement.

An opportunity to rebuild the latter section came with the building of hydro-electric works at Ardnacrusha between 1925 and 1930. The old locks were now eliminated, the navigation channel remaining in the river to Parteen, where a new navigation cut led to the power station and a staircase pair of locks, one 60ft and one 40ft deep. While these have by far the largest fall of any locks in the British Isles, they were built 105ft by 19ft 6in, still narrower, curiously, than those above Killaloe.

On the outbreak of war in 1914, the railway-owned canals were placed under the control of the Railway Executive Committee, which controlled the railways themselves. Nothing was done to control the independent waterways, however, and tonnages fell as boatmen left for the forces or for more lucrative war work in factories. Not until early 1917 were the canals, but not most carriers, brought under a Canal Control Committee of the Board of Trade. This committee tried to restore traffics, and introduced the use of soldiers to assist in the manning of boats, for instance on the Leeds & Liverpool Canal in 1917–8. But much traffic had gone for good, the 31,585,909 tons carried in the British Isles in 1913 being reduced to 21,599,850 tons in 1918.

On 31 August 1920 the canals reverted to private control, although the Ministry of Transport agreed to continue nominal Government control of certain waterways for a time after 1920 in order to raise tolls to an economic level pending new legislation. The removal of control placed a number of navigations into crisis: the war had disrupted trade, maintenance had been neglected during the period of control, and the prices of materials and labour were rising without any corresponding increase in revenues. The main railway-owned canal-carrying concern, the Shropshire Union, ceased to carry in 1921 as losses were too great, owing to the eight-hour day, higher wages and higher costs of materials. Before the war this concern had operated 670 craft of various kinds. Other canal companies with carrying departments, such as the Rochdale and Leeds & Liverpool, soon followed.

Bye-traders could not offer the same integrated services as their predecessors and tonnages carried soon dropped. The Rochdale Canal, for instance, had carried 554,597 tons in 1905, much in company boats, but tonnages declined to 180,269 in 1922, 100,092 in 1927, 38,638 in 1932 and 19,187 in 1937.

Much of this was local coal traffic around Manchester, as road competition and mill closures had reduced traffic across the summit to a minimum by 1925. This company, like small independent concerns such as the Neath and Stroudwater, increasingly focused upon revenues from property and water supplies.

The postwar inflation made it unlikely that the Royal Commission improvements would ever be carried out, and the Coalition Government appointed Neville Chamberlain MP, leader of the Waterways Association, to head a committee to consider the post-war position. Its second report, in May 1921, recommended against nationalization on the grounds of financial liabilities, as the waterways had deteriorated and both prices and wages had risen. However, it suggested that seven regional groups of waterways, which would include railway-owned canals, should be formed. Unlike the four great railway groups, these were to be acquired and controlled by public trusts. These would represent interests involved, from central and local Government to stockholders, and would be financed partly by Government. Neither these recommendations, nor those of the 1930 Royal Commission on Transport (which recommended voluntary amalgamations prior to compulsory acquisition by public trusts), were followed up. The Waterways Association viewed this as a defeat and disbanded, although a National Council for Inland Waterways was formed to continue the campaign for development.

The Chamberlain Committee had recommended that action begin with the Trent group, partly because Nottingham Corporation was already committed to an improvement scheme on that river. Amalgamations with feeder navigations were unlikely in this case. The Grantham Canal and most of the Nottingham Canal were disused by the 1930s, while part of the Chesterfield Canal had been disused since the collapse in 1908 of the summit Norwood tunnel, with much traffic local only. The length of the Nottingham Canal through Nottingham, part of the through Trent route, would be leased from 1937 to the Trent Navigation Company, which also approached the Fossdyke in 1939. This took place after major improvements up to Nottingham.

The River Trent had always been a significant navigation, and the opening of the Trent & Mersey Canal made it a link in a through route from the Humber to the Mersey. The original Trent Navigation Company, formed in 1783, was concerned with the state of the river, especially that part below the canal entrance at Wilden Ferry, while the Newark Navigation Commissioners controlled the cut of 4 miles at Newark. Later the Humber Conservancy Board was formed to control the portion of river from Trent Falls, where the river joins the Humber, to Gainsborough, where the control of the Trent Navigation Company began.

The navigation was good from Trent Falls to Newark, but between there and Nottingham lay a shallow and fast-running part of the river, with a fall of up to 19in to the mile. This meant that goods had to be transhipped at Newark to smaller craft, which added to the transport costs of those carried up to Nottingham. In 1906 the Trent Navigation Company obtained an Act to dredge the river to 5ft minimum and to build six new locks and cuts. By 1914, financial shortages meant that only Cromwell Lock, 188 by 30ft, had been built, while the river had been dredged so that 120 ton vessels could pass up to Newark.

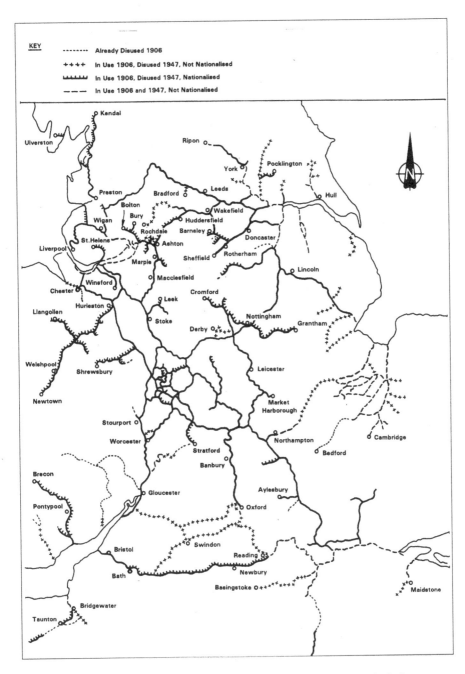

This map of the main waterways in England and Wales shows the way in which the system contracted between 1906 and 1947. Those shown in thick black lines show the most significant waterways to be nationalized.

The oil terminal at Colwick, shown here in the early 1960s. The craft operated by John Harker of Knottingley carried petroleum from the 1930s until 1971. There was a short-lived revival of traffic, using grant assistance to refurbish the wharf, in the 1980s. (British Waterways)

As the 1906 Act powers were expiring, Nottingham Corporation obtained a further Act in 1915, against railway company opposition, allowing it to finance the remaining works. Financial and labour shortages meant that only after the war was the river dredged and new locks built. The latter could take three Trent boats and a cargo-carrying tug, totalling 600 tons. Newark Nether Lock was also replaced, and a new channel at Holme Lock later allowed the largest river craft through to Trent Bridge, Nottingham. Above Nottingham the lines to Shardlow and Leicester only took Upper Trent boats of 71ft 6in by 14ft 6in.

Nottingham was now less than twenty-four hours away by river from Hull, where craft could be loaded direct from seagoing ships. The work authorised under the 1906 Act was completed in 1927, and Nottingham Corporation, which had spent about £450,000, took over the navigation. In 1932 the corporation opened a new basin at Trent Lane, forming a major new head of navigation, while a new oil terminal opened at Colwick in the early 1930s. Traffic increased from 66,960 tons in 1928 to 230,514 tons in 1936; oil carrying rose from 7 per cent to over 50 per cent of the tonnage. The delays involved reduced the value of the amalgamations with smaller waterways.

A second important development was the formation of the Grand Union Canal Company and the modernization of its route. In 1894 the Grand Junction

Lock widening on the Warwick section of the new Grand Union Canal in the early 1930s, with the original narrow locks still in use on the left. Note the broken balance beam on the offside bottom gate of the nearest lock. The new locks were built partly on the site of wide pounds and side ponds serving the narrow locks. Replacement side ponds are shown under construction. (British Waterways)

Company had absorbed the line to Leicester, and in 1929 joined with the Regents Canal in London and the three Warwick canals, to form a new company, the Grand Union. A through route from Regent's Canal Dock (now Limehouse Basin) and Brentford in London to Birmingham was now under one ownership, with running powers over a short length of the Oxford Canal.

Three years later the amalgamated company absorbed the Leicester and Loughborough navigations and the Erewash Canal, extending the line past Leicester and Trent Junction to Langley Mill. The length of the new combined waterway was over 300 miles. With the help of a Government guarantee of interest for a number of years about £1 million was then spent on the London to Birmingham route. As constructed, this was built as a barge canal to Braunston, while the remainder was narrow. On the Braunston to Birmingham section 51 new broad locks were built to take two narrow boats at once. In order to work 14ft beam barges through the canal it would, however, have been necessary to rebuild so many bridges that it was decided for the time being to maintain the 14ft standard from London to Berkhamsted, and a 12ft 6in standard from there to a newly developed depot at Sampson Road, a mile from Birmingham. While the Grand Union Company intended to build boats of 12ft 6in beam, and prototypes were constructed, there were so many lengths where two 12ft 6in craft could not pass that the canal north of Berkhamsted continued to be worked by narrow boats in pairs.

Much dredging was done, and over many stretches of the canal the cross-sectional area was increased by walling and piling the sides, thus enabling the boats to travel faster. Most of this programme was completed by 1934.

Meanwhile the canal company had begun carrying by buying the small firm of Associated Canal Carriers Ltd in 1930, changing its name in 1934 to the Grand Union Canal Carrying Co. Ltd, and greatly expanding its fleet. It also acquired the Erewash Canal Carrying Company, formed by the Erewash owners in the 1920s to carry from Leicester and Loughborough, developed shipping and property subsidiaries and provided lorries for deliveries in the Birmingham area.

It proved to have over-expanded: there were shortages of crews and many boats were laid up. The carrying operation had to be considerably cut down and reorganised before heavy losses could be ended. These had repercussions on the canal company itself, which paid no dividend on its ordinary shares between 1933 and 1945.

The Weaver Navigation formed part of the proposed Wolverhampton–Mersey route of the Royal Commission. The rebuilt Anderton Lift passed craft more rapidly, and through traffic increased to a record 226,000 tons in 1913. Much of this traffic served the Potteries, but further plans for a new canal there only got as far as a conference of Potteries local authorities in 1912.

Plans for a Birmingham Ship Canal, to the Severn or Mersey, were revived in the early 1920s, but all that emerged was a guarantee to cover losses on the Worcester & Birmingham Canal, to prevent its closure and thus safeguard the Severn route. The Weaver Navigation cleared its debts in 1934 and the Trustees promptly reduced tolls. New opening bridges, similar to those on the Manchester Ship Canal, had been built, and the last low bridge at Hartford was removed in 1938.

Until the 1930s only one seagoing vessel regularly used the river, most traffic relying on transhipment at Weston Point, Liverpool or Birkenhead. From 1938 the Weaver trustees sought to develop direct traffic to waterside industries, especially to the ICI works around Northwich, using diesel-engined coasters with a greater carrying capacity. Improvements, mainly dredging and the easing of corners, continued into the war years. In 1944–45, the trustees promoted a Bill to extend navigation up the Weaver valley to Audlem, and then south along an enlarged Shropshire Union Canal to Wolverhampton. This endorsed wartime Government proposals for a new line for 100 ton craft, but railway opposition limited this to an extension to Nantwich; this was never built.

The Manchester Ship Canal had a considerable effect on the trade of Manchester, in the growth of waterside industries in Trafford Park and near its waterside, served by its private railway. The first oil installations had opened at Mode Wheel in 1896, along with Barton Oil Berth in 1902, but the growth in oil traffic was increasingly focused on to the lower reaches up to Runcorn. In

1922 the Ship Canal Company opened a new dock at Stanlow to accommodate imported petrol, while refining started on the opposite bank in 1924, where there was soon established a major centre for oil storage and distribution. Distribution routes included the canal to Chester and the Midlands, and up the Weaver, but rail, pipelines and road transport were increasingly used.

Before 1907 the whole canal had been deepened from 26ft to 28ft in order to accommodate larger vessels, and in 1927 it was deepened still further between Eastham and Stanlow by 2ft. By the 1920s plans to complete the final Dock No. 10 at Salford had been shelved.

Ellesmere Port was also gradually developed for Ship Canal traffic, especially after 1922, when the Shropshire Union leased its property there to the Ship Canal Company. This built on existing installations based on the Shropshire Union, in milling, ironworks and a cement works, and that benefited both waterways. In the interwar years the importance of the smaller canals diminished, with greater reliance on direct shipments to Ship Canal locations and forwarding via the Ship Canal Railway.

The Sheffield & South Yorkshire Navigation had remained unmodernised, partly because of its effective domination by the Great Central Railway. Between 1918 and 1920 Sheffield Corporation promoted an unsuccessful plan for Government acquisition and improvement of the main line to Tinsley, with 18 new 300-ton locks. Traffic, much of it in coal and in goods upstream to Sheffield, revived in quantity during the interwar period, to 815,000 tons in 1937. This was increasingly short-haul, however, although in the early 1930s improvements allowed larger boats to reach a new warehouse at Doncaster and Aire & Calder compartment boats to access Hatfield Main Colliery through an enlarged Bramwith Lock.

The branches of the S&SYN fared worse during this period. After 1928 the private Park Gate branch, and the Elsecar Branch of the much larger Dearne & Dove Canal, were disused. Extensive mining caused much damage, and bridges and locks would have had to be rebuilt, along with bank raising. Much of this was the subject of complex legal negotiations with coal owners, a general issue that was not properly resolved until the 1950s. Faced with these costs and declining traffic, the S&SYN sought closure of the Dearne & Dove after the last through traffic to Barnsley ended in 1934. Objections prevented formal closure, but the line was left to become derelict, bar a short section at Swinton retained for coal and sand traffic.

During the interwar period, after much traffic had disappeared during the 1914–18 war, traffic on most smaller waterways further declined. In Britain, national tonnages carried diminished from about 17 million tons in 1924 to about 13 million in 1938. The condition and use of most waterways deteriorated, and a number became disused entirely. These included all the remaining waterways in the South Wales valleys, apart from traffics on the lowest part of the

Glamorganshire Canal. The latter was also affected by mining subsidence, and its owners left breaches unrepaired, above Pontypridd in 1915, and Nantgarw in 1942. By then, only the company's own boats used the canal, and it transferred remaining traffics to road. The other South Wales canals continued in use for water supplies, but apart from a section of the Swansea Canal, required for railway development, there were neither moves to close these, nor any attempts to revive traffic.

Disuse also overtook a number of mainly rural English canals by 1939, such as the Stratford, Pocklington, Grand Western, Wisbech, Louth, and almost all of the Huddersfield Narrow Canal. Earlier, traffics had ended on the upper part of the St Helens Canal and on the Droitwich Barge Canal after the 1914 war, and both were formally closed in the 1930s. Formal closure of the St Helens was promoted in 1931 to facilitate new road crossings around St Helens. The Bradford Canal, an urban canal with limited traffics, readily transferred to road, was closed in 1922 to save considerable costs in back-pumping round locks.

Among sparsely populated, mainly agricultural areas of England, traffic was especially badly affected by the flexibility of the motor lorry, such as in the fen districts, characterised in 1907 as:

> … the only district where navigation is utilized by the agriculturist…the roads in those districts are abominable; the soil is magnificent, soft alluvial deposit; they float barges or small craft up these drains; they load and take them off to some staith, where they can put the produce on to a railway truck or take it to their own yards.[4]

Once roads and vehicles were improved, traffic disappeared rapidly, although barges serving the beet industry and fuel deliveries to isolated pumping stations lasted until after the Second World War.

Traditional traffics by wherry and keel in the Broads area similarly declined, although new traffics developed by coaster to Norwich and to Cantley. While the Fens waterways were kept in being largely for drainage use, pleasure boating, which became dominant in the Broads, also grew.

Between 1919 and 1939 the number of licensed road goods vehicles in Great Britain increased almost eightfold from 62,000. Road competition removed much short-haul and rural canal traffic, serving waterside locations that railway sidings and railway cartage could not have reached economically. This also forced down railway rates, which sharpened competition with canal traffic and made their operations even less remunerative. However, competition was not always aggressive, as the 1933 agreement between the four main rail companies and the Canal Association suggests. This provided for the elimination of price cutting and the quotation of uneconomic rates.

In Ireland, after 1932 the Grand Canal Company began to carry some traffics by road, and canal traffic fell rapidly, as it did upon the Royal Canal. The rural waterways of the north gradually became disused: the Ulster in 1929, the Strabane in 1932 and the Newry Canal, oldest of them all, in 1938 outside Newry. Traffic on the Coalisland Canal, mostly in imported grain, had revived until road competition started to undermine it in the early 1930s. The Lower Bann, which featured some limited commercial and pleasure traffic, remained threatened with closure by drainage and hydropower schemes. The Lagan Navigation's traffic declined such that between 1938 and 1954 the Stormont Government made up any financial deficits, as the waterway would revert to its ownership if it became moribund.

Many traffics disappeared when customers either closed or changed the nature of their operations. The Monkland Canal, upon which traffic was negligible by 1934, demonstrates the effects of the working out of coal seams and quarries on canal routes. The replacement of coal as a source of power by electricity from the grid, developed between 1926 and 1937, did bring significant new traffics in coal to new power stations. However, the switch to new power supplies resulted in the loss of many dispersed canalside industrial customers. Examples of canalside power stations include three new ones served by the Leeds & Liverpool at Wigan and Whitebirk (Blackburn), and Kirkstall; the last involved a new branch in 1927 and the deepening of the canal to Leeds.

Neglect affected traffics on the Edinburgh and Glasgow Union, where the last coal traffic ended due to a lengthy stoppage to rebuild an aqueduct near Edinburgh in 1937. At the Falkirk end, where traffic had long been minimal, the lock flight was closed in the early 1930s, partly to replace a railway bridge with an embankment.

The Nottingham and Grantham Canals illustrate the difficulties in securing formal closure, processes that would delay decisive action over many declining waterways until amenity use had developed from the 1950s onwards. Both canals passed to the London and North Eastern company (LNERCo) on grouping. These suffered from the stifling of trade through night and Sunday closures, water shortages exacerbated by industrial sales of water, objections to the use of steam-powered boats, a lack of ice-breaking and refusals to quote through tolls. By 1905 only 18,802 tons were carried on the rural Grantham Canal, much of it in manure from Nottingham conveyed a short distance to local farms. This had reduced to 1,583 tons by 1924 and none in 1929. Almost all traffic had left the upper part of the Nottingham Canal by 1928, and the prospects of renewed traffic from the decrepit Cromford Canal (see Chapter Eleven) were remote.

The LNERCo., seeking to reduce costs, only managed to obtain a closure Act in 1936 after agreeing to maintain water levels and measures to ensure public safety. While closure allowed locks to be converted to weirs, with bridges replaced by low crossings, the watercourses had to remain. The LNERCo. thus saw little financial benefit in closure, or in the closure of other lines, like the Hollinwood and Stockport branches of the Ashton Canal, also disused in the 1930s. Parts of

Unloading porter barrels at Ballinasloe, the extension of the Grand Canal across the Shannon, around 1954. This was a part of a network of stores owned by Guinness and served by the Grand Canal Company (later CIE) fleet. The Ballinasloe branch closed in 1961 and much has since been destroyed by turf workings. (Guinness Museum)

the Grantham would be revived after the 1960s, but the Nottingham Canal would survive only in part as an amenity.

Similar objections inhibited plans by Shropshire County Council in 1935 to close parts of the Newtown and Shrewsbury lines of the Shropshire Union Canal in order to build new low road crossings. This was defeated by objections over the loss of rural water supplies and safety, although a major breach, at Perry Aqueduct on the Newtown line, was left unrepaired after 1936, and both lines were closed in 1944.

The Kennet & Avon Canal from Bath to Newbury was almost devoid of traffic by the interwar period, due partly to railway competition and poor maintenance. Objections caused the Great Western Railway to abandon closure plans in 1929, and it embarked on a programme of repairs, albeit to low standards. Traffic did not revive, although boats were able to struggle through until the late 1940s, after which there was a long campaign for restoration until completion in the 1990s.

Working conditions on waterways continued to be hard, and practices increasingly outmoded. The life of boat crews and canal workers, whether in carrying or

The Nottingham Canal at Wollaton Top Lock at the beginning of the twentieth century. Note the poor condition of the lock brickwork and the leaking top gates – indications of neglect. Even by this date traffics from this colliery and others along the line were very limited. (British Waterways)

maintenance, was a hard and often dangerous one. One of the last narrow-boat carriers later asserted that boat people 'worked eighteenth century hours, for nineteenth century wages, until three-quarters of the way through the twentieth century.'[5] Long hours, poor pay and harsh working conditions indeed drove many from the waterways in the twentieth century.

For the Irish Republic, the following account, albeit from a pleasure exploration in 1946, of Grand Canal transport bore out the 1923 commission's assertion that 'primitive conditions still exist':

We soon discovered that our 'tug' was the canal equivalent of an ordinary goods train on the railway, and in consequence our day's journey proved as slow as it was eventful. Our first stop was at Philipstown Wharf to pick up some empty porter barrels…After performing this arduous task the crew adjourned to the bar which was conveniently situated near the canal bridge and proceeded to do their best to empty another porter barrel…

At the next bridge…we stopped again, this time to deposit two bags of sugar. There was no wharf or warehouse, in fact no sign of habitation. Apparently the sugar was destined for the shop in the little village of Road just over a mile distant. Here there was no convenient bar to detain us, and we were just congratulating ourselves on having got under way smartly when our 'tug' suddenly slewed across the canal and ran her bows into the bank while one of the crew jumped ashore. He had apparently arranged to call at the neighbouring cottage upon some errand or other.[6]

Ireland's leading canal historian, Ruth Delany, described conditions on the Grand and Barrow:

> The position of lockkeeper in particular stayed with the same family through several generations. The house and garden were the attraction, because the wages were very poor: the Barrow lockkeepers were still getting as little as 11s. per week in 1930 and others not much more. The hours were very long, as boats had to be locked through at all hours of the day and night. On one occasion, Thomas Murphy, lockkeeper at Lowtown, was asked by the chairman of the company how long he had worked in the service of the company and he received the reply, 'A hundred years, fifty by day and fifty by night'.
>
> The boatmen were also drawn from the same families…It was a hard life and poorly paid. The four men lived in the tiny cabin in the bow, conditions were very primitive and they often shared their meagre meal from a communal enamel basin. Until 1946 they were expected to travel night and day, with twenty-four hours a week off on Sundays.[7]

Two examples from barge work in the Mersey area in the 1930s illustrate that work continued to be unpleasant and difficult. James Unsworth, born in 1906, recalled moving from regular work on the Leeds & Liverpool to work with Dick Abraham, who:

> … owned his own barge, the *Mary*, and carried anything – coal, wheat or muck. If there was nothing else, we could always get refuse from Liverpool Corporation, but the last load finished us off, 3½ tons of dead cats followed by a load from Hartley's jam works on a hot summer's day. I don't know which was the worst the smell the flies or the wasps. When we got to the dump we shouted for the unloaders, and beat it as fast as we could to the nearest pub.[8]

Another witness was Charlie Morris, who worked during the 1930s around Chester and the Mersey. He related how:

> … an owner thought more of his horses' welfare than the men and women who worked his craft. The horses must be in the stable for 7 pm bedded down, watered and fed, but the boaties could go hungry, and many times they did…All the boaties I knew had a dog, a good safeguard against hunger, many a rabbit or pheasant went into the pot that way, and I went to the cook on many a ship looking for food.[7]

The numbers of families living on narrow boats in lowland England declined, but conditions did not improve, especially when compared with other workers. There were renewed attempts to prohibit children from living on boats, but none succeeded. In 1921 a Ministry of Health committee reported that less than 1,000 children of school age lived on boats, but 85 per cent of these were almost illiterate. It recommended that such children should be prohibited from living on boats during school terms. The 1921 Education Act did not provide for this, and many children received no regular schooling. There were further attempts to remove children from boat crews, notably by the Labour MP Harry Gosling in 1929–30, but this foundered on the opposition of canal carriers, voluntary societies and the boatpeople themselves. A petition with 1,006 signatures of boatpeople against the Bill was delivered to Parliament on May 7 1930.

The opposition of boatpeople was based mainly upon concerns that both their homes and livelihoods could be lost, especially at times when working conditions generally failed to improve even to the limited extent that they had in competing industries. There were limited attempts at improvements in conditions, notably by the Grand Union Canal Carrying Company in the late 1930s, which formed a conciliation board with union representation. Some boatpeople did join unions, with 30 strikes recorded in the interwar years, the most notable involving Fellows Morton & Clayton workers in 1923, promoted by a dispute over reduced rates. The strike, which lasted sixteen weeks, was settled with a smaller reduction in rates.

Chapter Ten mentioned some early pleasure boating on the canals, although river cruising and the Broads remained more popular. The Great Ouse between St Ives and Bedford was kept open for a short period from 1906 by a River Ouse Locks Committee, representing pleasure users. Not until after the war would a long campaign, between 1950 and 1978, secure the re-opening of this river to Bedford.

Despite many examples of individual canal trips, the practice of owning or hiring craft year after year was confined mainly to the Thames and the Broads. More regular canal cruising was encouraged by George Westall, who became the President of the National Inland Navigation League, which existed for a time after the 1914 war. His *Inland Cruising* (1908) described a twenty-five-day tour in a motor boat in 1907, through 870 miles of waterway from the Thames to the Trent and Yorkshire Derwent to Malton, over the Leeds & Liverpool Canal, and via the Macclesfield, Coventry and Oxford Canals. It provided much practical information about canal routes and boats, including comments on hotels (for overnight stays) and the location of fuel supplies.

Some encouragement was provided by the growth of regular holidays for middle-class people, and by the availability of more suitable craft. Motive power was a major problem until the development of reliable marinised diesel and petrol engines, including the outboard motor, although their application to pleasure craft was gradual.

A hazard to early pleasure boating: an example of one of the Shropshire Union Canal 'swing' bridges (actually lift bridges) which gave A.E. Neal's friend William so much trouble. Most of the original bridges have been modified, but this one, Allman's Bridge, on the Prees Branch and thus in lesser use, survived until 1997, when it disintegrated. Its replacement, in replica appearance but widened, proved difficult to operate.

Further literature on canal boating included P. Bonthron's *My Holidays on Inland Waterways* (1916) with staccato descriptions of explorations of many canals, including some, like the Royal Military, which are no longer navigable. Bonthron's background is somewhat obscure. From Scottish origins, he was a wealthy London shipping agent, able to afford to own a car before 1914 and to hire small craft upon various canals and elsewhere. Less obscure was E. Temple Thurston, a minor Irish writer, whose *The Flower of Gloster* (1911) was a possibly fictional account of a tour through the Oxford, Stratford and Thames and Severn.

In Scotland, passenger steamers had run for many years on the Crinan and Caledonian Canals, and on the Forth & Clyde the five *Queens* plied between 1893 and 1939. There were some regular trip boats on smaller canals, such as the three steamers run by Arthur Beech from Compton on the Staffordshire & Worcestershire and Shropshire Union Canals. Largely confined to the summits of those canals, services in *Compton Queen* lasted until around 1930. Beech also hired small rowing boats, and had had 30 craft when he began at Compton in 1895. Small craft featured on many canals elsewhere, such as the Union Canal in Edinburgh, or the Shropshire Union at Whitchurch.

Early pleasure boating was not without incident, as a detailed log of a trip just before the First World War suggests. A.E. Neal owned a succession of craft at Derby, from where he travelled to Llangollen in 1913, near where on 19 July:

Poor William got his hand rather badly bashed against the wall in Chirk Tunnel while he was holding a flashlight over the side to guide my steering; but he soon forgot the pain caused by this in the agitation resulting from his dealings with the swing bridges. As he was a shorter man than Basil he could only just reach the uplifted bridge with the boat-hook, and being unable to give a sufficiently long and strong pull to return the bridge to the horizontal, it occasionally took command of the proceedings, and, when about a third of the way down, majestically uplifted itself again, carrying the struggling William into the air with it.[10]

These difficulties with a canal operated for transport rather than pleasure were also marked by Neal's trip to Oxford in the summer of 1914, when he succeeded in draining a pound at Claydon, which held up traffic. Technically infringing the by-laws, he was 'discharged with a caution' by the lock-keeper.

The attitudes of canal owners towards pleasure boating varied. Some, like the Birmingham Canal Navigation or the Bridgewater Department, were very reluctant to admit pleasure craft, while the London, Midland & Scottish Railway strongly discouraged boats on its Lancaster and Manchester, Bolton & Bury canals, but welcomed enquiries about the Shropshire Union and Trent & Mersey canals. The London & North Eastern Railway positively welcomed pleasure boating on its Ashton, Peak Forest and Macclesfield canals, with reasonable charges. Pleasure use was often discouraged on the more congested waterways. As one Grand Union worker at Brentford later recalled:

In my youth, we would do anything in our power to prevent pleasure boats, and we would make it pretty plain to them. The boatmen regarded them as a nuisance, that's all. The idea of people using the canal for pleasure didn't seem to occur to us then.[11]

Usually an exception to this was the annual outing, often on Sundays or bank holidays, when there was less traffic. On the Swansea Canal, for instance, trips at Whitsun were part of an annual celebration:

The carnival field, usually the local farm fields such as Norton fields at Ynystawe or the tinplate works field such as the 'Bryn' tinplate works at Ynysmeudwy was the destination for the boat trips. Tents and stalls would be erected on the field and all types of sports and games would be played throughout the day…

A canal barge would be hired from one of the local industries or the Great Western Railway Company, which had several maintenance barges on the canal…

On the Friday and Saturday preceding the event the barges would be scrubbed clean and sawdust sprinkled on the floor. The barges were decorated in various ways, principally to brighten the boats up but also to protect the best clothes of the occupants… Seats or benches would be placed in the boat for the older passengers whilst the youngsters stood up.[12]

These outings lasted until the last trip from Pontardawe to Ynysmeudwy in 1939, after which the canal became unnavigable. Another canal in Wales, the Shropshire Union, featured a number of early pleasure boating initiatives. The horse-drawn passenger boats from Llangollen continued into the 1930s and even, on a very reduced basis, during the Second World War. The popularity of the longer trips to Chirk, which connected with the Glyn Valley Tramway, declined with the growth of short charabanc outings and the ending of passenger carrying on the tramway in 1932. A shorter-lived service, run by a coach proprietor, ran from Ellesmere in the 1930s. While various individuals began to hire out their own boats at this period, from about 1933 one carrier at Whitchurch began to hire out a narrow boat, complete with horse and boatmen, during slack trading periods. This was a precursor of the later camping boats.

Both the Whitchurch and Ellesmere operations had ceased by 1937, despite their location on one of the most attractive, if increasingly decrepit, canals in Britain. An early operation that drew on this attraction, including the Newtown line, was the firm of Samuel Bond, which began to hire out *The Rambler* from Stoak, near Ellesmere Port, in 1932. Bond mainly built river and seagoing pleasure boats on the Mersey at Rock Ferry, Birkenhead, and started this sideline when orders for boats dropped during the depression. At this time, boat owners often hired out their own boats when they were not on holiday themselves. This was the initial basis for the Inland Cruising Association, founded in 1935 by G. F. Wain and others at Christleton, a week's round trip away from Llangollen. This became the first successful hire boat firm on a British canal, expanding rapidly to run a fleet of purpose-built craft by 1939; this had declined to a much smaller operation after the war.

The supply of private boats was augmented by the conversion of a range of former working craft. Lifeboats from scrapped ships was one source, but there were also conversions of narrow boat hulls. There may have been one as early as 1906–7, but by 1939 several boats had been converted.

Boat clubs began to be formed in the 1930s, of similar character to the many river cruising clubs like the Ripon Motor Boat Club, founded in 1931 on the short Ripon Canal. This was the consequence of a rare example of the removal of pleasure boats from a regularly cruised length, in this case the Yorkshire Derwent Navigation, upon which several motor boats were moored at Kirkham Abbey during the 1920s. Following flooding in 1931–2 and damage to Kirkham Lock, the LNER Co. sought closure and transfer of the navigation to the local Catchment Board. A River Derwent Protection Association was formed to raise funds to repair Sutton Lock in 1935. Boats from the length moved to the Ripon Canal, the lower lock and pound of which was repaired to facilitate moorings. Although the main cruising grounds were the Ure, Ouse and Derwent, RMBC boats visited the Pocklington Canal in 1933, just before it became impassable.

The earliest canalboat club, as such, was the Mersey Motor Boat Club, founded at Litherland on the Leeds & Liverpool Canal in 1932, with some boats moored around Maghull. Both this and the West London Motor Cruising Club, founded in 1938 at Alperton on the Grand Union Canal, were on heavily trafficked, urban, broad canals, but close to major rivers. The North Cheshire Cruising Club, at High Lane on the narrow and mainly rural Macclesfield Canal, was formed in 1943 in order to oppose the rating of boathouses. This formalised moorings that dated back to before the First World War.

Fuel restrictions brought most pleasure boating to an effective close in 1939, some for good. This included the steamers on the Forth & Clyde Canal from Port Dundas to Craigmarloch, where the *Gipsy Queen* was withdrawn and sent to the breakers in 1940. No service would be revived after the war, although this canal stayed open for a time and saw the sea-to-sea passage of pleasure yachts. The traditional annual outings, usually in working craft, still operated, although charabanc excursions reduced their appeal.

In Britain, wartime conditions brought the main connected traffic waterways, along with all of the railway-owned waterways, under central control, an arrangement that would persist until nationalization. At first the Ministry of War Transport did not bring the independent canals under control, on the grounds of cost and the assumption that much traffic would find its way to them without assistance. The war caused a major shift in trade, away from east coast ports facing Europe towards those on the west coast, while traffic also changed in character and usual destination. The limited mileage and flexibility of the waterways compared with rail and road transport meant reduced traffic, and the canal companies began to lose revenue. Subsidies to canal carriers were introduced in June 1940, aiming to make canal transport competitive with other forms of transport, along with pegged tolls. The latter soon proved insufficient to enable the canal companies to maintain their waterways, which deteriorated in consequence.

In 1941 the Government appointed Frank Pick, the head of London Transport, to investigate the use of canals in the war effort. Pick recommended that the Government should assume responsibility for them, and the advisory central and regional canal committees that had been set up at the beginning of the war were strengthened. He also recommended amalgamations of ownership on certain routes and the closure of lightly used canals. One major owner, the London Midland and Scottish Railway, implemented part of these proposals, transferring part of the Huddersfield Canal to the Calder & Hebble Navigation in 1945. The London Midland and Scottish Act of 1944 involved the largest single closure of canal mileage, including much of the Cromford, Huddersfield and Shropshire Union canals. This mostly involved similar conditions to those for the Nottingham and Grantham canals, so that water levels had to be maintained.

Pressure on transport in Britain became such that it was clearly necessary to maintain in reasonable order those waterways that could contribute to the war effort. Eighteen undertakings and a number of carriers were therefore taken into State control in 1942. All income went to the Ministry of War Transport, which paid fixed annual sums equivalent to average revenue in the last three pre-war years, plus outgoings considered necessary for war purposes. The cost to the Government up to the end of the war was £2.6 million.

While efforts were made to direct and divert as much traffic as possible to the waterways, the canals suffered from the previous poor standards of maintenance, and from the drain of skilled men and women, not only from the boats themselves, but from such ancillary industries as the boat-building and repairing yards. The different gauges of the canals made it almost impossible to transfer craft from less used parts of the system to others, such as the Mersey and Severn areas, where more traffic could have been carried by water if boats had been available.

The main transfer carried out was that of petroleum tank barges from the Humber to the Severn. These helped to build up what later became a substantial trade in petroleum by water from Avonmouth to Gloucester, Worcester and Stourport. The Severn line had suffered from the interwar depression, railway competition, and fragmented management, and its fortunes were only revived by the growth in oil traffic after depots were established in 1927 at Stourport and Diglis, Worcester. Sharp bends and draught restrictions above Gloucester prevented fully loaded petroleum craft from passing.

The carrying of general merchandise on the Severn was also improved by wartime developments. The link provided by the narrow Worcester & Birmingham Canal was of reducing importance, and Pick suggested that most of it could be closed. From the early 1930s new riverside wharves had been developed at Worcester and Stourport to serve large craft that could not pass up to the canal basins there. Pick recommended the enlargement of the Severn to take estuarial craft directly from Avonmouth and elsewhere to new depots at both towns for forwarding by road. New wharves were opened below Stourport and at Diglis in 1942 and 1944 respectively.

Towards the end of the war the coalition Government considered the prospects for postwar redevelopment and commissioned four schemes for the waterways of the Cross. Based wherever possible on the enlargement of river navigations rather than canals, these were to use the Severn to Stourport; the Weaver to Audlem and Shropshire Union south to Wolverhampton; the Trent and Tame to Tamworth; and the Thames between London and Oxford, the Oxford Canal and the Grand Union line into Birmingham. While none of these schemes proceeded, those for the Weaver and Severn spurred further studies to enlarge and extend those navigations.

Women had long partnered men on some canal boats, sometimes being captains in their own right. As a result of the enterprise of two, later three, women who ran a boat in 1941 on the Worcester & Birmingham Canal, a scheme was started to train women to work pairs on the Grand Union. While only a maximum of eleven pairs of boats was worked by women at the same time, it was none the less valuable. The scheme was later taken over by the Ministry of War Transport and was wound up at the end of 1945, when the last woman volunteer left. Four books, by Emma Smith, Susan Woolfitt, Eily Gayford and Margaret Cornish, describe these experiences. A smaller scheme involved women on Leeds & Liverpool Canal boats in 1945.

Damage from the Blitz disrupted traffic on waterways in major English cities. Among the worst affected was Liverpool, in which traffic was disrupted by a major breach caused by explosive bombing. Even the Leeds & Liverpool head office was evacuated to a house in Formby. Direct damage elsewhere, to track, buildings and boats, was generally limited to urban areas, although even the lock-house at the wholly rural Wharton Lock, on the Shropshire Union in Cheshire, was destroyed by a stray bomb. Stop planks were placed in bridgeholes most nights, to isolate sections that might be damaged. Much greater was the disruption to trade caused by the call-up of many canal workers, the destruction of factories and other sources of traffic, and in transport for collection and delivery services. Even by 1940 many boats were idle on the Leeds & Liverpool Canal, and again military personnel were brought in to assist. Later, labour shortages led to attempts to recruit canal boatmen from Ireland to the Leeds & Liverpool, Grand Union and Trent navigation, among others, in 1942–3.

The tonnage carried on canals had dropped to 13 million in 1938. The wartime dislocation of trade caused a further fall to about 10 million tons by 1946, of which about half was coal. As well as the major closure in 1944 the war years saw the closure of most of the Glamorganshire and Manchester, Bolton & Bury canals. On both canals, breaches had been left unrepaired.

Much public interest in waterways was raised from December 1944 by the publication of L.T.C. Rolt's *Narrow Boat*. This was written in 1940–1 about a journey made on the eve of war in his converted narrow boat *Cressy*. It portrayed, in somewhat arcadian terms, a world of narrow-boat carrying, which was in danger of disappearing, over canals that could also be lost. The various perspectives of those whose interest was aroused by *Narrow Boat* were reflected in the six people who met in 1946 at the flat of Robert Aickman, owner of a London literary agency. These founded the Inland Waterways Association, with officers that included Aickman, Rolt, and Charles Hadfield and Frank Eyre, authors of *English Rivers and Canals* (1945). The new association began to publicise the case for waterways revival. It campaigned for the revival of derelict waterways like the Suffolk and Essex Stour, and against closure proposals, such as those affecting the Llangollen line, and the Derby, Rochdale and Huddersfield Canals. Tom Rolt's book about the Irish canals, *Green and Silver* (1949), increased public interest and goodwill in the Republic and helped to influence the founding of the Inland Waterways Association of Ireland in 1954.

The nationalization of most British waterways, which had been seriously debated since 1888, came about almost without controversy through the Transport Act of 1947. This was part of a much broader nationalization of transport, centred on railways and road transport; the battle over the Bill was mainly fought over the nationalization of road transport and there were few mentions of canals in the debates. Waterway concerns represented by the Canal Association soon concentrated any opposition on the grounds of compensation, which proved fairly generous. Companies like the Stourbridge and Staffs & Worcs, owning waterways upon which traffic was fast disappearing, would have faced a disastrous financial future once wartime subsidies had ended, and the main campaign against nationalization concerned the publicly-owned Weaver Navigation, where the loss of local control was opposed.

In the south of Ireland partial nationalization came with the Transport Act of 1944, followed by the setting up of the road–rail amalgamation, Coras Iompair Eireann (the Transport Company of Ireland), in 1945. This took over the railway-owned Royal Canal, upon which the minimal remaining traffic would cease in 1951. During the Emergency of 1939–45 severe restrictions over fuel for road transport brought increased traffic in new turf boats to the Grand Canal, but after 1945 this declined as road transport revived.

State ownership of transport throughout the Republic was authorised in 1949, and the 1950 CIE, now a public corporation, acquired the Grand Canal Company, and thus the Grand and Barrow. This was not without controversy, although the Grand company had been subsidised for some time. CIE's main interest was, however, in the company's road services. Under a different form of public ownership, that of the Shannon by the Board of Works, the main issues were water and drainage, navigation was secondary, and soon threatened by proposals to fix opening bridges.

In the north the nationalization of rail transport took place through the Ulster Transport Authority from 1948, but no waterways were in railway hands and none were nationalised. However, in 1954 the Lagan Navigation Company was dissolved and its property, the Lagan, Coalisland and Ulster canals, transferred to a succession of Government departments, largely in connection with their drainage functions. Traffic on both the Coalisland and the canal section of the Lagan had ceased by 1948, and both were closed in 1954. It would remain to be seen whether this would be the effective fate of many other publicly owned waterways in the British Isles.

CHAPTER THIRTEEN

Between Transport and Amenity

The period between the Transport Act of 1947 and the end of the 1960s involved a transformation for the smaller canals, on which amenity uses largely replaced carrying, while the larger waterways retained a significant transport role.

Although most artificial canals in Britain were nationalised, many important inland waterways, including estuarial navigations and those in East Anglia, were not. The most significant exception was the Manchester Ship Canal, viewed as a port, and the Bridgewater Canal, viewed as part of that port operation rather than as part of a national transport system. From 1948, the Bridgewater Department concentrated its canal carrying services on lighterage from the docks into the Trafford and Warrington areas, the canal being deepened to the Kelloggs mill at Stretford in 1947. Other carrying services were withdrawn, although bye-traders continued to use the canal, including long distance traffics to the Midlands until the 1960s. From 1952 pleasure boating was encouraged on the canal, along which several boat clubs were formed in the 1950s. This new role for one of Britain's oldest canals, concentrating solely on the development of profitable traffics, and developing revenues from pleasure boating and water sales on the rest, indicated a possible course for those newly in public ownership.

Many other waterways which stayed in private hands were canals with minimal or no traffic, like the Stroudwater, Basingstoke, North Walsham & Dilham, or Rochdale, for which water and property revenues were significant. Such revenues were also important on some canals, especially those in railway ownership, taken over by the British Transport Commission (BTC) and its subsidiary Docks and Inland Waterways Executive (DIWE), of which the 'Inland Waterways' component was very much the junior partner.

The BTC attempted to integrate all transport in Britain, in place of competition between transport modes, but financial and organizational problems thwarted progress in this direction, and policies to re-introduce competition followed the change of Government in 1951. Competition for freight traffic between the partly denationalised road haulage and the state-owned railways intensified after 1953, when the DIWE was abolished and substituted by a Board of Management, still under the BTC. Until 1963 the inland waterways were a very small part of a large transport organization, whose centre, the BTC, was much more sceptical about the future of waterways than those who managed them on a day to day basis. From 1963 waterways were fully separated, along with other transport sectors, removing the cross-subsidization which had shielded the loss making parts of the BTC's operations, including most waterways and carrying operations.

Many canals were irrelevant to a national transport system; as early as 1949 the DIWE asserted that 'the future of the artificial waterways is obviously considered doubtful'.[1] It then considered only the Severn, Weaver and Trent routes as worthy of major improvement, later adding the lower Lee (to Enfield), lower Grand Union and Aire & Calder and Sheffield & South Yorkshire Navigations to form a group, linked to the major estuaries, which were capable of enlargement to take larger craft.

While most of the smaller DIWE canals formed a network throughout lowland England, this primarily relied on narrow boat carrying. Pick had dismissed this in 1941 in the following terms:

> ... canals are heavily handicapped in competing with the roads, except where craft carrying large loads are concerned, or where narrow boats worked in pairs are possible. For all canals with locks capable of holding only one narrow boat at a locking, the prospect is bleak and unpromising, and should be faced. They are definitely uneconomical and their financial position is unsound.[2]

While some long distance traffics survived between the major navigations and the Midlands, most traffics on the smaller waterways were short distance, with especially large tonnages around the Birmingham Canal Navigations (BCN) area. The DIWE wished to retain those canals which still held traffic but doubted the wisdom of investment to develop them. Investigations revealed that while many canals had no serious traffic future, they could be retained for pleasure boating, water supply or general amenity; early candidates included the Lancaster Canal and the canal to Llangollen, but not the Kennet & Avon, for which the costs of retention for pleasure boating were considered prohibitive.

The BTC, however, refused at first to allow the DIWE to foster pleasure boating or amenity, ordering the transfer of non-trafficked waterways to other authorities such as catchment boards, river boards or local councils, which could develop these for other purposes. In the early 1950s these orders were largely thwarted, except for parts of the Nottingham and Dudley Canals, when these authorities refused to take over the heavy responsibilities and minimal revenues involved. Meanwhile, while tonnages carried on DIWE waterways increased, by 1953 98 per cent of traffic was generated on only 1,250 out of 2,072 miles. A Board of Survey was appointed to consider future policy. In 1955 its report proposed to retain (for the time being) the Class II canals, mainly narrow trafficked canals, but endorsed the BTC policy to transfer 771 miles to other bodies. Proposals to close the Kennet & Avon and other canals followed, and protests in Parliament and elsewhere led to the appointment of an independent committee, the Bowes Committee, whose brief was to consider the future of all inland waterways in Britain.

Meanwhile, considerable disquiet was raised in Parliament over two independent disused canals, where closure involved a further loss of amenity. Most of the

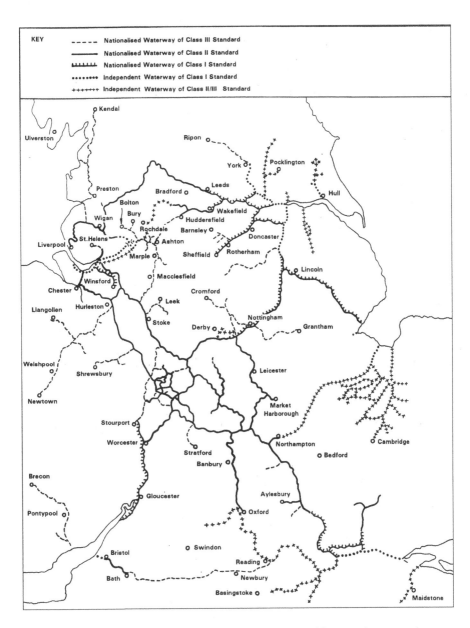

KEY
- - - - - Nationalised Waterway of Class III Standard
───── Nationalised Waterway of Class II Standard
⊔⊔⊔⊔⊔ Nationalised Waterway of Class I Standard
•••••••• Independent Waterway of Class I Standard
++++++ Independent Waterway of Class II/III Standard

The classifications produced by the Board of Survey in 1955, with suggestions as to the status of linking independent waterways. These roughly correspond to the usefulness of such waterways for traffic purposes. The very limited mileage of Class I waterways will be noted. The Bowes Committee would follow much the same classifications except for the Avon from Bristol to Bath, which was placed in Class A.

Rochdale Canal was closed in 1952. Local authorities in Lancashire had failed to force its owners to fill in sections and to pay to culvert former bridges; this canal soon became an unsightly water channel but a profitable source of water sales. The closure of the Stroudwater Canal in 1954 aroused a different controversy, carefully orchestrated by the IWA, over the loss of a potential cruising route solely to culvert highway crossings. The Bowes Committee's remit included the problems posed by disused canals, including those in private ownership, first raised in the 1930s over the Nottingham and Grantham Canals.

The Government rejected the Bowes Committee's recommendation that transport waterways (Class A and B, similar to those of the Board of Survey) should be put in good order and maintained for at least twenty-five years. It refused to subsidise the Class B waterways, but did agree that the future of the remaining waterways, along with disused private canals, should be considered by an independent Inland Waterways Redevelopment Advisory Committee (IWRAC), which could recommend whether to retain sections for pleasure boating, to eliminate, or find other uses.

IWRAC, which included L.T.C. Rolt, and Lionel Munk, owner of a major hire boat firm and later leader of the IWA, began work in 1959; many of its recommendations over the next three years were accepted, and several waterways were closed up to 1962. These included sections which were still navigable, such as parts of the Chesterfield Canal and part of the Erewash. One controversial closure in 1962, of the Dudley Tunnel line, soon led to the formation of a preservation society, which secured its restoration in 1973; this was probably the first formally closed navigation to be reopened.

Bowes also fostered investigations into the enlargement of the London–Birmingham and Weaver–Wolverhampton lines, but no firm proposals emerged, probably due to Government investment in parallel motorways, and the difficulties of developing sufficient new traffics.

After the Board of Survey, the docks were separated from the inland waterways. Improvements to the major Group I waterways were embodied in the Development Plan of 1956, and put into effect over the period to 1962. The largest expenditure involved widening, deepening and dredging to ease the passage of larger craft, while the enlargement and duplication of locks, such as those at Brentford, and on the Lee to Enfield, accounted for £1 million out of £5.5 million. New craft and improvements to handling facilities were also provided. Further developments on some of these waterways continued in the 1960s.

Public support for waterways was partly reflected in, and partly encouraged, by the growth of a waterways literature from the late 1940s onwards, much written by early IWA members. This included L.T.C. Rolt's outstanding *Green and Silver* (1949) and *The Inland Waterways of England* (1950); Robert Aickman's popular *Know Your Waterways* (1954); Eric de Maré's superbly illustrated *The Canals of England* (1950); and Charles Hadfield's *Introducing Canals* (1955). These together fostered interest in cruising and in canal history, and began a continuous stream of waterways publications, encouraged by journals like the IWA's *Bulletin* and the BTC's *Lock and Quay* and later *Waterways*.

From 1950 the detailed history of canals in Britain began to be studied in depth. In 1950 Charles Hadfield published the first edition of *British Canals*, and in 1955 *The Canals of Southern England*. The latter became the first in what became the *Canals of the British Isles* series, which eventually covered the detailed history of every area, ending with *The Canals of Eastern England* in 1977. Much historical work has since been developed, but little then was accurately known; only fieldwork made it clear that canals like the Chard Canal had been built at all. Nationalization inadvertently helped students of history by bringing together the scattered archives of canal and railway companies into a single collection, *British Transport Historical Records*, publicly accessible from 1951. Later these were transferred to the Public Record Office (since 2003, the National Archives). The *British Isles* series helped to inspire many individual waterways histories.

While the history of the IWA has been detailed elsewhere, some developments can be emphasised. It became involved in a campaign to acquire and revive the Basingstoke Canal in 1949, but also pressurised successive Governments to produce a national waterways policy for both carrying and pleasure boating; as Robert Aickman asserted in 1950:

> ... our impoverished economy can no longer afford to ignore what is the cheapest form of transport for a wide range of loads; and holidays with pay for millions require that the waterways be made available for pleasure boating on a vastly increased scale.[3]

While this proved unrealistic for the commercial use of narrow canals, it was brilliantly prophetic for the amenity use of canals, which was very limited in the late 1940s; public support grew considerably into the 1960s, reflected in the changing views of Parliament and local authorities. Public interest was greatly increased by a series of national and local boat rallies, beginning with that attended by a hundred craft at Market Harborough in 1950. Around this time, there was a major split within the IWA, much of it over personalities and power, with original members like Tom Rolt and Charles Hadfield expelled. Several local waterways societies, like the Kennet & Avon Canal Association, were formed as a result, and, following further divisions in 1958, the Inland Waterways Protection Society. Under Aickman, the IWA grew rapidly in size and influence into the mid-1960s, although its often confrontational approach perhaps limited its direct influence over Government and other decision-makers.

IWA efforts to support carrying by narrow boat developed partly at the expense of the support of larger craft and traffics, and new and enlarged waterways. The latter had to await the formation of the Inland Shipping Group, when many opportunities

The last regular traffic on the Macclesfield Canal was in coal to the Goyt Mill at Marple, which ended in 1953. The mill, built in 1905, has since been converted to other purposes. There were traffics in domestic coal on this canal in the 1970s.

had been lost. The decline of narrow boat carrying in the 1950s left the Ashton, Macclesfield, Erewash, Chesterfield, eastern Trent & Mersey and the Leicester line without traffics, while many others had minimal traffics. Campaigning helped to save some waterways for amenity use, but the decline in traffic proved inexorable, especially after British Waterways ceased to subsidise its own carrying by narrow boat.

The goodwill created by rallies and local campaigns for retention was enlarged by the onset of restoration schemes, which began in 1949 on river navigations with the revival of Linton Lock. The first major scheme sought to rescue the Lower Avon in Warwickshire, from Evesham to the Severn at Tewkesbury. This had decayed until only the lower reaches were navigable (and those barely), as the navigation company could not afford repairs, which were largely carried out by the sole trader using the river to Pershore. Douglas Barwell, a businessman prominent in the Midlands IWA, acquired the navigation early in 1950, passing it to a Lower Avon Navigation Trust, formed by Midlands IWA members. This first commissioned new gates for Strensham Lock to enable its reopening, and organised volunteer working parties, starting with brickwork at Nafford in 1951. Probably the first of its kind, this practical work paralleled similar work on the Talyllyn Railway from 1951, which was also revived and run by a preservation group. In both cases, during the 1950s, military units provided assistance.

The Lower Avon was reopened in 1962, after much fund-raising by volunteers, who also assisted in the reconstruction of weirs, the renewal of lock gates, and the removal of the remains of both watergates. Barwell's approach demonstrated the value of voluntary involvement, allied to professional support, to restore and manage the waterway.

The earliest canal restoration project to be completed (several began in the 1950s) was that of the southern Stratford Canal, a waterway disused after 1935 and unnavigable after 1947. Warwickshire County Council refused the DIWE's offer of a transfer, but sought abandonment in 1958 in order to lower a bridge near Wilmcote. The Stratford-upon-Avon Canal Society had been formed in 1956 to seek restoration, and combined with the IWA and the National Trust to defeat the Council's proposals. The IWA had pressed for an independent conservancy to own and run waterways, and it mooted the National Trust to take over lines like the Southern Oxford, Staffs & Worcs and the Caldon; the Trust was persuaded to lease the southern Stratford from 1960 for five years, and then to take the freehold.

David Hutchings, who had revived the Midlands IWA, was appointed manager, and funds were contributed by the Pilgrim Trust, the IWA, public subscription and the BTC/BWB, which also provided free water supplies. Work began at Kingswood in 1961, and the canal was reopened to Stratford in 1964, after major rebuilding work on the 13 miles and 36 locks. Almost every lock gate was replaced, many lock chamber walls were rebuilt, and the whole section dredged, with much bank repair.

Much work was carried out to limited standards (including paddle gear salvaged from locks disused since the 1920s), but it ensured that the canal was reopened, if not fully restored. This provided much publicity and inspired efforts elsewhere, including the rebuilding of the Upper Avon link between Stratford and the Lower Avon, again under David Hutchings. Differences here included the formation of a new Upper Avon Navigation Trust and the building of entirely new locks and weirs, altered water levels and major dredging. Work began in 1964 and was completed, after major difficulties, in 1974.

The Stratford Canal proved an unhappy venture for the National Trust, given the inevitable and continuing losses on the canal's operation. By the early 1980s even closure was under consideration, until it was transferred back to BWB with an endowment of £1.5 million towards maintenance arrears; the latter included almost a total lack of dredging.

The transfers of the Wey and Godalming Navigations to the National Trust in 1963 and 1967, were more successful, despite later controversies over management, as they were in reasonable order, and accompanied by property income. An Taisce, the Irish National Trust, took over part of the derelict Boyne from private owners in 1969, but resources for restoration have proved limited.

Pleasure boating had revived slowly after 1945, with shortages of fuel and suitable craft; the latter included many converted wartime pontoons and lifeboats, along with a growing number of converted narrow boats. A growing number of boatyards increasingly began to design and build purpose built canal craft, including Taylors of Chester, with *Teal* in 1954, later preserved (as *Amaryllis*) at Ellesmere Port, and the fleet for hire and private use built by Holt Abbott of Canal Pleasurecraft Ltd at Stourport from 1950.

One unintended consequence of nationalization was that the amenity use of certain waterways was allowed to develop for the first time, and that the need to obtain permits from separate authorities for different waterways was removed. By 1958 the toll system had been replaced by a general system of licensing, which encouraged long distance cruising. By contrast, on the privately owned Chelmer & Blackwater Navigation, pleasure boats were not permitted to use locks before the last timber traffic ceased in 1972.

By 1950, the much-reduced fleet of the Inland Cruising Association had been joined by new hire firms at Stone and Market Drayton. Hotel boats began with New-Way Holidays of Leighton Buzzard in 1950, joined by the more successful Waterborne Tours of Penkridge in 1951. There were sufficient hire firms to form a trade association, the Association of Pleasure Craft Operators, in 1954.

Day trip boats were also developed on a commercial basis. One early example, between Hest Bank and Carnforth on the isolated Lancaster, operated from 1948 to 1953. Despite bus and publicity links with the seaside resort of Morecambe, this collapsed with heavy debts. Other trip boats, on a more modest scale, were more successful, such as that started in 1951 by John James and *Jason* along the Regent's Canal in London.

The number of cruising licences issued on BTC canals rose from 1,500 in 1950 to 10,500 in 1961. New boat clubs were formed, often formalising existing moorings. Some were founded with a campaigning role, such as the Wey Cruising Club, formed in 1950, which campaigned for the Basingstoke Canal, rapidly becoming derelict; or the Nantwich & Border Counties Yacht Club, formed in 1953, whose early members were prominent in the North Western Branch of the IWA. Both clubs included sailing sections which later separated from the parent club.

The administrative changes within the BTC from 1955 coincided with a more proactive leadership under Sir Reginald Kerr. While he firmly favoured the retention of only selected waterways, the BTC encouraged the promotion of pleasure cruising, publishing a series of cruising guide booklets from 1956 onwards, and developing a small hire fleet, based first at Chester in 1956, and later at Middlewich and Oxford. As well as these self-drive boats, the BTC inaugurated hotel boats on the Oxford Canal and the Trent, which lasted into the 1960s, and day trip boats, running regular trips or on charter, of which the best known (and longest lived) was the *Zoo Waterbus*, serving London Zoo, alongside the Regent's Canal, which began to operate in 1959.

Basin End, Nantwich, in 1993, just before British Waterways last hire boating operation, in the distance, closed. Since then the moorings of the Nantwich & Border Counties Yacht Club, on the right, have been vacated, with the Nantwich Canal Centre occupying the terminal site.

Despite these beginnings, transport remained the remit of the BTC. Nationalization involved the carrying fleets of the Aire & Calder Navigation, including the coal compartment fleet, and the large narrow boat fleet of the Grand Union Canal Carrying Co. While much carrying remained in private hands, the BTC could acquire fleets by agreement, and acquired Fellows Morton & Clayton (in which it was a major shareholder) when this went into voluntary liquidation in 1948. This added 176 craft, along with road vehicles, warehouses and depots, to make the DIWE fleet the largest recorded, at almost 1,500 craft, although this was soon reduced as traffics diminished. The BTC tended to retain loss-making fleets wherever toll revenues exceeded their losses, and later acquired firms like Mersey Weaver, attempting to retain their traffics and toll revenue.

The Transport Act of 1962 abolished the BTC, and in January 1963 the new British Waterways Board (BWB), took office; members included Sir Frederick Parham, who had chaired IWRAC, and Charles Hadfield. Under the Act, the canals were to be maintained until firm policies could be decided. Despite the end of the cross-subsidization ensured by common BTC ownership, BWB sought to shift emphasis away from transport and towards amenity. It decided to cease most abandonments of canals, and sought to end the antagonism that had existed between the BTC and the IWA and canal societies, and to create instead a feeling of partnership.

BWB soon produced a policy report, *The Future of the Waterways*, which noted:

> We have taken over an undertaking which cannot as a whole be any longer regarded
> solely as a national transport system. As such, some of it is manifestly out of date. On
> the one hand, the waterways cannot be neatly and separately arranged as those usable,
> and those, not usable, for transport; nor in fact can they be each separately labelled
> as particular waterways usable for single particular purposes … the rational way of
> managing them is probably to manage them as one single, though varied, whole.[4]

BWB became the first public body to positively identify what the IWA had long
advocated, and the Bowes Committee had acknowledged, namely, that most
waterways had amenity value and that this should be the subject of subsidy. It
enlarged this case by stressing that ownership, even of unnavigable waterways, presented an irreducible deficit for which Government subsidy would be required,
and that a larger subsidy could secure the future of much of the system for pleasure boating. It was not then clear that all navigable canals could be kept open,
but that water sales, general amenity and pleasure boating would form additional
criteria for retention, and that pleasure use required a coherent network rather
than individual stretches. Once any network had statutory long-term protection,
private investment in hiring, moorings and boatbuilding could take place, and
their future would then be unquestioned.

The Facts about the Waterways, published in 1965, attempted to estimate the additional costs involved in retaining navigation for traffic or pleasure purposes. This
principle had to be fought for inside Government as well as with external pressure. The Treasury was very reluctant to accept subsidy, and the closure of many
waterways was seen as a candidate for public expenditure cuts. At one point, not
only might revival and restorations be stalled, it seemed probable that the major
loss-makers in the system, the Leeds & Liverpool and Grand Union line (especially the Leicester line) might have to be sacrificed to retain a smaller network.
It was perhaps fortunate that the Minister of Transport, Barbara Castle, was both
MP for Blackburn, through which the threatened Leeds & Liverpool ran, was
ideologically opposed to public expenditure reductions, and had taken canalboat
holidays. Much might have been lost had a different Minister been less support-
ive. In the event, the White Paper which followed in 1966 proposed five-yearly
reviews of canal viability that would have stultified enterprise; after widespread
protests headed by the IWA a new White Paper led to the Transport Act of 1968.

This Act provided that a small group of Commercial waterways were to be maintained and developed for 'the commercial carriage of freight'. BWB had rapidly given
up most of its own narrow boat carrying, introducing an experimental licensing system for specific carriers. It had also sought to continue the work of the Development
Plan, examining the potential of the Sheffield & South Yorkshire Navigation, and
enlarging the Aire & Calder to accommodate new oil and coal traffics.

The 1968 Act classified a large network, including waterways previously retained for transport purposes, as Cruiseways, which were 'to be principally available for cruising, fishing and other recreational purposes', with their operations subsidised. By then there was very little traffic on such waterways, and even less on the final group, classified as Remainder Waterways. These were to be 'dealt with in the most economical manner possible', including retention for cruising, water channelling, elimination or disposal. An Inland Waterways Amenity Advisory Council was established to advise BWB and the minister on developments for amenity purposes, and on any changes in the classification of waterways.

This effectively provided, twenty years after nationalization, a future for most waterways for cruising purposes. The IWA had played a major part in arousing public opinion, and convincing successive Governments, that this was a proper use for canals originally nationalised to develop a national transport system.

The 1960s saw the growth of a large movement of volunteers interested in practical involvement with the restoration of derelict waterways. Partly spurred by the Stratford restoration, which recruited volunteers from a distance, the voluntary movement became more organised in the 1960s. In 1966 *Navvies Notebook* (*Navvies* since 1971) was founded by Graham Palmer, initially based on the work of the London Working Party Group, which was involved with the decaying Basingstoke Canal in the early 1960s. This informed volunteers about the growing number of schemes throughout England and Wales, and enabled major working parties to be organised to coordinate voluntary efforts on distant canals.

Restoration was spurred by a co-operative approach from BWB. This began with the Stourbridge Canal, barely navigable in 1961, and upon which, with closure expected, the BTC had opposed the IWA campaigning rally of 1962. This was succeeded by co-operation between the new BWB and volunteers from the Staffordshire & Worcestershire Canal Society. The main line was restored with volunteer input alongside renewed BWB maintenance operations, and reopened in 1967.

Navvies Notebook enabled major working parties to be organised; perhaps the most celebrated example was 'Operation Ashton' in 1968. This was held at Droylesden on the Ashton Canal, which had been unnavigable since 1961–2, for which several local authorities had favoured elimination. Working parties had started on the adjacent Lower Peak Forest Canal in 1965, mainly clearing undergrowth. As the greatest opponent of restoration was Droylesden Council, 'Operation Ashton' aimed to clear a 700m section of the canal there to demonstrate that it could be an amenity. Graham Palmer pictured activities on the first morning, on 21 September 1968:

> To stand on Crabtree Lane Bridge and look down the site was a very emotional experience. As far as could be seen were hundreds of volunteers scurrying here and there clutching large, heavy, muddy objects, hauling on ropes, pushing wheelbarrows.

The eastern end of 'Operation Ashton' in Droylesden was marked by the two Fairfield Locks which lead to the summit level of the Ashton Canal. The pound between the locks has been used since 1977 by the Water Adventure Centre, showing that waterways in urban areas can be put to wider use than summer voyages by holiday-makers. Two lock chambers, one gateless, can be seen through the bridge; traffic was so heavy before the railway era that the two locks here were duplicated.

> Amongst them were the brightly painted dumpers and looming over the whole scene a string of old cars suspended from the jib of a red mobile crane brought along by our friends from the Caldon Canal Society. To add atmosphere were the raging orange-yellow flames from countless fires and billowing black smoke from the old car tyres found in abundance in the canal – and it still kept raining![5]

Despite the poor weather, some 2,000 tons of rubbish were removed by over 600 volunteers in one weekend. Methods used then would not be possible later, on safety and environmental grounds, and the clearance work had little lasting value, but the way was paved for more organised efforts that made a major impact. The canal was classified as a Remainder waterway in 1968, but local authority support for restoration grew, full restoration was agreed in 1971, and the canal was reopened in 1974.

The *Navvies* organization, renamed the *Waterway Recovery Group* in 1970, coordinated the work of growing numbers of local restoration bodies from the 1970s, going from the recently derelict waterways such as the Ashton to assist the gradual revival of the Kennet & Avon, last fully navigated in 1949, and on to work on canals like the Rochdale or Huddersfield canals which had long been derelict. For a time in the mid 1970s, a similar group, around *MacNavvies*, worked in Scotland, starting restoration and improvement works on the Forth & Clyde and Union canals, which had closed in 1963 and 1965 respectively.

The 1968 Act provided a secure framework for Commercial waterways, but this could not reverse trends in traffic. One area of traffic growth in the 1950s was the bulk carriage of liquids, especially on the Severn line, one of the large commercial waterways which the DIWE had considered worthy of improvement.

Nationalization unified the administration of the Severn Commission's line to Worcester and Stourport with the Gloucester & Sharpness Canal, owned by the Sharpness New Docks company. Improvements enabled estuarial craft to bring oil, grain, metals and general merchandise directly from Bristol Channel ports, especially Avonmouth, to depots at Stourport and Worcester for onward road distribution to the Midlands.

Petroleum traffic from the Bristol Channel ports grew after nationalization, to Diglis and Stourport on the Severn, and increasingly in coastal tankers, to Monk Meadow Dock in Gloucester. New oil wharves were added at Diglis in 1954, but despite further improvements under the Development Plan, traffics fell away in the early 1960s, especially above Worcester. Petroleum movements to Stourport, using smaller craft, declined from 201,477 tons in 1956 to 35,779 tons in 1963, as a result of pipeline developments. These later affected traffics to Worcester, where only small loads unsuitable for pipeline transfer were carried; by 1971 these had transferred to road and rail transport and regular movements above Gloucester had ceased.

The BTC handled the carrying of general merchandise, for which four new craft were built under the 1956 plan. However, the opening of the M5/M50 route helped to divert traffics from Avonmouth and Sharpness to the road-served South Wales ports, while all Bristol Channel ports were affected by the general diversion of shipping towards continental Europe. When Sharpness revived, this largely relied on rail or roadborne forwarding. Facing increasing losses, BWB withdrew its fleet in 1969, after which the main regular traffic above Gloucester was a long-standing grain traffic to Healings' Mills at Tewkesbury (and one up the Avon to Pershore), which continued until 1984, with later revivals.

The greater capacity of the Canal to Gloucester enabled the development of larger craft. A new oil depot opened at Quedgeley in the early 1960s to relieve congestion at Monk Meadow; this was mainly served by coastal tankers. Traffics in grain to mills in Gloucester Docks continued until the last one closed in 1977, while timber shipments to various waterside wharves in Gloucester lasted into the 1970s. While BWB opened a new depot at Monk Meadow in 1965 for timber and general traffics, diminishing trade led it to cease all handling at Gloucester in 1987. Quedgeley was to close in 1985, while the last petroleum was delivered to Monk Meadow around 1991. By 1993, there were no major regular traffics above Sharpness, and the Severn Corridor plan, to enlarge the line for 2500t craft to

Healings Mill on the Avon on Tewkesbury, the source of grain traffic between its opening in 1865 and the transfer to road transport in the 1980s. *Chaceley* was photographed during a revival of traffic between 1993 and 1998. The mill closed in 2006.

Gloucester, and 1500t on to Worcester, which had been agreed in 1983, had been quietly shelved.

Coal remained a major, if declining, canal-borne cargo between 1947 and the early 1970s. Some traffic was diverted to road or rail, with the growth, from the 1960s, of merry go round trains between pits and power stations. Traffics were affected by the declining use of domestic coal, through smokeless zones, changing energy use in industry, the closing of old waterside power stations and the opening of new non-coal stations, and the closure of gasworks as gas-making from coal ended in the 1960s. This was exacerbated by the obsolescence of much loading and unloading equipment, and the failure to invest in new facilities.

Positive developments were mainly confined to the opening of new waterside power stations such as Skelton Grange (1949) and Ferrybridge C (1967) on the Aire & Calder. Walsall Power Station, at Birchills on the narrow BCN, opened in 1949; by 1963 one of the busiest points on the whole BWB system was the length between this and Holly Bank Basin, with trains of narrow boats hauled by tugs, but this traffic ended in 1965.

The Leeds & Liverpool Canal relied heavily on coal carrying, mainly to power stations, gas works and waterside factories. General merchandise traffics mainly originated in Liverpool for delivery to a network of warehouses on both sides of the Pennines, along with grain movements.

Westwood Power Station at Wigan in the early 1960s. This was served only by canal and rail from its inception; only when the loading equipment needed to be renewed, in 1972, was a road access constructed and the canal traffic brought to an end. (British Waterways)

The opening of Westwood Power Station, Wigan, in 1952, fuelled largely by canal-borne coal brought through the Leigh Branch, added to existing traffics to stations at Whitebirk and Kirkstall. Two gasworks and sugar refineries in the Liverpool area also received coal from the Wigan area in the 1950s.

Most general merchandise was carried in BTC craft, and a number of new craft were constructed in high-tensile steel in the 1950s; this increased carrying capacity by 10 per cent. By the mid-1950s many warehouses were being used for road-borne storage, as few traffics could undercut rates by road. Pit closures and changes to industrial fuel use ended traffics, such as that to Tate & Lyle in Liverpool, in 1958. The BTC acquired a Bootle coal carrying fleet in 1962 in a bid to retain traffics, but the hard winter of 1962–3 had a major impact. Most coal traffic was suspended, and most was switched to road during this period, and did not return afterwards. By the end of 1964 the only traffic bar that to Wigan power station was a lighterage traffic in grain at Liverpool, which lasted till 1966. Grain carrying from Liverpool by H & R Ainscough, to their own mills at Burscough and Parbold, and into storage at Wigan and elsewhere, had ceased in 1961.

The Leeds & Liverpool presented major financial problems for the BTC, accounting for 30 per cent of its deficit in 1956. Maintenance and operating responsibilities included major mining subsidence on the Leigh Branch,

A rather grey view of Litherland Lift Bridge and Calder, one of the BTC general merchandise craft built of high tensile steel in the 1950s. The bridge was removed in 1975; before this it formed a discouragement to the passage of pleasure craft. Ironically, the earliest canal boat club was located near here. (British Waterways)

numerous locks, large reservoirs, two tunnels, and a large number of old warehouses inherited from the Leeds & Liverpool company.

Once the coal revenues collapsed in 1963, closure became a serious possibility, especially when pleasure boats were rarely seen outside the Lydiate and Keighley/Skipton areas; the heavy traffic and locks had deterred many boats. There were problems at both Liverpool and Leeds ends; a pleasure boat passage of River Lock, Leeds, took 6 hours in 1964, while crowbars were needed to open the swing bridges on the Yorkshire side. The terminal length into Bootle and Liverpool was subject to vandalism, while prior notice was required to raise Litherland Lift Bridge. BWB stated gloomily in its *Future* report of 1964 that 'given the present and (as far as they can foretell) the future usage they must give serious consideration to further reduction of expenditure even though this may mean a reduction of facilities.'[6]

The 1965 report estimated the annual costs of maintaining the main line to water channel standards at £77,800, and to navigable standards at £122,653; it appeared that £44,853 pa was required to allow a few pleasure craft to pass. It was thus clear that 'On the main line ... the deficit could be reduced considerably – though it would remain very substantial – by conversion to a water channel.'[7]

The IWA perceived the threat to navigation, and organised a National Rally at four sites on the canal in August 1965, with 130 boats reaching the main site at Blackburn alone. Its *Bulletin* stressed:

> ... the genuine delight of all British Waterways lock-keepers and maintenance men along the entire route of the canal, that now, at last, someone was determined that traffic should return... Immediately craft entered the canal, both at Leeds and at Wigan, there was startling evidence of the willingness of British Waterways men to offer every assistance. Lock-keepers turned out on duty at all manner of unaccustomed hours feverishly tarring and painting gates and balance beams, and greasing swing bridges. While the work they did was sometimes of a superficial nature, the waterway was generally easy to navigate; it cannot be too strongly emphasized that increased use by boats will improve conditions.[8]

This rally, as with earlier ones, helped to demonstrate the potential amenity value of the canal to local authorities which would not then support any closure proposals. As the canal formed a significant link in the future Cruiseway network, it was so retained under the 1968 Transport Act, except for 8 miles at the Liverpool end. There were proposals to use the latter for a road, and local campaigns to fill it in to remove danger to local children (there were several drownings), while most of this length remained behind gates, with the towpath inaccessible. This would remain one of the least used sections of navigable canal, although the towpath was later opened up. In 2006 work began on a new canal, the Liverpool link, to link the terminal end at Stanley Dock, Liverpool, with the historic Albert Dock, which was expected to bring many more boat movements and contribute to waterfront regeneration after completion in 2009.

The several lines of the Shropshire Union illustrate the fate of narrow boat carrying, and of campaigns for the retention and restoration of disused sections.

The main line to Autherley took mainly long distance traffic to and from Ellesmere Port and, via the Middlewich Branch, from the Weaver and Port of Manchester. By 1947 the 243,527 tons carried in 1937 had diminished to 72,591 tons. The main traffic through Ellesmere Port was in fuel oil carried from the Ship Canal at Stanlow, to Langley Green. By the time that this ceased in 1955, all general merchandise traffic through Ellesmere Port, largely in BTC craft to the Midlands was also lost, some to road transport. Traffics from Weston Point were mainly in metals and bentonite, which benefitted from backloads of coal and gravel on the Trent & Mersey Canal, as well as one in 'tank house slime' carried from Darlaston to Manchester; as these backloads were lost, the viability of this carrying operation diminished further.

The BTC kept its Northern fleet operating, despite growing losses in the face of increasing competition from road transport, so as not to lose both traffics and accompanying toll revenues. It even provided new craft in the late 1950s, but the

This bridge at St Martins on the Llangollen Canal was programmed by Shropshire County Council to be rebuilt without navigable headroom, but it was rebuilt in 1952 after the Denbighshire, Shropshire and Cheshire county councils agreed to retain navigation. The 1952 bridge has been replaced since this photograph was taken in 1993.

loss of Midlands traffics continued, dropping from 29,012 tons in 1957 to 5,779 tons in 1960.

In 1964 BWB closed its narrow boat fleet, and Willow Wren, one of the more enterprising carriers, took over the remaining traffics. This, however, could not make these pay, and gave up after the loss of aluminium traffics to Wolverhampton in 1967. The recently formed Anderton Canal Carrying Company then took over the aluminium traffic briefly, carrying final traffics in 1970 in silicon carbide for a Stafford factory, forwarded by tractor from Norbury. As maintenance priorities increasingly centred round the summer passage of pleasure craft, a satisfactory service to customers could no longer be assured. Nevertheless, a final traffic in oil for Bloxwich, from Ellesmere Port, developed in 1971 with BWB assistance.

The closure of the branches to Newtown, Llangollen and Shrewsbury in 1944 was based on the maintenance of water levels, so that while locks and bridges could be dismantled, draining and infilling would require Ministry of Agriculture approval.

The Llangollen line had remained navigable after 1944, supplying water to the lower Main Line and various industrial users. The closure Act transferred highway bridges to local highway authorities, which soon proposed two culverted crossings in Denbighshire and one in Shropshire. As maintenance was mainly waterborne, the Divisional Waterways Officer in the North West, Christopher

Marsh, convinced Denbighshire that the culverting of Wenffrwd Bridge, near Llangollen, would involve the Council in heavy future maintenance costs, and it was agreed in 1949 to build a new bridge instead. This approach was confirmed by all the canalside highway authorities in 1951.

In the early 1950s the DIWE offered the canal to the Mid and South East Cheshire Water Board, which planned to use it to transfer domestic water abstracted from the Dee near Pontcysyllte into Cheshire, using the canal reservoir at Hurleston for storage. The Water Board refused to take over the canal, and in 1952 produced alternative plans for a pipeline to Cheshire. Only when loan sanction for this scheme was refused was it agreed that the BTC should retain ownership and obtain powers to permit the water supply scheme. The canal was duly put into good order between 1956 and 1959, when the abstractions began. The water sales revenue made the Llangollen line one of a handful of profitable canals by the mid-1960s, and this enabled it to stay open for pleasure traffic. The line's popularity expanded rapidly in the 1960s, so that it was classified as a Cruiseway in 1968.

While water supplies to industry were long known in Britain, the use of canals to transfer domestic water was new; a further scheme followed on the Gloucester & Sharpness Canal (for Bristol), and later the Bridgewater & Taunton Canal. In 1993 studies suggested that midlands canals could be used to transfer water between regions, and a partnership, Watergrid, was set up in 2003 to develop this and other water sales. In Ireland, the Grand Canal supplies the Guinness brewery in Dublin.

One of the DIWE's few successful transfers in the 1950s was of the terminal length of the Shrewsbury Canal to the local council; while this was drained and filled in, the rest of the line remained, obstructed by a number of road crossings north and west of Wellington. IWRAC approved plans to dewater both the Shrewsbury and Newtown lines once alternative drainage and farm water supplies could be secured; negotiations had reached a late stage on the Shrewsbury line by 1965, when a restoration campaign was launched, partly inspired by the Stratford example. While there were limited physical obstacles to restoration on the eastern length, BWB declined support due to the high restoration costs and the advanced stage of negotiations; the draining of the canal and its sale to local farmers began in 1966, and by 1970 much had been sold and filled in. A later revival of interest involved some work near Berwick Tunnel. Later campaigning safeguarded the remaining line, but with little progress yet on the ground.

The Shrewsbury and Newport campaigners formed the Shropshire Union Canal Society, which turned its attention to the line to Newtown (now known as the Montgomery Canal). By 1949 this was obstructed by five low road crossings and two dry sections, and by the mid-1960s the length into Newtown was destroyed and a dewatering scheme prepared for the rest, although negotiations with landowners were not completed. In 1967 the campaigners tried to persuade BWB to repair the supplies to the Tanat feeder and hence the centre section of

Welshpool Lock on the Montgomery section of the Shropshire Union Canal; the building
in the offside distance, formerly the Shropshire Union warehouse, now houses the
Powysland Museum. For 25 years after the restoration campaign started, this length was
an isolated cruising section of 2 miles, but after 1995 it formed part of an 11 mile section
between Berriew and Burgeddin. The trip boat, owned by Montgomery Canal Cruises, ran
four trips daily in summer for many years until it ceased operations at Welshpool in 2003.

the canal. A new Welshpool bypass was proposed along the line of the canal in
1969, and in October a campaigning dig, including volunteers from the Navvies
group, cleared the canal in Welshpool. This assisted the defeat of the bypass plans
in 1972, and BWB decided to repair the Tanat feeder.

Restoration began on Welshpool Lock, aiming to develop a length of
2 miles between lowered road crossings either side of Welshpool. A further 6
miles north to Burgedin re-opened in 1978; volunteers gradually restored the
locks at Carreghofa, Frankton and later Aston, and BWB improved the channel
of the watered lengths. Meanwhile, amid much disquiet, further road crossings
were lowered, but plans for restoration south of Welshpool were enhanced by the
insertion of a navigable culvert under the new Abermule bypass in 1973.

Developments in lowland England and North Wales were not followed elsewhere. Following concerns about plans to block the Shannon Navigation in 1952,
and contact with the IWA in Britain, the Inland Waterways Association of Ireland
was formed in 1954. Founders included Colonel Harry Rice, author of *Thanks
for the Memory* (1952), about the Shannon, and Vincent Delany. Both were boating
enthusiasts, and the latter, and his wife Ruth, became Ireland's leading waterways

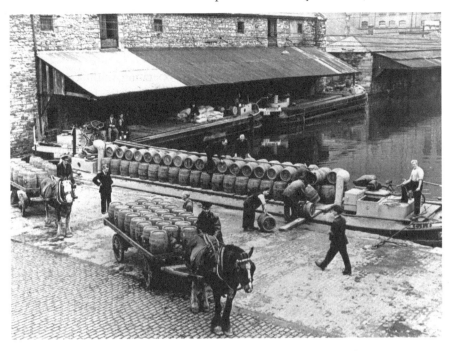

Loading porter barrels into CIE boats and discharging empties at James Street Harbour, Dublin, towards the end of the carrying era, around 1957. Note the simple loading methods, the use of the horse and cart (still viable over short distances for collection and delivery), and the numerous staff. This harbour and the connecting length of canal were filled in during the early 1970s. (Guinness Museum)

historians. The IWAI was spared the internal problems which afflicted its British counterpart, although the position of Irish waterways was potentially desperate. It first fought plans to replace opening bridges over the Shannon with low fixed spans, and persuaded CIE to introduce passenger launches on the river that required 18ft headroom, in 1955.

Unlike in Britain, the IWAI could do little to campaign for carrying on the waterways. The CIE fleet continued to operate on the Grand, Barrow and Shannon into the 1950s, but after the Transport Act of 1958 CIE transferred its services onto the ailing rail network. The final traffics, for the Guinness Brewery, were carried in 1960. IWAI intervention prevented immediate closure of the canals, although CIE were authorised to close canals that had been disused for three years, and thus closed most of the Grand Canal branches and the Royal Canal in 1961.

Hire boating in the Republic had been as limited as that in Britain; in 1946 Tom Rolt located only three craft on the Shannon, and found that only through traffic was permitted on the Grand Canal. After the 1950s, encouraged by the IWAI campaigns and the annual Shannon rallies from 1961, several hire firms started operations on the Shannon, while private pleasure boating grew. Albert Lock, in the northern part of the Shannon at Jamestown, was used 70 times in 1959, 1,672 times in 1964 and 2,240 times in 1969 (By 1997 12,076 passages were recorded). In the mid-1960s three hire firms were operating on the Grand Canal, although growth was not inexorable; by the 1990s there were only two.

Proposals by Dublin Corporation to fill in the Circular line, linking the Grand to the Liffey at Ringsend, were defeated by a long IWAI campaign between 1963 and 1969. Campaigning included picketing the City Hall, then an unusual form of protest in Ireland. The Circular line remained open, but the terminal length of the main line in Dublin was filled in by 1974. In 1969 IWAI campaigning led to the reopening of Richmond Harbour, at the western end of the Royal Canal, although most in the IWAI then saw the rest of the canal as a lost cause.

Little public interest was aroused in the waterways of the north of Ireland, although the IWAI covered this area and an active Erne branch was formed. In the 1960s the construction of a new motorway destroyed 8 miles of the canal line of the Lagan, including the aqueduct at Spencer's Bridge. The Lower Bann Navigation had limited commercial and pleasure traffic, but from 1962 the Lower Bann Association successfully opposed proposals for closure. The last major traffic left the Newry Ship Canal in 1966, and this closed in 1974, when the owning trust went into liquidation; the development of alternative port facilities at Warrenpoint made this canal obsolete. After 1970, the only traffics on the island were in the North: a coal traffic on the tidal Lagan and sand dredging on Lough Neagh, the latter still in being.

In Scotland, the final traffics had passed on the Monkland and Union canals in the 1930s; the Monkland closed in 1950, and part of its line was used to construct the Monkland motorway (M8) in the 1960s. The Union was also a barrier to road developments, and was closed in 1965, after a brief period during which British Waterways introduced small hired pleasure craft. While the Forth & Clyde had long been obsolete for most seagoing traffic, a small oil traffic developed in the early 1950s, and fishing boats and seagoing yachts regularly used it. The Bowes report viewed its costs of operation as subsidizing part of the fishing industry, and closure in 1963 obviated the need to provide new opening bridges. Despite individual campaigners like Douglas Russell, the Scottish Inland Waterways Association was not formed until 1971.

There was little public support for the retention of canals in South Wales. Both the Swansea and Monmouthshire Canals were closed in stages to 1962, with parts being retained for water supplies; on the Monmouthshire through Cwmbran New Town, locks were converted to ornamental cascades, with new roads crossing at water level.

Only the Brecon & Abergavenny length, disused since 1938, remained navigable. Maintained primarily for water supply, it was only used by rowing boats until an IWA rally of trailed boats at Brecon in 1952 awakened interest, helping to defeat

Unloading lime juice in barrels for Roses' of Boxmoor from a British Waterways' narrow boat in the early 1960s. Note the rather primitive, but mobile, crane and the pleasure boat in the background. This was BWB's last narrow boat traffic. (British Waterways)

closure plans to facilitate highway crossings. After the partial restoration of the locks south of Talybont from 1959, boating grew on the lower length. A section was filled in at Brecon in 1960, and the canal was classified as a Remainder waterway in 1968. However, the extension of the Brecon Beacons National Park to include much of the canal, (making it the only canal in a National Park), and an agreement with local authorities to fund restoration, enabled the length from Talybont to Brecon to be reopened in 1970. Between 1969 and 1971 the number of boats on the canal increased from 136 to 217. While a major breach closed the canal in the 1970s, it was later repaired and the canal reclassified as a cruiseway in 1983.

Long-distance carrying by narrow boat was seen to end in 1970, when the coal traffics from Warwickshire to Croxley and Southall ceased. Of the carriers involved, Willow Wren soon went into receivership, while Blue Line concentrated on hire boating. The remaining major carrier by narrow boat, the Birmingham & Midland Carrying Company, launched with much optimism in 1964–5, mainly used its fleet as camping boats after 1971. Decreasing financial viability accompanied lack of traffics and crews, exacerbated by declining maintenance standards, including winter closures, on Cruiseways. This effectively ended the way of life of people living on narrow boats, although enthusiasts would continue carrying.

The Regent's Canal and lower Grand Union (to Berkhamsted and Uxbridge) had been classified as major transport waterways in the 1950s, although improvement works were mainly confined to the duplication and mechanization of the locks at Brentford, and the development of the depot there. While BWB closed its south eastern fleet in 1963, ending most traffics from Brentford to Birmingham, it retained one traffic, lime juice in barrels to Roses' at Boxmoor, transhipped at Brentford. In other hands, this lasted until 1981, perhaps the last medium distance narrow boat traffic carried on strictly commercial lines, which outlived barge traffics on the Regent's and lower Grand Union. In 1966 numerous timber yards and manufacturers such as Heinz at Harlesden or J. Lyons at Greenford were still receiving goods imported through the London docks; by 1972 increasing craft size, and dock reorganization, especially the closure of Surrey Commercial Docks where much of the timber traffics originated, had reduced regular barge traffics to a minimum. These waterways were classified as Cruiseways in 1968.

The long level of the Paddington Branch and Regent's Canal above the locks at Camden had developed for pleasure boating since the 1950s, with trip boats which introduced many people to waterways. From the early 1970s BWB removed the restrictions on the weekend use of locks, converting the duplicate locks on the Regent's Canal to weirs by 1975.

One unusual long-term traffic began in 1967 on a Remainder waterway in the Potteries, the Caldon Canal. Johnson Bros, a subsidiary of Wedgwood, began carrying tableware between two factories in Hanley and a packing plant four miles away in Milton, using a special narrow catamaran, *Milton Maid*. This would later expand to further craft, but reduced to *Milton Maid* and a shorter run after the Milton plant closed in the 1980s. This only ended finally in 1995 with a further factory closure. These effectively used a roll-on, roll-off principle, loading cargoes onto trolleys which were wheeled off onto ramps at the unloading points.

After 1960, inland waterways traffic would develop in ways which bore little relation to the traditional craft, track and trading of the canals of the industrial revolution; by the end of the 1980s, even regular movements by barge would be rare. Concerns that traditional carrying might disappear altogether were met by varied responses. These included the development of boat preservation, sometimes allied to museums, and the development of carrying on a partly commercial basis. The assertion in *The Future of the Waterways* in 1964 proved prophetic:

> … the scale of commercial transport operations over the narrow waterways is small.
> It appears that, if there is a future for it, it may lie more in the use of some kind of
> relatively small, and perhaps 'profit-sharing', organization than in normal terms of
> large scale company undertakings.[9]

The remaining carrying by narrow boat into the 1970s mainly involved domestic coal. Perhaps the most professional operator was the Ashby Canal Association, which succeeded in retaining traffics from Gopsall Wharf until 1981, on a canal upon which carrying had almost ceased in 1959. From here and from Atherstone

The Boat Museum at Ellesmere Port, showing the top gate of the Whitby Locks, the entrance opened in 1993 (remodelled in 2006), and the associated trip boat. Before the museum opened in 1976, on a much smaller scale, there were proposals to build a container terminal to serve the Manchester Ship Canal on this site.

Wharf, coal was carried to various canalside locations in Southern England. Several other individuals or groups became coal merchants, supplying bagged coal to various locations, some of which, like the Macclesfield Canal, had seen no traffic since the 1950s. The Narrow Boat Trust, formed in 1971 to preserve working narrow boats in action, acquired three Willow Wren craft; volunteers would assist the carrying of domestic coal on to the Thames into the 1990s. A periodic short-haul gravel traffic developed on the Soar near Leicester, initially in wide craft, then in narrow boats, and finally in special narrow craft.

Another aspect of the preservation of craft and historical sites was the development of museums. The earliest museum, based traditionally on artifacts in glass cases, was opened by BWB at Stoke Bruerne in 1963. Visitor numbers grew from 14,000 in 1963 to 48,000 in 1970, when the original displays and visitor facilities had been enlarged. Stoke Bruerne itself became a major attraction, with boat trips to Blisworth Tunnel from 1968. By 1974, when visitors were at a record level of nearly 108,000, it had been joined by the Canal Exhibition Centre at Llangollen, linked to the horse-drawn trip boats there, and the small private Dewsbury Canal museum, which focused on the waterways of Yorkshire.

Other museums which involved waterways were founded in the 1960s as open-air museums. These reflected a development which had begun in Sweden in 1891, featuring a broad industrial setting, often with relocated, reconstructed, or replica structures. These served to introduce many visitors to the historic built environment rather than historic artifacts, and may well have inspired much interest in historic canals. Ideas behind three had been developed in the 1960s, the earliest to open, at Morwellham Quay in Devon in 1969, at the end of the Tavistock Canal. That at Blists Hill in Ironbridge (1973), included the visual restoration of part of the Shropshire Canal and the Hay inclined plane, although plans to remove the Longdon Aqueduct and erect it at Blists Hill were abandoned. Volunteers were involved in clearance work here, albeit for a canal that was not intended to be restored for navigation.

Volunteers also fostered a museum with a very different aim, but which came to conserve many buildings and structures within the historic canal port at Ellesmere Port. The North West Museum of Inland Navigation had been planned in 1970 as a small private collection of historic boats, but once the site at Ellesmere Port was secured, this proved to expand in size and purpose after it opened in 1976. Finally, the Black Country Museum, which included some floating exhibits, opened in 1977, on a site next to Dudley Tunnel. A separate but related activity there were the Dudley Canal Trust's boat trips into the tunnel, which intensified in the 1980s, so that this became one of the most extensively visited points on the English canal system. The last traffic had passed along this line in 1951, it had been closed in 1962, and yet within 25 years it was a popular amenity. The transformation which this reflected will be discussed in the final chapter.

CHAPTER FOURTEEN

Into the Second Canal Age

The growth in amenity uses of waterways, encouraged by the Transport Act of 1968, led to the expansion in use and extent of the then navigable network. Public perceptions of canals changed, so that local authorities, like those in Tameside, which had once sought the destruction of their local canals, came to regard them as important recreational assets. The same period brought one consequence of this new popularity – a somewhat insidious commercialization which, to some, compromised the essential character of historic waterways environments. Leisure facilities upon canals had changed greatly since the beginnings of pleasure boating in the interwar years, and new interests and concerns had developed.

The formal administration of most of Britain's waterways did not greatly change after 1970, despite unsuccessful attempts in 1973 to merge BWB, as a manager of watercourses and minor supplier of water, into the new regional water authorities in England and Wales. Previously independent river navigations, such as the Thames, Nene and Great Ouse, came under the remit of the new authorities, the largest number being under the Anglian Water Authority. These retained navigation as one priority alongside others such as water supply, wastewater management, drainage and flood protection, and increasingly, nature conservation. This could lead to conflicts and limited support for navigation facilities, as would transpire with the Yorkshire Derwent. When many water authority activities were privatised in 1989, navigation was one of the responsibilities transferred to the new National Rivers Authority, itself subsumed within the wider remit of the Environment Agency from 1996. BWB did acquire control of further waterways, including the southern Stratford Canal from 1988, the Linton Lock and Yorkshire Ouse Navigations, and, via The Waterways Trust, the Rochdale Canal. This, along with new navigations, reflected various purposes, including a more secure future for navigation and the securing of restoration.

In Ireland, the Grand and Royal Canals were finally transferred in 1986 from CIE control to the Office of Public Works, which had long controlled the Shannon. The OPW, operating as the Waterways Service, was able to develop pleasure boating and amenities in ways beyond CIE's remit, including the fostering of the new Shannon-Erne link from 1990. In turn, the OPW's role was replaced in 1999 by Waterways Ireland, one of six cross-border bodies, that took over the Lower Bann Navigation from the Rivers Agency in the North, where the disused navigations remain under various ownerships.

The 1968 Transport Act provided legal protection for Cruising and Commercial Waterways, but did not directly guarantee finance or maintenance provision. Government funding for the latter proved insufficient, and, during the 1970s, there were lengthy closures of Harecastle, Blisworth, Netherton and Braunston tunnels, Pontcysyllte and Alvechurch aqueducts, and Anderton lift, all on Cruiseways. The engineers Peter Fraenkel & Partners surveyed the condition and maintenance for BWB in 1974, identifying arrears of maintenance to both commercial and cruising waterways standards of £60 million at 1975 prices (£380 million at 2008 prices). While, 30 years later, much of this backlog had been cleared, with the aid of special grants, major problems remained. Had significant commercial traffic persisted on cruiseways, it could not have survived for long, as enthusiasts discovered. Parliament somewhat reluctantly accepted the need to continue financial support for maintenance, while the Transport Act 1978 placed a duty on the relevant Secretary of State 'to promote a national policy for the use of inland waterways for commercial transport.'

The Conservative Government elected in 1979 began to pursue policies of privatization or commercialization of state assets. In line with the latter, a Statement of Objectives for BWB, agreed in 1984, insisted that it 'should, as far as practicable, run its affairs on a commercial basis',[1] attract private finance and investment, and thus minimise its calls on public funds. BWB nevertheless continued to stress its 'traditional role and commitments as custodians of part of the National Heritage'[2]. Consequences included BWB's sale of the last of its carrying fleet in 1987, followed in 1988 by the sale of its remaining freight depots. Cargo handling was privatised at Weston Point Docks (where traffic collapsed after 1993), and at Sharpness from 1997. Hire boating was abandoned in 1993, but BWB assumed new roles in property development, with an early joint venture to develop property at Gloucester Docks and elsewhere. In 1999 the new Labour Government announced that BWB would no longer be viewed as a nationalised industry, but as a public corporation acting as a guardian of leisure and heritage assets. In 2000 *Waterways for Tomorrow* set out what then appeared to be a secure future.

After 1968 the IWA increasingly focused on issues of interest to pleasure boat navigation and amenity, including canal restoration, within a framework of critical support for, and co-operation with, BWB and other canal owners. However, in 1971 it helped Charles Hadfield, now restored to membership, to form what became the Inland Shipping Group (renamed Inland Waterway Freight Group in 2005). The ISG focused interest away from traditional carrying, and from ambitious yet impractical schemes such as J. F. Pownall's Grand Contour Canal. The latter, first suggested in 1942 and endorsed by IWA as late as 1965, had advocated a new canal for 1,350 ton barges (and water supply), mostly at the 310ft contour, between Preston and Hertford, with branches to the Midlands. Instead, ISG soberly investigated new traffics, new approaches to cargo and cargo handling, and track improvements. Apart from an early scheme for a trans-Anglian waterway, linking the midlands to Eastern ports, most attention was devoted to large tidal waterways for low-profile coasters and short-sea traffic. These reflected the growth of trade with the European

Union, linking the Eastern coast ports with ports and inland waterways on mainland Europe. This included many waterways that are very different from the traditional smaller canals and river navigations discussed earlier in this book. These were now found to contribute much more to domestic waterborne freight than the BWB-controlled waterways. Revised statistics indicated that in 1980 87 per cent of inland waterway traffics moved in ships, and 81 per cent passed to the open sea. By 2000 the latter had increased to 92 per cent, demonstrating the limited role of inland waterways – much of that proportion passing over the tidal Thames.

To admit seagoing traffics onto the larger inland waterways, barge-carrying ships, such as the LASH (Lighter Aboard Ship), used in the Medway, or BACAT (Barge Aboard Catamaran) were developed. Craft could move directly inland from these vessels without any need to tranship cargoes, although the heavy capital cost of the specialised ships necessitated long-term traffic commitments. While BACAT was introduced into the Yorkshire waterways, it was withdrawn in 1975 due to unofficial union opposition at Hull. The use and development of barge-carrying ships continues to be advocated from time to time.

BWB suggested modest improvement schemes in the early 1970s to develop transhipment depots at Winsford and Rickmansworth, to provide barge feeder services to the congested Mersey and London. The decline of the former, and the need to destroy historic structures to enlarge the lower Grand Union from Brentford, led to their abandonment. Regular traffics had ceased on the Grand Union and on the Weaver above Anderton by 1974. Only the modest Sheffield & South Yorkshire enlargement was completed, in 1983. Nevertheless, experience in Continental Europe suggested (and continues to suggest) a considerable potential for new and enlarged waterways, such as the Rhine-Main-Donau Canal, finally completed in 1992.

The collapse of regular narrow boat carrying was matched by a decline in barge traffics by the 1990s, due both to the reorganization of traffics and to the need for increased carrying capacities of craft. The closure of coal mines and power stations ended many coal traffics, like that in the final West Country barges on the Calder & Hebble Navigation to Thornhill Power Station in 1981. The decline led BWB to abandon its compartment fleet in 1986, although the need to modernise these historic vessels was also a factor. Developments in timber packaging and the distribution of imported timber, increasingly via continental ports, helped to end important traffics on the London waterways, to Gloucester and the Lydney Canal, the final traffic on the latter. The oil crisis of the early 1970s accelerated the reorganization of petroleum distribution, and the closure of depots like Quedgeley on the Gloucester & Sharpness followed smaller ones like that at Exeter in 1972.

Traffics in bulk grain, which mostly relied on port storage and overside loading, declined with the increasing use of home-grown grain and the concentration of most imports into two major terminals at Seaforth (Liverpool) and Tilbury. This removed much traffic upstream from Hull, including Beverley Beck in

The Aire & Calder Navigation above Pollington Lock in the 1960s. Craft include *Esso Leeds*, *Liliane* and British Waterways' *Waterdog*. This remains the busiest of the BWB waterways, dealing mainly with bulk liquids and quarry products. (British Waterways)

1981, and onto the Sheffield & South Yorkshire and Aire & Calder Navigations. The closure of smaller upstream mills ended many traffics, such as that revived between Tilbury and the Wey at Coxes Mill, Weybridge, which closed in 1983. New highway developments improved the capacity, flexibility and speed of road transport, serving growing ports with no upstream connections, which made it increasingly competitive with waterborne transport. This affected the use of general terminals; of the BWB depots sold in 1988, those at Knostrop, Brentford, Enfield and Nottingham had not been used for water transport for some time, while others at Anderton, Newark and Gainsborough were soon diverted to other uses or redeveloped.

Opportunities for new traffics were increasingly lost as waterside wharves became attractive for commercial or residential property development, especially during the property booms of the late 1980s and the 2000s. This was a consequence of major investment in urban regeneration initiatives and a new demand for waterside residences, which also affected smaller canals. While this was most marked in the development of London's docklands, it also affected such sites as the timber yard and mill in Norwich which provided the last traffics there in 1989. The relocation of industrial customers to larger sites nearer motorways was a further factor. This inhibition was partly mitigated by policies to protect significant wharfage, such as that on the Thames from 1997, but much potential was lost.

Two commercial BWB waterways that were developed were the adjoining Aire & Calder Navigation (ACN) and Sheffield & South Yorkshire Navigation (SSYN), whose main lines, serving Goole, Leeds, Wakefield and Sheffield, had been identified for development soon after nationalization. The depot at Knostrop, provided under the 1956 Development Scheme, was soon enlarged, as was the ACN for new traffics in oil to Leeds and in coal, especially to the power stations at Ferrybridge. The latter included new coal compartment boats, in push-towed trains of pans carrying 500t, a more efficient development of the earlier Bartholomew system. These were emptied by a special boat lift at Ferrybridge C Power Station, opened in 1967. Served by a declining number of pits, this traffic nevertheless became by far the largest upon BWB waterways, accounting for a large proportion of tonnages carried by the end of the twentieth century, over 2 million tons in 1993.

In 1978 the line to Leeds was further improved to carry 700-ton craft; in 1977 *Humber Jubilee*, the first craft to be built for the ACN since 1968, began to carry petrol from Immingham to Leeds. Of the 2 million tons then carried, 400,000 T was in liquids. The ending of the BACAT trade, the later closure of depots at Castleford and Wakefield, and the relative failure of the Caldaire terminal, opened in 1985 to assist transhipment at Goole, demonstrated a decline in general merchandise traffic. Coal traffics to the Skelton Grange Power Station and into Leeds ended by the mid-1970s, while Ferrybridge B closed in 1992. This left Ferrybridge C served from the deep mine at Kellingley, which had opened in 1965, the Astley/St Aidan's open cast site, where the original wharves opened in 1974 were replaced by a new loading point in 1988, and a smaller loading point at Wakefield, served by road.

Most petroleum traffics would decline by 2000 as fuel taxation changes advantaged road transport, but those to the terminal at Fleet, near Leeds, would be revived in the 2000s. Sand and coal traffics to Leeds and Knottingley, and traffics from and to Wakefield, had long ceased by then, while the last grain traffic on the smaller Selby Canal was carried in 1981. Finally, one consequence of electricity generation privatisation and improved air quality standards was the reduced demand for coal, especially sulphurous coal, which led the Ferrybridge owners to switch to imported coal with lower sulphur content. Coal traffic thus ended in 2002, leaving only petroleum and aggregates traffics, along with traffics into South Yorkshire. The premature closure of the Selby coalfield, close to the ACN but never served by it, and the St Aidans site, removed much potential for revival.

This loss of traffics, reflecting the loss of customers rather than direct competition from road or rail, was even more manifest on the SSYN. Under the Development Plan, the lock at Long Sandall was enlarged in 1959 to allow compartment boats through to Doncaster and Hatfield. After 1963 the Sheffield terminal was replaced by one downstream at Rotherham, leaving the Sheffield Canal as a Remainder waterway, with the last traffic to the basins at Sheffield in 1970.

BWB had resisted attempts in 1964 to close the whole line, or at least that between Hatfield and Keadby, when British Rail sought to close its opening bridge at Keadby and transfer remaining traffics to rail. BWB's plans to enlarge the whole line were rejected in 1966, but its revised scheme of 1971 proposed enlargement from the New Junction to Rotherham. Not until 1979 did work begin, after EC and County Council financial support, to provide a 700t waterway to a new depot south of Rotherham. The scheme, which involved channel widening and realignment, dredging and piling, bridge alterations and 10 new locks, opened in 1983, with the new depot in 1985. BWB improved the 1905 waterway, the New Junction to the ACN, at the same time. The total cost was about £12 million.

This scheme was paralleled by proposals elsewhere, including the Severn corridor to Worcester and the Trent into Nottinghamshire. However, by 1985, many traffics, including coal from Denaby to Doncaster, had ended, while some potential customers had failed in the recession and industrial closures of the early 1980s. Few new traffics materialised beyond a limited increase in general merchandise carried from Goole to Rotherham and Swinton, and tonnages proved to be one-tenth of those anticipated.

Traffics on other Yorkshire waterways continued over generally unimproved lines, albeit ones with modernised facilities. Traffics to York, on both the Ouse and Foss, including general imported traffics, and sand won from the river upstream, ended in the 1990s. This left traffics to Selby, some in former LASH lighters, and this in turn ceased in 2007. Smaller traffics on the Trent, to West Stockwith and along the Fossdyke to Lincoln, ceased by the early 1970s, while larger petroleum and general traffics on the Trent to Newark and Nottingham had ceased by the mid-1980s, with a short revival to Colwick in the 1990s. Sand and gravel were loaded at various Trent valley wharves for Hull and points on the ACN, with a large traffic between Besthorpe and a new wharf for Lafarge at Whitwood on the ACN Wakefield line, developed from 2002 with a substantial Freight Facilities Grant. Downstream on the tidal Trent, which was controlled by Associated British Ports after the privatisation of the British Transport Docks Board, traffics in 3,000t ships were extensively developed, with wharves at Keadby, Gunness, Grove Wharf, Neap House, Flixborough, Burton-on-Stather and Gainsborough. While by 2000 traffics to Gainsborough had ceased, the lower wharves continued in use. Over 2,000 seagoing vessels were handled in 1990, although this had reduced to around 1,300 by 2003. Like Goole, a port further inland, these reflected rising trade with the European Union, linked by the North Sea.

Other East Coast ports that featured inland waterways traffic, along improved tidal waterways, included Wisbech on the Nene, Fosdyke Bridge (revived from 1979) on the Welland, Boston on the Witham, Mistley on the Stour and Colchester on the Colne. Among these, traffic into Colchester, which involved 2,501 ship arrivals carrying over 1 million T in 1984, ended in 1999 with the closure of this municipal port, which had been unprofitable for a number of years.

The Manchester Ship Canal at Barton, viewed from the Swing Aqueduct looking upstream. The *Arklow Villa* is carrying grain from France to the Cerestar wharf, in the far distance. In the right foreground is Barton Oil Berth, whose use ended in the early 1990s.

The Manchester Ship Canal Company (MSCCo.) was affected by similar factors to the smaller commercial waterways, especially those whose traffics relied upon ports, and also by the changing direction of trade towards continental Europe. It would feature unprecedented campaigns both to retain navigation and for company takeover, which would result in most of the Canal remaining open but controlled by the property company Peel Holdings.

The MSCCo. had steadily disengaged from smaller canal traffic, closing Runcorn Locks in 1966 in order to develop traffic at Runcorn Docks, where tonnages handled had grown from 52,832 tons in 1958 to 435,318 tons in 1968. New customers had been gained after the Runcorn Bridge opened in 1961, but later road developments, notably the M62 to Yorkshire and Humberside, would reduce traffics into the Manchester area. Although the MSCCo's attempt in 1959 to close Walton Lock and the lines into Warrington were defeated, it compensated the final lighterage customer in 1984 and allowed Walton Lock to fall derelict. Lighterage to Howley Quay, through the Black Bear Canal, had ended in the 1960s, and this length was closed in 1976. On the Bridgewater Canal, lighterage into Castlefield and coal to Trafford Park Power Station had ended by 1973, while grain to Kelloggs mill at Stretford ended in 1974 when the traffic was transferred to road from Seaforth. On the line to Runcorn, a major breach at Lymm brought unexpected proposals for closure, but the IWA National Rally there in 1972 encouraged its repair and reopening in September 1973. Local authorities then formed a Bridgewater Canal Trust to cover operating losses, and the development of pleasure boating continued. After the property company Peel Holdings acquired the MSCCo, much property development, some of it controversial, followed.

As early as 1962 the Rochdale Committee of Inquiry had endorsed the MSCCo. policy to concentrate development at the Ship Canal's deeper western end, which could accommodate larger ships, and on bulk liquid traffic, concluding that:

> … we cannot believe that the port has any great development potential. The ability of ships to berth right inland is a factor of decreasing importance in these days of cheap and rapid road transport, whereas the limitations on the size of ship which can use the port are likely to become more serious as the average size of ship continues to grow. [3]

At the end of the 1960s the upper reaches, above Runcorn, were still much in use. Regular liner services linked the Terminal Docks at Salford with Canada and the Mediterranean. Between Mode Wheel and Barton there were several oil installations, with grain carried to Barton; while below Barton Lock, sewage sludge was loaded for dumping in Liverpool Bay. Partington Coaling Basin, whose facilities dated back to 1894, handled coal for export, chemicals and petroleum products. Much distribution had been carried out by the Ship Canal Railway, which followed the canal line to Runcorn, but this was closed in 1976.

Container handling, which was to transform dock handling processes, and to greatly speed the turn-round of ships, had begun on the Canal in 1965. Britain's first container terminal for fully-cellular dedicated container ships opened in November 1968 at No.9 Dock; this was developed for Manchester Liners vessels for Canada, and the Mediterranean from 1971. Growing containerization overseas, coupled with the long transit time up the Canal towards Manchester, and proposed motorway links, fostered the development of a container terminal at Ellesmere Port; after this opened in 1972, Ellesmere Port's export trade exceeded that of Salford.

In 1981 the MSCCo. chairman asserted that 'No longer is there any demand for deepsea general cargo vessels in the heart of the greater Manchester area'. [4] In 1980 the National Coal Board had declined to modernise the coal exporting facilities at Partington, moving operations to Garston, while in 1983 Manchester Liners moved its remaining container service to Ellesmere Port. By 1984 only scrap exports for Spain, and occasional heavy-lift ships to Pomona Docks, remained at the terminal docks.

In April 1984 the MSCCo. announced its intention to close the upper reaches after 1987, when the North West Water Authority would withdraw its sludge ships, with a major loss of revenue. This announcement aroused controversy in Parliament, and a Steering Committee that included local authorities was soon formed to consider the future of the upper reaches. However, the MSCCo. chairman stressed that in 1985 the upper reaches lost £2.2 million while the lower part made a profit of £1.6 million, and:

> the only commercial solution which I can see is to run a viable port on the canal between Eastham and Runcorn and to turn the Upper reaches back into a river, a safe river but with no through navigation…Should it be that an overriding public interest requires an ocean link to be retained, then I believe that the public should meet that cost.[5]

As with the smaller canals, the MSC involved irreducible maintenance costs; its course drained much of the Greater Manchester region, and if it was not dredged to navigation standards, the consequent silting might cause flooding. Dredging vessels would probably need to pass through locks and bridges, whether or not the waterway was open to shipping or even to pleasure craft alone. The Steering Committee suggested that the least expensive solution was to keep the Canal open, attracting new traffics and fostering property development and leisure use. While the MSCCo. rejected this, it was soon embroiled in a major takeover bid that eventually resulted in its full ownership by Peel Holdings, for which the site of what would become the Trafford Centre was a critical asset. As part of arrangements whereby most City Council directors were removed in 1988, it was agreed that the Canal would stay open indefinitely, while property development unrelated to water transport would be encouraged on its banks. After a major planning battle, the out-of-town retail and leisure centre, costing £900 million, opened in 1998.

About 300 ships still used the upper reaches annually, although traffic was in decline. The final length closed to shipping after the Trafford Road Swing Bridge was fixed in 1992, but substantial annual traffics of about 400,000t continued in imported grain to Cerestar (later Cargill) at Barton, for which special ships were commissioned in 1993.

After 1983, when Salford City Council acquired much of the former Salford Docks, these were transformed into Salford Quays, with extensive office, retail, leisure and residential development. Much former dockspace was isolated by new locks in order to improve water quality, with two new short canals, Chandler's (opened 1988) and Mariner's (1989). Ironically, these were probably the first canals to be constructed in the UK solely for pleasure use. From 1995 they were linked to the Bridgewater Canal by the new Pomona Lock, replacing the difficult route through Hulme Lock. Redevelopment in this and the Pomona area continued into the 2000s. New traffics, assisted by Freight Facilities Grants, were developed in the area, including cement for export and grain barged from Seaforth. In 2004 Peel Ports opened a new container terminal, dealing with a coastal feeder service, at Irlam, with plans for a larger tri-modal facility at Port Salford upstream. The turn towards leisure use was evidenced by a plan, unveiled in 2005, to build a new canal to link the Trafford Centre with a passenger service to Salford Quays. The potential loss of the major traffic in imported grain after 2008 will leave the upper reaches with very limited traffic.

At the time that this was photographed, in 1993, this presented a somewhat contradictory scene, but this is one which has since become commonplace in waterside areas. This shows one of the terminal docks of the Ship Canal, now Salford Quays. Although there would be a very doubtful future had this land been retained for freight use, the conversion of handling and storage space to commercial and residential property elsewhere has meant the loss of useful wharves, notably on the tidal Thames. This does represent the fate of many canalside areas, with the water space preserved, but the past dressed up to add flavour to the present and the use of navigable waterways to enhance the value of residential and commercial property.

The reduced traffics in the Port of Manchester also affected the lower reaches. Total tonnages declined from 16 million T in 1970 to 12.5 million T in 1980, 8.7 million in 1990 and 7.7 million T in 2000. Tonnages, mostly along the first few miles up to Ince, stabilised at around 6 million in the 2000s, of which about 1 million was in the upper reaches. Losses included the Ellesmere Port container terminal, which closed in 1992, while changes in Shell's distribution arrangements also reduced traffics to Stanlow. Finally, there was some traffic on the Weaver Navigation, but the closures of Anderton Depot and industrial customers at Weston and Wallerscote left a single coaster traffic until 1999. This was transferred to road after dredging problems, toll costs and delays caused by a bridge reconstruction. Prospects for a later ship traffic in salt from Winsford collapsed over questions of maintenance and lock dimensions.

Traffics on the London area waterways were similarly affected by port changes. This mostly relied on lighterage to and from the docks, a substantial industry that declined steeply in the 1970s. The 1956 Development Plan sought to develop the line to Brentford, dualling and mechanising the lock there, with similar work on the lower 13 miles of the Lee to Enfield, which halved the transit time from the docks. The Regents and lower Grand Union, which served factories and timber yards, relied on

Timber traffics and wharves on the Lee navigation in the early 1960s. Before the development of modern timber handling techniques and packaging, such traffics were easily handled by lighters, stowing logs and planks with ease, and emptying ships carrying imports rapidly. Timber yards grew up alongside the Lee, Regent's, the lower Grand Union and the Grand Surrey Canal, but while traffics remained significant in the late 1960s, most had ceased by the end of the 1970s. (British Waterways)

smaller lighters that became uneconomic, and diminished after the closure of Regents Canal Dock in 1969. The loss of lighterage firms led BWB to form Lee & Brentford Lighterage in 1982, to try to retain traffics, but when this collapsed in 1984, carrying to Brentford ended. Factors included the rundown of the older London docks, road competition and the reorientation of trade around Tilbury. One of the largest movements on the Lee, in metal to Delta Enfield Metals, ended when the cargo ceased to be imported through London. By the 1990s even traffic to Bow Creek had ended, although later there was a modest revival and trials of a new waste traffic along the Lee. One unanticipated consequence of plans both to restore the Bow Back Rivers, and to stage the 2012 Olympics in London, is that freight transport might be revived, in the first example of the freight transport use of a restored waterway.

The Transport Act 1968 secured a long-term future for the Cruising waterways, and thus marked the end of the general campaign to retain waterways which had remained navigable, and strengthened campaigns to revive those that were unnavigable or excluded from its protection. In the Republic of Ireland, these battles had, effectively, been fought in the early 1960s by the IWAI, although a later attempt to remove the safeguards for the CIE canals in the Transport Act 1958 had to be defeated.

One consequence was increased investment in both private and hire boats, as illustrated by the following table for BWB canals and rivers:

	1965	1975	1984/5	1994/5	2004/5
Private licences	9,241	19,356	18,872	29,767	25,244
Hire craft	441	663	1,590	1,546	1,648

While the basis of licensing changed during this period, the trends, most marked for the growth of hire boating in 1965–75, are clear. The expansion of hiring involved more professional management and better craft than those of the pioneers. However, it was not particularly profitable and proved volatile, like much of the leisure industry, with the failure of companies and the withdrawal of fleets, especially during the recession of the early 1980s. This was a period of major expansion in world tourism, with cheaper transport and the end of exchange controls upon travel abroad. The notorious British weather and the difficulties and dangers in canal operation, along with long closures and congestion in places, deterred some holidaymakers. This was balanced by the increased numbers of people able to afford holidays in expanded annual leave and, indeed, in early retirement at reasonable pensions. Some of the latter expanded the numbers leaving conventional employment to cruise continuously for much of the year.

Craft changes were reflected in the boatbuilding industry, which developed from the conversion of working craft, often reduced in length or cut in two, through new plywood and clinker boats and fibreglass hulls. The latter developed from dinghy-making in the 1960s, the largest firm being Norman Cruisers of Lancashire, which lasted until the 1980s. As with caravan design, upon which boat interiors were often based, standards of amenity and fittings rose, and were usually accommodated within the steel-hulled craft which became commonplace from the 1980s. Some of the latter were mass-produced, but much fitting out remained craft-based, making boats for hire or ownership increasingly expensive.

The development of waterways for cruising did arouse some objections, recalling earlier controversies about the commercialization of the Broads. In 1968 BWB noted that linear moorings could present problems, and from 1974 sought to control their growth by encouraging the development of off-line moorings and marinas. Some canals became congested at peak times; thus a duplicate line of locks was suggested in the 1970s for the Grindley Brook flight on the Llangollen line. Another solution was to develop new cruising grounds.

Concerns about the growth of cruising reflected those about the growing numbers of visitors to the countryside. Planning controls did not always prevent the development of unsympathetic canalside properties and facilities, and one view was that a form of over-development for leisure had removed much of the tranquillity that attracted some to the smaller historic canals. However, it was this economic activity, including enhanced property values, that formed a major and growing justification for the retention and later restoration of waterways.

An unanticipated controversy lay in the damage and disturbance to habitats and species caused by boat wash and towpath walking. Older maintenance practices had paid scant regard to this, with vegetation stripped to ensure boat and horse passage, but traffic decline had allowed the survival of some species in canals that were lost elsewhere as agriculture became increasingly industrialised. The long-standing nature conservation movement, that had loosely allied itself to waterways retention, began to attack the disturbance caused to waterways whose future was assured or that could be revived for navigation. An early instance of this was the Prees Branch of the Llangollen line, where objections by Shropshire Wildlife Trust in 1971 prevented restoration of one section, retained as an unnavigable water-course, with only a short length to the main line revived for navigation. From the late 1980s the designation of Sites of Special Scientific Interest by the Nature Conservancy Council (later Natural England) inhibited navigation on the restored Basingstoke Canal, with restrictions upon boat movements and the need to create an artificial bat roost to replace that in the Greywell Tunnel, which remains unre-stored.

The planned designation of part of the BCN as one of only two EU Natura 2000 sites on canals indicated the dilemmas of nature conservation. While much of the Cannock Extension had closed in 1963 after massive mining subsidence had ended coal traffics in 1961, a short length remained open south of the A5. Neither the banning of motor boats nor their extensive use would be satisfactory, as:

> The population of *Luronium natans* in this cul-de-sac canal is dependent upon a balanced level of boat traffic. If the canal is not used, the abundant growth of other aquatic macrophytes may shade-out the Luronium natans unless routinely con-trolled by cutting. An increase in recreational activity would be to the detriment of Luronium natans. Existing discharges of surface water run-off, principally from roads, cause some reduction in water quality.[6]

Measures to improve water quality, much inspired by European legislation, tended to enhance the amenity of navigation on rivers and canals in Britain, especially on the Broads, which were badly affected. The IWA helped to campaign against the effects of detergents in treated wastewater discharged to the summit of the Staffs & Worcs Canal after 1960, and improvements to urban water quality and on waterways like the Manchester Ship Canal, to which salmon returned in the 1990s, were welcome.

In the Irish Republic, nature conservation concerns did not arise to the same extent, but the IWAI began to perceive a threat to the character of the Shannon from pollution and its development for powered boats, and sought the develop-ment of sympathetic harbour facilities.

IWA's organisation and approach to campaigning had changed after the 1960s, especially following the effective departure of Robert Aickman, forthright but vituperative. His confrontational approach, and the need to involve local people, had encouraged the formation of many smaller canal societies, mostly campaigning bodies. The Upper Avon Navigation Trust, in which he remained heavily involved until his death in 1981, not only campaigned for, but organised and financed restoration (with the help of a benefactor), and became the navigation authority for the river from Evesham to Stratford. This was one model of IWA involvement in amenity waterways, the alternatives being those of critical support of waterways owners, practical support or action in working parties, or attempts to persuade local authorities, by protest or through shifting the consensus, to support retention or restoration. Before turning attention to the remainder waterways, it is worth focusing upon a restoration campaign upon a waterway that had been used by pleasure boats in the 1930s, but was partly derelict: the Yorkshire Derwent.

Part of this had remained navigable since the 1930s, but only visited by river boats that would pass through the tidal Ouse onto its lower reaches. While drainage works had destroyed two locks, the scenic reaches between locks remained navigable. A society had been formed in 1959 to support restoration, but this had proved ineffective. From 1974 the newly-formed Yorkshire Water Authority, which had drainage and pollution control responsibilities, proposed powers to control navigation, including measures of restoration, along similar lines to the Thames and Anglian authorities. An alternative model was pressed by the Yorkshire Derwent Trust, formed to take over and restore navigation on similar lines to the Upper Avon Navigation Trust, with Aickman as one of its officers. This pursued a policy of opposition to the YWA, which withdrew support for restoration, and continued to regulate the river. The restoration of one lock, and the consequent increase in boating, with a trip boat running between former locks in 1980, inspired opposition that remains hard to place. This seems to have been a coalition between local landowners who disliked powered boats and visitors on the river, and nature conservationists concerned about the damage and disturbance that visitors could bring. In the face of this opposition, the IWA was persuaded to promote litigation to argue that highways rights of way legislation provided a right of navigation on the river, a right taken away from BWB waterways by the 1968 Act. A long legal battle ensued, lost in the House of Lords in 1991. The waterway remains unrestored and lacks any new navigation authority.

The Pocklington Canal, which joins the lower course of the Derwent, was also affected by the designation of SSSIs, but with more positive results. An early IWA campaign had inhibited plans by Sheffield Corporation to use the Canal line to deposit sewage sludge in 1959, and the Pocklington Canal Amenity Society was founded in 1969. Local farmers now supported restoration, having earlier favoured the slurry scheme, and the canal was restored, lock by lock, from the junction, with five of the nine miles restored by 1983. The designation of much of the canal as SSSIs, due to its wildlife (the only canal site protected under the Wild Birds Directive), slowed down the restoration of navigation on the final section to Canal Head, although the PCAS fostered gradual improvements. A further complication was the designation of several bridges and all but one lock as listed structures, conserving historic character but increasing the cost of restoration. The small numbers of visiting and resident craft, and the severe lack of dredging, prevented damage from boat wash, but also endangered some features of the SSSIs, with algal growth due to the low depth and lack of flow.

BWB's remit was to treat all remainder waterways in the most economical manner possible; for the Pocklington Canal, this meant maintenance confined to the ensuring of safety. While most of the BCN system, bar the through routes, was so designated, several lengths were still being used for commercial traffic in 1967–8. The final traffic in waste between the Chemical Arm and the Gower Branch ended in 1975, and floating tube storage at Coombswood in 1976, leaving occasional movements, mainly of refuse by Alan 'Caggy' Stevens, before his death in 1997. While the BTC had organised trips south from Gas Street in the early 1960s, pleasure boating had been slow to develop, apart from moorings on the Cannock Extension and Longwood Boat Club at Daw End. The 1969 IWA National Rally in Birmingham helped to foster support for the retention of the remainder lengths and the promotion of pleasure boating.

BWB argued successfully that waterborne maintenance was essential for the BCN's water supply and drainage functions to continue, and thus most sections that were still navigable in 1968 were retained, albeit in limited use. Exceptions were perhaps insignificant, although the last loss, the blocking in 1992 of the Ridgacre branch to accommodate a low road crossing, aroused major protest on a national scale.

Some revivals and restorations followed, including the Titford Canal and the Dudley Canal to Coombswood, where work was completed in 1974; in the late 1970s, Hawne Basin, disused since 1967, was cleared by volunteers and the Coombswood Canal Company for moorings. The most significant reopening had been that of the Dudley Tunnel, although headroom and ventilation problems, followed by a collapse for a long period between 1981 and 1992, meant that it was only used occasionally as a through route. However, the northern part became extensively used by trip boats after the Dudley Canal Trust promoted the driving of new tunnels in 1984/5 and 1989/90 to create a circular route through limestone mines. Increasing demand led the Trust to support an unsuccessful major lottery fund bid in 2008 to enlarge the trip boat operation through further tunnels into limestone caverns; the scheme remains.

Most other remainder waterways that were revived after 1968 would be re-classified as cruiseways under the BWB Act of 1983. These included the Ashton and lower Peak Forest, Erewash and Caldon Canals. Once the future of many remainder waterways appeared secure, more attention could be devoted to

The Rochdale Canal at Hebden Bridge, with the re-excavated wharf between the two boats on the offside. During the late 1960s there were proposals (and much local support) to fill in the whole of the canal within Hebden Bridge.

the restoration of other waterways. Among many schemes, covering almost every historic waterway by 2008, two trans-Pennine waterways can be highlighted as outstanding examples.

The Rochdale Canal restoration, involving 33 miles of canal with 92 locks, grew to maturity and completion from an improbable start. Within twenty years after most of it closed in 1952, its line had been obstructed in several places by road crossings, including two motorways, and with culverted sections, one in Failsworth with a large store built on its site. The only continuous section was that which linked the Ashton and Bridgewater canals in Manchester, whose closure was authorised in 1965 should the Ashton Canal also close. This length was barely navigable, and the subject of many voluntary working parties, while the remaining 3 miles within Manchester were shallowed to 6in depth by 1970. Water sales and property had long been the concern of the Canal Company, and its study in 1973 of possible uses for the discontinuous canal did not include boating.

Interest in the canal as a local amenity began at Littleborough in 1971, and the local IWA and the Calder Navigation Society, which had helped to secure the retention of the adjacent Calder & Hebble Navigation, investigated revival. Some enthusiasts doubted whether full restoration should be sought, and it was stressed that 'the object is to consider all possibilities not only to restore a through route but also to link up existing pounds by restoring locks to form linear parks and to permit boating'.[7] The Rochdale Canal Society, founded in 1974, aimed initially

The remains of Old Double Locks on the Sankey Canal. The oldest surviving example of a staircase pair, these closed in 1931 and were partly bulldozed to form 'cascades;' in the early 1980s, some time before the formation of the Sankey Canal Restoration Society, The restoration of Brtain's earliest canal, and its possible extension to join the Leeds & Liverpool, is a long-term project, but parts are still in water and sections of its later extensions have been restored for the mooring of craft using the River Mersey.

only to restore an isolated section near Todmorden. This held working parties and a trail boat rally on the summit pound in 1975.

Early support for eventual restoration came from Calderdale Council and Greater Manchester Council, and work began unexpectedly in the Rochdale area, under a job creation scheme. This restored, visually, two locks and various other lengths as part of local environmental improvements. In 1981 Calderdale Council obtained approval to restore a 3 mile section, including ten locks, between Todmorden to Hebble End Bridge, in order to introduce a trip boat. This opened in summer 1983, and was extended in April 1984 through a new Hebble End Bridge, the first bridge in Britain to replace a culverted crossing. By 1986 the basin and wharf at Hebden Bridge had been re-excavated to form a base for a horse-drawn trip boat, while the first hire boat had been introduced onto the steadily expanding but isolated section.

Meanwhile campaigning had begun, to provide a navigable crossing at Chadderton, under what was later built as the M60 Manchester Outer Ring Road. A working party cleared the area in 1981, with a trailed boat rally there in 1986. This helped to build public support, so that by the public inquiry in 1988 only the Department of Transport favoured blocking, which was rejected in favour of a diversion and bridges. By then navigation had been restored through

THE INLAND WATERWAYS ASSOCIATION OF IRELAND
Cumann Uiscebhealaigh Intire na h-Éreann

RALLY & FESTIVAL
to celebrate the Re-opening of

THE NAAS BRANCH OF THE GRAND CANAL

The Weekend of the 9th - 10th May, 1987

**RALLY OF BOATS TO ARRIVE AT NAAS BRANCH HARBOUR
THE MORNING OF SATURDAY, 9th MAY.**

**RE-OPENING CEREMONY
SATURDAY AFTERNOON
FOLLOWED BY RECEPTION**

*Watersports ● Exhibitions ● History Excursions
Social Functions ● Etc.*

A large assembly of boats is expected to mark this Historic event

FURTHER DETAILS FROM –

DES LEYDEN	KEN SHAW
Chairman IWAI Dublin Branch	Chairman Naas Branch
6 Foxrock Avenue	12 The Grove
Dublin	Celbridge
Phone 895593	Phone 271253

The Naas Branch of the Grand Canal, closed in 1961, was the first branch to be restored. Restoration proposals began in the early 1970s, with the lowest lock reopened in 1978, and it was restored with voluntary and Government employment scheme assistance.

four new road bridges to Sowerby Bridge, where a major blockage included two infilled locks and a section covered by a road, Tuel Lane. This section was replaced by a tunnel and a new deep Tuel Lock, with the largest fall in Britain at nearly 20 feet. When this opened in 1996, after over £3 million had been spent, this connected half the canal, 15 miles to Littleborough, to the main system. Unlike earlier schemes, restoration had involved extensive engineering works, with a much smaller practical role for voluntary working parties. Funding came partly from Calderdale Council, West Yorkshire County Council before its abolition in 1986, and various job creation, urban regeneration and derelict land measures.

Between Littleborough and Manchester, much clearing and visual restoration had been carried out, but without any restoration of navigation. This restoration would rely largely on regeneration agencies and National Lottery funding, specifically from the Millenium Commission. A lengthy campaign ensued, with much local authority, IWA and Canal Society pressure, to secure the transfer of the Rochdale Canal Company to the recently-formed The Waterways Trust (a condition of funding), against much resistance from the property company that owned it. Major engineering works included the rebuilding of the terminal A629 (M) roundabout at a slightly higher level, and, two miles south, the adjustment of canal levels to route the line through a former farm underpass below the M62. Further south, the regeneration of Failsworth included the demolition of the store blocking the canal line, while the shallowed section was removed, with many subsidiary works. This enabled the *Millenium* scheme to be finally completed for reopening in July 2002!

At much the same time the Huddersfield Canal, closed earlier but still navigable in 1948 (when the Rochdale was not), was also restored. Its 20 miles included the 3-mile summit tunnel, which had collapsed by 1972, with its restoration alone estimated at £12 million. By then, three sections had been piped and infilled, with the canal line in Stalybridge built over and obscured, and all but five of the lock chambers demolished or capped. Initial pressure for restoration came from Peak Forest Canal Society members, as the reopening of that canal and the Ashton approached in 1974. This new Society commissioned a report, published in 1977, which suggested that restoration was possible, using new lines through Stalybridge, and part of Huddersfield. Most of the line was protected from further destruction, and short lengths, at Uppermill and between Slaithwaite and the summit at Marsden, were revived, including the rebuilding of several lock chambers.

One difference here was the heavier involvement of the Huddersfield Canal Society, which formed a subsidiary that contracted for part of the restoration works. This was one of the partners, including the local authorities and BWB, in the Huddersfield Canal Company, which oversaw the final restoration of £30 million. Funding was similarly through English Partnerships and the Millenium Commission, and the restoration, including the rebuilding of much of the town centre in Stalybridge, locks at new levels, and tunnels under buildings in Huddersfield, was completed in April 2001.

Although the Stratford restoration had involved many locks, dredging and the raising of an ornamental bridge blocking the terminal lock, there were no major engineering works to recreate the line of the canal. Such works would be beyond the scope of volunteers, however skilled many had become. The transformation in public and Government attitudes partly reflected a renewed view of the social, economic and environmental benefits that a working canal could bring. One evidential basis for this lay in cost-benefit analysis, an appraisal process that had been first used in the US as early as 1902, and was extensively used there from the 1950s. It was used in Britain to appraise the M1 motorway in 1959 (after construction had begun), the Victoria Line and, most notoriously, the London airport schemes.

More detailed factors, including economic, social and environmental costs and benefits, would be incorporated. Many of these indicated that the small direct financial income from any restored waterway would often be greatly augmented by non-financial benefits, that could outweigh the capital cost of major engineering works. One of the earliest studies was produced in 1983 by W.S. Atkins for the restoration of the Montgomery Canal. This suggested major net economic benefits and that the full restoration costs, including an excavated section into Newtown, should be incurred within 3 years so as to reap early benefits. Despite this, the public expenditure involved was rejected in 1989, on the ground that regeneration in South Wales presented a higher priority. A more gradual approach

The *Saint William* was one of the last coasters to use the Newry Ship Canal to Newry, in the 1960s. Since Newry & Mourne District Council acquired the canal, pleasure boats have been allowed to use the canal. The gates of the lock were pulled open for the first time in 1987, and may be automated to encourage greater use. (McCutcheon Collection)

followed, enlarging the Welshpool navigable length and restoring the line south to Refail (near Garthmyl) by 1996. The line below Frankton towards Maesbury was rebuilt, but re-opening of the Aston Locks was held up by the need for volunteers to construct a Nature Reserve in which to transplant floating water-plantain, and thus seek to relocate the SSSI status of the canal below the locks.

Perceptions of the high nature conservation value of the Montgomery line partly went back to the 1950s, and not only was the restoration expenditure heightened by the increasing demand for mitigation measures, but outright opposition developed from the Countryside Council for Wales and (to a lesser extent) English Nature (now part of Natural England). British Waterways produced a Conservation Management Strategy in 2005 that presented the linking of the Maesbury length with the Welshpool length as the first priority, citing the economic benefits of linking the under-utilised Welshpool section with the main system.

The Rochdale restoration demonstrated some general developments, which underlay the acceleration of completed schemes in the late twentieth century. An early emphasis was a move away from protest and pressure towards a more consensual gaining of public support, and especially the support of those involved in planning controls and regeneration, public funders, and politicians. Thus interests in Hebden Bridge had gone from favouring the culverting of the whole canal there and the building of a new Calder Valley road along much of its route, to supporting its revival and the increased tourist and local amenity benefits that this could bring. Initially, decisions to protect the line from further destruction were made, and then the first steps towards the tidying up and partial restoration of short sections. Protests aimed, as in the M60 campaign, to build public support and thus isolate parties like the Department of Transport. Voluntary work no longer aimed to completely restore navigation or to carry out maintenance, but sought to demonstrate how improvements could be made before others could produce the actual restoration. An instance where this faltered was in those parts of the Huddersfield Canal that had already been partly restored, and whose completion and slight enlargement of lock chambers could not be funded, which caused problems after reopening. In the 1970s and 1980s various job creation schemes funded partial restoration, but from the 1990s onwards full-scale schemes were promoted. These aimed to fund total restoration, albeit sometimes broken down into separate projects that would amount to full restoration by stages.

This extended to the promotion of new lines entirely for leisure use. The leading example was the Ribble Link, which aimed to reconnect the Lancaster Canal, which had always been isolated from the main system, bar sea connections via Glasson Dock. This sought to canalise the Savick Brook, which the Canal crossed near Preston, to link the Ribble and Douglas to the Rufford Branch of the Leeds & Liverpool, which had itself been saved from closure at the last moment. It took advantage of the peculiar circumstance that all major bridges over the Brook had been constructed to standards that would permit canalization to the right height and width. After 1979, the Lancaster Canal Boat Club and Lancaster Canal Trust promoted a scheme to convert this to a canal. Costings were produced by 1982, and with Millennium Fund and development agency finance, the Link opened in July 2002.

Other river navigation proposals – the Higher Avon and the Upper Severn, foundered over concerns about environmental damage. Similarly, plans to extend the Great Ouse upstream from Bedford to join the Grand Union at Wolverton were replaced, partly due to its circuitous line, by an alternative Bedford-Milton Keynes canal, including a tunnel. A more ambitious series of schemes was promoted from 2003 by the Environment Agency and others as the Fens Waterway Link. This, described as one of the largest schemes of rural regeneration, would link Boston to the Great Ouse via the Welland Navigation, and open up extensive new cruising grounds for broad craft. Although running through flat terrain, this would involve extensive excavations, including several miles of new waterway. Work on the first stage, a new lock and barrage below Boston, began in 2006.

Other new waterways have been suggested to ensure adequate use after restoration. These included plans to link the Leeds & Liverpool to the isolated Sankey Navigation, much of which was destroyed in the late 1970s, and whose revival has been gradual.

Canals that were long-disused and partly destroyed became the subject of viable, if slow-moving, restoration schemes. The Wey & Arun Junction Canal, disused since 1867, with sections built over, had 10 locks and several short lengths restored by 2008, as a result of campaigning and practical work that began in 1970. The Herefordshire & Gloucestershire Canal had been disused after 1882, with the section through and south of Ledbury built over by a railway, itself later closed. A long campaign began in 1983, to protect and gradually restore structures and amenities. One unexpected development arose near the Severn entrance lock at Over, where the redevelopment of a hospital site, built over the line, received planning approval on condition that the canal basin should be restored. Against a tight timescale, and with major involvement by WRG, this was completed in 2000, although any restoration of the canal upstream may well be decades away. Another proposal, to link the short gap in the Dudley Canal between Hawne and Selly Oak, embodied similar ambitions. This includes the rebuilding of the 3,795 yard Lapal Tunnel, which collapsed in 1917 and was largely filled by concrete; the provision of two major road crossings; and the re-excavation of most of the line.

Other schemes have aimed to restore short lengths for amenity purposes, such as the Swansea Canal, of which only the 5 miles between Clydach and Ystalyfera had not been destroyed by 1981, when revival began. There are plans to link this via a new River Tawe Navigation, and the Tennant Canal to the Neath Canal, of which two long sections separated by an infilled section near Resolven have been restored. The Wilts & Berks Canal Amenity Group, founded in 1979, aimed to restore local amenities on this 51-mile-long canal. Although the whole section in Swindon is destroyed, eventual restoration was later envisaged. Some structures have been restored by working parties, while the IWA partly celebrated its 60th anniversary in 2006 by financing the building of a short new section off the Thames at Abingdon, initially to provide new moorings.

In Scotland, the restoration of the Forth & Clyde and Union Canals proceeded on a piecemeal basis, but accelerated to completion for the millennium. The earliest works restored isolated sections near Edinburgh and Glasgow, with new road crossings under the Glasgow Canal Project of the late 1980s, and a new crossing at Linlithgow extending navigation. Millennium funding provided two massive restorations, including the entire Forth & Clyde, including relocated locks, numerous new crossings, and a diversion to the Carron River to avoid Grangemouth. Much more audacious were new structures, including the world's first drop lock, at Clydebank. The lock flight on the Union Canal at Falkirk was bypassed by the Falkirk Wheel, a completely new type of structure, which has become one of Scotland's biggest tourist attractions. Conceived in 1994, this was opened in 2002, with a fall of 24m (79ft), linked to a new line by an aqueduct, a 160m tunnel under the Antonine Wall, and new locks. New road crossings, and a lengthy re-excavated section near Edinburgh, completed the Union Canal restoration. Further ambitious works have included the extension of the Glasgow Branch in 2004–6 into Port

Dundas, at a cost of £5.7 million; and the plans, due to start in 2008, for an extension of the eastern end towards Grangemouth, including a new lift to link the canal back to the Forth, part of a much wider Lottery-backed scheme known as Helix.

In the Irish republic, the IWAI developed schemes to restore most of the Grand Canal branches, with that to Naas reopening in 1987, and proposals to reopen its Corbally extension to encourage traffic over this little-used route. As the Ballinasloe branch was heavily damaged by turf-digging, a new Suck Navigation to Ballinasloe, was constructed between 1997 and 2001. The Shannon was restored back into Lough Allen in 1996, and in 2006 Waterways Ireland proposed a further extension upstream to Annagh Upper, a section that has never been navigable.

The IWAI had not felt it practicable to restore the Royal Canal, whose main line is 90 miles long with 56 locks, last navigated in 1955 and closed in 1961. By 1974 the section west of Mullingar had been drained, with eight major obstructions, and plans to use the line in Dublin for a motorway. The Royal Canal Amenity Group was rapidly formed to promote restoration; the motorway and further obstructions were defeated, and local authority and CIE support for protection gradually won. An early practical step came in 1977 when CIE was persuaded to repair the top gates at Lock 12, to allow work on the seven-mile pound west to Blanchardstown. Support from job creation schemes (similar to those in the UK) enabled the building of lock gates, and the transfer to the OPW accelerated works, so that restoration had reached Mullingar, 46 miles from Dublin, by 1990. A hire boat firm began operating on this length from 1997. The restoration of the final section of 15 miles between Ballybrannigan Harbour and Richmond Harbour was anticipated for 2010.

The most significant early restoration project in the British Isles was the former Ballinamore & Ballyconnell Canal, disused since the 1860s. European funding, for waterways that crossed the border, through an area of exceptional rural depression, secured reopening in 1994 as the Shannon-Erne Waterway, for a scheme upon which work began only at the end of 1990. At a cost of £28 million, work on this canal, 28 miles long with 16 locks, included the rebuilding of several lock chambers, the raising of the level of Lough Scur and dredging through two other loughs, and the widening of the former channel. Land acquisitions alone involved 450 farmers and 650 acres.

In the North, restoration had been proposed for all the major canals by the early 1990s, although progress on the ground was limited to short lengths, like a section of the Lagan Navigation at Lisburn and the re-excavation, as part of the Blackwater Valley Museum, of a short section of the Ulster Canal. The site of the latter, 10 miles of which has been filled in, crosses the border, and in 1997 both Governments commissioned reports into its restoration. Restoration costs were estimated at £90 million at 2000 prices, for a project that would take at least 7 years. However, EU funding was refused, on grounds of insufficient economic benefit, late in 2004, and more modest interim plans to restore sections in Clones and at the Lough Erne end have been put forward for EU funding.

Earlier plans for the Newry Canal saw voluntary clearance work near Scarva in 1982, but the entrance locks on the Ship Canal and the 4 miles to Albert Basin were reopened in the late 1980s. By 1992 all four local authorities had acquired their sections, and an ambitious project to restore navigation, bypassing low crossings in Newry, has support in the long term. Local authorities also supported the restoration of the Lagan Navigation, including a new line to bypass that destroyed by the M1, and the Coalisland Canal. Local support grew from the 1990s, so that the IWAI, which had had very few members in the North, had several branches there.

The first years of the twenty-first century perhaps completed the transformation of the smaller canals into a Second Canal Age. Their use for freight carrying was largely limited to heritage/enthusiast movements, often with much public support, but reflecting a kind of 'museumification'. The new scene, for leisure and amenity, involved their development in ways never anticipated by those who originally promoted, engineered, used and developed them.

The growing popularity of towpath walking from the 1970s was reflected in expanding numbers of publications. Towpaths had long been used for informal walking where routes offered access, so that some became classified as public rights of way, and increasing numbers viewed walking as a leisure activity or as a means of visiting waterways. However, as BWB stated in 1967:

> Hitherto a 'trespassers will be prosecuted' policy has been traditional – in the distant past because the towing paths were extensively used for their original purpose, and in the more recent past because the uncertainty surrounding the future of the smaller waterways made it difficult to do anything which would tend to establish rights of way.[8]

This resistance could be reduced once most horse (and tractor) towage had ended, while the security provided by the 1968 Transport Act enabled more positive policies. The concurrent Countryside Act 1968 reflected new emphases on outdoor recreation near to urban centres, with the designation of country parks, while from the 1970s many local authorities funded improvements to paths both in urban and rural areas. Devon County Council acquired and restored the remainder Grand Western Canal in 1972 and opened it as a linear country park in 1974, with limited boating use. This reflected the growth of country parks. Local authorities next to the London canals, many of which had retained horse and then tractor towage into the early 1970s, opened up inaccessible towpaths. The City of Westminster was the first local authority to adopt its section of towpath, in 1968, and to open up access, albeit on a restricted gated and patrolled basis at first. This became part of the London Canal Way, opened in 1977. Part of the Regents Canal line was used to lay underground cables and surfaced for walking.

After 1978 BWB formally permitted the use of all its towpaths. Long distance public footpaths, using the enabling legislation of 1949, began to be completed in the 1960s, starting with the Pennine Way in 1965. The Offas Dyke Path, which opened in 1971, included a short length of the Llangollen Canal near Pontcysyllte. In 1993, the 145-mile long Grand Union Canal Walk opened, the first signed long-distance canal towpath. This followed the expenditure of £1 million on bank protection, path laying and signposting. The more multi-purpose Trans-Pennine Trail, formally opened in 2001, included the Sankey Canal between Widnes and Warrington.

In Ireland, the OPW and later Waterways Ireland encouraged the clearance and development of towpaths, including that along the unrestored Royal Canal. The Newry Canal towpath and part of the Lagan formed part of the (incomplete and indistinct) Ulster Way, established in the 1970s. These were especially useful in an island which, like Scotland, has far fewer public footpaths than England and Wales.

While many ramblers are keen walkers of towpaths, no specific group campaigned for towpath walking until the Towpath Action Group was formed in 1987/8. This focused initial attention on obstructions to the newly restored towpath of the Rochdale Canal in Manchester, and continued to campaign for the removal of further blockages on that Canal and other canals upon which navigation was restored. This works with rambling groups both to promote towpath walking and to campaign for improved conditions and accessibility.

A further use of towpaths was for cycling, which BWB had permitted by license, but began to restrict in 1983. Formal use, including resurfacing of towpaths with zoning for walkers and cyclists, began with the formation of Sustrans from a Bristol group of cyclists in 1977, which began to develop routes from 1979. One of these used a disused railway between Bristol and Bath, and this was followed by the route of the Kennet & Avon, then partly under restoration, from Bath to Devizes, between 1984 and 1988. This became the focus both of a BWB experiment in 1989 in charging for cycling (abandoned after major protest by cyclists), and controversy over conflicts between cyclists, walkers and anglers.

Attempts to rescue and rehabilitate historic waterways (and indeed promote new ones) for the future were matched by attempts to conserve traditional working boats and practices, the growth of museums, and developments in waterways history. The preservation of craft was partly linked to the decline in traditional carrying, and attempts to not only retain and restore historic craft, especially narrow boats, but also to develop their use. In part, this reflected the ending of narrow boat- and indeed barge-building, the closure of yards and the loss of skills. The earliest development was the formation of the Narrow Boat Owners Club at the IWA Marple Rally in 1966, after many traditional narrow boats experienced problems navigating the Macclesfield Canal. Later renamed the Historic Narrow Boat Owners Club, as many new pleasure boats had 'narrow boat' hulls, this aimed to preserve former working narrow boats built before 1962, and to campaign for the maintenance of waterways facilities to secure their use. This has also fostered an interest by private owners and others in what may be termed 'boat genealogy', striving to record comprehensive and minute details, and achieve authenticity; this has sometimes extended to the genealogy of boatpeople and canal workers, reflecting the explosion of interest in family history since the 1970s.

In 1990, a group of owner/carriers grouped together to form the Commercial Narrow Boat Operators Association, combining enthusiasm with professional organization. Based mainly in the South Midlands, with 40 vessels by 1993, this was renamed the Commercial Boat Operators Association in 1999, reflecting new membership by barge operators. This has helped to retain carrying by narrow boats, albeit often in small quantities, much of it in bagged domestic coal. The Narrow Boat Trust and the Wooden Canal Boat Society (founded as the Wooden Canal Craft Trust in 1974) aimed mainly to preserve the boats, their appearance and skills involved, rather than to carry cargoes on a commercial basis.

While enthusiasts helped to preserve the appearance of traditional narrow boat carrying operations, large traditional canal craft did not attract the same enthusiasm, or indeed the levels of interest in preserved Norfolk wherries, for which the Norfolk Wherry Trust had been founded in 1949. Some of these were preserved in floating collections, the largest of which became that at Ellesmere Port after the Boat Museum opened there in 1976. Into the 1980s, this expanded to conserve much of the port site, as well as craft, exhibits and archives. Until 1981, this was run by volunteers, after which it was professionally managed with much help from job creation schemes.

By contrast, the then National Waterways Museum at Gloucester, housed in a historic dock warehouse, was largely founded by BWB when it opened in 1988. The setting would become one popular for residential and commercial property development over the following 20 years. The restoration of historic buildings make the docks a tourist attraction in its own right, with the museum one attraction. The smaller Stoke Bruerne operation, still run by BWB, was renamed the Canal Museum in 1989.

Smaller museums or exhibition centres elsewhere highlighted the history of local waterways, inter alia, including that founded at Nottingham (1982) and the London Canal Museum (1992). Developments like that at Wigan Pier, with *The Way We Were* exhibition in a converted canal warehouse linked by trip boat to the nearby Trencherfield Mill, helped to conserve historic buildings rather than to develop canal history or research. In Scotland, part of the Monkland Canal was re-excavated to form part of the Summerlee Heritage Park at Coatbridge in the 1980s, although the main attraction was the former ironworks, and plans for further excavations have not materialised.

One effect of these developments was to conserve elements of craft, buildings, engineering and townscapes that were no longer commonplace, and to introduce members of the public to historic canals and landscapes. The 1980s, however, saw a literature-led backlash against the growth of 'heritage' and the sense that this could portray a false history, against the full forces of postmodernist doubt. The Wigan Pier attraction came in for especial scorn, with allegations of unconscious cultural ideological dominance.

In Ireland, much more sparsely populated, canal-oriented museums were slower to develop, and on a more modest scale. That at Robertstown, in the former Grand Canal Hotel, succumbed to financial problems in the 1990s. Although a heritage centre operated there between 1999 and 2003, the building was sold for refurbishment as a hotel. The OPW opened what would become the Waterways Ireland Visitor Centre at Ringsend in 1993. The Heritage Boat Association, founded in 2001 after the World Canals Conference in Dublin, has sought to preserve both working and pleasure craft throughout Ireland, but generally afloat and in private ownership. Survivors include Grand Canal and Shannon lighters, many of which have been converted for leisure use. In the North, despite the area's pioneering involvement in industrial archaeology, formal museum coverage is limited, although in 1992 a small museum opened in the former stables at Moneypenny's Lock, by the Newry Canal.

Some of the growth in museum and visitor centres reflected the growth of the heritage industry, in which the selling of heritage places and objects, authentic or not, proved profitable in its own right or contributed to the viability of tourist destinations and facilities. There were many currents to this movement, but one feature was the growth in private or privately funded attractions, and the increasing need to sell the attraction to visitors, day or tourist, for whom there were many other attractions, from the expansion of weekend leisure shopping to visitor attractions outside the British Isles. Rather than a crisis of historical authenticity, many museums experienced increasing financial difficulties in the 1990s. This included the closing of the museums in Nottingham (2000) and Birchills (2003) in Walsall.

Where there were prospects for the incorporation of 'heritage' into newly viable property development, as with the Wigan Pier Quarter and many former canal-served buildings and areas, this could lead to the refurbishment and conservation of older buildings and the development of former wharves and boatyards. At Wigan, for instance, the much-criticised exhibition finally closed in December 2007, with the former canal warehouse proposed for conversion, along with the new development on the site of Mayors' boatyard. This paralleled the development of much of the historic waterside for apartments and commercial uses.

Financial instability led to the formation of The Waterways Trust (TWT) in 1999 to take over the running of the three main museums at Stoke Bruerne, Ellesmere Port and Gloucester, renamed the National Waterways Museum in 2006. Resignations and further financial problems caused much public criticism of this apparent saviour. Although the position was stabilised, with the modernization of the exhibitions at Ellesmere Port largely completed in 2007, the condition of much of its boat collection, 30 years after rescue and founding, was poor. Those attractions that set out to entertain seem to have proved more viable than those that aimed to conserve history and to educate.

This uneasy relationship between the waterways past and its representations extended into the loss of everyday heritage of canals and canalside scenes. Despite the preservation and presentation of some scenes, often recreated, within museum contexts, much that gave many transport waterways their everyday character has disappeared. This disappearance has been gradual but incremental, including the early removal of obsolete handling facilities, and the redevelopment or conversion of canalside warehouses and canalside industries and wharves. The attractiveness of waterside locations, sometimes sanitised, fostered the redevelopment of many canal wharves, such as the former coal depots on the Bridgewater Canal, mostly redeveloped with the encouragement of its property company owner.

Against this, measures for landscape and built environment conservation were strengthened, enabling some protection for the character of waterside landscapes. Among the first seven UK World Heritage Sites, designated in 1986, was the Ironbridge Gorge, which included the surviving parts of the Shropshire Canal, the Hay inclined plane, and the Severn. Later designations included Blaenavon (2000), which took in part of the Brecon and Abergavenny Canal, while the Pontcysyllte Aqueduct, along with the canal between Chirk and Llantysilio, has been proposed for listing in 2008. In the Irish Republic, where WHSs have developed more slowly, the Clonmacnoise religious site next to the Shannon fulfils the criteria for designation. In the UK, on a more local scale, many smaller scale conservation areas incorporated extensive sections of canal from the 1970s, one of the earliest including most of the Macclesfield Canal in the Macclesfield area in 1975. After 1974 these influenced the demolition of buildings and other changes that might affect the character of canalside areas, with some success.

These changes to physical landscapes and places were perhaps matched by changes to the cultural landscape. After the 1970s living on narrow boats had ended, as had, sadly, the lives of many who had lived on boats or engaged in canal carrying or maintenance. While much could be recorded visually or aurally, the everyday life that had persisted, with variations, on the lowland canals, had passed into memory. Even the lives of those who boated for pleasure changed, with much more luxurious craft, and with the discovery of the waterside increasingly replaced by the orchestration of leisure facilities. Developments at least partly reflected movements outside – the era of protest from the mid-1960s to the late 1970s was related to some of the attitudes of those campaigning for restoration and practical protest in voluntary working parties. One development was that in popular arts and crafts, which greatly increased over this period, from those who followed and copied narrow boat painting (which declined as an everyday practice), sometimes helping to conserve traditional practices. In other cases, 'roses and castles' appeared as a decoration for trinkets and items like painted wooden spoons. Varied standards of authenticity and completion led to the founding of the Waterways Craft Guild in 1997, to set and maintain standards.

A further development was the development of travelling theatres that sought a form of outreach, like that pioneered by the travelling Century Theatre in the 1950s. The Mikron Theatre, a company founded in 1963, began to perform at waterside locations, using the converted narrow boat *Tyseley*. Mikron began with Shakespearian plays, but from 1972 it began to compose its own plays, based on research into canal history. Between 1982 and 2003 Day Star, a company with somewhat different aims, also toured waterways. Music around waterways themes was much more limited, although there were attempts to preserve or mimic the instruments and songs of boatpeople, linking these to the folk song revival. Similarly, many novels were published with a waterways background, contrasting with A.P. Herbert's *The Water Gypsies* (1930); some took historical themes. Finally, some painting had partly developed from book illustration, but became an art form in its own right, with the Guild of Waterways Artists founded in the 1980s. In all of these developments, there was a tension between historical authenticity and the need to achieve artistic qualities and the need to entertain. In a sense, the canals, especially those of lowland England, had become a palimpsest of all manner of cultural meanings, sometimes in conflict with contested space, sometimes reflected in the physical fabric of canals and watersides, sometimes not. To trace and explain this would, however, require the skills of a cultural historian. Despite some moves within transport history towards a 'cultural turn', notably in the experience of railways, there is little evidence of work of this emphasis for waterways history.

The major waterways histories completed in the 1970s were followed by many smaller, often locally produced, publications on canal history, and ventures into new fields. The growth of local archives, supplementing the collections in the National Archives (Public Record Office until 2003), provided historians with solid written evidence on a subject which had, as Charles Hadfield commented in an earlier version of this book, 'been somewhat at the mercy of guesswork and catchwords'. Some re-examinations of documentation have led to some revision of what had been accepted wisdom, such as the respective roles of Brindley and the Gilberts, in Peter Lead's *Agents of Revolution* (1989). Charles Hadfield directly queried the roles of Telford and Jessop in *Thomas Telford's Temptation* (1993), while my own book about Charles' work, *Canal Man and More* (1998), began to consider alternative perspectives on the postwar revival of waterways.

Publications in academic journals remained sparse, but there were a number of magazines that published historical articles, beginning with *Waterways World* in 1972. This was joined by the annual *Waterways Journal* from 1997, while the Railway and Canal Historical Society *Journal* increasingly featured waterways themes from the 1970s. 2006 saw the founding of *Narrowboat*, a new magazine devoted to waterways history.

New fields of history have also yielded insights. Social historians' studies, like those of Harry Hanson and Wendy Freer, have examined the working and living conditions, organizations and everyday lives of canal workers. Industrial archaeology, extending in its popular sense to excavations on the Bude and Grand Western Canals, or to the history of canal-served industries, yielded many insights after its first formulations in the 1950s. The early 1990s saw interest begin in the history of pleasure boating, reflecting perhaps the demise of many early pleasure boaters and their craft.

Oral history, as both technique and source, had begun in the late 1940s in the US, but increased from the 1960s with the development of cheap and portable tape recorders. One astonishingly early researcher was Ian L. Wright, whose informal interviews of (mainly) Glamorganshire Canal workers in the 1940s greatly informed his two-volume study (with Stephen Rowson) of *The Glamorganshire and Aberdare Canals* (2001/4). Many articles based on the recorded memories of former boatpeople and canal workers appeared from the 1970s. Perhaps the most prominent exponent has been Mike Taylor, whose work has preserved memories from many whose testimony is no longer available, especially on the Yorkshire waterways. Much material has been recorded and deposited, sometimes untranscribed, and this forms a treasury for future interpretation and analysis. Oral history may provide one foundation for cultural history work, while attempts to evoke and resurrect the meanings of past worlds, backing imagination with information, must lean on oral testimony. The use of photographic evidence, itself fortunately expanding with digital photography, is a significant adjunct to this potential 'history from below'.

In the first decade of a new century, it could seem that a transition to a Second Canal Age, of leisure, heritage and modernised transport, has been completed. The first canal age, in England at least, was largely self-supporting in economic terms, but this one is partly dependent upon public support. For two of the largest owners, the EA and the Broads Authority, income from users has to be supplemented by subsidies for navigation and amenity. BWB has been the subject of various proposals, including its transformation into an independent trust or outright privatisation. It has steadily come to rely upon the income from its inherited property portfolio to limit the need to rely upon direct Government grant. Sudden cutbacks in the latter in 2006/7, caused by EU penalties over unrelated problems with rural support, and cuts in real terms until at least 2011, demonstrated the need for long-term secure funding for both BWB and EA waterways. It became clear that not only would large-scale restorations prove difficult, shown by the withdrawal of BWB from the Cotswold Canal restoration early in 2008, it could prove difficult to finance the everyday maintenance of waterways. Cutbacks in staffing and planned maintenance followed. That financial problems were not confined to BWB was shown by the vicissitudes of the local authority-backed Basingstoke Canal Authority, and the financial problems of the private Chelmer & Blackwater Navigation in Essex. IWA found a new role in campaigning for better waterways funding, and, from 2005, in directly managing the Chelmer & Blackwater, through its subsidiary Essex Waterways Ltd. Whether the promise of *Waterways for Tomorrow* and completed and planned schemes like those in Scotland will prevail, or a series of crises and general neglect, remains to be seen. The First Canal Age did end, and it is hoped that the second will not.

What might be the future of waterways in the British Isles? Like Charles Hadfield, I will resist the temptation to offer predictions. Two patterns, however, can be discerned. The first is that before and during the Middle Ages, people and light goods moved by road, many heavy goods, if they could, by water. In those days the maritime link was strong, sailing vessels navigating rivers and the sea alike. The widening and improvement of road facilities was spurred by the turnpike mania, and the concurrent canal mania did the same for waterways.

The two, along with maritime-linked rivers and canals, helped to foster the first industrial revolution. Then came railways, to sweep away much unmotorised road and water transport. But now railways are of minor importance for most freight carrying, bar specialised traffics, and roads and waterways are fulfilling their old functions, but upon much-improved roads and (perhaps) improving waterways, and using very different vehicles and craft. There are some changes: rail and to a lesser extent road have lost passengers, though little freight, to air transport; both have lost traffic to pipelines; while both road and rail have gained maritime links by means of the Channel Tunnel and RoRo ferries.

The second is that in the Second Canal Age the functions and purpose for which canals of the First Canal Age were developed have been largely superseded, with their flowering for leisure, amenity, historic and nature conservation, and general contributions to well-being. The multiple concerns about the adaptation of rivers in the Middle Ages, and the past conflicts therein, have returned in an age where transport, amenity, water resources and nature and historic conservation have sometimes clashed. Those concerns now also apply to the canals, for which conservation and amenity are now paramount. In both eras, problems of finance and institutional governance failed to be fully resolved. For the historic canals, though, the development of transport must lie only in niche and heritage movements, and in this sense a history of transport, covered by the original *British Canals*, is completed.

Notes

Chapter One

1. Cl.33, British Library translation, available at www.bl.uk/treasures/magnacarta/translation.html, accessed February 2008.
2. L.T.C. Rolt, *The Inland Waterways of England*, 1950, p.69.
3. Quoted in T.S. Willan, *River Navigation in England 1600–1750*, 1936, p.106, referring to the Medway Navigation.
4. Quoted in Keith Fairclough, 'A Survey of the River Lea by Sir Christopher Wren' in *Journal of the Railway and Canal Historical Society*, Vol. 31, Pt 1, No. 153, March 193.
5. *A Report of the Committee of the Commissioners of the Navigation of the Thames and Isis, appointed to survey the rivers from Lechlade to Whitchurch...*, 1791.
6. H.C. Darby, *The Mediaeval Fenland*, 1940.
7. L.F. Vernon-Harcourt, *Rivers and Canals*, 1882, p.81.
8. Quoted in H C Darby, *The Draining of the Fens*, 1940.
9. Quoted from the *Journals of the House of Lords* in T.S. Willan, *River Navigation in England, 1600–1750*, 1936.
10. Kennet Navigation Minute Book, 20 May 1761.
11. Mersey & Irwell Act, 7 Geo I c 15.
12. 2 Geo I c 12 (Ireland).
13. *Dublin News-Letter*, 30 March 1742.
14. Obituary notice of Henry Berry, *Liverpool Mercury*, 7 August 1812.
15. *Annual Register*, 1760, p.160.

Chapter Two

1. Thomas Telford, *A Survey and Report of the proposed extension of the Union Canal from Gumley Wharf, in Leicestershire, to the Grand Junction Canal, near Buckby-Wharf, in Northamptonshire*, 1804.
2. H.F. Killick, 'Notes on the early history of the Leeds & Liverpool Canal' in *The Bradford Antiquary*, July 1897.
3. J.A. Langford, *A Century of Birmingham Life*, 1868, quoting a local newspaper.
4. W. Cobbett, *Rural Rides*, Vol. 2, 1912, p. 93 (Everyman edition).
5. *Thames Navigation. Observations upon the evidence adduced before the Committee of the House of Commons upon the ... Hants and Berks Canal*, 1825.
6. *Felix Farley's Bristol Journal*, 22 March 1794.
7. E. Meteyard, *Life of Josiah Wedgwood*, 1866.
8. J.S. Padley, *Fens and Floods of Mid-Lincolnshire*, 1882.
9. Gloucester & Berkeley Canal Minute Book, 23 December 1794.
10. Thames & Severn Canal Records (Glos CRO).
11. J.A. Langford, *A Century of Birmingham Life*.
12. Ashby de la Zouch Canal Minute Book, 1 July 1794.

13 Birmingham Canal Minute Book, 14 July 1769.

14 J.S. Padley, *Fens and Floods*.

15 H.F. Killick, *Bradford Antiquary*.

16 Kennet & Avon Canal Minute Book, 10 April 1797.

17 Quoted in D.R. Phillips, *The History of the Vale of Neath*, 1925.

18 Unidentified newspaper cutting (Charles Hadfield collection).

Chapter Three

1 C. Nicholson, *The Annals of Kendal*, 2nd edn, 1861.

2 Swansea Canal Minute Book, 9 June 1803

3 J.A. Langford, *A Century of Birmingham Life*, 1868.

4 J. Plymley, *A General View of the Agriculture of Shropshire*, 1813. Article by Telford on 'Canals' dated 1797.

5 Grand Junction Canal Minute Book, 9 July 1811.

6 Charles Dickens, 'On the Canal' in *Household Words*, 11 September 1858.

7 Grand Junction Canal Minute Book, 10 November 1825.

8 W. Hutton, *A History of Birmingham*, 2nd edn, 1783.

9 Grand Junction Canal Minute Book, 13 September 1808.

10 Driffield Navigation Minute Book, 6 July 1841.

11 J. Plymley, *A General View*.

12 L.F. Vernon-Harcourt, *Rivers and Canals*, 2nd edn, 1896.

13 Birmingham Canal Act, 23 Geo III, c 92.

14 A. Rees, *Cyclopedia*, 1819. Article on 'Canals' written 1805.

15 Staffs & Worcs Canal Minute Book, 14 September 1832.

16 Basingstoke Canal Report, 20 May 1802.

17 *Illustrated London News*, 10 October 1874.

18 Swansea Canal Minute Book, 3 March 1818.

19 Peak Forest Canal Minute Book, 16 May 1806.

20 Staffs & Worcs Canal Minute Book, 23 August 1823.

21 Quoted in F.S. Thacker, *The Thames Highway: A History of the Locks and Weirs*, 1920.

22 Regent's Canal Minute Book, 1 December 1830.

Chapter Four

1 *Case of the Birmingham Canal Committee, in opposition to the Dudley Canal Extension Bill*, nd.

2 J. Phillips, *A General History of Inland Navigation*, 4th edn, 1803.

Chapter Five

1 *Exeter Flying Post*, 2 January 1794.

2 J. Latimer, *The Annals of Bristol in the Eighteenth Century*, 1893.

3 Salisbury & Southampton Canal records.

4 Peak Forest Canal Minute Book, 7 July 1794.

5 Article by Thomas Telford in J. Plymley, *A General View of the Agriculture of Shropshire*, 1813.

6 Kennet & Avon Canal Reports, 14 June 1797 and 26 June 1798.

7 Letter to shareholders, 29 January 1798. Kennet & Avon Canal records.

8 Grand Junction Canal Minute Book, 5 July 1797.

9 Basingstoke Canal report, 26 October 1803.

10 *Records of the Borough of Nottingham*, 1760–1800, Vol. VII, 1947.

11 Grand Junction Canal Minute Book, 5 May 1801.
12 Tavistock Canal Report, 16 March 1803.
13 Tavistock Canal Report, 27 September 1816.
14 *Ibid.*

Chapter Six

1 J. Knox, *A View of the British Empire, more especially Scotland, with some proposals for the improvement of that country, the extension of its fisheries and the relief of the people,* 1784.
2 J. Phillips, *A General History of Inland Navigation,* 4th edn, 1803.
3 Quoted in E.A. Pratt, *Scottish Canals and Waterways,* 1922.
4 *Prospectus of the advantages to be derived from the Crinan Canal,* 1792.
5 Daniel Defoe, *A Tour thro' the whole Island of Great Britain,* 1724–6.
6 H.W. Dickinson, *James Watt,* 1936.
7 English & Bristol Channels Ship Canal Report, 23 June 1828.
8 *Canals and Waterways Journal,* January 1982.
9 J. Phillips, *A General History of Inland Navigation,* 2nd edn, 1795.
10 Gloucester & Berkeley Canal Minute Book, 28 October 1794.
11 *Ibid.,* 11 August 1795.
12 *Ibid.,* 2 June 1797.
13 *Ibid.,* 5 October 1871.

Chapter Seven

1 Basingstoke Canal Report, 21 October 1816.
2 *Ibid.,* 11 October 1822.
3 Kennet & Avon Canal. Minutes of a meeting of the Western sub-committee, 10 November 1840.
4 E.T. Meteyard, *Life of Josiah Wedgwood,* 1866.
5 H.F. Killick, 'Notes on the early history of the Leeds & Liverpool Canal' in *The Bradford Antiquary,* July 1897.
6 T. Grahame, *Essays and Letters on … Inland Communications,* 1835.
7 Quoted in 'The Lancaster Canal and its Connection with Railways', *LMS Railway Magazine,* November 1928.
8 J. Farey, *A General View of the Agriculture of Derbyshire,* 1817.
9 Prospectus of the Stirling Canal, 1813 (Charles Hadfield collection).
10 *Exeter Flying Post,* 22 November 1810.
11 B.T. Barton, *History of the Borough of Bury,* 1874.
12 Birmingham Canal Proprietors' Minute Book, 14 May 1841.

Chapter Eight

1 Bridgwater & Taunton Canal records.
2 *A Report of the Committee of the Commissioners of the Navigation of the Thames and Isis, appointed to survey the rivers from Lechlade to Whitchurch … ,* 1791 (Institution of Civil Engineers).
3 *Report from the Committee of the Hon the House of Commons appointed to enquire into the progress made towards the amendment and improvement of the Thames and Isis,* 1793 (Institution of Civil Engineers).
4 *Report of a Survey of the River Thames from Lechlade to the City Stone …,* 1811 (Institution of Civil Engineers).

Chapter Nine

1 Thames & Severn Canal Report, 25 January 1825.
2 Report of Canal Conference of 1888. Royal Society of Arts. Paper on the *History, Rise and Progress of Canal and River Navigation in Great Britain and Ireland*, by M.B. Cotsworth.
3 Quoted in D. Trevor Williams, *The economic development of Swansea and of the Swansea district to 1921*, University of Wales Press, p.129.
4 Basingstoke Canal, Notice of Meeting, 12 September 1831.
5 Kennet & Avon Canal Report, 21 July 1835.
6 Staffs & Worcs Canal Minute Book, 7 May 1840.
7 *Ibid.*, 4 September 1845.
8 Grand Junction Canal Minute Book, 23 October 1845.
9 Minutes of Evidence of the Royal Commission on the Canals and Inland Navigations of the United Kingdom. Answers to questions 23965 and 23970.
10 Kennet & Avon Canal Report, 21 July 1845.
11 Birmingham Canal Navigations Minute Book, 22 February 1878.
12 Staffs & Worcs Canal Minute Book, 12 December 1844.
13 *Ibid.*, 30 December 1844.
14 James Wheeler, *Manchester: Its Political, Social and Commercial History, Ancient and Modern*, 1836.

Chapter Ten

1 Grand Junction Canal Minute Book, 28 May 1841.
2 *Ibid.*, 16 July 1845.
3 *Ibid.*, 21 May 1846.
4 *Ibid.*, 2 October 1857.
5 *Ibid.*, 7 January 1859.
6 Swansea Canal Minute Book, 5 September 1809.
7 *Journal of a Somerset Rector*, 1930.
8 Unpublished journal of Josiah Baxendale, edited by G.L. Turnbull, 'A Tour by Canal', *Journal of the Railway and Canal Historical Society*, Vol XXIV No. 3, November 1978, 102 and 105.
9 Recounted in *IWA Bulletin 71*, June 1964.

Chapter Eleven

1 *Report of the Canal Conference of 1888* (Royal Society of Arts). Letter from W.M.T. Campbell.
2 *Ibid.*, paper on *The Relative Cost of Transport by Railway and Canal*, W. Shelford.
3 *Minutes of the Royal Commission on the Canals and Inland Navigations of the United Kingdom, 1906–10*. Answer to Question 1468, 15 May 1906.
4 *Ibid.*, Answer to Question 19214, 6 November 1906.
5 Report to the Board of Trade on the Thames and Severn Canal, 1888 (Glos CRO).
6 Grand Junction Canal Minute Book, 6 March 1835.
7 *Birmingham Daily Post*, March 1875, quoted in Harry Hanson, The Canal Boatmen *1760–1914*, 1975, p.129.
8 Quoted in Stephen Rowson and Ian L. Wright, *The Glamorganshire and Aberdare Canals*, Vol.2, 2004.

Chapter Twelve

1 *Report of the Royal Commission on the Canals and Inland Navigations of the United Kingdom, 1907–9*. Vol VII. Final report, para 28.

2 *Ibid.*, para 20.
3 *Ibid.*,para 442.
4 Minutes of Evidence of the Royal Commission on the Canals and Inland Navigations of the United Kingdom. Question 22588, 27 February 1907.
5 Michael Streat, owner of Blue Line, quoted in Tom Chaplin, *The Narrow Boat Book*, 1977, p.115.
6 L.T.C. Rolt, *Green and Silver*, 1949, pp.83-4.
7 Ruth Delany, *Ireland's Inland Waterways*, 1st edn, 1986, p.143.
8 James Unsworth, 'Life on the Leeds & Liverpool' in *Waterways World*, April 1981, p.52.
9 Charlie Morris, private correspondence 25 November 1991 and 20 October 1993.
10 Austin E. Neal, *Canals, Cruises and Contentment*, Heath Cranton, London, nd (*c.*1921), p.134.
11 V. Gregory, quoted in *Waterways News*, January 1976, p.4.
12 Clive Reed, Social Outings on the Swansea Canal, Swansea *Canal Society Newsletter*, October 1993.

Chapter Thirteen

1 BTC Supporting Papers, 9/9/1949, PRO AN85/2.
2 Frank Pick, *Report on Canals and Inland Waterways to the Ministry of War Transport*, unpublished document, 1941, pp.49–50.
3 Foreword to Lewis A. Edwards, *Inland Waterways of Great Britain and Northern Ireland*, London, 1950.
4 British Waterways Board, *The Future of the Waterways*, 1964, p.17
5 Graham Palmer, 'In The Beginning', *Peak Forest Canal Society Newsletter*, No. 23, October 1968, p.9.
6 British Waterways Board, *The Future of the Waterways*, 1964, p.44.
7 British Waterways Board, *The Facts about the Waterways*, 1965, p.84.
8 Quoted in *IWA Bulletin* 75, November 1965, p.39.
9 British Waterways Board, *The Future of the Waterways*, 1964, p.28.

Chapter Fourteen

1 Department of the Environment, *BWB Statement of Objectives agreed with the DOE*, 26 July 1984.
2 BWB Annual Report, 1985.
3 Ministry of Transport, *Report of the Committee of Inquiry into the Major Ports of Great Britain*, HMSO, September 1962.
4 Manchester Ship Canal Company, Annual Report and Accounts, 1981.
5 *Ibid.* 1985, p.3.
6 Joint Nature Conservation Committee, the Habitats Directive: selection of Special Areas of Conservation in the UK, www.jncc.gov.uk/protectedsites/sacselection/n2kforms/ UK0012672.pdf, accessed February 2008.
7 Ralph Kirkham, letter in *Waterways World*, December 1978.
8 British Waterways Board, *Annual Report and Accounts*, 1967, p.17.

Further Reading

Previous editions of *British Canals* included a long bibliography. There are bibliographies for pre-1916 material in W.T. Jackman's *The Development of Transportation in Modern Britain* (1916) and more recently in Edward Paget-Tomlinson's *The Illustrated History of Canal & River Navigations* (second edition, 1993). Mark Baldwin's *Canal Books* (1985) usefully discusses the literature of waterways up to the 1980s. During the currency of this book, there will be more publications to be reflected in online bibliographies. I have therefore provided below only a selected short list of books pertinent to the general history of waterways in the British Isles. This has meant, sadly, the omission of many excellent studies related to individual waterways.

Journals of interest, historical and current, include the *Journal of Transport History*, the *Journal* of the Railway and Canal Historical Society, *Transactions* of the Newcomen Society, *The Engineer*, *Engineering*, *Proceedings of the Institution of Civil Engineers*, *Industrial Archaeology*, *Transport History* and the annual *Waterways Journal*. Along with numerous private canal society and local history publications, there are also periodicals like *Waterways World*, *Canal Boat*, *Canal and Riverboat*, *Narrow Boat*, and *Narrow boat*.

I should mention that, as a former academic, it goes somewhat against the grain not to reference every statement and to provide a comprehensive bibliography, but this would render the book too long for the benefit of a small number of readers.

Albert, William, *The Turnpike Road System in England, 1663–1840*, 1972.
Baldwin, Mark, *Canal Books*, 1984.
Blair, John (ed.), *Waterways & Canal-Building in Medieval England*, 2007.
Bonavia, Michael R., *The Nationalisation of British Transport*, 1987.
Bonthron, P., *My Holidays on Inland Waterways*, 1916.
Boughey, Joseph and Hadfield, Charles, *Charles Hadfield: Canal Man and More*, 1998.
Boyes, John and Russell, Ronald, *The Canals of Eastern England*, 1977.
Burton, Anthony, *Canal Mania*, 1993.
Burton, Anthony, *The Canal Builders*, 2nd ed., 1993.
Chaplin, Tom, *Narrow Boats*, 1989.
Compton, Hugh and Carr-Gomm, Anthony, *The Military on English Waterways 1798–1844*, 1991.
Crowe, Nigel, *English Heritage Book of Canals*, 1994.
Cumberlidge, Jane, *Inland Waterways of Great Britain*, 1998.
Cumberlidge, Jane, *Inland Waterways of Ireland*, 2002.
De Mare, Eric, *The Canals of England*, 1950.
De Salis, H.R., *A Chronology of Inland Navigation in Great Britain*, 1897.
De Salis, H.R., *Bradshaw's Canals and Navigable Rivers of England and Wales*, 1904, 1918 and 1928 eds.
Delany, Ruth, *Ireland's Waterways: Celebrating 300 Years*, 2005.
Delany, V.T.H. and D.R., *The Canals of the South of Ireland*, 1966.
Foxon, Tom, *The Industrial Canal - Volume 2, The Railway Interchange*, 1998.

Freer, Wendy, *Women and Children of the Cut*, 1995.

Freer, Wendy and Foster, Gill, *Canal Boatmen's Missions*, 2004.

Gladwin, D.D., *Passenger Boats on Inland Waterways*, 1980.

Hadfield Charles, *The Canal Age*, 2nd ed., 1981.

Hadfield, Charles, *The Canals of South and South East England*, 1969.

Hadfield, Charles, *The Canals of South Wales and the Border*, 2nd ed., 1967.

Hadfield, Charles, *The Canals of South West England*, 1967.

Hadfield, Charles, *The Canals of the East Midlands*, 2nd ed., 1981.

Hadfield, Charles, *The Canals of the West Midlands*, 3rd ed., 1985.

Hadfield Charles, *The Canals of Yorkshire and North East England*, 1972–3.

Hadfield Charles, *World Canals: Inland Navigation Past and Present*, 1986.

Hadfield Charles, and Biddle, Gordon, *The Canals of North West England*, 1970.

Hanson, Harry, *The Canal Boatmen 1760–1914*, 1975.

Hanson, Harry, *Canal People*, 1978.

Harford, Ian, *Manchester and Its Ship Canal Movement*, 1994.

Harris, Robert, *Canals and their Architecture*, 1980.

Jeans, J.S., *Waterways and Water Transport in Different Countries*, 1980.

Lead, Peter, *Agents of Revolution: John and Thomas Gilbert - Entrepreneurs*, 1989.

Lewery, Tony, *Flowers Afloat: Folk Artists of the Canals*, 1996.

Lewery, Tony, *Popular Art*, 1991.

Lewis, M.J.T., *Early Wooden Railways*, 1970.

Lindsay, Jean, *The Canals of Scotland*, 1968.

McCutcheon, W.A., *The Canals of the North of Ireland*, 1965.

McKnight, Hugh, *Canal and Rivercraft in Pictures*, 1969.

Paget-Tomlinson, Edward, *Britain's Canal and River Craft*, 2nd ed., 2005.

Paget-Tomlinson, Edward, *The Illustrated History of Canal and River Navigations*, 3rd ed., 2006.

Porteous, J.D., *Canal Ports: The Urban Achievement of the Canal Age*, 1978.

Quinlan, Ray, *Canal Walks of England and Wales*, 1994.

Ransom, P.J.G., *The Archaeology of Canals*, 1979.

Ransom, P.J.G., *Scotland's Inland Waterways*, 1999.

Rolt, L.T.C., *Narrow Boat*, 2nd ed., 1947.

Rolt, L.T.C., *Green and Silver*, 1949.

Rolt, L.T.C., *The Inland Waterways of England*, 1950.

Russell, Ronald, *Lost Canals and Waterways of Britain*, 1982.

Russell, Ronald, *Walking Canals*, 1984.

Russell, Ronald, *Waterside Pubs*, 1974.

Shill, Ray, *The Industrial Canal – Volume 1, The Coal Trade*, 1996.

Smithett, Robin, *Precious Cargo – 50 Years of Hotel Boats*, 2000.

Squires, Roger W., *Britain's Restored Canals*, 2007.

Tew, David, *Canal Inclines and Lifts*, 1984.

Uhlemann, Hans-Joachim and Clarke, Mike, *Canal Lifts and Inclines of the World*, revised ed., 2002.

Vernon-Harcourt, L.F., *Rivers & Canals*, 1896.

Vine, P.A.L., *London's Lost Route to the Sea*, 5th ed., 1996.

Vine, P.A.L., *Pleasure Boating in the Victorian Era*, 1983.

Ward, J.R., *The Finance of Canal Building in Eighteenth-Century England*, 1974.

Ware, Michael, *Britain's Lost Commercial Waterways*, 2005.

Weaver, C.P. and C.R., *Steam on Canals*, 1983.

Westall, George, *Inland Cruising on the Rivers and Canals of England and Wales*, 1908.

Willan, T.S., *River Navigation in England, 1600–1750*, 1936.

Wright, Ian L., *Canals in Wales*, 1977.

About the Authors

JOSEPH BOUGHEY is one of Britain's lead-ing canal historians. Interested in British and Irish waterways since boyhood, he taught estate management and environ-mental management and planning at Liverpool John Moores University until 2010. He wrote Canal Man and More (Sutton, 1998) about Charles Hadfield's involvement with waterways. He is espe-cially interested in twentieth century waterways history and the history and politics of conservation.

CHARLES HADFIELD (1909–1996) was a pioneer in the history of British canals, and was, for much of his lifetime, the world's leading canal historian. He wrote twen-ty-two books and played a major part in the making of post-war waterways history.

Index

The destination for history
www.thehistorypress.co.uk